The Call of
Conscience

Studies in Rhetoric/Communication
Thomas W. Benson, Series Editor

The Call of Conscience

Heidegger and Levinas,
Rhetoric and the Euthanasia Debate

Michael J. Hyde

University of South Carolina Press

UNIVERSITY OF SOUTH CAROLINA **BICENTENNIAL**

© 2001 University of South Carolina

Published in Columbia, South Carolina, by the
University of South Carolina Press

Manufactured in the United States of America

05   04   03   02   01   5   4   3   2   1

Library of Congress Cataloging-in-Publication Data

Hyde, Michael J., 1950–
    The call of conscience : Heidegger and Levinas : rhetoric and the euthanasia
debate / Michael J. Hyde.
        p.   cm. — (Studies in rhetoric/communication)
    Includes bibliographical references and index.
    ISBN 1-57003-388-9 (alk. paper)
    1. Conscience.   2. Heidegger, Martin, 1889–1976—Contributions in concept of
conscience.   3. Levinas, Emmanuel—Contributions in concept of conscience.
    4. Rhetoric—Moral and ethical aspects.   5. Euthanasia   I. Title.   II. Series.
BJ1471 .H93   2001
170—dc21   00-011421

For my wife, Bobette

Contents

Series Editor's Preface

Michael Hyde's *The Call of Conscience* offers a fresh and vital exploration of the interplay of philosophy and rhetoric in the debate he investigates. Professor Hyde grounds his work in a rhetorical exploration and extension of the ethical thought of Martin Heidegger and Emmanuel Levinas, which is then put to work reading the rhetoric of the debate over euthanasia. The result is a model of philosophical rigor and originality. From my perspective as a teacher of rhetoric the book proves to be a vivid and compelling exercise in ethical close reading, which achieves its effects in both the lessons it draws and the patterns of reflection it rehearses with the reader.

Professor Hyde's book is the work of years of research and reflection, but also of personal experience, teaching, and conversation. The subject of euthanasia is a minefield for the critic: the language of the debate is rich in fear, sentimentality, equivocation, and absolutism on all sides, and Professor Hyde skillfully engages with these mines and their results without losing sight of the virtues of all sides of the debate.

The work is rigorous at the same time that it is deeply personal and conversational. Because Professor Hyde speaks with a compelling voice, this book will not only appeal to teachers of rhetoric and philosophy but also command the attention of anyone who thinks about medical ethics and education. It is the sort of book that can transform the lives of students.

THOMAS W. BENSON

Preface

This book is about the phenomenon of conscience. We typically speak of conscience as something that "speaks" to us; hence, the evocative "voice of conscience" whose "call" summons us to do what is good, right, and just.

The call of conscience demands our attention. Imagine what our lives would be like if we were incapable of hearing and responding to what conscience has to say. I am particularly interested in how this happens, how conscience functions as a call that needs to be answered. The phenomenological theories of conscience set forth in the works of Martin Heidegger and Emmanuel Levinas form the basis of this study. Although these two philosophers differ in their assessment of the phenomenon, I nevertheless believe that both are instructive in understanding the nature of the call.

This book is also about the relationship between the call of conscience and the practice of rhetoric, especially as this practice lends itself to being a voice of conscience to others and thus a voice that has a crucial role to play in the establishing of community. Like conscience, rhetoric also "calls"; it summons its audience into the space of practical concerns so that the one who speaks or writes and those who witness and are acknowledged by this activity may judge and "know together" (Gk. *sun-eidesis;* Lat. *con-scientia*) matters of importance. Maintaining the health of our communal existence requires nothing less. There is a "physicianship," if you will, to rhetoric's calling.

As a way of illustrating in concrete terms how the relationship between the call of conscience and the practice of rhetoric shows itself in our everyday existence, I turn to the ongoing debate in the United States over the justifiability and social acceptability of euthanasia and physician-assisted suicide. The rhetoric informing the debate admits a constant call of conscience, for there is so much at stake: the meaning of life and death, the truth of God's word, the future of American medicine, the individual's right of choice, the communal and moral welfare of society. The rhetoric of euthanasia is wide in scope and quite involved. It can be no other way. There is no "science" of ethics from which to calculate when, if ever, one's "good (*eu*) death (*thanatos*)" ought to be allowed to happen.

While I certainly hope that my discussion of these matters may be of some value to anyone who is interested in the workings of conscience, rhetoric, and the euthanasia debate, I have specifically designed this project so that it might contribute to a literature concerned with finding ways of healing a long-standing rift between the enterprises of philosophy and rhetoric. Focusing on the call of conscience is, I think, an especially fitting way of dealing with the matter; for the rift between philosophy and rhetoric begins to take form with a

certain interpretation of the call advanced by Socrates and enshrined throughout the writings of Plato. I will have more to say about this interpretation in
the introductory chapter as I supply readers with pertinent background material regarding the concerns in question here and thereby clarify the way in
which my specific treatment of these concerns defines a project dedicated to
showing how philosophy can serve rhetorical theory, how rhetorical theory
can return the favor, and how specific teachings of philosophy and rhetorical
theory can aid in the assessment of a rather intense ethical controversy.

Without knowing it at the time, I started writing this book, at least in my
head, many years ago. The project began when I suffered my first "mental
breakdown" at a too-early age. I think this breakdown had much to do with
what Kenneth Burke describes as a human being's oxymoronic tendency to be
"rotten with perfection." Another major contributing factor was the loss of significant others in my life. Something similar occurred when I again broke
down twenty-five years later. With this second existential crisis and my reaction to it, the project came together like never before. Indeed "there *is* a way,"
I thought, to connect certain ideas and concerns that I had struggled with over
the years and that reflected some of what was on my mind as I attempted to
heal and get well. The main title of this book identifies one of the phenomena
that haunted and challenged me for so long. I am less haunted now, but the
challenge remains, as it must. We are all fated to hear the call of conscience,
for it comes with our finite existence, a way of being that sooner or later fal-
ters and breaks down and thereby makes known how the call never goes away
as long as we live and breathe and are capable of knowing as much.

Acknowledgments

I am indebted to the faculty, staff, and students of the Department of Communication, Wake Forest University, for providing me with a community that makes teaching and research an immense joy. Special thanks are also due to Fred Antczak, Wes Avrams, Connie Chesner, Thomas E. Clark, David Cohen, Matthew Ferebee, Aaron Harmon, Chris Johnstone, Walter Jost, Bob Mills, Angela Rose, Peter B. Rosenquist, Ken Rufo, Calvin Schrag, Craig R. Smith, Kathleen Turner, Roy Wood, Jamie Wright, and Ken Zick. These colleagues and friends provided scholarly advice and much-needed psychological support. I also thank those groups who heard earlier versions of some of my chapters at the Universities of Denver, Pittsburgh, and Washington; Indiana, Northwestern, and Purdue University, and the London School of Economics. I am grateful to Wake Forest University for a semester research leave that enabled me to complete the writing of certain sections of this book. And for their expertise and kindness, I wish to thank Thomas Benson, Studies in Rhetoric/Communication Series Editor, and those from whom I have received help in working with the University of South Carolina Press: Barry Blose, Barbara Brannon, Christine Copeland, Catherine McGrady, Warren Slesinger, and Elizabeth Yoder.

Chapters 1, 2, and 4 contain portions of my previously published journal articles: "The Call of Conscience: Heidegger and the Question of Rhetoric," *Philosophy and Rhetoric* 27 (1994): 374–96; and "Medicine, Rhetoric, and the Euthanasia Debate: A Case Study in the Workings of Postmodern Discourse," *Quarterly Journal of Speech* 79 (1993): 201–24. Chapter 6 contains portions of my "The Call of Conscience, Rhetorical Interruptions, and the Euthanasia Controversy" (with Ken Rufo), *Journal of Applied Communication Research* 28 (2000): 1–23. Grateful acknowledgment is made to the editors and publishers of these journals for their permission to use the material in question. Its present adaptation represents various degrees of revision and expansion of those first versions.

Abbreviations

Works by Heidegger

BC   *Basic Concepts,* trans. Gary E. Aylesworth (Bloomington: Indiana University Press, 1993).

BP   *The Basic Problems of Phenomenology,* trans. Albert Hofstadter (Bloomington: Indiana University Press, 1982).

BT   *Being and Time,* trans. Edward Robinson and John MacQuarrie (New York: Harper and Row, 1962).

DT   *Discourse on Thinking,* trans. John M. Anderson and E. Hans Freud (New York: Harper and Row, 1966).

EB   *Existence and Being,* trans. Douglas Scott, R. F. C. Hull, and Alan Crick (South Bend, Ind.: Henry Regnery, 1949).

EGT   *Early Greek Thinking,* trans. David Farrell Krell and Frank A. Capuzzi (New York: Harper and Row, 1975).

ET   "On the Essence of Truth," trans. John Sallis, in *Basic Writings,* ed. David Farrell Krell (New York: Harper and Row, 1977), 117–41.

FCM   *The Fundamental Concepts of Metaphysics,* trans. William McNeill and Nicholas Walker (Bloomington: Indiana University Press, 1995).

GBAPh   *Grundbegriffe der Aristotelischen Philosophie* (an unpublished transcript of Heidegger's 1924 Summer Semester lecture course at Marburg, in the Marcuse Archiv in the Stadtsbibliotek in Frankfurt am Main).

ID   *Identity and Difference,* trans. Joan Stambaugh (New York: Harper and Row, 1969).

IM   *An Introduction to Metaphysics,* trans. Ralph Mannheim (New Haven: Yale University Press, 1959).

KPM   *Kant and the Problem of Metaphysics,* 4th ed., trans. Richard Taft (Bloomington: Indiana University Press, 1990).

LH   "Letter on Humanism," trans. Frank A. Capuzzi, in collaboration with J. Glenn Gray, in *Basic Writings,* 193–242.

PAR   *Parmenides,* trans. Andre Schuwer and Richard Rojcewicz (Bloomington: Indiana University Press, 1992).

PLT   *Poetry, Language, Thought,* trans. Albert Hofstadter (New York: Harper and Row, 1971).

PR   *The Principle of Reason,* trans. Reginald Lilly (Bloomington: Indiana University Press, 1991).

PS   *Plato's Sophist,* trans. Richard Rojcewicz and Andre Schuwer (Bloomington: Indiana University Press, 1997).

QCT   *The Question Concerning Technology and Other Essays,* trans. William
        Lovitt (New York: Harper and Row, 1977).
SZ   *Sein und Zeit* (Tübingen: Niemeyer, 1979).
TB   *On Time and Being,* trans. J. Stambaugh (New York: Harper and
        Row, 1972).
WCT   *What Is Called Thinking,* trans. J. Glenn Gray (New York: Harper
        and Row, 1968).

Works by Levinas

AT   *Alterity and Transcendence,* trans. Michael B. Smith (New York:
        Columbia University Press, 1999).
CPP   *Collected Philosophical Papers,* trans. Alphonso Lingis (The Hague:
        Martinus Nijhoff, 1987).
DF   *Difficult Freedom: Essays on Judaism,* trans. Sean Hand (Baltimore:
        Johns Hopkins University Press, 1990).
EE   *Existence and Existents,* trans. Alphonso Lingis (The Hague: Marti-
        nus Nijhoff, 1978).
EFP   "Ethics as First Philosophy," trans. Sean Hand and Michael Temple,
        in *The Levinas Reader,* ed. Sean Hand (Cambridge, Mass.: Black-
        well, 1989), 76–87.
EOF   "Ethics of the Infinite" (interview with Richard Kearney), in
        Richard Kearney, *Dialogues with Contemporary Continental Thinkers:
        The Phenomenological Heritage* (Manchester, UK: Manchester Uni-
        versity Press, 1984), 49–70.
EP   "Ethics and Politics," trans. Jonathan Romney, in *The Levinas Reader,*
        289–97.
EI   *Ethics and Infinity,* trans. Richard A. Cohen (Pittsburgh: Duquesne
        University Press, 1985).
OB   *Otherwise Than Being or Beyond Essence,* trans. Alphonso Lingis
        (Boston: Klumer, 1991).
GCM   *Of God Who Comes to Mind,* trans. Bettina Bergo (Stanford: Stanford
        University Press, 1998).
ITN   *In the Time of the Nations,* trans. Michael B. Smith (Bloomington:
        Indiana University Press, 1994).
NTR   *Nine Talmudic Readings,* trans. Annette Aronowicz (Bloomington:
        Indiana University Press, 1990).
OS   *Outside the Subject,* trans. Michael B. Smith (Stanford: Stanford
        University Press, 1994).
PM   "The Paradox of Morality" (interview with Tamra Wright, Peter
        Hughes, and Alison Ainley), trans. Andrew Benjamin and Tamra

	Wright, in *The Provocation of Levinas: Rethinking the Other* (New York: Routledge, 1988).
PN	*Proper Names,* trans. Michael B. Smith (Stanford: Stanford University Press, 1996).
TI	*Totality and Infinity,* trans. Alphonso Lingis (Pittsburgh: Duquesne University Press, 1969).
TIHP	*The Theory of Intuition in Husserl's Phenomenology,* trans. Andre Orianne (Evanston: Northwestern University Press, 1973).
TO	*Time and the Other,* trans. Richard Cohen (Pittsburgh: Duquesne University Press, 1987).
US	"Useless Suffering," trans. Richard Cohen, in *The Provocation of Levinas: Rethinking the Other,* 156–67.

The Call of
Conscience

Bringing Together
Theory and Practice

"Without the existence of conscience," Erich Fromm once wrote, "the human race would have bogged down long ago in its hazardous course."[1] Indeed people whose lives are uninformed by conscience are otherwise known as psychopaths. Such people cannot be trusted, for they lie without compunction, injure without remorse, and cheat with little fear of detection.[2] In a world where distrust is the norm, civility becomes impossible. All that one could reasonably expect from the conscienceless inhabitants of such a world would be self-serving, uncaring, and manipulative behavior. Forget about such things as guilt and shame, compassion and fairness, duty and justice. Respecting others would be a waste of time. Giving one's word would be, at most, a joke. Using language to discuss matters in a sincere, appropriate, and truthful manner would be a meaningless endeavor. When conscience leaves the scene and fails to return, the fate of a body politic's moral ecology is sealed. Perhaps, then, Fromm's observation should be amended: Without the existence of conscience, there never would have been a "human race" in the first place—at least none worthy of the name.

Conscience is integral to our being. One might therefore agree with Ernest Becker that "any philosophy or any science that is going to speak intelligently about the meaning of life has to take it [conscience] into account and treat it with the highest reverence."[3] To treat conscience this way requires that one know and respect its truth: what it is and how it works. The Judeo-Christian scriptures provide, perhaps, the most "popular" source of guidance for assessing the matter. Other noteworthy and competing assessments of the nature and function of conscience are found in the writings of such thinkers as Immanuel Kant, David Hume, Adam Smith, Charles Darwin, Friedrich Nietzsche, and Sigmund Freud. For the purposes of this study, it will be helpful to recall some of what these authorities have to say about the matter at hand. The dispute over the truth of conscience that unfolds as one moves from the Bible to Freud makes it clear that there are various ways to go about revering the phenomenon. The dispute also highlights something that is equally important to this study—that when trying to offer a respectful account of what conscience is and how it works, many other related phenomena must be considered.[4]

Some Theories of Conscience

With the Bible in hand, one might swear that conscience is, of course, the "voice of God" instilled in our souls. Within the Judeo-Christian tradition, however, things are more complicated than that. The Old Testament speaks of conscience in terms of the "heart": "I will give them a heart to know Me, that I am the Lord" (Jer. 24:7).[5] With this gift, we are made capable of being open to, concerned with, and awed by, the happenings and mysteries of life. According to Rabbi Abraham Joshua Heschel, awe "is the cardinal attitude of the religious Jew." Awe draws one near to its inspiring object; it is "evoked not in moments of calculation but in moments of being in rapport" with what is being witnessed.[6] In a moment of awe, one's orientation toward the world assumes a way of being whose watchword is this: Let there be! The moment is "holy," for now the manner in which one experiences the presence of things is most like the "saying" that first called life into being: "And God said, Let there be light" (Gen. 1:3).

In moments of awe, things "speak" in mysterious ways. The experience is humbling. It is a time of wonder. What does this mystery mean? What should one do? For the religious Jew, wonder "is the state of our being asked,"[7] the state where one is addressed and acknowledged— "Where art thou?" (Gen. 3:8–9)—where one is thereby given the opportunity to respond and be accountable— "God . . . said unto him, Abraham: and he said, Behold, here I am" (Gen. 22:1)—and where one's capacity for moral feeling is called forth and directed: "And now . . . what doth the Lord thy God require of thee, but to fear the Lord thy God, to walk in all his ways, and to love Him, and to serve the Lord thy God with all thy heart" (Deut. 10:12).

All of this requires the heart (or conscience), but it does not first come from the heart. The prophets admitted as much; their teachings came not out of "their own heart" (Ezek. 13:2). A person's conscience may call with the wisdom it has acquired over the years, but the voice of God calls from beyond the heartfelt and interpretive workings of one's moral sense. "His is the call, ours the paraphrase."[8] Moreover, the Old Testament also teaches that this sense is not infallible; its paraphrase may be utterly mistaken ("The heart is deceitful above all things, and desperately wicked: who can know it?" [Jer. 17:9]).

In the New Testament this fact of life is acknowledged by the Apostle Paul in 1 Corinthians 8 and 10 when he discusses how the socially conditioned "conscience" of certain Christian converts forbade them to eat meat that had been offered in sacrifice to idols. Paul considers this conscience to be misguided and therefore "weak," for "we know that an idol is nothing in the world, and that there is none other God but one" (1 Cor. 8:4). It is significant, however, that Paul advises against the use of force to enlighten those of a "weak conscience" because this could lead to their destruction (1 Cor. 8:11). For Paul conscience (*suneidesis*) is a person's knowledge ("consciousness") of his or her own conduct, especially as this conduct is consistent with whatever moral standard the person has appropriated. Conscience thereby functions to inform and defend one's psychic health, self-respect, and personal integrity.[9] Requiring the "weak" to disobey their conscience is thus tantamount to inflicting a potentially fatal wound on their well-being. Paul regards such an act as sinful (1 Cor. 8:12) and encourages the "weak," whenever they learn that the meat before them is sacrificial, to behave according to their own standards so as to avoid the pangs of conscience (1 Cor. 10:28–29). An individual's conscience is not something to be taken lightly. As Thomas Aquinas would later put it: "Every conscience, whether it is right or wrong, whether it concerns things evil in themselves or things morally indifferent, obliges us to act in such a way that he who acts against his conscience sins."[10] When the paraphrase of the call of conscience is in error, Paul recommends a showing of respect for the circumstances at hand and preaches tolerance and patience as ways to reform. For him conscience calls for such virtues.[11]

With the Scriptures, then, one learns that the workings of conscience are intimately connected with the fabric of human emotion as well as with our hermeneutic or interpretive capacity to come to terms with the meaning and significance of our situations and actions. However, owing to this connection, rooted as it is in the contingency of experiential reality, the call of conscience may end up communicating errors in judgment. Conscience, therefore, must be cultivated and instructed. In both Judaism and Christianity this educational task gives rise to a casuistic approach for thinking about and resolving perplexing cases of conscience. As can be seen in the case of Paul and the Corinthians, for example, this approach favors moral deliberation that takes into account the attending circumstances of those who seek to be in good conscience.[12] The world of practice and the existence of conscience go hand in hand.

In the thinking of Immanuel Kant, however, all of this is questioned. "Morality," claims Kant, "does not need religion at all . . . ; by virtue of pure practical reason it is self-sufficient."[13] For Kant we are rational and dutiful creatures by nature; "the law of morality" is incorporated in our very being as a "categorical imperative": "Act only according to that maxim [or principle of conduct] whereby you can at the same time will that it should become a universal law."[14] Kant makes much of how this "supreme principle of morality" is imposed and legislated by reason itself; it is not derived from our existentially conditioned needs, inclinations, desires, aversions, sensibilities, or emotions. He thus maintains that our actions ought to be guided first and foremost by the dictates of pure practical reason.

According to Kant, conscience comes into play when reason assumes its role of judging whether an action is really right or wrong. Kant emphasizes that it is reason, not conscience, that performs such a judgment. "But," he says, "concerning the act which *I* propose to perform I must not only judge and form an opinion, but I must be *sure* that it is not wrong." Conscience, for Kant, is the enactment of this requirement: "It is *the moral faculty of judgment, passing judgment upon itself*"; it is reason judging itself "as to whether it has really undertaken that appraisal of actions (as to whether they are right or wrong) with all diligence, and it calls the man himself to witness for or against himself whether this diligent appraisal did or did not take place."[15] It thus makes no sense to Kant to speak of a misinformed conscience. Conscience is innate; it does what it does, "involuntarily and inevitably." As rational beings, we have an obligation "to cultivate our conscience, to sharpen our attention to the voice of this internal judge, and to use every means to get it a hearing." To hear and obey the voice of conscience is to be extremely and unconditionally conscientious about one's effort to act dutifully. Conscience calls for nothing more nor less than this. Hence, for Kant, there can be "no such thing as an erring conscience."[16]

Conscience is infallible; its workings are free of all influences from empirical, contingent grounds, according to Kant. A more "religious" take on the matter might have us think otherwise. Theories of "moral sentiment," such as those advanced by David Hume, Adam Smith, and Charles Darwin, would have us do just that. For here the argument is advanced that conscience *does* arise from the contingency of social relationships, especially as these relationships are based on the natural disposition of human beings to have certain emotions. "Reason," says Hume, "can never be the source of so active a principle as conscience, or a sense of morals"; rather, "morality . . . is more properly felt than judg'd of."[17] Hume points to "sympathy" as the central emotion inspiring moral consciousness.

Adam Smith affirms and extends Hume's treatment by discussing how our sympathetic orientation toward others, which promotes our sociability, enables us to develop a sense of what pleases or offends people. We thereby acquire an understanding of what constitutes "appropriate" modes of conduct. Standards of moral judgment arise from the reciprocity of this ongoing process. We feel for and judge others, and they feel for and judge us. Based on this process, we also learn to judge the "praise-worthiness" of our own behavior. Human beings desire "not only to be loved," says Smith, "but to be lovely."[18] That is, we are creatures who want to feel that the approval (or disapproval) of others is truly warranted. "The love of praise is the desire of obtaining the favourable sentiments of our brethren. The love of praise-worthiness is the desire of rendering ourselves the proper objects of those sentiments."[19] Smith emphasizes, however, that when genuinely attending to this love of praise-worthiness, our judgments are directed not merely by the drift of current "public opinion" but rather by "the eyes" of those people whose character and conduct admit "excellence" and who thereby inspire in us a habit for acquiring a "real love of virtue." For Smith conscience (or what he also terms "the man within the breast") develops in accordance with our ability to sympathize with and appropriate the moral sentiments of such people. The love of praise-worthiness and the call of conscience inform each other.[20]

Kant would have us regard this understanding of conscience as being "lax" and "superficial" because it is not grounded *solely* in the a priori workings of reason.[21] Approaching the matter "exclusively from the side of natural history," Charles Darwin, on the other hand, is much more supportive of the teachings of moral sentiment theory. Like both Hume and Smith, he emphasizes how the development of conscience is made possible by our "instinctive sympathy" for others.[22] He also makes much of three additional factors that inform the evolution of this "most noble of all the attributes of man." First, conscience, Darwin maintains, presupposes the intellectual ability of comparing past and future actions or motives and, as a consequence, feeling "dissatisfied" with how one has heretofore attended to his or her "social sympathies." Second, our moral sense also requires "the power of language" so that "the wishes of the members of the same community . . . [can] be distinctly expressed," thereby allowing a "common opinion" to form regarding "how each member ought to act for the public good."[23] And finally, if the call of conscience is to maintain a strong influence in our lives, we must, with the help of others, develop habits of recollection, reasoning, and instruction that promote and strengthen our "social affections and sympathies."[24]

There is definitely something "progressive" about Darwin's evolutionary view of conscience. He associates the development of our moral sense with the "very idea of humanity," with "our sympathies becoming more tender and more widely diffused until they are extended to all sentient beings."[25] For Darwin the evolution of conscience is a communal endeavor. For someone like Friedrich Nietzsche, however, the Darwinian view of conscience is, to say the least, misleading.

Nietzsche's philosophy is informed by what he understands to be the "true" call of conscience: "The man who does not wish to belong to the mass," writes Nietzsche, "needs only to cease taking himself easily; let him follow his conscience, which calls to him: 'Be your self! All you are now doing, thinking, desiring, is not you yourself.'"[26] For Nietzsche the call of conscience defines "the fundamental law" of "the self": its "will to power." To speak of the self as will to power is to speak of a being whose existence is marked by a constant struggle to assert itself, to transform and transcend itself, to actualize its potential for becoming more than the herd-influenced creature that it typically is conditioned to be by the restrictive communal and moral codes of social, political, and religious institutions. "The tendency of the herd is directed toward standstill and preservation," says Nietzsche, "there is nothing creative in it."[27] The self as will to power, on the other hand, is a creative force that exhibits its essential nature by way of the self's "instinct for freedom." To hear, affirm, and enact the truth of the call of conscience is to cultivate this instinct. Conscience calls the self to affirm its freedom such that it can develop and make use of its "ability to contradict" and thereby promote "the revaluation of all values." For as Nietzsche would have it, "the ability to contradict, the attainment of a good conscience when one feels hostile to what is accustomed, traditional, and hallowed" constitutes "the step of steps of the liberated spirit."[28]

Might it be said, then, that the call of conscience is a call for "progress"? Nietzsche would deny such a proposal unless one is willing to equate progress with "the eternally self-creating" and "eternally self-destroying" acts of individuals bent on sustaining their own will to power. For this power, proclaims Nietzsche, is what "life itself" is and what shows itself in the "ebb and flood" of the whole marvelous uncertainty and rich ambiguity of existence.[29] Moreover, the call of conscience, at least as Nietzsche perceives it, is not something that beckons the self to find comfort and security in the company of others. For here the morality of the herd more often than not rules the day. And thus here, according to Nietzsche, the self's instinct for freedom, because of its potentially disruptive influence, must be "turned backward *against man himself*" so as to guard against the creation of any new values that might undermine the authority of the extant herd morality. Nietzsche associates this repression of freedom with what he terms "the origin of the 'bad conscience'"—a conscience that breeds self-contempt because it makes one believe that his or her instinct for freedom is a source of sin, guilt, and shame.[30] The bad conscience speaks the authority, the commands and taboos, of the herd morality; it says "No" to the self's will to power. The bad conscience, in other words, is nihilistic. But with Nietzsche we are forever reminded that there still exists a more truthful call, one that emanates from a "conscience behind . . . [our] 'conscience'" that is always uttering "Yes" before it is made to say "No."[31]

There is some similarity between what Nietzsche labeled the bad conscience and what Sigmund Freud terms the "super-ego." This "agency" of conscience takes form as the child internalizes the rules of conduct that are initially imposed by the parental relationship and are later reinforced by authorities (educators, teachers) who assume the parental role and provide "ideal models" of conduct. According to Freud, the "super-ego applies the strictest moral standards to the helpless ego which is at its mercy"; it "observes, directs, and threatens the ego in exactly the same way as earlier the parents did with the child"; "it calls the ego to account not only for its deeds but equally for its thoughts and unexecuted intentions."[32]

As an internalized authority that has become part of oneself, the superego cannot be avoided. It is ever present, always on call, "like a garrison in a conquered city."[33] The conscience of the superego is an "other" who lives, so to speak, in one's head—an other whose critical ways may become so debilitating that one may find it necessary to seek out the therapeutic efforts of psychoanalysis. Freud aligns these efforts with the "intention . . . to strengthen the ego, to make it more independent of the super-ego, [and thereby] to widen its field of perception and enlarge its organization."[34] In order to do this certain of the ego's ties to the past must be questioned, if not severed. The superego, maintains Freud, represents more than anything else the cultural past, for its contents are the "ideologies" or "time-resisting judgements of value" that inform a society's current moral tradition. "In the establishment of the superego we have before us . . . an example of the way in which the present is changed into the past."[35] Perhaps Nietzsche would have credited the therapeutic efforts of psychoanalysis with trying to rehabilitate the self's will to power by getting it to feel "hostile to what is accustomed, traditional, and hallowed."

Yet unlike Nietzsche, Freud does not appeal to this "conscience behind [one's] 'conscience'" when addressing the existential crises that can arise due to an overly restrictive superego. Although it may play havoc with our psychological well-being, for Freud the superego is the one and only agency of conscience, that which "civilization" sets up in individuals so as to obtain "mastery over . . . [their] dangerous desire for aggression."[36] Moreover, the necessity of the superego is the result of the human being's need to admire, to strive for, and to identify with, some ideal; to be acknowledged and loved by others for doing this; and thereby to avoid the dread of "anxiety" that often accompanies the condition of being rejected and isolated by those who are deemed important for one's personal welfare.[37] The superego, in other words, performs an important communal function. With its call of conscience, it ensures that the voice of the other will always be with us, offering moral guidance and attending to our need to feel a sense of belonging. It does this by speaking to us with a voice rooted in the past, a voice that "has been determined by the earliest parental imago[e]s." The formation of one's superego is not, therefore, an ongoing process. Somewhere along the line (Freud does not specify when), the development of a person's conscience comes to a standstill. This makes conscience a very conservative influence in a person's ongoing life. Open-mindedness is contrary to its ways of being. Notions such as "freedom" and "liberated spirit" are not part of its vocabulary. Freud "reproaches" the superego because of this.[38] But for him, there is nothing else to listen to if we want to hear the call of conscience.

Heidegger and Levinas

I think it is fair to say that all of these theories would have us treat conscience with the "highest reverence" (at least as this attitude of respect is defined by the respective authors). It is also fair to say that with the theories we are given a formidable list of variables to consider when thinking about what conscience is and how it functions: the voice of God, emotion, responsibility, interpretation, human fallibility, practical wisdom, respect for others, the contingency of existence, moral deliberation, reason, duty, appropriateness, praiseworthiness, character, language, community, power, freedom, the ability to contradict, guilt, authority, tradition, ideals, and the importance of being acknowledged, among others.

Two quite original theories of conscience that have yet to be mentioned form the basis (part 1) of this study. These theories unfold throughout the influential writings of Martin Heidegger and Emmanuel Levinas. Both of these philosophers' theories take form by way of a phenomenology of human existence, and both theories speak of the truth of conscience by focusing on how this all-important feature of our being reveals itself first and foremost as a "call," a primordial "saying" of existence that summons us to be responsible in all that we say and do and that is always already at work before any moral system is instituted in our daily lives. For both Heidegger and Levinas, if we want to know what conscience is, *we must first attend carefully to the way in which it calls.* The act of listening is as important to the truth of conscience as is its own evocative voice; the call of conscience is consummated only in the hearing and the understanding of what it has to say.

With their investigations of this eventful happening, Heidegger and Levinas clarify how the call of conscience is fundamentally related to other specific and essential features of existence that, along with the act of listening, structure our everyday lives. What ends up being disclosed about these features, especially when the findings are read together, enables one to understand how the workings of conscience can at least be associated with any of the variables that were included on the list above. I am particularly drawn to Heidegger and Levinas for precisely this reason. Their combined theories allow for an understanding of conscience that is unprecedented in its richness of detail and comprehensiveness and that thereby has much to offer those who would treat the phenomenon with the highest reverence.

Yet to involve oneself with these philosophers' theories is necessarily to become caught up in a specific philosophical and political controversy. Simply put, with Heidegger we are eventually led to understand that the call of conscience is rooted in "the temporality of Being," in one's ongoing receptiveness to the "presencing" of what is. Taking unending exception to this ontological view of the matter, Levinas maintains instead that the call originates in "the temporality of the interhuman," in the "face-to-face" encounter between the self and the other, an encounter whose fundamental ethical nature extends beyond the reaches of ontology such that it forever holds a "trace" of what is "otherwise than Being": God. When dealing with this philosophical controversy, I adhere to the view that Levinas' position presupposes at least certain aspects of Heidegger's. Still, what Levinas has to say about the face-to-face encounter offers a significant extension of Heidegger's all-too-brief treatment of how the call of conscience is related to the indelible communal character of human existence, or what Heidegger terms our "being-with-others." Here the controversy takes on a political dimension.

Heidegger is primarily interested in describing the workings of conscience as they relate to "one's own" (the self's) existence. With the call of conscience, one can also hear the call of Being. Heidegger would never have us forget the importance of our being able to think about and respond to this call—of conscience, of Being—for he felt that only by way of such activity can we learn to appreciate who we really are and how we might better our lives as we confront, for example, the nihilistic tendencies of technology that presently rule our fate. Heidegger's lifelong devotion to this matter, however, spawns its own forgetfulness; for he continually fails to clarify how the call can make its way to our ears via the pain and suffering of others. Such forgetfulness also shows itself in Heidegger's political engagements beginning in 1933.

Motivated by an ultraconservative sociopolitical outlook and a sense of his own intellectual genius and importance, Heidegger lent his voice to the movement of National Socialism, naively believing that his intellectual endeavors could provide philosophical direction for the movement and thereby free it from the hands of Nazi ideologues who erroneously justified the revolution on biological and racist grounds. We learn something of the Nazi reaction to this philosopher's vision by listening to the complaints of ideologues like Erick Jaensch, who in 1934 maintained that Heidegger's philosophy, with its hair-splitting distinctions, is similar to Talmudic thought, holds "extraordinary fascination" for Jews, and is the product of a disintegrative mind "on the borderline between mental health and illness."[39] Still, Heidegger remained a party member until the end of the war. For him the "inner truth and greatness" of National Socialism was not to be found in what the Nazi made of this movement, but rather in its potential for challenging the ways of technological nihilism.[40] The Nazi, to be sure, epitomized such nihilism with what they did to the Jews and other non-Aryans. Sadly, Heidegger had nothing to say about this horrifying event. He opted for silence and forgetfulness when it came to the pain and suffering of fellow human beings. Heidegger was intensely attuned to a call, but it was not one disclosed by the afflicted flesh of others.[41]

Levinas tells us that anyone "who undertakes to philosophize in the twentieth century cannot not have gone through Heidegger's philosophy, even to escape it. This thought is a great event of our century" (EI 42). Levinas also tells us that Heidegger's forgetfulness concerning the Other, especially as it surfaces in his political engagements, is both unforgettable and unforgivable (EI 37–44). I agree.[42] But like many others who have gone through Heidegger's philosophy, even to escape it, and who, as John Caputo puts it, have learned that "it is not safe to love Heidegger unless you also hate him," I remain convinced that in the thinking of this philosopher there is much that is valuable for understanding who and how we are as human beings inhabiting a world.[43]

What Heidegger reveals about the call of conscience (Being) is a case in point. Moreover, as I hope to show before concluding my examination of Heidegger's theory, what he tells us about the type of response that the call of conscience requires the self to make to others provides readers with a credible way of gauging Heidegger's tragic lack of judgment in 1933 and beyond.[44] The Other does have a seminal role to play in Heidegger's philosophy, although he could (and should) have said much more about the topic. Levinas helps to remedy this deficiency in Heidegger. The call of the Other warrants careful attention and respect. But so does the call that arises from "one's own" existence. Neither Heidegger alone nor Levinas alone is sufficient for developing a comprehensive phenomenological understanding of the workings of conscience.

I deal with Heidegger's thinking on the call of conscience in chapters 1 and 2. Chapter 1 first offers a brief discussion of how Heidegger conceives of phenomenology as a genuine way for describing the ontological workings of the call of conscience, which is always heard and comprehended against the backdrop of everyday existence. Hence, some of Heidegger's key observations concerning the nature and operation of everyday existence will also be discussed in chapter 1 in order to prepare the reader for appreciating the full scope and function of the ontological workings of the call of conscience (the topic of chapter 2). Levinas' thinking on the call is the focus of chapter 3. Limiting a discussion of Levinas to one chapter is possible because a good deal of the groundwork that is needed to appreciate his phenomenology of conscience and of the place where it comes to call will have already been worked out in the chapters on Heidegger.

Conscience and Rhetoric

My critical assessment of Heidegger's and Levinas' theories of conscience is also intended to show how a fundamental relationship exists between the call of conscience and the practice of rhetoric. Rhetorical scholars have yet to produce a sustained investigation of this topic—a topic that certainly goes to the very heart of the long-running quarrel between philosophy and rhetoric. As one of its initiators, Plato fueled this quarrel as he told the story and recorded the teachings of his mentor, Socrates; hence, those most famous philosophical critiques of rhetoric laid out in the *Gorgias* and *Phaedrus*. The story told of Socrates in the *Apology,* however, is the one I want briefly to recall now, for it is with this dialogue that we learn most specifically how the quarrel between philosophy and rhetoric is rooted in a certain interpretation of the call of conscience advanced by Socrates.

Socrates describes the call as a "prophetic voice" that first came to him in early childhood and remained his "constant companion."[45] The voice commanded his "service to God" (23b), which he took to mean that his life's calling must be that of "leading the philosophical life" (28e), of "elucidating the truth" for others (29d) and encouraging them "not to think more of practical advantages than of . . . [their] mental and moral well-being" (36c). To those who accused him of corrupting the minds of the youth, Socrates said, "I am . . . a gift from God" (31a). He could not say this if he did not believe it to be true, he said, for the voice, his daemon, always spoke up and prevented him from committing any wrongdoing (40a–b). When the call came, lying was out of the question, as was any involvement in the politics of public life, "corrupted" as they were by the teachings of those who were eloquent but unwise, who were skilled in the oratorical practice of making "the weaker argument defeat the stronger" by employing "flowery language . . . decked out with fine words and phrases" (17b–18b), but who apparently felt no shame as they engaged themselves in such a crowd-pleasing and unconscionable rhetorical exercise, and who, as evidenced by Socrates' trial, could pose a serious threat to his life. Although he accepted being called an "orator" as long as that was defined to mean "one who speaks the truth" (17b), Socrates "would much rather die" as the result of his philosophical ways and commitments than engage himself in the unethical maneuvers of sophistry (38d–e). His constant companion never balked at this decision. During his defense Socrates thus had little trouble admitting to his fellow citizens that "no man on earth who conscientiously opposes either you or any other organized democracy, and flatly prevents a great many wrongs and illegalities from taking place in the state to which he belongs, can possibly escape with his life. The true champion of justice, if he intends to survive even for a short time, must necessarily confine himself to private life and leave politics alone" (31e–32a).

When Socrates drank his dram of hemlock and Plato assumed his mentor's "calling," the destiny of the rhetorical tradition was more or less set. From that time forward, those who wished to speak more favorably of the orator's art would have to answer to charges of sophistry brought by these two Greeks by clarifying, if possible, how the art has a necessary and thus legitimate role to play in cultivating the moral ecology of the body politic. Aristotle, of course, was the first to take up the challenge as he worked out in the *Rhetoric* the artistic nature (*logos*) of a practice whose essential purpose is to deal with what is, in the main, contingent: those matters that we recognize as pressing and that require careful deliberation and judgment, but whose meaning and significance are presently ambiguous, uncertain, and contestable. The contingency of human existence stares us in the face every day. It is a fact of life, one that constantly tests our moral ability to make right and just decisions. Rhetoric is necessary, given this fact of life. The point is repeated throughout the rhetorical tradition: "Lacking definitive evidence and being compelled to act are the prerequisites of the rhetorical situation."[46]

There is, however, another and related justification of the orator's art that was also set forth early on in the rhetorical tradition and that, as repeated and developed by Cicero, goes even further in contesting what Socrates had to say as he listened to and interpreted the call of a prophetic voice. Commenting on the cultural and educational influence exerted by this interpretation, Cicero accused it of bringing about "the undoubtedly absurd and unprofitable and reprehensible severance between the tongue and the brain, leading to our having one set of professors to teach us to think and another to teach us to speak."[47] Although made by one who was certainly committed to the theory and practice of rhetoric, this accusation was not intended as a mere put-down of philosophy. Like Socrates, Plato, and Aristotle before him, Cicero held firmly to the belief that "if we bestow fluency of speech on persons devoid of . . . [the] virtues [of integrity and supreme wisdom], we shall not have made orators of them but shall have put weapons into the hands of madmen" (*De oratore* 3.14.55). Hence, Cicero insisted that "philosophy is essential to a full, copious and impressive discussion and exposition of the subjects which so often come up in speeches and are usually treated meagerly, whether they concern religion, death, piety, patriotism, good and evil, virtues and vices, duty, pain, pleasure, or mental disturbances and errors."[48]

But Cicero also insisted that "we are not born for ourselves alone," that "our country claims a share of our being," and that if we intend "to contribute to the general good," we must not disparage and retreat from the politics of public life but instead use "our skill, our industry, and our talents to cement human society more closely together, man to man."[49] The obligation stated here speaks to the importance of rhetoric. Philosophy is essential for the education of the orator, but it is the "art of eloquence" (*oratio*) practiced by this advocate of the *vita activa* that instructs one on how to equip (*ornare*) knowledge of a subject in such a way that it can assume a publicly accessible form, and function effectively in the social and political arena. The severance between the tongue and the brain is an impediment to this civic-minded, persuasive, and moral endeavor. For the good of the community, philosophy and rhetoric must work together. Cicero—who admitted "that whatever ability I possess as an orator comes, not from the workshops of the rhetoricians, but from the spacious grounds of the Academy" (*Orator* 3.12)—would have it no other way. Conscience calls. Cicero heard it. And his interpretation was clear:

"To be drawn by study away from active life is contrary to moral duty" (*De officiis* 1.6.19). No wonder Cicero felt obliged to offer counsel in the ways of rhetoric. For "what function is so kingly, so worthy of the free, so generous, as to bring help to the suppliant, to raise up those who are cast down, to bestow security, to set free from peril, to maintain men in their civil rights? . . . The wise control of the complete orator is that which chiefly upholds not only his own dignity, but the safety of countless individuals and of the entire State" (*De oratore* 1.8.32).[50]

What I have to say about rhetoric and its relationship to the call of conscience is supportive of this position. Philosophy informs my discussion of the topic. With Heidegger's and Levinas' theories of conscience a far-reaching understanding of the phenomenon emerges that has much to tell us about its existential, ontological, and metaphysical nature. I argue that these theories encourage one to see how the call of conscience requires the development of rhetorical competency, of knowing how to evoke from others a response to a particular situation so as to engage them in collaborative deliberation. With this evocation, this acknowledging call to others, rhetoric demonstrates its "physicianship" as it helps to promote reasoned judgment and civic virtue and thereby lends itself to the task of enriching the moral character of a people's communal existence.[51]

Although my argument regarding rhetoric's relationship to the call of conscience is informed by the thinking of Heidegger and Levinas, the present study is not intended to be only an affirmation of philosophical insight. For although these philosophers' theories of conscience are instructive for remedying a lack in rhetorical scholarship—that is, for suggesting how rhetoric is related to a phenomenon that humankind could hardly afford to be without and that thereby provides a major source of legitimation for an art that was long ago fated to be ever on the lookout for things that justify its activities— neither Heidegger nor Levinas commit themselves explicitly to advancing a favorable assessment of rhetoric. In fact their overall philosophical projects contain elements that would have one think about rhetoric in ways that are reminiscent of philosophy's long-standing prejudices against this art. My discussion of how rhetoric is related to the call of conscience proceeds as I draw on the insights of various rhetorical theorists in order to deal with this irksome problem. Philosophy has much to tell us about a phenomenon that deserves to be treated with the highest reverence, but so do the teachings of the rhetorical tradition.

From Theory to Practice: The Euthanasia Debate

The rhetorical tradition is made up of a vast array of observations detailing the ways symbolic action has taken form in situations marked by what Thomas B.

Farrell describes as "the intrusion of the contingent" in the moral lives of human beings.[52] The tradition is also characterized by an equally vast array of theoretical directives based on these observations that promote rhetoric to the status of an art and that offer guidance for cultivating the ability to engage this contingency. From the world of practice to the realm of theory and from the realm of theory to the world of practice, the rhetorical tradition unfolds in such a dialectical manner.

Guided as it is by the thinking of Heidegger and Levinas, my discussion of the call of conscience and its relationship to rhetoric will perhaps appear to be heavily weighted on the side of theory. Indeed, I am concerned with two philosophers who offer us phenomenologically oriented theories of conscience. Phenomenology, however, is a way of doing philosophy (and constructing theory) that is quite committed to forming an appreciation of the everyday world of practical affairs. For only by attending carefully to the workings of this "ontic" domain can the phenomenologist do what he or she is supposed to do: disclose and elucidate the phenomena of human experience as they present themselves in their existential immediacy. Getting as close as possible to the truth of what is, to "the things themselves" (den Sachen selbst), is the principle goal of phenomenological inquiry. And the movement begins with an immersion into the "everydayness" of human being. Heidegger's and Levinas' "appreciation" of rhetoric is based, in part, on their assessments of this domain of situated, practical concerns.

Yet as these assessments are worked out in order to offer a phenomenological account of the ontological and metaphysical underpinnings of the everyday world and the way in which the call of conscience presents itself here, Heidegger and Levinas definitely head us in the direction of theory. Rhetoricians who journey too far in this direction risk being accused by their colleagues of being out of touch with the true place of rhetorical practice. A homecoming is expected. To meet this expectation is to show respect for the tradition that grounds the rhetorician's calling. It is a matter of conscience.

My move from theory back to practice (part 2) takes place as I consider how the relationship between the call of conscience and the practice of rhetoric informs the ongoing controversy regarding the justifiability and social acceptability of euthanasia, of helping people who are suffering unbearably from some terminal illness or bodily injury die a "good death." If focusing on the nature and function of conscience is a fitting way of dealing with the long-standing rift between philosophy and rhetoric, then I think it is fair to say that this controversy too is an especially appropriate topic for my purposes. I say this having Socrates once again in mind, for certain key issues raised in the euthanasia debate are also a part of the circumstances surrounding this philosopher's final days on earth.

Socrates heard an inner voice that not only summoned him away from the rhetorical and political practices of everyday life but also called him toward his death. During the month that elapsed between the end of his trial and his downing the hemlock, he refused to take advantage of an escape arranged for him by his friends. In the *Phaedo* he explains how it is "natural that a man who has really devoted his life to philosophy should be cheerful in the face of death, and confident of finding the greatest blessing in the next world when his life is finished."[53] And Socrates' philosophical life, at least as it could be lived in Athens, was finished. The sentence of the jury made sure of that. Hence, just before "he drained the cup in one breath" (117c), and at an earlier hour than was necessary, he informed his friends that "I should only make myself ridiculous in my own eyes if I clung to life and hugged it when it has no more to offer" (117a). No objection came forth from his inner voice. A life without philosophy supposedly was not worth living. Socrates had lived a good life. Now it was time to die a good death, surrounded by loved ones and true friends who, according to Socrates, should realize that although "it is not legitimate to do oneself violence," putting "an end to ourselves" is justified whenever "God sends some compulsion like the one which we are facing now" (61d–62c).

The outspoken conflict between philosophy and rhetoric that begins with Socrates is, to be sure, a matter of conscience; thus right from the start it is also necessarily a matter of life and death—or better, a matter of the good life and the good death and how each of these goods are to be achieved. These related matters lie at the heart of the euthanasia debate. Owing to an illness or an accident and to the excruciating pain and suffering that can accompany such misfortune, a person's way of living a good life can come to an end. Owing, however, to the powers of medical science and technology, something of this life may be revived and sustained. Like Socrates' friends, modern medicine grants those whom it is obliged to serve an all-important option, for it is in the business of helping people escape from the throes of death. But what if their conscience speaks against accepting such help? What if they, like Socrates, can point to their particular circumstances and compulsions and say in good conscience that the time has come to put "an end to ourselves"?

Socrates voluntarily ended his life with the assistance of God. (Remember: his conscience did not tell him *not* to drink the hemlock; it did not call him to escape his death sentence.) Patients have a constitutional right to seek and receive such assistance from their physicians, although the legality of their suicide is restricted to an act of "passive" euthanasia: the withholding or withdrawing of life-prolonging and life-sustaining technologies. Anything more "active" than that (injecting a patient with potassium chloride, for instance) constitutes "murder."[54] But should it? Is there truly a moral difference between passive and active euthanasia, between "letting die" and "killing"? Are not both acts directed toward bringing about a merciful, peaceful, and dignified end? If so, then should not patients have the right, and physicians the license, to make use of the ways and means of active euthanasia?

Answers to these and related questions offered by all sorts of people—patients young and old, family members, clergy, physicians, nurses, lawyers, politicians—make up the rhetoric of the euthanasia debate, a debate that medicine long ago helped to initiate when its Hippocratic ancestors appropriated religious directives from Pythagorean philosophy and thereby conceived of suicide as being a sin against God. With the taking of their Hippocratic oath, physicians promise never to assist in this unholy deed: "I will use treatment to help the sick according to my ability and judgment, but never with a view to injury and wrong-doing. Neither will I administer a poison to anybody when asked to do so, nor will I suggest such a course."[55] In the Hippocratic *law,* however, it is written: "There are in fact two things, science and opinion; the former begets knowledge, the latter ignorance."[56] The physician who utters the Hippocratic oath is necessarily making a promise that is based not in "science" but rather in the "opinion," the rhetoric, of a religious ideology. It would seem, then, that medicine's traditional stance against suicide is essentially rooted in a matter of "ignorance."

Medicine, of course, would rather have science than opinion speak on its behalf, for its reputation and social standing are predicated on a scientific understanding of the body and on the definitive evidence about disease that such understanding makes possible in the form of a "true" *techne,* a true realm of technical knowledge that can be used to cure the body of what ails it. Medical ethics, however, is not a science, although science certainly can be helpful when trying to gauge how a patient's quality of life will be affected by some disease. Take away the rhetoric of philosophy and religion that supports medicine's moral mission, and what you have is a rogue profession doing whatever science enables it to do, be it "good" or "bad." Not even Socrates—who called for a "scientific rhetoric" to combat the illness of ignorance that threatens the health of "men's souls"—was able to avoid being opinionated when it came to "knowing" what God's call of conscience demanded. The hemlock did its work before the philosopher could say with *absolute certainty* where his "good death" would lead him. Moral codes and visions, and the calls of conscience that accompany them, presuppose the workings of rhetoric.

The euthanasia debate, with its definitions of, and arguments and narratives about, the meaning and value of life and death, marks out a rhetorical situation of immense proportions. What I have to say here about the rhetoric going on will in no way cover everything that can be said about the matter.[57] I trust this failing is acceptable since, as noted in the preface, my investigation of the debate is primarily directed toward an assessment of how the relationship between the call of conscience and the practice of rhetoric shows itself in our everyday existence. The four chapters in which I do this unfold around five related topics that will emerge as I discuss Heidegger's and Levinas' thinking on the call of conscience and that allow one to account for some of the key definitions, arguments, and narratives that are a part of the rhetoric of the euthanasia debate, especially as the debate has evolved since the late 1980s. These topics include the phenomena of deconstruction and acknowledgment (chapter 4), emotion and the reconstructive power of language (chapter 5), and the discursive creation of heroes (chapters 6 and 7). In the concluding chapter I suggest what ought to become of the euthanasia debate in light of the present philosophical and rhetorical study of the workings of conscience.

Part I

Theory
Conscience and Rhetoric

Chapter 1

Heidegger and the Call of Conscience

A Question of Being

> We constantly comport ourselves toward beings and are beings. We discern not only about ourselves that we are beings, but about our being that we are concerned, one way or another, with ourselves and how we are. Being concerns us, whether it is a matter of the being that we are ourselves or those beings that we are not and never can be. We are always that being that is concerned with being, who, thus concerned and struck, finds in being what is most reliable. Being remains everywhere reliable, and yet considered in respect to its rank within what is worthy of reflection, it is the most forgotten. Despite this forgottenness, however, it remains in everyday comportment not only the reliable, but is, prior to that, already something that grants us awareness of beings and permits us to be beings in the midst of beings. (BC 55)

Martin Heidegger's philosophy unfolds as an answer to a question: What is the meaning, the truth, of Being? The question raises an issue whose philosophical relevance is documented throughout the Western tradition of metaphysics as the contributors to this tradition wonder about why there is "anything at all" (Being) rather than "nothing" and then go on to make a case for what Being "truly" is. Yet as Heidegger makes clear in his wide-ranging critique of metaphysics, the thinking devoted to this ontological task is continually hampered by a limitation inherent in its manner of inquiry. That is, metaphysics approaches the question of Being by restricting its thinking to an investigation of thing-like beings and what these beings consist of in their present existence. Metaphysics thereby promotes a certain understanding of the relationship between existence and Being: as a thing exists, so it is. Being presents itself in this "it is" of the thing's existence. To experience, interpret, and express something about the thing's existence is to determine not only what type of being "it is," but also to denote its present status (that is, *its* truth) in the order of Being. Metaphysical thinking stops here, however. Being is granted the status of "the most universal concept," reified as the ultimate ground of all beings, and oftentimes transformed into the concept of God. Metaphysics thus defines

Being as something indefinite yet self-evident (that is, as "continuous presence"), as something that presents itself in beings yet is different from them.

The thinking of metaphysics acknowledges what Heidegger terms the "ontological difference": Being is distinguishable from beings. But that is as far as this thinking goes. Metaphysics, for the most part, leaves the question of the truth of Being unexamined. Hence, Heidegger writes: "Metaphysics does indeed represent beings in their Being, and so it thinks the Being of beings. But it does not think the difference of both. Metaphysics does not ask about the truth of Being itself. Nor does it therefore ask in what way the essence of man belongs to the truth of Being" (LH 202–3). To ask about the truth of Being requires, according to Heidegger, that one pay special attention to how the "presencing" of Being discloses itself in beings whereby it may then be understood to some extent. For Heidegger this occurrence presupposes a conception of temporality that eludes metaphysics and its emphasis on the "present" existence of thing-like beings. Hence, if the truth of Being is to achieve clarification, and not merely to be accepted as an a priori enigma, one must account for its temporality by investigating how Being *becomes* present and therefore truthful. With Heidegger we must understand that Being refers not merely to a thing but rather to the *coming to presence* of that which is. Being is more of a verb ("to be") than it is a noun (a name for something: for example, that thing called a "fence"); it is active, not static. For something "to be" means for it to be revealed, disclosed, made manifest—time and again. This is Being's way, that which must be thought through as much as possible so as to come to a genuine understanding of its meaning and truth.

In *Being and Time* Heidegger initiates his performance of this ontological task by offering a phenomenology of human existence. Heidegger's analysis of the call of conscience begins here. The analysis is quite involved; the phenomenon under consideration has much to tell us about what it means *to be* a human being. As a way of orienting the reader to how Heidegger would have us appreciate what it is that we are listening to when the call announces itself, I want to say a few words about his mode of inquiry, his phenomenological approach to the question of Being. This approach is itself a response to a call—a call not unlike the one that gives voice to conscience.

A Phenomenological Approach

For Heidegger phenomenology is a way of thinking devoted to interpreting, analyzing, and describing how the immediate content of experience actually presents itself. It seeks to disclose with "demonstrative precision" the appearing or "presencing" of some phenomenon, "to let that which shows itself [*phainesthai*] be seen from itself in the very way in which it shows itself from itself" (BT 58). Phenomenology, in other words, attempts to generate a discourse that is especially attuned to the way in which some phenomenon happens, to how it reveals or manifests itself within the temporal horizon of human understanding. The discourse of phenomenology assumes the task of disclosing a phenomenon's own disclosure, *its* being and truth. It may thus be said that phenomenology is a truth-telling activity, for as Heidegger points out in his discussion of the matter, truth *happens* first and foremost as a disclosing of the world, a revealing or uncovering of the "givenness" of something that is perceived to be (BT 256–73).

What Heidegger is referring to here is not "the truth" that may be disclosed in some verbal judgment ("The sky is blue"), in some epistemic correspondence of some reified proposition with some equally reified state of affairs. The truth of such a disclosure presupposes a more original happening of truth, a more original instance of disclosing: the actual presencing of that which shows itself and thus gives itself for thought and understanding. This is the truth (of Being) that Heidegger is after; his phenomenology is directed toward a hermeneutic assessment of *how* this primordial showing and giving take place. Heidegger describes this task as requiring one to "listen" to the "call of Being." Moreover, he tells us that in order to do this "the point is not to listen to a series of propositions, but rather to follow the movement of showing" (TB 2). This may sound a bit strange. How is it that this "showing" calls?

Phenomenology goes about telling the truth by "letting-something-be-seen" with its discourse. Heidegger identifies such a disclosive or evocative use of discourse with what he defines as the "essential being of language" (*Logos*): its "saying" power, its capacity to "speak" by pointing to and showing us something (OWL 122–24). "Language speaks," insists Heidegger, and it does so especially in discourses that warrant praise for being revelatory and perhaps even awe-inspiring because of the way they call forth and disclose their subject matter, thereby enabling us to better our understanding and appreciation of what is being talked about. For example, in order to understand and appreciate what Lincoln is trying to tell us with the Gettysburg Address (a most evocative discourse, to be sure), we must listen not only to him (which of course we can no longer do) but also to the power of his language as it displays a capacity for making manifest certain matters of importance, for saying something to us by showing us what this something is thought to be. If the Gettysburg Address is to speak to us in a truthful manner, this, at the very least, is what it must do: through an act of saying, of showing, it must give us something to understand.[1]

Heidegger reminds us that the oldest word for "saying" is *logos*: "Saying which, in showing, lets beings appear in their 'it is'" (OWL 155; BT 56). The saying power of language is what enables any discourse to give expression to things that call for attention. Heidegger further reminds us that the word for "saying" (*logos*) is also the word for Being. Indeed, Being is constantly disclosing and showing itself in how things are, in the presencing of all that lies before us, in the circumstances of life that call for thought. The truth of Being is a saying, a showing, a phenomenon that presents itself for understanding. This is what Heidegger is referring to when he speaks of the "call of Being": that primordial "saying" whose showing is thought-provoking. And this is why Heidegger tells us that if we are to listen attentively to this call, we must "follow the movement of showing" so as to let whatever concerns us speak for itself. Heidegger insists that this is the one true way of phenomenology; its discourse must be responsive to a most fundamental calling (TB 25, 44–45, 65–67, 82).

As we have already noted, *Being and Time* marks Heidegger's first systematic attempt to address the question of Being. Here he directs his attention to the presencing of what he terms "Dasein": the "to be" of human existence. The reasons given for this focus are noteworthy; they make much of how "Dasein is an entity which does not just occur among other entities. Rather it is ontically distinguished by the fact that, in its very Being, that Being is an *issue* for it" (BT 32). Put another way, the "special distinctiveness" of Dasein that differentiates it from other entities is that this entity *is concerned with* its existence, its being, its way of becoming what it is. This concern for being is constantly demonstrated in our everyday involvement with things and with others. Reflecting on the meaningfulness of what is being demonstrated, we can and oftentimes do (as in times of personal crisis, for example) raise the question of what it means to be. The question makes explicit our concern for being. Only the human being is concerned enough to do this—to ask the question, think it through to some extent, and then say something about what is thought.

W. B. Macomber notes that "Heidegger wishes to make a concerned attitude fundamental to all human activities including the most detached and disinterested speculative inquiry." This position, Macomber perceptively points out, "has a peculiar status: it is not incontestable, but in contesting it we exhibit the concern which we wish to deny."[2] Indeed the human being is that entity that is much concerned with its existence. Heidegger emphasizes that in being this way, Dasein reveals itself as the "place," the "site," the "clearing" or "opening" wherein Being is disclosed and made meaningful. "Disclosedness," according to Heidegger, is the fundamental characteristic of Dasein; it denotes how human being is authentically related to Being. Human being is the witness for Being, the only creature capable of hearing and responding to a call that announces itself in the presencing of all that lies before us and that may then again be disclosed to a certain degree in the interpretive workings of discourse or other symbolic activities (see, for example, BT 256–73; BPP 300; IM 205; ID 31; BDT 323–39; PAR 140–44).

We go about offering this response as beings who are perpetually caught up in the temporal-historical process of understanding our existence, of trying to come to terms with the meaning of what was, what is, and what may continue to be. The question of Being and this process go hand in hand. Being is related to human concern, to this concern's disclosive capability, and thus to the temporal horizon of human understanding wherein Being is interpreted and made manifest as something meaningful. For Heidegger this relationship defines the fundamental way that human being "belongs to the truth of Being"—*how it happens* that we are open to that which gives itself for understanding and thereby calls for thought. The occurrence of this specific happening of truth—especially since it can be attended to and described by the one who is actually living it—thereby offers special access to yet another primordial occurrence: the happening of "the truth of Being itself." This is why Heidegger's project of "fundamental ontology"—devoted as it is to overcoming a specific problem inherent in the thinking of traditional metaphysics—begins with a phenomenology of human existence. For here is the "place" where Being shows itself every hour, minute, and second of each day. The call of Being is essentially a temporal occurrence. Human existence offers living proof of this in and through the temporality of its own being, its own presencing. Being calls. Human existence shows how.

There are moments in our everyday lives when what is disclosed here can make itself known in a most dramatic and personal manner, as when one is witnessing the wonders of nature's ways, for example. But such an awe-inspiring occurrence may also come from a source that is no further away from us than the issue of our own existence. Being calls, and thus so does *human* being. When this happens, according to Heidegger, we are listening to a call "which *we ourselves* have neither planned nor prepared for nor voluntarily performed, nor have we ever done so. 'It' calls, against our expectations and even against our will." Moreover, notes Heidegger, the call "does not come from someone else who is with me in the world. The call comes *from* me and yet *from beyond and over me*" (BT 320).

What Heidegger is saying here is quite relevant for my present purposes. Heidegger is speaking of "the call of conscience"—a call whose saying is a showing, a revealing, a disclosing of our "potentiality-for-Being," of our "projective" involvement with the temporal process of becoming and understanding that which we are: our possibilities. The call of conscience, in other words, confronts us with the question of what it means to be. When hearing this call, we are concerned with the truth of our temporal existence and with the decisive challenge that comes with it—trying to determine how to live out this truth in some meaningfully significant way. Hence, with what it discloses, the call of conscience brings us face-to-face with the fact that we are creatures whose desire for the "good life" requires us to assume the personal and ethical responsibility of affirming our freedom through resolute choice.

Moral systems, with their institutionalized principles, precepts, and laws, are made possible by the enactment of this responsibility; they stand and fall on that which the call of conscience discloses. The call *is* this disclosure; it originates in the temporal openness of that entity whose concern for its being enables it to perceive and care enough about what it is hearing and what is in need of a response. The call of conscience calls upon the "resoluteness" of our response-ability, and it does this constantly. As long as we exist, the call is there, although what it has to say and show, according to Heidegger, is all too easily forgotten and forsaken as we become conditioned to think and act in accordance with the conventions and rituals of everyday life. More will be said about this last point as this chapter unfolds.

It is important to keep in mind that what Heidegger says about the call of conscience is phenomenologically oriented; his discourse speaks to us, not of some particular instance of "herd morality" (Nietzsche), but of what such morality presupposes. Heidegger attends to the call's ontological constitution. This is what he is doing when he maintains that "the call comes *from* me"—that is, from the temporal openness of human being— "and yet *from beyond and over me.*" This last point of emphasis acknowledges the "ontological difference" marking the relationship between human being and the truth of Being. We hear the call of conscience as we stand in the midst of our temporal openness, struggling with the whence and whither of our existence, and getting ready to choose, to act, and perhaps to change our lives for the better. For Heidegger, however, this fundamental way of being, this calling, is not "Being itself"; rather, it offers but a robust indication of what the truth of Being might very well be. The call of conscience sounds the call of Being, but the two are not identical. Heidegger devotes himself to thinking the difference so that he can hear the call of Being as clearly as possible. Moreover, he maintains that the task at hand constitutes the most "authentic" and thus "responsible" way of coming to terms with such moral and ethical issues as how it is that "God" speaks to us (if indeed this is the case), and how we might best deal with the problems of technology that presently confront us (QT 3–49). Although Heidegger would not have us associate his philosophical investigations with moral and ethical motives, these investigations do lay out a path of thought where, when all is said and done, we come to learn that the way of thinking that is called for by Being (and that Heidegger thereby engages in quite *conscientiously*) defines an "activity" requiring the highest degree of personal commitment and responsibility. I take this to mean that, given what Heidegger insists it calls for, the call of Being also sounds a call of conscience.

In the remainder of this chapter and the next one, I will be following Heidegger's path of thought so as to listen to what he has to say as he listens to the call of Being (conscience) and to the call of conscience (Being). To hear one is to hear something of the other. So far, by way of introduction, I have presented only an overview of Heidegger's project. A more in-depth treatment is offered in what follows.

The primary objective here is to further our understanding of the ontological workings of the call of conscience. Heidegger initially assists us in achieving this end when he offers at the beginning of *Being and Time* an analysis of the common and everyday way we go about understanding our environment. Here Heidegger uncovers a world of circumspective concern, purposeful behavior, and know-how; a world that is never without the influence of the Other; a world whose routines, conventions, and discursive activities promote community as well as provide a breeding ground for the evils of conformism; a world that owes much to the disclosive capacity of emotion; a world where time and space assume a most definite character; and a world whose discourse both reveals and conceals the truth. The call of conscience comes to us as we inhabit this world of "everydayness." Its "voice" interrupts our habits, complacency, and states of indifference by confronting us with the challenge of freedom, choice, and personal responsibility. The call of conscience thus brings about a momentary modification of our day-to-day existence—a modification that may, in turn, prove helpful in cultivating and improving a community's moral ecology and evolving world of everydayness. With this modification, conscience "summons" us from a world to which we are bound to return. It can be no other way. Like the call itself, everydayness is an unavoidable ontological structure of human being.

The call of conscience is always heard and understood against the backdrop of the ways and means of this structure. Hence, if we are to further our understanding of the ontological workings of the call of conscience, we must first be clear about how the everydayness of our lives manifests itself as the place where conscience comes to call.

Everydayness: Where Conscience Comes to Call

A world of know how.   Everydayness manifests itself as "that environment which is closest to us" and wherein we show ourselves to be the purposive and pragmatic creatures that we are. In the world of everydayness our fundamental way of understanding existence consists of knowing how to deal with the immediacy of our everyday, goal-directed tasks. As creatures of know-how, we embody and exhibit a hermeneutic competence for coming to see and involve ourselves with the world in an instrumentally oriented manner. For the competence or interpretive outlook of know-how is that of "circumspection," of being concerned with the world in such a way that it becomes and remains *useful* for one's purposes. Here, in accordance with what Heidegger terms the "existential-hermeneutical 'as'" of "primordial understanding" (know-how), things first manifest themselves *as* "equipment," *as* instruments and materials of work (BT 200–201). For example, with my writing of this chapter, the computer in my office immediately presents itself, not to the theoretical stare of my "speculative eye," but to the know-how of my carefully conditioned (practiced) hands. As it is understood by the "circumspective interpretation" of my know-how, I appreciate the computer *as* a tool that, when handled well, facilitates the doing of a specific task.

Our successful involvement in the everyday world of know-how also has much to do with how well equipment goes unnoticed as it is being used. A "good technology" does not call attention to itself; rather it "withdraws" in use and becomes transparent so as not to impede the endeavor that it is helping to facilitate. A shoe that pinches, a hammer that is too heavy, a pen that skips, a phone connection whose static prevents us from hearing a pin drop, a VCR whose gadgetry confronts us with a "design hell," a television without high definition, or a computer that is too slow—all these lack the necessary transparency that would otherwise enhance the user's absorption in the performance of some activity. The more inconspicuous the technology, the more we can preoccupy ourselves with the situation at hand. Preoccupation, and the forgetfulness that goes with it, *is the way of being* favored by the world of know-how and catered to by technologies that are "user friendly" and thus, with a little practice, allow us to forget their presence as they weave themselves into the fabric of everyday life.

Our lives necessitate the hermeneutical competence of such comportment in order to be skilled at existing, to do what is appropriate given the circumstances, to perform a job well. Hermeneutical competence is productive of, and maintained by, the practical wisdom (*phronesis*) that forms the habit of right insight into human action and that shows itself in the activities of our knowing how to do things correctly. Although these activities are performed by individuals, they nevertheless owe much to what the Other has to offer. In fact the everyday world of know-how is nothing without the Other.

Being-with-others.   As Heidegger readily acknowledges, being-with-others is an inevitable condition of one's existence. Even being "alone" presupposes a being-with-others, for an individual can be alone only because the Other is not present. "So far as Dasein *is* at all," writes Heidegger, "it has Being-with-one-another as its kind of Being" (BT 163). What an individual is now in her life carries with it a history that has "always already" been influenced by the Other. Human existence is marked with an indelible communal character. "The world of Dasein is a *with-world* [*Mitwelt*]. Being-in[-the-world] is *Being-with* Others" (BT 155).

This communal character of our existence registers itself as the historically informed and common ways that members of a community see, interpret, and become meaningfully involved with things and with others, thereby sustaining a world of common sense and common praxis, a world of "public-ness." In his description of this world Heidegger tends to emphasize its "mass"-like (Plato), "crowd"-like (Kierkegaard) and "herd"-like (Nietzsche) propensity to bring about a mindless conformism amongst its adherents. For example, he notes that in our publicness

> the real dictatorship of the "they" is unfolded. We take pleasure and enjoy ourselves as *they* . . . take pleasure; we read, see and judge about literature and art as *they* see and judge; likewise we shrink back from the "great mass" as *they* shrink back; we find "shocking" what *they* find shocking. . . . In this averageness with which [the "they"] prescribes what can and may be ven-tured, it keeps watch over everything exceptional that thrusts itself to the fore. Every kind of priority gets noiselessly suppressed. Overnight, every-thing that is primordial gets glossed over as something that has long been well known. Everything gained by a struggle becomes just something to be manipulated. (BT 164–65)

Perhaps anyone who has ever become dismayed over the thought and action of some collectivity may find Heidegger's assessments to be on mark. But such assessments of publicness define only a part of what Heidegger is telling us about the everydayness of our being-with-others. For he also admits that publicness "belongs to Dasein's positive constitution" (BT 167). That is, owing to the traditions, customs, rules, and norms that inform its way of being, publicness provides a sense of order to what would otherwise be a state of chaos and confusion. In his acclaimed reading of *Being and Time* Hubert Dreyfus emphasizes this very point when he notes that, for Heidegger, "the source of the intelligibility of the world is the average public practices through which alone there can be any understanding at all."[3] Although such practices can and oftentimes do provide a breeding ground for the evils of conformism, they nevertheless also provide the necessary background for coming to terms with who we are as social beings and for determining whether or not our extant ways of seeing, interpreting, and becoming involved with things and with others might be changed for the better. The primordial understanding of know-how and the publicness of our being-with-others go hand in hand. In Heidegger's terms they are "equiprimordial."

Emotion. Heidegger also makes much of how our everyday way of being-with-others defines a realm of emotional orientations and attachments ("moods") that are constantly "attuning" us to, and helping to disclose, the sit-uations of which we are a part and that are forever unfolding before our eyes. By way of its disclosive function, human emotion informs and gives focus to the circumspective interpretation of the primordial understanding of know-how. "Understanding," writes Heidegger, "always has its mood," and thus so does the publicness of our being-with-others (BT 182). Emotion, in other words, has a fundamental role to play in organizing and structuring our every-dayness.

Heidegger recognizes that emotions function primordially as vehicles for the active sensibility of human beings; that is, they provide the perspectives for seeing the world as interesting, as something that matters and that warrants interpretation. Emotions are not primarily psychic phenomena originating purely from one's "inner condition"; rather, they take form in the interaction between a person and the world as the world is perceived by the person through an act of consciousness. In this way an emotion orients a person toward the world in a "concernful" manner (BT 172–82).

When any mode of emotional consciousness (for example, joy) is pro-longed through time so that it continually influences how a person perceives and thinks about the world, the emotion becomes mood-like in nature. Moods are generalized emotions permeating a person's existence. Even one's passive indifference to the world, wherein thought appears to vanish into the "pallid, evenly balanced lack of mood," still warrants recognition as being an emotional orientation between a person and the world; it is still a mood. Moods are therefore an ever-present quality of human existence. "The fact that moods can deteriorate . . . and change over means simply that in every case Dasein always has some mood" (BT 173), some mode of emotional consciousness that enables it to disclose and understand the world in a specific and meaningful way.

In performing this interpretive or hermeneutical function, emotions serve a "truthful" purpose. Recall that, for Heidegger, truth *happens* first and fore-most as a disclosure of the world, a revealing of something that directs our concern for being. It may thus be said, for example, that the emotionally intense visions of suffering that Picasso was able to disclose in his 1937 paint-ings *Guernica* and *Head of a Horse* are displays of truth—displays that, in their own concerned way, are as reasonable and rational as the assertion that two times two makes four. Unlike this "objective" assertion, which need only func-tion on an intellectual level for its content to be apprehended, Picasso's dis-plays are "subjective" and function primarily on an existential level. His paintings project a protest against the brutality of fascism in particular and modern war in general. At the same time, they project the *real* suffering that he was experiencing and living as he visualized the pain of creatures under attack and being destroyed. The paintings are not what Picasso thinks, but what he is as an emotionally concerned being. They express an existential truth: "something which one *is* rather than *has,* something which one *lives* rather than *possesses.*"[4]

Heidegger insists that any form of cognitive determining owes at least something to the disclosive capabilities of emotion. Reason itself poses no exception here. Even when reason is couched in the most positivistic language (such that it can be "objective" in its registration of "facts"), its announcements will always be rooted in what emotion makes possible—that is, an interpretation of some matter of interest, a concern for being. Hence, the so-called dispassionate claims of reason—as made by science, for example—can never escape the emotion that begets their existence. By adhering (passionately) to the belief that man is a rational animal, Western philosophy devotes much of its twenty-five-hundred-year history to teaching us that this escape is not only possible but necessary if "truth" is to be discovered. But with his investigations of our everydayness, Heidegger teaches otherwise. Moreover, Heidegger would have us understand that the relationship between emotion and our everydayness is one that also has much to do with the temporality and spatiality of human existence.

Time and space.   As that which orients and directs our concern for being, emotion also functions to structure what Heidegger describes as the essential meaning of this human phenomenon: temporality. Recall that for Heidegger, "*The 'essence' of Dasein lies in its existence,*" in its constant "projective" involvement with the temporal process of becoming and understanding its possibilities. This "potentiality-for-Being," a potentiality that constitutes the "not yet" of a person's future development, is what Heidegger refers to when he writes of the temporality of human concern, or what he also terms the "primordial time" of Dasein's "authentic temporality," which "lies in advance" of our common everyday understanding of time (BT 377–78; BP 266). The distinction here is crucial if one is to appreciate fully how emotion functions to structure the temporality of human concern.

The terms *future, past,* and *present,* for example, are those of common, everyday time. They suggest what time is in a language of measurement and standardization; a language that separates time into a linear progression of discrete units; a language of seconds, minutes, hours, days, years, and so on; a language that *spatializes* time by representing it as an infinite succession of instants or "nows"; a language that makes its appearance in clocks, calendars, and maps. Such a language, however, does not account for the actual nature of the temporality of human concern, for the way this phenomenon happens before it is transformed, segmented, and reified by expressions that compose common parlance.

The way of temporality is that of a unity where future, past, and present are interpenetrating and inseparable *ekstasies* (in the literal sense of the Greek *ek-stasis:* a standing outside and beyond oneself) rather than juxtaposed dimensions defined within an objectified spatiotemporal coordinate (BT 377). A human being is not a "thing" that merely lives "in" time; a human does not exist just "now" and "then" as does a coin in a pocket. Rather, a human being *exists as time,* as a being who is presently living its "having been" that once was its future, and who, at the same time, is presently living out the possibilities that are yet to come. The temporality of human concern is a "unitary phenomenon." The future, past, and present presuppose the ekstatic character of this phenomenon's existence. Hence, Heidegger writes: "The character of 'having been' arises from the future, and in such a way that the future which 'has been' (or better, which 'is in the process of having been') releases from itself the Present. This phenomenon has the unity of a future which makes present in the process of having been; we designate it as '*temporality*'" (BT 374).

Notice here how the future becomes the pivotal *ekstasis* in Heidegger's definition of the temporality of human concern. Indeed, for Heidegger, "*The primary phenomenon of primordial and authentic temporality is the future*" (BT 378): a person's existence is always "on the way" (*unterwegs*) toward understanding what can or will be in her life but is "not yet." Along with the disclosive capacity of our emotional dispositions, this potentiality-for-Being makes possible our "openness to the world." Without this potentiality, we could not be open to the world because, as should be quite obvious, we would not exist; our time on earth would be over. However, without some emotion or mood to orient and direct our concern for being, we could not actualize our potential for being open to the world by seeing it as interesting, as something that matters and that warrants interpretation. With this in mind, we are now in a position to understand more fully not only how emotion functions to structure the temporality of human concern but also how this structuring gives rise to the way in which we live a spatial existence.

Emotion structures our temporality by spatializing it. The primordial occurrence of this phenomenon takes place by way of our emotionally disclosive ability to see the world as a matter of interest. Owing to this ability, according to Heidegger, we are able to become involved in an "encounter" with "what has presence environmentally" and thus with what can now be made into an object of concern (BT 134–38). This immediate making-present function of emotion exists throughout our lives. As long as we are conscious of what is going on in the world, we are never without some emotion or mood to direct our attention toward those objects with which we must deal circumspectively on a daily basis in order to live a meaningful life. Following Heidegger, it can thus be said that the making-present function of emotion has the effect of situating our concern for being in the here and now, in the immediacy of our everyday existence, in that time and place called "the Present" (BT 374).

Earlier I alluded to this structuring of the temporality of human concern when mentioning how time is commonly conceptualized as a spatialized succession of measurable units. When structured this way, time becomes a tool, an instrument, a piece of equipment—something that is "ready-to-hand" and can be used for the practical purpose of managing moment by moment the everydayness of one's present existence. Is it not the case, as is often said, that in everyday existence "time is of the essence" because here and now there is so much to do and so little time to do it that "he (or she) who hesitates is lost"? Yes, there are only twenty-four hours in a day, yet still the clock ticks—every day. We created this ticking to help orchestrate the tempo of our lives. The ticking is there, however, because we first used our emotional capacity to see time as interesting, as something that matters and that warrants interpretation. The interpretation gives a certain structure to time. In everyday existence, time is "spaced" and space is "timed."

But as Heidegger points out, emotion has a more primordial relationship with time and space than this. With its making-present function, emotion first and foremost situates our concern for being in a lived and attuned space (the everyday world of know-how), where distance is experienced, not as metrical measurement, but as existential remoteness and closeness. Heidegger illustrates this primordial spatiality of our existence when he notes, for example, that while walking down the street, "one feels the touch of it at every step as one walks; it is seemingly the closest and Realest of all that is ready-to-hand, and it slides itself, as it were, along certain portions of one's body—the soles of one's feet. And yet it is farther remote than the [friend] whom one encounters 'on the street' at a 'remoteness' . . . of twenty paces when one is taking such a walk" (BT 141–42). In the situation of this lived space, the presence of the street is of little concern compared to the presence of the friend. The street is a matter of indifference; the friend is a matter of joy. Indifference makes what is close become remote; joy makes what is remote become close.

Again, the spatiality of such an existential configuration is not initially apprehended as one would measure the distance between two points in space. Rather, the primordial spatiality of our existence (which makes possible any such measurement) is always there with it, immediately and constantly, by way of our being open to the world through our emotional dispositions and our potentiality-for-Being. The making-present, or disclosive, function of emotion allows for what Heidegger describes as "Dasein's making room for itself" in its everyday involvements with things and with others (BT 419). The space of this room will vary in accordance with the different emotions at work defining the situation at hand. As H. F. Ellenberger notes, "Love, for instance, is 'space-binding': the lover feels himself close to the beloved in spite of distance, because in the spatial modality of love, distance is transcended. Happiness expands the attuned space; things are felt as 'aggrandized.' . . . Sorrow constricts attuned space, and despair makes it empty."[5] Be it large or small, empty or full, the presence of our lived space owes much to the ways of emotion.

We must not forget, however, that there is something else to which our emotionally directed spatiality is indebted, something that its existence pre-supposes. Heidegger emphasizes this fact when he writes, *"Only on the basis of its ecstatico-horizontal temporality is it possible for Dasein to break into space"* (BT 421). In other words the basis of our spatiality is our potentiality-for-Being, our primordial and authentic temporality, our essential way of living a "future which makes present in the process of having been." Heidegger makes much of this fact in stressing the importance of another fact: the present and the future status of our lived and attuned space is always being modified by the past, by our constant involvement in the process of having been. Although this second fact may appear to be something less than profound, its development by Heidegger is essential to the purpose of this discussion.

According to Heidegger, the modification of our lived and attuned space is rooted in our repeatedly being influenced to use our emotions for the pur-pose of seeing, interpreting, and becoming involved with the world in specific and meaningful ways. This influence shows itself as soon as we are "thrown" into the world through birth. We are subjected from then on to the manners in which the members of our culture employ its emotional dispositions to cre-ate and sustain a world of common sense and common praxis, a world of pub-licness, a world of "the everydayness of Being-with one another." Throughout our having been and continuing to be a subject of and in this world, we come to understand the "appropriate" ways for structuring our temporality into a lived and attuned space that puts us in touch with others. In this world of know-how, of emotion, of time and space, our being in touch with others is sustained and modified by yet another essential feature of everydayness: dis-course.

Discourse. Heidegger's understanding of this phenomenon was pre-viewed at the beginning of this chapter. In his later philosophy Heidegger developed an expansive appreciation of discourse, associating it with the "Say-ing" (*Logos*) of "Being itself"— that is, with the presencing of all that lies before us and that calls for thought. More will be said about this matter in chapter 2. In *Being and Time,* however, discourse (*Rede*) is more closely aligned with the unthematized and nonverbal "articulation" (the hermeneutical "as") of under-standing that is operating in the world of know-how, as well as with any the-matized and verbal articulation of understanding that functions to make explicit in some manner how people are faring in their everyday relationships with things and with others. The interpretive understanding that belongs to this second mode of discourse thereby shows itself as a "derivative mode" of the primordial, hermeneutical "as" of circumspective interpretation. Heideg-ger discusses this derivative mode of interpretive understanding in terms of how it operates as an assertion, as "apophantic" discourse (*apophansis:* to make manifest) that *points out* something by *predicating* it in a definite way such that what is being talked about can be *communicated* and shared with others (BT 196–99). One finds such an articulation of intelligibility happening with all types of discourse—from the specialized assertions of science and logic to the more common assertions that periodically punctuate the practice of everyday life.

What Heidegger finds especially noteworthy concerning an assertion's apophantic mode of operation is how it brings about what he terms a "leveling of the primordial 'as' of circumspective interpretation" (BT 198–201). One sees this phenomenon unfolding, for example, when physicians, trained as they are to abide by and express the scientifically oriented "voice of medicine," engage in the practice of "properly" writing up a patient's "medical case history." I want to elaborate on this specific example because it is especially pertinent to the long-range goals of this book and will serve as a topic for thought in most of the remaining chapters.

Medical case histories are rooted in the "illness stories" of patients. Such stories, according to Eric Cassell, "are different from other stories because they almost always have at least *two* characters to whom things happen. They always have at least a *person* and that person's *body*."[6] Of these two characters, it is the body, the place where a disease happens, that must assume priority as a matter of interest to the physician who hopes to find a cure. Directed by this priority, the physician can now begin constructing a story that will—or at least should, so far as his or her peers are concerned—cut like a scalpel through the personhood of the patient, thereby leaving intact only those portions of the patient's history that can be used to make a good case about some disease, in some body, in some bed. Medical case histories mark out an effort in dissection directed toward offering a depersonalized perception and account of the patient. They are prized for their self-effacing objectivity and efficiency, both of which are registered via the antiseptic language of "disease theory" and what it has to say about such things as "angina pectoris," "rheumatic mitral valvular disease," and "oat cell carcinoma of the lung." Medical case histories employ a language that tells a *body story,* not a *person story.* From the standpoint of medical science, these two stories are not meant to go together. They employ different language games; their respective characters are incommensurate. Indeed the idiosyncratic subjectivity of the *person* gets in the way of the scientific objectivity of the *body*. When this occurs, the medical matter at hand may become too time consuming, too existential, too uncertain and opinionated. Remember the Hippocratic law: "There are in fact two things, science and opinion; the former begets knowledge, the latter ignorance."[7] Medical case histories offer stories that are law abiding.

Anyone who has ever benefited from a physician's ability to tell such a story may have little trouble testifying to its importance. When complaints surface, however, they often bear on the fact that, during one's encounter with the medical profession, he or she was treated by physicians whose scientific conditioning and outlook blinded them to the difference between physiology and life. What tends to be forgotten when such blindness occurs is that patients are also *persons* and should be treated as such. A diseased body is also a *lived* body that brings to the medical encounter a host of personal concerns, involvements, and values (a world of know-how) that the patient may want to have taken into account in the designing of a prescribed treatment regimen. Patients have the right to do this; they have the right to affirm who they are while in the presence of Medicine. This large dimension of the patient's humanity is left out of the picture by the ways and means of a well-told body story. Here, then, is an instance of the "leveling of the primordial 'as' of circumspective interpretation." The assertions of a body story point out and predicate their object in a very restrictive way. Their apophantic mode of operation, as Heidegger would say, "no longer reaches out into a totality of involvements" (BT 200), that is, into the patient's hermeneutically informed world of know-how.

Manifesting itself in the ways people are involved with the everyday concerns and contingencies of life, the world of know-how has a richness that has much to tell us about who we are and what it means to be. Heidegger speaks of this richness as a philosopher, a phenomenologist, a thinker of Being who seeks to disclose with his discourse the ontological structures that make possible the intricate dynamics of know-how. Something similar is going on, according to Heidegger, in "poetical" discourse, for "poetry, creative literature, is nothing but the elementary emergence into words, the becoming uncovered, of existence as being in the world [of know-how]. For the others who before it were blind, the world first becomes visible by what is thus spoken" (BP 171–72). Although far more "philosophical" in tone and structure than poetry, Heidegger's discourse has something poetic about it. The poet attempts to reach out into existence and disclose a "totality of involvements" whose truth (disclosure) has yet to be genuinely understood by others. Thus the poet is engaged in the constant struggle of using discourse in such a way as to avoid as much as possible its "leveling down" tendencies. Perhaps this is why it has been said that physicians should read a little poetry as part of their training. What they might learn there is how to widen and deepen their understanding of those whom they are obliged to serve; and this, in turn, could result in "a more total embracing of the patient's condition."[8]

In our everyday being-with-others there is no getting away totally from the leveling-down tendency of discourse. No discourse can say it all; there is always something being concealed in the revelatory assertions of what one has to say about some matter of interest. The more a given discourse conceals about its subject matter, the more its leveling-down tendency is at work. According to Heidegger, the presence of this tendency is especially apparent in what he terms the discourse of "idle talk" (*Gerede*)—a type of discourse that, for Heidegger, has no small role to play in our everyday being-with-others. Heidegger describes idle talk as discourse that "discourages any new inquiry and any disputation," encourages people to follow "the route of gossiping and passing the word along," and "releases [them] from the task of genuinely understanding" how they are faring in their relationships with things and with others (BT 211–14). The scope of such discourse is far ranging: idle talk is the stuff of hearsay, innuendoes, and stereotypes. It prevails in the surface understanding of the "news" of the day that the media generates with its pseudoevents, sound bites, and "Now . . . This" mentality.[9] It announces itself in the well-worn and reified language of an ideology that is more easily and mindlessly repeated than it is truly understood and appreciated for what it is actually disclosing *and* concealing with its slogans and doctrines. Idle talk is heard whenever we say the "appropriate" things to people ("Be my guest," for example) more out of habit than out of a genuine concern and respect for their being. Idle talk is the "chatter" of "small talk" that helps to sustain the average understanding of our publicness, of our everyday manner of being with things and with others.

Concentrating, as he does, on the way in which the leveling tendency of idle talk lends itself to promoting the baseness of conformism, Heidegger's assessment of this discursive practice is rather unflattering. He nevertheless makes it clear, however, that the interpretive understanding that manifests itself in and through idle talk defines an essential aspect of our existence: "This everyday way in which things have been interpreted is one into which Dasein has grown in the first instance, with never a possibility of extrication. In it, out of it, and against it, all genuine understanding, interpreting, and communicating, all re-discovering and appropriating anew, are performed" (BT 213). With idle talk the "rhetorical" grounds are set for disclosing and concealing the truth of some matter of importance.[10]

Heidegger maintains that the effort in truth-telling brought about by the first of these two options defines an activity that is crucial for cultivating the social, political, and moral welfare of our everyday being-with-others. In order to engage ourselves in this activity, we must listen carefully to what is being said in the discourse of idle talk so as to determine how our prevailing ways of seeing, interpreting, and involving ourselves with the world might be changed for the better. "Being-with develops in listening to one another," writes Heidegger (BT 206). By listening to the discourse of others, we open ourselves to the ways in which they are employing language to say something about the world. This is how we learn to think and speak like others and thereby to form a communal bond with them. Listening, in other words, helps make possible our publicness; it is our primary way of responding to the discourse of others and to the "call" that this discourse emits as its language speaks.

Remember, language does indeed "speak," insofar as it says something to us, points something out to us, shows us something through an act of disclosure. We may affirm what is being said with this disclosure or, finding it to be too concealing of its topic, we may opt to see and hear things differently. The existential status of our publicness is maintained and modified in accordance with the consequences that follow from these decisions, based as they are on a certain perceptual ability. Although it is easily taken for granted because we supposedly do it all the time, *knowing how* to listen is not something we should dismiss as being unimportant to how we live our lives in the company of others. Human existence is nothing without this company. Remember, "so far as Dasein *is* at all, it has Being-with-one-another as its kind of Being" (BT 163). Our existence is marked with an indelible communal character. For the benefit of others, as well as for ourselves, we have an obligation to listen and respond to the call of their discourse.

But such a call comes not only from what others have to say, point out, and show. It also comes—and in a most ontologically original and thus authentic way—from a presence that is much closer to us and that Heidegger describes as "the voice of the friend whom every Dasein carries with it" (BT 206). As long as we exist, this friend is present before us, forever calling, forever demanding a hearing. For the friend being referred to here is our "ownmost potentiality-for-Being," our own "projective" involvement with the temporal process of becoming and understanding that which we are: our possibilities. Hence, when Heidegger speaks of "the voice of the friend," he is directing our attention toward a happening whose truth, as briefly noted earlier in this chapter, manifests itself as the primordial occurrence of the call of conscience.[11] Human existence and the call of conscience go hand in hand. As beings whose existence is marked with an indelible communal character (publicness), we are bound to hear the call within the context of our everyday being-with-others. Our response to what the call has to say, show, and disclose must therefore contend with how our thinking and behavior are conditioned by this world of everydayness.

What I have said so far about the nature and mode of operation of our everydayness was intended to set forth a basic understanding of what this conditioning entails so that the reader might be better prepared to appreciate the full scope and function of the ontological workings of the call of conscience. To listen to the call of this most indispensable of friends is to learn something essential about what it means to be. Although Heidegger emphasizes that such an act of listening constitutes a "personal" undertaking on the part of a human being, he also admits, as will be discussed later, that what is learned here has much to tell us about the respect that is owed to others. There is something quite educational about the call of conscience. Hence, for the benefit of ourselves as well as for others, we have an obligation to listen and respond to a call that is embedded in the very fabric of human existence.

The Ontological Workings
of the Call of Conscience

Human Being and the Challenge of the Call

Conscience calls. The everyday discourses of religion and other moral systems remind us of this fact as they instruct us about doing the right things and living the good life. These instructions function in terms of a challenge-response logic. That is, the evocation of a moral system's call of conscience is simultaneously a provocation whose "voice" commands: "Thou shalt" do this! "Thou shalt not" do that! The prescriptions advanced by this voice are meant to be taken *to* heart, not merely known *by* heart. When it comes to responding to the challenging dictates of conscience that constitute some system of morality, being able to recall and recite them, although important, is not good enough. Moral systems emit a call of conscience that calls for concerned thought *and* the "appropriate" (prescribed) behavior to go with it. A moral system's call of conscience is action-oriented: even when it tells us *not* to do something, it still is telling us not *to do* something. By putting into practice what the call brings to mind, we display what it supposedly takes to be an "upstanding" member of the community, a model citizen, a person whose character (*ethos*) warrants praise and imitation. The challenge-response logic of a moral system's call of conscience is a character-building operation.

Heidegger makes much of this operation in his phenomenology of conscience. There is, to be sure, a challenge-response logic at work when conscience calls. No moral system could exist without it. Heidegger certainly wants us to realize this, but he also wants us to realize something more: namely, that the challenge-response logic of any moral system defines an operation that originates in something greater, and thus *other,* than the system's specific ethical prescriptions and prohibitions. I have already given some indication of what this something is for Heidegger: the operation shows itself originally in the way in which our temporal existence is itself a challenge calling for a response. We are creatures who are always caught up in the play of time, always on the way toward understanding what can or will be in our lives but is not yet, and thus always confronted with the task of trying to make sense of, and to do something with, our lives.

Human being (Dasein) is its own evocation and provocation: it calls for the responsiveness of concerned thought and action, for that which enables us, even in the most distressful situations, to take charge of our lives as we assume the responsibility of affirming our freedom through resolute choice and thereby become personally involved in the creation of a meaningful existence. This is how systems of morality come into being in the first place. The language of morality is the language of responsiveness and responsibility. The challenge-response logic at work in a moral system's character-building call of conscience is always already operating in the very being of our temporal existence. Human being emits its own challenging call, its own call of conscience, which is constantly forthcoming and which demands a heartfelt response— much like a friend in need. Hence, for Heidegger, if we are to develop a genuine appreciation of the call of conscience, we must pay particular attention to how this phenomenon manifests itself first and foremost as an ontological structure of our existence.

Conscience calls. This call is happening all the time. It discloses itself as the "giving-to-understand" of our temporal existence, of our "ownmost potentiality-for-Being." For Heidegger it thus makes perfect sense to speak of the "call" (or even the "voice") of conscience when describing the ontological workings of the phenomenon, for conscience does indeed function discursively: it has the formal structure of "discourse" (*Rede*), which, as noted in chapter 1, is a mode of "disclosure" in which something is said, pointed out, revealed, and shared. The call of conscience is human existence disclosing itself to the one living it. This is what is "talked about" when conscience calls: the givenness, "the bare 'that it is,'" of one's Being. Or, as Heidegger puts it, "*In conscience Dasein calls itself*" (BT 317–21).

This way of stating the matter alerts us to the fact that the call of conscience, understood ontologically, is not something that comes first and foremost from you or from me or from any other individual. Dasein is not a person; rather, it is the Being of a person's temporal existence—that which we live every day but did not create, that which warrants a response but that we "have neither planned nor prepared for nor voluntarily performed." The call of conscience is rooted in something other than the traditional ways of life that constitute and define the "I," the ego, of one's subjectivity. Hence, as he writes about conscience, Heidegger emphasizes that "'it' calls," and it does this "against our expectations and even against our will" (BT 320).

There appears to be something impersonal about the character, the *ethos,* of the call of conscience. Indeed "it" calls, "it" discloses, "it" gives! One might feel more comfortable "knowing" that what is disclosed and given here for understanding is, in fact, an indication of the wondrous ways of God. Although Heidegger neither affirms nor denies the feasibility of this explanation, he does maintain that with it we "pass over the phenomenal findings too hastily"; and he thereby insists that "the fact that the call is not something which is explicitly performed *by me,* but that rather 'it' does the calling, does not justify seeking the caller in some entity with a character other than that of Dasein" (BT 320–21).

For Heidegger, if we are to treat the call of conscience with the highest reverence, we must not jump to metaphysical and onto-theological conclusions before we have taken the time to consider most carefully (that is, phenomenologically) all that is involved as the call presents itself to us. In doing this, according to Michael Zimmerman, Heidegger "cannot decide for the religious person whether, in fact, God speaks in conscience, but he can show that such speaking could not occur unless we were ontologically structured to be able to hear it."[1] The workings of the call of conscience manifest themselves in the disclosive happening, and thus in the giving-to-understand of human existence. If there is something impersonal about this, so be it.

Yet in holding fast to this character of the call, we would be wrong not to notice that there is also something quite personal going on here. For although no particular person is its author, "the 'it' which does the calling" is nothing less than a person's *own* temporal existence, his or her essential way of being in the world as Dasein, as that entity capable of understanding "the fact 'that it is, and that it has to be something with a potentiality-for-Being as the entity which it is'" (BT 320–21). This is what the call of conscience discloses, what it gives us to understand. The call, in other words, brings us face to face with what Heidegger describes as the *"constancy of the Self."*

The Self of a human being is its temporality, its existence, its potentiality-for-Being its possibilities. A human being's "own Self" finds its existential origins here—in this ontological "ability to be" that makes possible, for example, one's becoming a teacher, a husband, a Christian, or whatever. For any human being this ability is uniquely his or her "own" (*eigen*); it defines the "authenticity" (*Eigentlichkeit*), the most primordial truth, of human being. Hence, in the truest and most authentic sense of the term, this self-activity can be claimed by any person to be personally and properly "mine." It forms the temporal basis of a person's historically situated and thus "finite" freedom, which is always anchored to and constrained by past decisions, present involvements, one's biological condition, and existing environmental factors (BT 67–68, 163–68, 369).

As its ability to be unfolds in and through time, a person's freedom is never without that which can and does make its life a task, a struggle, a continual effort in survival. The call of conscience discloses the *"Self-constancy"* of this challenging nature of our existence. Responding to this challenge is the fundamental vocation that a human being is called to by the evocation of conscience. The point is worth repeating:*"In conscience Dasein calls itself."* So as Heidegger says, the call is something that comes *"from beyond me and over me."* But it also can be said, following Heidegger, that the call comes *"from me,"* that is, from who I am as that entity (Dasein) whose ability to be is quite a personal matter, since it forms the basis of all that I say and do (BT 320).

Based on what has been said so far about Heidegger's analysis of the call of conscience, it should be clear that he wants us to understand how the phenomenon is fundamentally and inextricably related to the temporal character of human existence and thus to the authenticity of Dasein's "ownmost potentiality-for-Being-its-Self." When concerning ourselves with this relationship, we must therefore keep in mind that the call of conscience functions in accordance with, and discloses something other than, what time is made out to be once it is transformed into those discrete units of measurement (seconds, minutes, hours, days) that help to structure and regulate our everyday activities. The call comes to us from beyond this world of "public time." What it gives us to understand is not a set of standards for knowing how to tell and manage time, but rather that upon which these standards take form: the temporality of our Being (BT 464–72). To hear the call of conscience is to be made aware of this difference between the public time of our daily lives and the more "primordial time" of existence itself. I spoke of this difference earlier when discussing the nature of our common way of inhabiting the world ("everydayness"). Indeed there is no way of getting around the topic of our everydayness when one is attempting to comprehend the ontological workings of the call of conscience.

Like anything else that we are able to perceive and understand, the identity of the call of conscience must be distinguished from those things that it is not. For example, Heidegger would certainly have us recognize that the call itself is not "the moral faculty of judgment, passing judgment upon itself" (Kant); nor is it the result of some "evolutionary" process (Darwin) whereby we develop our ability to sympathize with, appropriate, and give expression to the "moral sentiments" of those whose character and conduct is deemed "praiseworthy" (Hume, Adam Smith); nor is it the embodiment of the "will to power" (Nietzsche); nor the voice of the "super-ego" exerting parental control over our freedom (Freud). Although such explanations of the call's nature introduce various topics that, from the standpoint of Heidegger's phenomenological perspective, must be taken into account when trying to assess its scope and function, they nevertheless fail to realize or to clarify specifically how the call is itself an ontological structure of our Being, embedded in the very fabric of our temporal existence.

The call of conscience speaks to us of this existence; it reveals how we are always "on the way" toward understanding what can or will be in our lives but is not yet; it discloses and opens us to our potentiality-for-Being. This is what the call does. It thus shows itself *to be* something that *is not* simply tied to, and identifiable with, the type of time that marks our everydayness and that, for example, weighs on our minds as we are rushing around in order to avoid being late for some engagement. For Heidegger this is the most existentially relevant and thus important distinction to be made when attending to the call's identity. For the distinction is specifically commended to us by the call itself, by what it discloses: the call of conscience makes an issue of the *temporal* character of human existence; it thereby also and necessarily makes an issue of our everydayness.

Everything Heidegger has to say about the call of conscience is in some way or another related to this practically oriented world of circumspective concern with its values, standards, and conventions for knowing what is right and wrong, and for knowing how to think and act accordingly, whatever the situation. As previously discussed, this world of everydayness offers a recurring lesson in hermeneutic competence, that is, in how one should see, interpret, and become meaningfully involved with things and with others so as to sustain a world of common sense and common praxis, a world of communal normalcy—which is to say a world of everydayness. Our everyday way of being in the world supplies us with the symbolic materials that help to shape our identities and selves, who we know ourselves to be as we are working with (and being worked by) these materials day after day. Heidegger recognizes the world of everydayness as defining an unavoidable ontological structure of human existence: its presence in our lives is the result of our being the purposive, pragmatic, and social creatures that we are. Importantly, Heidegger also recognizes that the world of everydayness is where the call of conscience is necessarily received. The call does not come *from* this world of know-how, but it does come *to* it. And it does this in the form of a challenge—one that we have been referring to all along.

The call of conscience confronts us with the challenge of our temporal existence, of how it is that we are always caught up in the process of having to deal with what is "not yet" in our lives (the future), and thus of how it is that our existence is constantly calling on us to face our possibilities with anticipation and to assume the personal and ethical responsibility of affirming our freedom through resolute choice. As Theodore Kisiel puts it, "Dasein is always first on the receiving end of existence, ever in need to be receptive and responsive to its demands."[2] This is what the call of conscience brings to our attention: it sounds an ongoing call for concerned thought and decisive action, for that which enables us to assess and perhaps change for the better those values, standards, and conventions that govern and normalize our everyday relationships with things and with others. The challenge exposed by the call of conscience, in other words, makes us aware of what is needed if our everyday existence is not merely to become a way of being where complacency and conformity rule the day and thus where, as Heidegger states it, "the real dictatorship of the 'they'" shows itself. The power of this dictatorship to condition, constrain, and reify our thought and behavior with its values, standards, and conventions is that which is directly challenged by the call of conscience.

The world of the "they," according to Heidegger, is one where "everyone is the other and no one is himself," and where assuming the personal and ethical responsibility of affirming one's freedom through resolute choice is uncalled for because others have already made the "proper" choices that are necessary for "leading and sustaining a full and genuine 'life.'" In the world of the "they," we are conditioned to forsake and forget what the call of conscience has to say, what it discloses and thereby requires from us: the "resoluteness" of personal commitment and responsibility. The call of conscience challenges us to own up to our own existence, even as we are led to do otherwise in the world of the "they." With Heidegger, then, it may therefore be said that, as it calls, "Conscience summons Dasein's Self from its lostness in the 'they'" (BT 310; also 165, 222).

With this summons comes an option: we must either choose the way we want to live our lives or allow others to do the choosing for us; we either achieve integrity through resolute choice or lose integrity through a retreat from choice. We cannot escape this either/or condition of existence. "As truly as there is a future," Kierkegaard once wrote, "just so truly is there an either/or."[3] Heidegger agrees. Human existence brings with it a challenge-response logic, a most primordial call of conscience that has a *constructive* ring to it. The future is constantly calling us to acknowledge our authenticity and thus to shoulder the responsibility of making thoughtful decisions about how to build and live a meaningful life. Heidegger notes, however, that if we are to remain "authentic" while living the commitment of our decisions, we must be prepared and willing at any moment to question the supposed correctness of what we are thinking and doing as a result of having made these decisions (BT 355). The constancy of the call demands as much, for it speaks to us of uncertainty: the future orientation of existence is forever opening us to the possibility of change, of things being otherwise than usual, of how what is yet to come in our lives may require us, for truth's sake, to rethink and revise what we currently hold to be correct about our ongoing commitments, involvements, and interpretive practices.

From the heart of existence comes a constructive call for concerned thought and decisive action, a call of conscience. But this call, related as it is to the future, also has a *de-constructive* ring to it, for it repeatedly calls into question our desire for certainty and stability—a desire that manifests itself whenever we assume the personal and ethical responsibility of affirming our freedom through resolute choice in an effort to bring meaning and order to our everyday existence. In short, listening to the call of conscience, we are constantly told of the importance of being both decisive and open-minded.

Owing to the changing circumstances of our lives, what appears to be "right" now may be "wrong" later. Our everyday way of inhabiting the world is always open to question, always being challenged by something other than itself. The call of conscience speaks to us of (discloses) this fact of life.

We are attending to the ontological character of the call of conscience— how it permeates human existence, how it functions in accordance with the temporality of our being, how it thereby calls us to be thoughtful, resolute, responsible, and self-critical. Making itself known in the midst of our every-dayness, the call of conscience summons us from our "lostness in the 'they'" and challenges us with the constructive and deconstructive task of living an authentic existence.

There is more to be said about the workings of this challenge than what has been discussed so far. Heidegger advances our understanding of the topic as he describes how our being open to the call of conscience defines an anx-ious and disorienting experience—one that brings us face to face with our fini-tude (our "Being-unto-Death") and the ever-present state of "Being-guilty" that is concomitant with this fact of life. In developing this description, Heidegger also reveals how the call of conscience, in addition to everything else, requires the building of community. A fuller treatment of these matters is offered below; it begins with a further consideration of how the call of conscience makes itself known in the midst of our everydayness. The "anxiety of con-science" emerges as this event takes place.

The Interruptive Nature of the Call

In order to hear the truth of what the call of conscience has to say, we must pay careful attention to the temporality of our Being. This "primordial truth" of existence (and its inherent challenge), we have seen, is what the call dis-closes as it makes itself known. Attending to the moment when this revelation actually happens in our everyday lives, Heidegger emphasizes that the call of conscience functions to "interrupt" the way in which we are currently "losing" ourselves "in the publicness and the idle talk of the 'they.'" What thus "gets bro-ken by the call" are our conditioned and typical involvements with things and with others, especially as these involvements admit little more than a compla-cent and conformist allegiance to those values, standards, and conventions that govern and normalize the perceptions, thoughts, and practices of our every-day existence (BT 316).

Living life in this manner secures one's status as a "they-self," whereby one's existence becomes primarily a matter of "going along with the crowd." Although such an existence certainly has its rewards in that it caters to our communal need of inhabiting a world of common sense and common practice, it also can prove to be quite a dangerous thing in that it provides the breeding grounds for the evils of conformism. For Heidegger conformism defines an "inauthentic" state of our "Being-with-others" because it operates to relieve us from the "burden" of explicitly dealing with a challenge that, as detailed above, is disclosed by the call of conscience: the personal challenge of assuming the ethical responsibility of affirming our freedom through resolute choice and of being self-critical.[4] The call of conscience interrupts our absorption in the world of the "they" as it confronts us with this challenge of authenticity, rooted as it is in the temporality of our Being.

Heidegger is rather vague, however, when discussing how this interruption initially occurs. We are only told that it manifests itself as an "abrupt arousal." One might therefore read Heidegger as suggesting that the call is its own catalyst of change. The abrupt arousal of its interruption is all that is needed to make us aware of how we are losing ourselves in the world of the "they" and thus of how we must assume the responsibility of "*making up for not choosing*" if we are to reverse this process (BT 313). What was said earlier about the deconstructive nature of the call's future orientation does lend some support to this reading: the call of conscience is human existence disclosing itself to the one who is living it. The call thus speaks to us of how our temporal Being is forever opening us to what is "not yet" in our lives and to the uncertainty and possibility of change that are concomitant with this way of being toward the future. The call thereby makes us aware of how our everyday understanding of the world is always open to question. Recall also that the call is not something that is "voluntarily performed." Rather, it happens "against our expectations and even against our will"; it reveals itself as something *other* than that which it calls for (concerned thought and decisive action) as it interrupts our lives. The call of conscience is "always already" at work before these capacities are put to use. It may therefore be said that the call of conscience is, in the way it functions, its own catalyst of change, its own interruption, which is constantly occurring, constantly calling and challenging us to be more than a "they-self," whether we realize it or not.

Our failure to hear the call, Heidegger maintains, is the result of how the world of the "they" conditions us to conform to its values, standards, and conventions. Under "the dictatorship of the 'they,'" we are not required to choose but only to be chosen; we are not required to be true to our "ownmost potentiality-for-Being" but only to enjoy and sustain the tranquility that comes from being one of the "they." But is the call's ongoing interruption, in and of itself, enough to make us aware of how we are faring in this social realm of human activity such that we can reform its influence by assuming the responsibility for our own acts as we respond to the call? The process, I submit, is not that simple and direct. The call of conscience does sound a constant interruption, but its "abrupt arousal" is not perceived until something happens to disturb or break down our conditioned and typical ways of understanding the world and of becoming involved with things and with others.

Although Heidegger fails to clarify this point while attending to the workings of the call of conscience, he does prepare us to understand its significance when, earlier in *Being and Time,* he discusses the process by which human awareness arises out of human activity. This discussion centers around what Heidegger discovers to be going on when a tool that we are using suddenly breaks in our hands (BT 102–7). A brief consideration of some of what Heidegger has to say about this phenomenon should therefore prove helpful in advancing our understanding of a specific issue that remains unclear in his ontological assessment of the call of conscience.

When using a tool to accomplish a given task, we find ourselves firmly situated in the practically oriented world of circumspective concern, demonstrating a competence for knowing how to deal with the immediacy of some goal-directed activity. As discussed in chapter 1, our successful involvement with what we are doing here is conditioned by the tool's transparency, by how well it goes unnoticed as it is being used, by how efficiently it facilitates an endeavor by not getting in our way, by not drawing attention to itself, by enabling us to forget its presence. The tool must be inconspicuous if we are to maintain our preoccupation with the situation at hand.

At the moment that the tool breaks, however, all of this changes. It now obtrudes on our awareness, revealing itself as a *factum brutum,* a "thing" divested of its practical significance. This thing gets in the way and impedes our progress. In so doing it also gives us pause for thought: What is going on here, and what can be done about it? We ask this question as beings who can step back from, contemplate, and theorize about our daily preoccupations so that we might understand them better and perhaps improve on their performance. The defective tool forces us to become engaged in this reflective process to some degree; it thereby brings about a modification of our circumspective and instrumental way of being situated in the world. That is, when the tool breaks, loses its transparency, and becomes an all-too-noticeable thing, we are abruptly dislocated from a preoccupation, from work in progress, and are situated in a more theoretically oriented position to understand the environment. For when the tool breaks, its status as a well-designed, ready-to-hand piece of equipment discloses itself differently, more fully and explicitly, and thus in a way that was not possible so long as the work was flowing smoothly. The tool's being—what it is and does—is no longer absent and forgettable but is instead quite present, memorable, and remarkable. The broken tool opens itself for inspection as it "announces itself afresh" (BT 98–105).

What we are thereby given to see (*theoria*) more vividly when this happens is not, however, restricted to a single piece of equipment. For the tool's "unusability" not only calls attention to the tool itself, but it also makes us more mindful of other pieces of equipment whose functions are connected to what the tool is supposed to do. For example, when a computer malfunctions and becomes conspicuous and thus questionable, it also calls into question the usefulness of the desk, printer, paper, work station, and well-lit room that once supported its operation. The everyday world of know-how marks out an instrumental matrix whose infrastructure entails the interconnectivity of equipment.[5] The broken tool gives notice of this; it discloses a "truth" about itself and related things that warrants thought, especially if we are to figure out and fix what went wrong so that we can get back to being preoccupied with the task at hand and to a world of practice where all is well once again.

Could something as simple as a tool that abruptly breaks in our hands alert us to the call of conscience? It's possible. For example, a malfunctioning computer might arouse its user not only to become more aware of what it takes to perform and complete a given task (working on a manuscript, for example) but also to give thought to how a sustained preoccupation with this task is leading this person to become too neglectful of others (such as family members) who deserve to be treated in a much more caring and respectful way. In this case, the question brought about by the defective tool—What is going on here, and what can be done about it?—is no longer merely restricted to knowing how to remedy a technological breakdown. A certain realization has made the situation more complicated than that. Another option for action is now apparent—one that, if taken, will further delay the person's preoccupation with completing a task as he attends instead to other pressing concerns. Hence, in this situation the person is necessarily confronted with the personal challenge of critically assessing his existence and of assuming the responsibility of *explicitly* choosing a course of action that is oriented toward reinstating a sense of order in the person's life. The call of conscience, in other words, has caught the person's attention and awaits a response.

Heidegger tells us that the call of conscience "makes itself known as a Fact only with factical existence and in it" (BT 313). The above example offers a concrete illustration of how this is so. We are alerted to the call by way of an occurrence that so disrupts our conditioned and typical ways of understanding and inhabiting the world that we are thereby brought face to face with the ever-present challenge of owning up to our own existence, our own "authentic potentiality-for-Being." Later on, I will discuss how such a disruptive occurrence can be brought about by the practice of rhetoric, which is one of the fundamental ways that the orator's art is related to the call of conscience. Much will be made of this point when I turn my attention to the euthanasia debate. Within this debate rhetors are obliged to hear and respond to the call, for the debate over the morality or immorality of euthanasia is itself rooted in a disruptive occurrence that reveals the call of conscience in a most vivid and personal way. This occurrence shows itself in the factical existence of people whose bodies and lives have been broken by a serious illness or accident and whose subsequent pain and suffering is so overwhelming that their response to the call is a plea to others to help them die a dignified death. The rhetoric of the euthanasia debate speaks to us of this situation; therefore, it cannot help but be somewhat disruptive in what it has to say.

Committed as he is to describing the ontological workings of the call of conscience, Heidegger omits any specific assessment of how disruptive occurrences in the everyday world facilitate our ability to perceive the call's disclosure. He does make clear, however, that there are additional matters that must be taken into account if we are to grasp the full existential significance of these revealing and thought-provoking occurrences. The first of these matters concerns the way human emotions and moods play a role in orienting us toward the call of conscience. When considering this matter, Heidegger keys on the emotion/mood of anxiety. He does this, not out of any morbidity of temperament, but simply because the revelatory character of anxiety, compared to that of other emotions and moods, is more fundamentally attuned to the call's disclosure.[6]

Other matters that warrant Heidegger's consideration as he elaborates on this point include how anxiety, in opening us to the call of conscience, transforms the lived time and space of everyday existence, how it thereby lets us be directly affected and touched by our mortality, and how it thus forces us to deal with another ontological condition of our Being. As mortal creatures we always find ourselves in a state of "Being-guilty"; we forever owe a debt to existence. A necessarily partial payment of this debt takes place when we respond to that which anxiety brings to our attention: the call of conscience.

The Anxiety of Conscience and Related Matters

The experience of anxiety signals a significant loss of meaning and stability in our lives. It arises when our daily progress is impeded, if not shattered to its very core, by occurrences (such as a serious illness) that disrupt our accustomed routines and relationships with things and with others and that thereby expose us to the uncertainty inherent in our temporal existence. Anxiety focuses on this uncertainty. That is what makes the emotion so disquieting and so dreadful, and thus quite distinctive.

In anxiety we remain open to how the future orientation of existence works to call into question the orderliness of our everyday habits of living. Anxiety thus attunes us most directly to the deconstructive dimension of our temporal existence; it concentrates our attention on the way in which human being makes an issue of itself every second, minute, and hour of the day. In anxiety we are anxious not merely because of some ontic occurrence raising havoc in our lives, but rather because that primordial condition of existence—the temporal openness of our Being—makes itself known by way of such an occurrence. This ever-present condition is the true source of anxiety. For example, a person may feel anxious when suddenly stricken by a serious illness, but the experience of this emotion is possible only if the person cares enough about *what is to become* of his or her existence now that it is no longer what it used to be and perhaps may never be again. In anxiety we stand face to face with the not-yet of the future and thus with the uncertainty that accompanies this dimension of existence that is always ahead of itself. Or, as Heidegger would have it, "Anxiety makes manifest in Dasein its *Being towards* its ownmost potentiality-for-Being," a potentiality "which it always is" (BT 232).

Perhaps it is clear, then, how anxiety is more closely attuned to the call of conscience than is any other emotion. Recall that the call of conscience is a phenomenon that we "have neither planned nor prepared for nor voluntarily performed"; it emanates from something *other* than the traditional ways of life that constitute and guide our everydayness; it is not something that we have created. Rather, the call of conscience is the givenness, "the bare 'that it is'" of human existence disclosing itself to we who are living it. The call thus conveys to us that very happening that anxiety brings to our attention. This is why Heidegger speaks to us of the "*anxiety of conscience*" (BT 342). The two phenomena go hand in hand. In anxiety we become witnesses to a most important, authentic, and challenging revelation: the temporal unfolding of our Being, the call of conscience.

The relationship of anxiety to this revelation helps to explain why we find the experience of anxiety to be so disorienting and distressing and thus to be something we commonly dread. The disorienting nature of anxiety stems from the way the emotion brings about an "existential modification" of our everydayness (BT 268). What is initially modified here is the temporal/spatial character of lived experience. Anxiety directs our attention toward the unfolding of our Being, toward that primordial happening of time that, as discussed earlier in this chapter, "lies in advance" of, and makes possible, the measurements and spaces of "public time" (the hours of the day, for example) that were created by human beings in order to regulate and standardize the tempo of their lives. Anxiety thus makes us especially receptive to, and involves us most intimately with, the "projective" character of our "authentic temporality"—how it is that we are always on the way toward understanding what can or will be in our lives but is not yet.

In anxiety we are caught up in that play of time that transcends the immediacy of the present, of the here and now, and that forms the ontological basis of our future-oriented existence. Hence, in anxiety we are situated in the world in such a way that no psychological distance exists between our "selves" and what this emotion reveals. Heidegger refers to this situation as one wherein we are likely to feel "uncanny" (*unheimlich*: literally, "not-at-home"). The feeling is disorienting; it arises because in anxiety we are dislocated from the familiarity of "Being-at-home" in the everyday world of public time and are delivered over to a different, unspatialized happening of time—wherefrom comes the call of conscience.

Anxiety holds us open to this call as it directs our attention toward the temporal unfolding of our Being. Such a disorienting experience can be quite distressing. Not feeling at-home is a strange and uncomfortable way of being-in-the-world. The situation affects us physiologically. Anxiety is well known for what it can do, for example, to the normal functioning of our cardiovascular system. But the physiological effects of anxiety are just that—effects; their presence is the result of our being brought face to face with the temporality of our "ownmost potentiality-for-Being" and with the uncertainty that accompanies this most basic condition of human existence. Following some disruptive occurrence, anxiety forces us, if only for a moment, to confront the issue of our Being, especially as this issue involves us in trying to come to terms with what is to become of our lives now that our present circumstances are in a distressing state of disarray. How this issue will eventually and finally be resolved is, of course, made clear by human existence itself.

As temporal beings we are radically finite. We not only die; we *know* that we will die. Our potentiality-for-Being is essentially a "Being-toward-the-end," a "Being-toward-death." When the end will come is indefinite; we can only anticipate its impending arrival. But come it will. "As potentiality-for-Being," writes Heidegger, "Dasein cannot outstrip the possibility of death" (BT 294). Putting the matter this way brings us back to the topic of anxiety. The disclosive function of anxiety attunes us most directly to our potentiality-for-Being. It thereby places us in close touch with our own mortality, with "the indefinite certainty of death" that permeates our existence. Anxiety is distressing, not only because it makes us feel *unheimlich* and fosters a host of adverse physiological reactions, but also because with what it discloses it exposes us to that "uttermost possibility" of life that marks the end of our very ability to be.

Our potentiality-for-Being is a Being-toward-death, a Being-toward the most personal and finalizing disruptive occurrence that life has to give. Life carries with it its own negation. The revelatory character of anxiety is far-reaching enough to bring to our immediate attention this primordial truth of existence—a truth that is awe-inspiring in that it is at once fascinating (I am!) and dreadful (But not forever!). Heidegger makes much of how in our everyday existence we are influenced by the "they" which "is constituted by the way things have been publicly interpreted" to avoid developing an authentic understanding of this truth, especially its dreadful aspect. "It is already a matter of public acceptance," he writes, "that 'thinking about death' is a cowardly fear, a sign of insecurity" and "weakness" on our part. In this and other ways, according to Heidegger, "*The 'they' does not permit us the courage for anxiety in the face of death*" (BT 298). The problem here is quite significant, as Heidegger sees it, in that it has much to do with a human being's authentic development. That is, without the courage to face up to our own mortality, to the way in which our potentiality-for-Being *is* a Being-towards-death, we lack the very thing that enables us to be most receptive and responsive to the call of conscience.

I hope this last point follows for the reader. The call of conscience, we should remember, comes to us from out of the temporality of our ownmost potentiality-for-Being, which is to say that it comes to us from the way in which we are each destined to live as a Being-toward-death. Life and death and the call of conscience all go together; they are equiprimordial. Anxiety reveals the relationship: it holds us open to the certainty of our ability-to-be, to the "definite uncertainty" of our ability-not-to-be, and thus to a challenge that is embedded in the temporal structure of our finite existence. Much has already been said about this challenge. It defines the primordial happening of the call of conscience, which makes itself known when our everyday lives are radically disrupted and which thereby summons us to assume, in the face of uncertainty (the not-yet of the future), the personal and ethical responsibility of affirming our freedom through resolute choice.

The call of conscience calls for the courage and commitment of concerned thought and decisive action—the very things that are needed if we are to put our ability-to-be to "good" use while we still have the time to do so. Our existence is so structured as to emit a call that our Being-toward-death makes it wise to answer as often as possible. This is why Heidegger takes exception to those social customs and conventions of the "they" that do not permit us the courage for anxiety in the face of death. For such courage makes it possible to take seriously the full significance of a fact of life whose instructive potential for alerting us to the *urgency* of the call of conscience remains unsurpassed by anything else that life has to give. Heidegger would thus have us understand that "authentic 'thinking about death' is a wanting-to-have-a-conscience" (BT 357), a wanting to be up for meeting the ever-present challenge of being receptive and responsive to a call that emanates from existence itself, from our ownmost potentiality-for-Being (toward-death). And that can make us feel quite anxious.

Being-Guilty

There is, however, an additional price to pay as we go about meeting this challenge: that of having to come to terms with our guilt. According to Heidegger, "The call of conscience has the character of an *appeal* to Dasein by calling it to its ownmost potentiality-for-Being-its-Self; and this is done by way of *summoning* it to its ownmost Being-guilty" (BT 314). Heidegger stresses that a human being does not merely *have* guilt; rather, this being *is* guilty. Guilt is an ontological structure of human existence; it is part and parcel of our existential finitude, of our having to live lives that, no matter how "full" they might be, are necessarily pervaded with negation.

The void of non-Being, the presence of an awesome absence, a "nothingness" (*Nichtigkeit*), penetrates the very core of human existence. Owing to this nothingness, we can never become fully sovereign over our Being. We are mortal creatures; we think and act within a finite understanding of Being. Thus we can never know with absolute certainty what the basis of our Being—its "why" or reason for Being—truly is. All we have before us is its givenness, "the bare 'that it is'" of existence disclosing itself to us and challenging us with its call for concerned thought and decisive action. This disclosure that sounds forth a challenge is not a human creation ("Dasein is not itself the basis of its Being," BT 330), although our everyday existence is certainly indebted to it and to what it constantly calls for.

Imagine what this sociopolitical realm would be like if it were not informed by the concerned thought and decisive action of conscientious human beings! Only by responding to the call of conscience—which comes to us from existence itself but whose ultimate origin must remain a mystery to any finite being—can we play a role in helping to maintain the well-being of our personal and communal existence. The task here is ever-present. The uncertainty of the future, which is always calling us into question, makes certain of that. As long as we are alive we owe a debt to existence, which it itself extracts from us with its call. For Heidegger it is this ever-outstanding debt that defines how our existence is ontologically structured as a Being-guilty.

We offer a necessarily partial payment of this debt as we respond to the call of conscience by assuming the personal and ethical responsibility of affirming our freedom through resolute choice. "Understanding the call is choosing" (BT 334). This is how we come to terms with the guilt that we *are,* whereby our Being-guilty further manifests itself in our "factical" existence. For when we answer the call of conscience and thereby make a choice to live our lives in some meaningfully significant way, we are at the same time necessarily excluding other possible avenues of thought and courses of action that perhaps could serve us equally well if not better. The call of conscience summons us to make such a sacrifice, for as Heidegger notes, "to hear the call authentically signifies bringing oneself into a factical taking action" whereby choices *must* be made (BT 341). Hence, as we respond to the call of conscience, we show ourselves as being guilty of committing a sacrifice, an act of exclusion. Our existence is so structured as to ensure that our lives, from the bottom up, are pervaded by guilt.

"*Dasein as such is guilty,*" claims Heidegger (BT 331). Why this is so should now be clear. We are guilty because of how we forever owe a debt to existence and because of the way this debt must be paid. The call of conscience constantly summons us to choose; and choice requires sacrifice, the excluding of possibilities. Of course, such acts of exclusion occur with all that we say and do every day. It is impossible to live one's life without making choices. The process is easily taken for granted and forgotten when things are going well with our everyday routines. Here our involvement with the process of making choices need be nothing more than an exercise in mindlessly going through the motions that are dictated by our habits of thinking and living. However, when our habitual routines are called into question by occurrences that disrupt our typical involvements with things and with others, the process of making choices is no longer something that can be taken for granted. For now we are confronted most directly with the challenge of having to make a conscientious decision about which of our past and present possibilities we can and ought to employ in trying to restructure our lives in a meaningful way. In other words, the situation here is one in which conscience calls.

Our involvement in the process of making choices must therefore become a personal matter. If, for example, I want to go on repeating what I was doing before my life was disrupted (given that this is still a possibility), the choice is *mine* to make. Others may offer helpful advice, but it is still *I* who must choose. This is why Heidegger speaks of our being "individualized" (BT 322) by the call of conscience. When it catches and directs our attention, we have to *own up to our own existence* and assume the responsibility for what we *are* and *are not* about to do. Shouldering this responsibility attests to our willingness to be open to the charge of being guilty for the choice/sacrifice we decided to make. Such open-mindedness is always what it takes to at least begin the corrective process of making amends and doing things differently.

These last two points bring us back once again to the topic of anxiety. For the more we remain open to our guilt so that we stand ever ready to rectify our perceived misdeeds, the more likely we are to experience that emotion that attunes us most directly to the call of conscience. Recall that anxiety functions by directing our attention to how the future orientation of existence is always calling us into question with its uncertainty. Arising as it does from a disruption of our everyday involvement with things and with others, anxiety brings us face to face with this uncertainty and the challenge that comes with it: having to assume the responsibility of affirming our freedom through resolute choice. Depending on how open-minded we are with respect to our guilt, such an anxiety-provoking disruption can take place as we are made aware of how our ongoing behavior might in some way be harming others and/or ourselves. The situation at hand would thus be one that calls for the remedy of concerned thought and decisive action. A choice must be made that perhaps can change things for the better as it reinstates a sense of order in our lives, thereby lessening the anxiety we are experiencing over whether the choice we are about to make is the appropriate one.

Being in any way uncertain about the correctness of this choice, we leave ourselves open to anxiety. We do the same thing when we remain open to our guilt. Heidegger speaks favorably of such open-mindedness, not because he advocates indecisiveness, but rather because he sees this orientation as being totally in line with the "truth" of our temporal existence. There is an "openness" to human being. We live lives that "stand open" to the future, to its uncertainty, and to the challenge (the call of conscience) that issues forth from this primordial happening of time. This challenge operates as the true source of anxiety and defines the basis of our Being-guilty. Moreover, as we have also seen, the call admitted by this challenge is always urgent, because in living a life that is a Being-toward-death, we can never know for sure how much longer we have to respond. And we must respond; it is a debt we have to pay for being the creatures that we are, for living an existence that, in its openness, is always calling us into question and is, at the same time, always calling for the concerned thought and decisive action that is needed to address this question of our Being in a meaningful and responsible way.

Furthermore, our existence is so structured as to ensure that answering the call of conscience is a never-ending task. We cannot be true to this task unless we are open to its challenge. The truth of our temporal existence—the disclosing of its openness—tells us as much. Being true to the call of conscience, to all that it calls for, is thus being true to ourselves, to the openness of our "ownmost potentiality-for-Being." Remember, "*In conscience Dasein calls itself*" (BT 320). It is a very personal ("individualized") experience.

A common criticism of Heidegger's ontology of conscience is that it is too locked into the "authenticity" of this self-affirming experience; it makes the resolute *self* into a "hero," but at the expense of the *other*. Indeed, Heidegger speaks to us of the "unshakable joy" (BT 358) that we should feel when the call of conscience catches and directs our attention; for then we find ourselves in the awe-inspiring and exhilarating situation where the moment has come for us to be more than a conformist, more than a "they-self," more than what others simply tell us to be. The "dictatorship of the they" is an affront to the "individual Dasein" struggling to live out an "authentic existence" by hearing and responding to the call of conscience, to that which is "other" than others. Of course, without this "other" there could be no talk about others, for neither they nor we would exist. The call of conscience *is* human existence disclosing itself to us who are living it.

Because he is so taken with the otherness of this call, and because the issue he makes of it entails a rather critical assessment of another source of otherness in our lives (that is, other people), Heidegger is open to the charge of offering us a theory of conscience that ends up disparaging the social nature of human being. But matters are not that simple. For although Heidegger emphasizes how the call of conscience "calls [us] back" from "the public idle talk of the 'they'" and toward our ownmost potentiality-for-Being (BT 322), he also acknowledges how our answering the call involves us in a process whereby a respect for others becomes necessary. Heidegger develops this point by showing how the call of conscience, in addition to everything else, calls for the building of community.

Conscience and Others

We are social creatures. Human existence is marked with an indelible communal character. "So far as Dasein *is* at all, it has Being-with-one-another as its kind of Being" (BT 163). The call of conscience makes itself known as we are living out this communal character of our existence; its appeal calls us to make some choice that is deemed appropriate for the situation at hand.

Choosing to make this choice is an act of self-affirmation, of authenticity, of freeing oneself from one's "lostness in the 'they'"; it is not, however, an act that detaches a human being "from its world" and isolates it "so that it becomes a free-floating 'I'" (BT 344–45). On the contrary, the resoluteness that shows itself with one's response to the call of conscience "is always the resoluteness of some factical Dasein at a particular time" (BT 345). Wanting to have a conscience is a situated occurrence. Although Heidegger makes much of how this occurrence speaks to the difference between one's being an "authentic self" and one's being only a conformist or "they-self," he would certainly have us understand that the occurrence does not dissociate a person from the *Mitwelt;* for as he notes, "Resoluteness brings the Self right into its current concernful Being-alongside what is ready-to-hand, and pushes it into solicitous Being with Others" (BT 344). Elaborating on this point, Heidegger offers the following important observation: "Dasein's resoluteness towards itself is what first makes it possible to let Others who are with it "be" in their ownmost potentiality-for-Being, and to codisclose this potentiality in the solicitude which leaps forth and liberates. When Dasein is resolute, it can become the "conscience" of Others. Only by authentically Being-their-Selves in resoluteness can people authentically be with one another—not by ambiguous and jealous stipulations and talkative fraternizing in the "they" and in what "they" want to undertake" (BT 344–45).

Heidegger is speaking to us here of a self who has heard the call of conscience and who has moved beyond the depersonalizing tendencies of the "they" by assuming the personal responsibility of affirming its freedom through resolute choice. He is also speaking to us of a self who is now in the position of taking on the additional responsibility of becoming a voice of conscience for others. Abiding by what Heidegger says elsewhere in *Being and Time* about "the [authentic] solicitude which leaps forth and liberates," such a voice would have to maintain its own supposedly "truthful" point of view while at the same time encouraging, by way of "considerateness" (*Rücksicht*) and "forbearance" (*Nachsicht*), an authentic response from the others. In Heidegger's terms the goal here is to have all concerned "devote themselves to the same affair in common," "become authentically bound together," and thereby engage in a codisclosing of the situation at hand (BT 159).

Hence, with Heidegger's analysis of the call of conscience there emerges a consideration of how the resolute self has a responsibility to bring about an authentic community by calling upon others to assume the responsibility of affirming *their* freedom through resolute choice. In doing this, the resolute self not only displays a willingness to test before others the integrity of its affirmed authenticity—a test that the call of conscience requires us to take time and again (BT 355)—but also engages others in the related tasks of trying to cultivate all that is good in their "heritage," so that they too might have a say in the establishing of their collective "destiny." Summarizing this entire process, Heidegger makes a point that critics of his analysis of conscience skip over too quickly or omit completely: "Only in communicating and in struggling [with others] does the power of destiny become free" (BT 436).[7]

The call of conscience, the self, and others are related by way of a process of communication and struggle. Although Heidegger does not elaborate on the intricacies of this community-building process, it is still possible to advance with his help a more nuanced appreciation of its nature than has been noted so far. "Communicating" and "struggling"—how do these activities, specifically, work together to inform and direct the process? Heidegger's assessment of "communicating" is developed in conjunction with his thinking on a topic covered in chapter 1: the way the "apophantic discourse" of an "assertion" functions to make explicit to those who are "listening" to how one is faring in his or her everyday relationships with things and with others. In answering the question before us, we thus will have to recall certain things that were said about this topic. Moreover, we will also have to get a better handle on what Heidegger has in mind when he refers to the activity of "struggling."

When Heidegger speaks of the struggle that characterizes the communicative interaction between the self and others, he is pointing to an activity that also informs the practice of phenomenological inquiry. Such an inquiry defines an effort in truth telling; it seeks to disclose with "demonstrative precision" the "appearing" or "presencing" of some phenomenon. In order to do this—"to let that which shows itself be seen from itself in the very way in which it shows itself from itself"—the phenomenologist must bracket out and set aside preconceptions of the phenomenon so to be as *open* as possible to the phenomenon's own disclosure, to how it in fact is actually (truthfully) happening. Remaining open to the disclosure allows the phenomenon to be what it is and to speak for itself. Phenomenology is a way of "listening" attentively and being receptive to the "saying" (*logos*), the disclosing or unconcealing of truth that is going on here. Hence, the type of inquiry it calls for requires one to become engaged in what Heidegger terms a "struggle for unconcealment"—that is, a struggle that involves trying to understand what some being truly is, and then trying to find the most fitting and telling words for communicating this understanding to others.

One sees such a struggle going on throughout *Being and Time* as Heidegger attends to and interprets how human existence (Dasein) reveals itself. This struggle is not rooted in some dominating and dictatorial worldview that desires ultimate control over its subject matter. Phenomenology does not work that way. Its struggle begins by letting things be what they are. As Heidegger made clear throughout his works, to "let things be" is to treat them with great care and respect and to safeguard their being. It is no different than what Heidegger tells us must take place in the case of the self communicating and struggling with others in an attempt to build an authentic community. The struggle here requires the self to *open* itself to others by becoming thoughtful and respectful of their rights, circumstances, and feelings ("considerateness") and by allowing them the time to share their interpretations of the issues at hand. This is what the self must do if it is "to let Others who are with it 'be' in their ownmost potentiality-for-Being." And this, in turn, might require great patience ("forbearance") on the part of the self, since what others have to say in response may indicate that they do not understand or they misunderstand what they are being told, or that they perhaps find the self to be "guilty" of maintaining a wrong point of view. Indeed trying to build an authentic community can be a time-consuming task filled with controversy.

Yet for the self that wants to be true to the call of conscience that is always calling it into question and thus always speaking to it of the importance of being open-minded, the struggle must go on. The self must remain open to the personhood of others and to their discourse, which tells of this personhood by giving some indication of how people are faring in their relationships with things and with each other. According to Heidegger, it is essential that the self listen carefully to this discourse, for "listening to . . . is Dasein's existential way of Being-open as Being-with for Others" (BT 206). Being open to others, listening to and taking seriously what they have to say, is how the self counters the egotistic and selfish tendency of becoming so engrossed in figuring out what it wants to express next that it misses or forgets what others are expressing. Authentic community is not built on egoism but on the altruism of being "for Others" and on the "empathy" that this makes possible.[8] Heroism on the part of the authentic self precludes selfishness.

This is not to say, however, that the self owes it to others to capitulate completely to their interpretations of the issues at hand. Heidegger speaks to us of a self whose struggle with others is essentially a "struggle for unconceal-ment," a struggle devoted to disclosing the "truth" of some matter of impor-tance, and thus a struggle given over to countering as much as possible what Heidegger, as noted earlier, terms the "leveling down" or concealing tendency of discourse. For Heidegger the reality and livelihood of authentic community is made possible by the willingness of the self and others to involve themselves continually in this interpretive struggle for truth (unconcealment). The self promotes this struggle with its own particular interpretation of the matter in question—an interpretation that was formulated in response to the call of conscience and that the self now seeks to have others appropriate as it com-municates with them about the truth of the matter. Displaying considerateness and forbearance toward others is necessary here, for they too may have some-thing instructive to say regarding this truth. For the sake of truth the self must be open-minded. The call of conscience demands as much. But this call, we must remember, also confronts the self with the challenge of being decisive, of having to assume the personal responsibility of affirming its freedom through resolute choice. The call of conscience calls for the courage of con-viction; it summons the self to take a stand on the issues. Failing to respond to this challenge is, for Heidegger, a "cowardly" way to live one's life (BT 298, 311).

How, then, might the self best structure its communication with others so that they in turn might become receptive to the self's interpretation of the truth? The question is as old as the rhetorical tradition itself. With his 1924/1925 lecture courses on Plato's *Sophist* (PS 214–44) and on Aristotle's *Rhetoric* (GBAPh 43–66), Heidegger makes clear his awareness of this fact, although in *Being and Time* the "rhetorical" workings of discourse are discussed generally in terms of the phenomenon of "communication."

Heidegger analyses this phenomenon in conjunction with his analysis of the discursive workings of an "assertion," which he designates as having three interdependent functions: "pointing out," "predication," and "communication." When a person asserts an interpretive understanding of something, the some-thing (for example, "the steps") is pointed out by predicating it in a definite way ("were too steep") so that the person's interpretive understanding of this something can be communicated and shared with others. Hence, Heidegger defines communication as a "letting someone see with us what we have pointed out by way of giving it a definite character. Letting someone see with us shares with . . . the Other that entity which has been pointed out in its definite character" (BT 197). Clearly, such sharing must take place if others are to understand what the self has to say, if only to dispute it. The self who would help bring about authentic community thus owes it to others to enhance the communicability of its discourse. The self, however, also owes it to itself to do this. For if others are to become receptive to the self's interpretation of the truth, they first have to comprehend what it is that they are being asked to take to heart. The building of authentic community is a heroic act requiring communicative (and rhetorical) competence.

Knowing how to enhance the communicability of its discourse is a skill that the self develops, according to Heidegger, by listening to the ways in which others employ language to manage their everyday lives (BT 205–7). The discourse at work here is itself a demonstration of know-how, of people exhibiting in various circumstances some degree of skill in knowing, for example, how to speak in an appropriate and timely manner, or how to structure and put forth a rational argument, or how to participate properly in conversations promoting "small talk." Moreover, as noted above, such discursive practices, given their respective topics, also provide evidence of how people are currently taking an interest in the world; that is, how they are seeing, interpreting, and involving themselves emotionally with things and with each other. Listening to what people have to say about these topics and to the ways in which they express their concerns, the self receives an education in how to think and act like others and thus how to form a communal bond with them. Without this education the self has nothing to go on in developing its communicative competence. A competent communicator is one who knows how to interact with others in acceptable and fitting ways so as to enhance the chance that they will comprehend and appreciate what he or she wants to point out, predicate, and share. A competent communicator is also one who knows how to secure the attention of others by attending to their ongoing interests. Commenting on the necessity of this talent, Kenneth Burke writes: "The factor of *interest* plays a large part in the business of communication. Even if one speaks very clearly and simply on a subject of great moment to himself, for instance, one is hardly communicating in the desired sense if his auditor does not care in the least what he is saying. . . . Communication cannot be satisfactory unless the matter discussed bears in some notable respect upon the interests of the auditor. Without the assistance of this factor, the entire paraphernalia of appeal—comprehensiveness, conciseness, cogency, construction, pliancy, and all the rest *ad lib.*—are wasted. . . . We interest a man by dealing with his interests."[9]

Burke expresses here a fundamental teaching of the rhetorical tradition. Heidegger's "ontologically broad" (BT 205) conception of communication affirms this teaching: the effectiveness of communication is contingent on how well one's discourse is attuned to the know-how of others; to their common sense and common practices; to how they are currently seeing, interpreting, and involving themselves emotionally with their environment. Heidegger credits Aristotle's *Rhetoric* with providing "the first systematic hermeneutic analysis" (BT 178) of this world of know-how. Indeed rhetoric makes its living first and foremost within the temporal and spatial confines of such a world. It discovers the materials that are needed for its work amidst the ways in which people are emotionally involved with the everyday concerns and contingencies of life. Here the available means of persuasion are found and people wait for their particular interests to be acknowledged by those who would engage them in collaborative deliberation about contestable matters. Rhetoric, in other words, helps to promote civic engagement and civic virtue; it thus lends itself to the task of enriching the moral character of a people's communal existence. For Aristotle, this is how the *hoi polloi* are granted a way of becoming more than what Plato called them: "the greatest of all sophists."[10] Heidegger offers an extremely concise formulation of the entire process that summarizes his thinking on how the self, in responding to the call of conscience, has the further obligation of engaging others in the task of building an authentic community: "Only in communicating and in struggling [with others] does the power of destiny become free" (BT 436).

Henry Johnstone Jr. reads *Being and Time* as a work that supports the view that "we will never really be competent at communication until we are ready to admit that in communicating we are also engaging in rhetoric."[11] My discussion of what Heidegger means by "communicating" and "struggling" lends support to Johnstone's position. When Heidegger's thinking on the call of conscience comes to an end in *Being and Time,* we find ourselves having to consider the importance of a certain type of know-how that has long been associated with the art of rhetoric.

There are, of course, other readings of Heidegger's work that do not see matters this way. Those like Paul R. Falzer, for example, contend that rather than being a supporter of the rhetorical enterprise, Heidegger conceives of the orator's art as being primarily a tool for bringing about mindless conformism and thus inauthenticity. One might read Heidegger this way because, as seen in *Being and Time,* rhetoric is associated with the use and production of "moods" or emotional orientations that sustain our "publicness"—the world of common sense and common praxis that too often inhibits critical reflection and conditions us to be creatures who are merely content to just go along with the crowd, the "dictatorship of the they." Yet in making this point, Heidegger is not necessarily dismissing rhetoric's potential for doing good.

Heidegger says this about the matter: "Publicness . . . not only has in general its own way of having a mood, but needs moods and 'makes' them for itself. It is into such a mood and out of such a mood that the orator speaks. He must understand the possibilities of moods in order to rouse them and guide them aright" (BT 178). I take this last sentence to be especially important. The original German reads: "*Er bedarf des Verständnisses der Möglichkeiten der Stimmung, um sie in der rechten Weise zu wecken und zu lenken*" (SZ 138–39). Macquarrie and Robinson translate "*in der rechten Weise*" as "aright." In her more recent translation of *Sein und Zeit,* Joan Stambaugh translates the phrase as "in the right way."[12] Keeping in mind, however, that the German *recht* carries with it a moral sense (as when, for example, one says "*es is nicht recht von dir*"—"it is wrong or unfair of you"), a still-less-condensed translation is possible: the orator "must understand the possibilities of moods in order to rouse them and guide them in a right and just manner."

With this translation, I believe, one sees Heidegger explicitly acknowledging something good about the practice of rhetoric, something that enables it to be more than a vehicle for generating mindless conformism. Like rhetorical theorists dating back at least to Aristotle, Heidegger thinks of rhetoric as something that can move (*emovere*) and thereby advance the moral consciousness and conduct of people.[13] Indeed rhetoric plays a crucial role in the articulation of good morale: it is evocative; it calls. Employed "in a right and just manner," it can help move people to ideas and ideas to people. The call of conscience, the practice of rhetoric, and the cultivation of a community's moral ecology go hand in hand. They work together to promote a process that operates in both a constructive and deconstructive way, that is directed toward the ascertaining of truth, and that would therefore have people remain open to the differing perspectives of others.

Yet Heidegger's philosophy is not directed toward the advancement of the orator's art. Unlike Aristotle, for example, Heidegger does not listen to the world of know-how in order to suggest how the self might best structure its communication with others so that in the struggle they might become receptive to the self's interpretation of the truth. Beyond what he says about the importance of listening to others and about how they deserve to be treated with considerateness and forbearance, Heidegger advances no specific recommendations for dealing with this rhetorical matter. Rather, he listens to the world of know-how, because this is what he maintains the phenomenologist must do, at least initially, in order to work out the question of the meaning and truth of Being. In *Being and Time* the question is answered by clarifying the ontological workings of the call of conscience. In his later writings Heidegger further develops his answer by paying ever more careful attention to the *Being* of this call. He thereby no longer speaks to us of the call of conscience, but he emphasizes instead the importance of listening to "the call of Being"—a task that, for Heidegger, calls primarily on the philosophical and poetical, not the rhetorical, talents of human beings.

In the next section I want to say a few things about where Heidegger leads us with his continual thinking on the call of conscience/Being. Taking a moment to remember some of what has been said so far about the ontological workings of the call will help us maintain our bearings as we follow Heidegger's unfolding pathway of thought and thereby come to see how his fading consideration of rhetoric defines a significant omission in his overall philosophical project.

From the Call of Conscience to the Call of Being

The call of conscience is rooted in the way the disclosing of human existence poses a constant challenge as it confronts us with the future, with what is not yet in our lives. This challenge calls us to assume the ethical responsibility of affirming our freedom through resolute choice so that we may have a say in determining our own destiny. We hear this primordial call of conscience while inhabiting the world of know-how; it makes itself known as something that interrupts our typical and ongoing involvements with things and with others. This interruption is likely to make us feel anxious because of the challenge it reveals and because of how it forces us to confront the guilt that necessarily marks our finite existence, the way in which our potentiality-for-Being is a Being-toward-death. The call of conscience is awe-inspiring; it brings us face to face with the issue of our own Being.

Responding to the call of conscience is an urgent task; one's life may end at any moment. It is also a task that calls us to test out with others the supposed truthfulness of our response. The future orientation of the call of conscience is forever calling us into question. What we consider to be correct now may be wrong later, at least in the opinion of those being affected by the consequences of some conscientious decision. An authentic response to the call of conscience includes remaining open to this possibility and thus to the need to communicate and struggle with others who are encouraged to share their interpretations of the matter at hand. The reality of authentic community is made possible by this communicative struggle for truth, this way of judging and "knowing together" (*conscientia*) what is right or wrong about our current assessments of some matter and about the behavior that follows from these assessments.

Systems of morality are designed to aid us in this task; their discourse sounds *a* call of conscience that prescribes what we ought to think and do in a particular situation. We must keep in mind, however, that *the* call of conscience discussed in this chapter is not itself a human creation; hence, it is not to be confused with some already institutionalized discourse that speaks to us of the morally good and the morally evil. Rather, the possible forms that morality may take are dependent on our response to a call that transcends the realm of moral categories and that speaks only of a challenge posed by our own potentiality-for-Being. What the call thus discloses, according to Heidegger, is something that functions in a "silent" way: our ongoing projective involvement with the temporal process of becoming and understanding our possibilities. This is why Heidegger maintains that "the discourse of the conscience never comes to utterance. Only in keeping silent does the conscience call" (BT 342–43). When this call catches our attention as it interrupts our everyday routines, we are made aware of the very thing—the Being of our temporal existence—that gives rise to the call but that, in so doing, "does not put itself into words at all" (BT 318).

With its interruption, the call of conscience reveals the silence that must be thought and then given expression in order to answer the question of Being. Hence, the thoughtful language of *Being and Time*. But what we read here, as Heidegger makes clear throughout his later writings, provides an answer to the question that is somewhat misleading because it is still too steeped in the ways of metaphysical thinking and because it thereby ties "the truth of Being itself" too closely to the needs, decisions, and actions of human beings—to what, for example, we have to do with and for others in order to offer an authentic response to the call of conscience.[14]

The question that interests Heidegger is not one that directs his thinking toward the interpersonal dynamics of such a practical activity. Although the call of conscience heads us in this direction, it also speaks to us of something that is *other* than, and that makes possible, our willful and purposive ways of being-with-others. That is, the call of conscience reveals the Being—or what the later Heidegger also describes as the "presencing"—of human being, which shows itself in the givenness of our temporal existence but whose "peal of still-ness [silence] is not anything human" (PLT 207). This is what Heidegger is after: not merely the presencing of human being (the call of conscience) but the presencing of Being itself (the call of Being), which is always there to behold in "the being of a being" but which is also "essentially different from a being, from beings," from you or me or any other concrete entity (BP 17). Being "is not itself a being"; rather, its truth is given in the "presencing of what is present" before us (EGT 39–58; OTB 1–24). Hence, Heidegger's ultimate goal in his later writings is to overcome as much as possible the restrictions of metaphysical thought by thinking "Being without regard to its being grounded in terms of beings" (OTB 2). His path of thinking must therefore move in a specific direction: from human being-and-time to time-and-Being.

Being and time are fundamentally related. As we have seen, the relation-ship is displayed in the "ecstatic" character of Dasein, in the "primordial" way a human being *exists as time,* as one who is presently living its "having been" what once was its future and who, at the same time, is presently living out the pos-sibilities that are yet to come. Before it is transformed into units of measure-ment (seconds, days, months, years), this "authentic temporality" of human being manifests itself as a "unitary phenomenon," as the mutual extending and opening up of the future, past, and present. For Heidegger, however, more can be said about the way in which the presencing of this phenomenon happens. Heidegger performs the task by maintaining a phenomenological orientation "toward the thing itself" ("presencing as such"); for he wants to think Being explicitly, "empirically" and "deeply," and without regard to its being grounded in terms of being. Here, for example, is Heidegger doing just that:

> In the approaching of what is no longer present and even in the present itself, there always plays a kind of approach and bringing about, that is a kind of presencing. We cannot attribute the presencing to be thus thought to one of the three dimensions of time, to the present, which would seem obvious. Rather, the unity of time's three dimensions consists in the interplay of each toward each. This interplay proves to be the true extending, playing in the very heart of time, the fourth dimension, so to speak—not only so to speak, but in the nature of the matter.
>
> True time is four-dimensional.
>
> But the dimension which we call the fourth in our count is, in the nature of the matter, the first, that is, the giving that determines all. (OTB 15)

Notice that Heidegger makes no mention here of human being. And this is because he has taken what he terms elsewhere a "step back from the representational thinking of metaphysics" (PLT 185) so as to think of the ecstatic nature (the Being) of time itself, the "true extending" of its three dimensions, which is also a dimension. This fourth dimension defines a "playing in the very heart of time" that simultaneously differentiates and unites the future, past, and present, that "holds [these dimensions] apart" and "holds them toward one another" (OTB 15). For Heidegger this playing is the "source" of time; it is that which "gives" (es gibt) time and thereby makes possible the temporality of human being (OTB 15–19). We are creatures who owe our existence to something other than ourselves.

With this description of the playing that happens in the very heart of time, Heidegger provides his most telling answer to the question of Being: the truth of Being, its presencing, is revealed as something at play. Heidegger stresses, however, that this revealing is at the same time a concealing, for the play of Being is also that which "holds itself back and withdraws" whenever one attempts to grasp the reason for its happening, for its Being the way it is. "The play is without 'why,'" writes Heidegger. "It plays since it plays. It simply remains a play: the most elevated and the most profound" (PR 113). Hence, following Heidegger, it may be said that the play of Being—which gives itself to us by way of the presencing of all that lies before us—is itself a "mystery," for it is never without an element of "absence." The play of Being "names a presence of absence" (OTB 18).

Heidegger equates the play of Being with the self-organizing workings of Nature in which beings are constantly appearing and disappearing, revealing and concealing themselves. In the specific case of a human being's temporal existence, the phenomenon shows itself in the way the present is given immediacy (presence) in its ecstatic relationship with the past and the future, with what is *no longer* present (absence) and with what is *not yet* present (absence). Heidegger also makes much of how the phenomenon is disclosed in the "Being of language," that is, in the fundamental way that "language speaks." According to Heidegger, language is not first and foremost "a mere human faculty"; rather, its essential nature comes to it from the play of Being. Language speaks the "Saying" (*Logos*)—the presencing, the silent call—of this play. This "speaking of language" shows itself in the way words both reveal and conceal their subject matter; in the way they, in their presenting ("naming") of things, also name "a presence of absence," an "otherness" that holds itself back and withdraws from the calculating power of the word (OTL 57–108). We may play with words at times, but it is always the case, says Heidegger, that "the nature [Being] of language plays with us" (WCT 118).

Heidegger is describing a phenomenon that discloses itself as that which differs from everything that is, but whose presencing is always there to behold in the existence of beings. This is necessarily the case. Beings cannot be without Being. But it is also the case that Being cannot be without beings. The presencing of Being needs the existence of beings in order to disclose itself. And the one being that is most needed here, according to Heidegger, is the human being. In emphasizing this point throughout his later works, Heidegger is not simply making a careless metaphysical mistake in his response to the question that directs his thinking, however. The play of Being is not a human creation; it is always already happening before we put our creative talents to use. Indeed without the play of Being, without what "It gives," we would not have the essential time that it takes to exist, to be. *Es gibt*! It gives! Like all other beings, we need what is given here!

But the play of Being also needs us in order to reveal itself as something meaningful and significant. Of all the beings whose existence is caught up in, and presupposes, this most primordial happening, it is only the human being that can respond to the play of Being by thinking and putting into words how it manifests itself in the presencing of anything that "is." We hold a special relationship with Being; we belong and are appropriated to it in a distinctive manner. Heidegger puts the entire matter this way:

> Man obviously is a being. As such he belongs to the totality of Being—
> just like the stone, the tree, or the eagle. To "belong" here still means to be
> in the order of Being. But man's distinctive feature lies in this, that he, as the
> being who thinks, is open to Being, face to face with Being; thus man

remains referred to Being and so answers to it. Man *is* essentially this relationship of responding to Being, and he is only this. This "only" does not
mean a limitation, but rather an excess. A belonging to Being prevails within
man, a belonging which listens to Being because it is appropriated to Being.
. . . Being is present and abides only as it concerns man through the claim it
makes on him. For it is man, open toward Being, who alone lets Being arrive
as presence. (ID 31)

For Heidegger "the proper dignity of man" lies in his being true to the
essential relationship he holds with Being (LH 210). This is what Heidegger is
doing with everything he has to say about human existence (Dasein) in his early
and later works, or when he discusses, for example, how the play of Being
manifests itself in the work of art (PLT 17–87), as well as in the simplest of
things, such as a jug (PLT 165–82). Heidegger is thinking about "that which
calls on us to think." He is responding to the presencing, the Saying, the silent
call of Being that reveals itself in what and how something is. The call of Being
is a revelation that, as Heidegger further explains by way of an etymological
analysis of the word *call,* "reaches out" to us, "invites" thought, and thereby "sets
in motion" a process that defines the existential basis of human understanding.

In responding to the call of Being, Heidegger is thus doing what he in fact
maintains must be done if human beings are to gain a genuine appreciation not
only of whatever it is that concerns them but also of that which makes possible the existence of everything that is, and that thereby ought to warrant their
utmost respect. "What calls on us to think," writes Heidegger, "needs thinking
because what calls us wants itself to be thought about according to its nature.
What calls on us to think, demands for itself that it be tended, cared for, husbanded in its own essential nature, by thought" (WCT 121). In meeting this
demand, whereby we are being true to the essential relationship that we hold
with Being, we assume what Heidegger stresses is our highest responsibility
and thus ultimate calling: to be "the shepherd of Being" by thinking its truth
and bringing it into language (LH 210).

With this last point in mind, might it be said that the call of Being also
sounds a call of conscience, a call that summons us to assume the responsibility of affirming our freedom through resolute choice? Heidegger never speaks
explicitly of the call of conscience in his later works. But he does speak of "the
heart"—a term that, as discussed in the introduction, is another name for conscience found in the Old Testament. Hence, he tells us that the call of Being,
the disclosing of the "beingness of beings," is something that needs to be "taken
to heart" so that its truth is placed in "safe-keeping" and remains "memorable"
(WCT 202–28). For Heidegger, taking to heart what the call of Being discloses constitutes an act of "devotion," "a steadfast intimate concentration upon
the things that essentially speak to us in every thoughtful meditation" (WCT

140). This is how we open ourselves to the call of Being, so that in a moment of "releasement," of "wonder" and "awe," we can experience "the marvel of all marvels: that what is *is*" (EB 355; DT 90).

By way of devotion, which Heidegger also describes as a "'letting be' of what-is" (EB 306), we return "Being's favor" (EB 358) by giving "thankful" thought to what Being first gives us. Heidegger writes:

> When we give thanks we give it for something. We give thanks for something by giving thanks to him whom we have to thank for it. The things for which we owe thanks are not things we have from ourselves. They are given to us. We receive many gifts, of many kinds. But the highest and really most lasting gift given to us is always our essential nature [the distinctive relationship we hold with Being], with which we are gifted in such a way that we are what we are only through it. That is why we owe thanks for this endowment, first and unceasingly. (WCT 142)

Giving thanks to Being is a matter of the heart, of "taking to heart" what calls on us to think the presencing, the disclosing, the truth of what is.

Referring to the heart in this way is certainly reminiscent of how the Old Testament speaks to us of conscience, of that wondrous gift that enables us to be awed by the happenings and mysteries of life and that thereby keeps us in touch with the Lord's call: "I will give them a heart to know Me, that I am the Lord" (Jer. 24:7), the One whose Saying—"Let there be . . ."—brought about the original letting-be of what is. In Heidegger's case, however, this Saying and the gift that goes with it comes from Being, the "purely 'Other' than everything that 'is'" (EB 353). Might this "Other" be God? Heidegger notes that with his philosophical project "nothing is decided about the 'existence of God' or his 'non-being'" (LH 229). Still, he sees his project as offering an authentic and enlightening approach to the question. As he puts it: "Only from the truth of Being can the essence of the holy be thought. Only from the essence of the holy is the essence of divinity to be thought. Only in light of the essence of divinity can it be thought or said what the word "God" is to signify. . . . How can man at the present state of world history ask at all seriously and rigorously whether the god nears or withdraws, when he has above all neglected to think into the dimension in which alone that question can be asked?" (LH 230).

Of course, in order to "think into" this dimension one must *choose* to do so. Heidegger's philosophical project presupposes his having made this choice in a most conscientious and resolute manner. He devoted himself to hearing the call of Being and taking it to heart. That was his highest responsibility, his ultimate calling. Remember: "What calls on us to think, demands for itself that it be tended, cared for, husbanded in its own essential nature, by thought" (WCT 121). Registering itself in the temporality of human being, this demand is the constant challenge posed by the future, by what is not yet in our lives.

This challenge calls for concerned thought and decisive action; it summons us to assume the responsibility of affirming our freedom through resolute choice. The summons is the call of conscience, a call that lies at the very heart of our existence and that is always calling us into question. The call of Being does indeed sound a call of conscience. Heidegger met the challenge here by offering a heartfelt response to what he describes as the "most thought-provoking" happening there is and that "speaks without a sound": the call of Being (WCT 207).

The call of Being and the call of conscience are related. The relationship is displayed in Heidegger's resolute way of responding to the call of Being, to that which calls for thought. Heidegger is first and foremost a "thinker." Yet as he would have it, this fact of his life in no way makes him any less of an "actor," for the thinker is also one who is engaged in what Heidegger maintains is the highest form of action: that of opening himself to the "innermost essence" of things. Hence, Heidegger tells us that "thinking does not become action only because some effect issues from it or because it is applied. Thinking acts insofar as it thinks. Such action is presumably the simplest and at the same time the highest, because it concerns the relation of Being to man" (LH 193; also see EB 359). When it comes to answering the call of Being, the decisive action called for by the call of conscience is such that it "surpasses all *praxis*" (LH 239).

The course of Heidegger's way of thinking/acting extends far, as it must. To think the truth of Being—how "it gives," how it calls—is to think a phenomenon that, as discussed above, both reveals and conceals itself at one and the same time. In the midst of the presencing of all that appears before us, lies an element of "absence." Being functions in a mysterious way: it "plays"; it is always in a state of "withdrawal" as it gives itself to us. Heidegger thinks about this withdrawal, this presence of absence, which he describes as the void of nothingness, the "Nothing" out of which the coming to presence of all that is appears. The ancient metaphysical question— "Why is there something rather than nothing?"—has it wrong. The Nothing of Being is real; it exists as the "nihilating" nature of Being itself, the way in which Being holds itself back and slips away from our grasp.

As a way of clarifying his thinking on this "uncanny" phenomenon, Heidegger discusses how the calculating logic of science, which presupposes the presence of the phenomenon, conditions us to believe that it is but "a horror and a phantasm," an absurdity unworthy of rational thought. "Science wishes to know nothing of Nothing," writes Heidegger. "Science, by adopting an attitude of superior indifference, abandons it as that which 'is not'" (EB 328–29). Science thus negates the Nothing as something that does not make sense and that is thereby forgettable. Heidegger emphasizes, however, that what science would have us forget, our own existence would have us remember; for something of the givenness of the phenomenon shows itself in how our potentiality-for-

Being is essentially a Being-toward-death, a Being-toward the final not-yet in our lives. Being and nothingness, life and death, are intimately related. "The essence of mortals calls upon them to heed a call which beckons them toward death" (EGT 101). Our finitude defines the starkest way that the Nothing, the presencing of Being's absence, reveals itself to us. What comes after death remains a mystery. We can never know for sure what the nihilating nature of Being is all about. It gives, and it takes away. What is given is our potentiality-for-Being; what is ultimately taken away is this potential and what we have made of it throughout our lives.

Heidegger's thinking on the presence of Being's absence returns us to a topic that, as discussed in *Being and Time,* is closely related to the call of conscience. Recall that in this work Heidegger explains how "authentic 'thinking about death' is a wanting-to-have-a-conscience" (BT 357), a wanting to be up for meeting the call's ever-present challenge that emanates from our ownmost potentiality-for-Being (toward death) and that can make us feel quite anxious. Recall also that anxiety holds us open to the call and thus exposes us to that "uttermost possibility" of life that marks the end of our very ability to be. The "anxiety of conscience" thereby calls for "courage" so that we can deal in a thoughtful and composed manner with the dread of knowing that we are bound to die.

The later Heidegger also speaks of anxiety (*Angst* or "dread") and courage. For example, he tells us: "The clear courage for essential dread guarantees that most mysterious of all possibilities: the experience of Being. . . . Courage can endure Nothing" (EB 355). Given the choice he made when answering the call of conscience, Heidegger must therefore have seen himself as being a courageous soul. For with his way of thinking/acting, one must be willing to bear the burden of unceasingly standing face to face not only with the dreadful reality of death but also with the mystery of nothingness, the presence of Being's absence that lies beyond the mortal reach of human beings. Heidegger maintains that assuming this burden defines an act of "sacrifice." What is sacrificed here is our common tendency to order and understand the world by way of "calculative thought" (EB 356–59). Such thought is willful, practical, and deliberative; as such, according to Heidegger, "its own great usefulness" can only take place as it discloses beings in terms of its own purposive inclinations and everyday activities (DT 46). "Calculative thought places itself under compulsion to master everything in the logical terms of its procedure" (EB 357).

The call of Being, however, does not call for this mastery, this mode of the "will to power"; rather, as detailed above, it calls for a way of thinking that is most in line with the essential relationship we hold with Being and that is thereby committed to a letting be of what is. Returning "Being's favor" requires that we relinquish a habit of thinking bent on domination and cultivate a much more caring, respectful, and receptive type of thinking. Heideg-

ger puts it this way: "In sacrifice there is expressed that hidden *thanking* [think-
ing] which alone does homage to the grace wherewith Being has endowed the
nature of man, in order that he may take over in his relationship to Being the
guardianship of Being" (EB 358).

Heidegger made this sacrifice "to fulfil the highest demand which alone
touches man to the quick" (EB 355). With the way he responded to the call of
conscience, he committed himself to being a thinker engaged in what he
describes as the "essential thinking" of "meditative thought" (EB 357–60; DT
46–57). Such thinking is the *modus operandi* of phenomenological inquiry given
over to disclosing the truth of Being (OTB 74–82), a truth that both reveals
and conceals itself in the presencing of what is. Heidegger thinks and puts into
words the play (revelation/concealment) going on here. He responds to a
call—of conscience, of Being. With this response he shows himself to be not
only a thinker but also a poet.

"The thinker utters Being," writes Heidegger. "The poet names what is
holy" (EB 360). In order to utter Being, one must give thought to the presence
of Being's absence, to the purely Other than everything that is. In order to
name what is holy, however, one's thinking need not extend that far (although
Heidegger's certainly does). The poet is more concerned with the positive
dimension of Being (the presencing of what is—the "holy") than with the negative (the withdrawal and concealment of Being).[15] As a meditative thinker, the
poet has entered into a state of "releasement," a "letting go" of beings so as to
allow them to be what they are. Thereby the poet is now better positioned to
speak *their* truth. For Heidegger, to be sure, it is the poet (and, of course, a
"thinker" like himself) who affirms the proper dignity of human being, its most
essential and thus authentic calling, by bringing into the language of "mortal
speech" a heightened sense of some happening of truth. The poet does this not
only as one who has entered into a state of releasement, but also as one who
has developed a sensitivity to the being of language, to its playful nature. The
devoted poet is forever trying to have language reveal more than it conceals so
that she or he can disclose some truth that remains unthought and unsaid by
those who have yet to learn how their calculative ways of thinking and speaking close them off to the "Saying" of this truth. Hence, for Heidegger the poet
is one who tries to maintain a thoughtful "conversation" with Being—a conversation dedicated to having language become more attuned with the way
things are disclosing themselves and thus with the truth of what and how they
are.

Putting all of this in terms of Heidegger's early philosophy, one would say
that the poet's conversation with Being constitutes a heroic struggle to avoid
as much as possible the "leveling down" tendencies of discourse (see above, pp.
35–37). Expanding on the example from medical science that was offered to

illustrate this topic, one could also say that such a struggle is apparent whenever a physician tries to hear and tell the story of a patient not only in terms of the objectifying and calculative language of disease theory but also in terms of the patient's personal concerns, relationships, and values. In communicating with one who is in need of help, the physician as poet, as a meditative thinker, opens herself not just to the diseased body of a patient but also to the lived body of a person and the totality of involvements that go with it. The illness story told by the physician/scientist/poet is one that displays respect for both the physiology and the personhood of some sick soul. The patient's being calls for nothing less than this. Coming as it does from one whose life has been interrupted by the ontological assault of illness, this call is rightly heard by both patient and physician as sounding a call of conscience. The responsibility of making personal decisions is at hand. Concerned thought and decisive action are needed. The patient deserves to be treated with considerateness and forbearance so to ensure that his or her voice, no matter how unscientific it may be, is granted the opportunity of having a say in what ought to be done with his or her life. The call of conscience demands as much.

It must be noted, however, that Heidegger never offers an example like this one to illustrate the dynamics of the poet's conversation with Being. Rather, in discussing how the poetry of those like Hölderlin and Rilke educates us about this conversation, or when assuming this instructive task himself with his own poetic thinking about some subject matter, Heidegger directs our attention primarily not toward the lived body of other human beings, but rather toward the presencing of fleshless things such as a jug, a stone, a river, a house, a windmill, a statue, a blossoming flower, a painting by Van Gogh of a pair of peasant shoes. Meditating on the truth of these shoes and on what they have to say about the one who wears them, Heidegger does convey some appreciation for the lived body: "From the dark opening of the worn insides of the shoes the toilsome tread of the worker stares forth. In the stiffly rugged heaviness of the shoes there is the accumulated tenacity of her slow trudge through the far-spreading and ever-uniform furrows of the field swept by a raw wind. . . . This equipment is pervaded by uncomplaining anxiety as to the certainty of bread, the wordless joy of having once more withstood want, the trembling before the impending childbed and shivering at the surrounding menace of death" (PLT 34). At least as Heidegger perceives it, Van Gogh's painting engages its viewers in a conversation about a woman's hard work, struggle, and suffering. But such an acknowledgment of the lived body is rare in the later Heidegger. When he discusses and practices the poet's art, when he responds to the call of conscience to answer the call of Being, his heart goes out most often and most directly to things other than human beings and, of course, to the purely Other than everything that is.

What I am noting here points to a much-discussed problem with Heidegger's thinking on the call of Being. As Heidegger goes about responding to this call, the poetic trajectory of his thinking ends up demonstrating a lack of concern for the welfare of others, or what John Caputo describes as the "flesh" and "vulnerability" of the body—"the body in need, the body of the suffering, the bodies of those who lay claim to those who are well-off."[16] Moreover, as Richard Bernstein points out, a way of thinking that is inattentive to the needs of others "is itself extremely dangerous . . . because it virtually closes off the space for attending to the type of thinking and acting that can foster human solidarity and community." Bernstein would thus have us remember what he feels the later Heidegger seems to forget: "Our dialogue, and communicative transactions, are not only with Being itself, but with other human beings."[17] And this being so, it makes good sense for members of a community to develop their rhetorical competence in order to encourage the further development of another essential aspect of authentic community: civic virtue.

A Lesson in Conscience

The charges brought against Heidegger by those like Caputo and Bernstein can be tempered a bit, I believe, by recognizing how Heidegger's thinking on the call of Being, related as it is to his earlier thinking on the call of conscience, lends itself to an analysis of communicative transactions (for example, the physician-patient relationship as discussed above) that necessarily entail the requirement of attending carefully to the body in need. I do not believe I have been overly generous with hermeneutic charity in reading Heidegger in this way. Although he never explicitly admits as much, the respect he shows for the call of Being is the same respect that the call of conscience requires us to grant to others. To "dwell poetically" in the presence of all that lies before us is to treat beings with considerateness and forbearance. Hence, it might be said that with Heidegger's thinking on the call of Being, we receive a lesson in what it takes to meet this requirement.

As we have seen, in *Being and Time* Heidegger associates the challenge of this requirement with the ethical and rhetorical task of trying to build an authentic community by communicating and struggling with others. In his later works the requirement remains aligned with this task, although now Heidegger speaks of the matter in a more ontologically expansive way: as a struggle to conduct a thoughtful conversation with Being whereby we open ourselves to the truth (disclosure) of what is by letting beings be themselves. This struggle requires that a sacrifice be made: the ways and means of calculative thinking must be put aside so that the more essential and revealing operation of poetic or meditative thinking can prosper. The conversation that is made possible by this manner of thinking is, for Heidegger, an "ethical" achievement in the most original sense of the term. The basic meaning of *ethos* refers to the "abode" or "dwelling place" that founds our communal relationships with others and wherein a person's moral character is developed (LH 233).

All of this is not to say, however, that I would totally dismiss the charges made against Heidegger, for these charges are not without foundation, and they are serious. Heidegger is primarily interested in listening to a call that operates in silence and that is not anything human. He is awestruck by what is Other than others, by that which must first offer itself before anything else can come *to be*. Heidegger ponders what is given here. He returns Being's favor by responding in a most conscientious way to its call   a call whose presence names an absence, a nothingness, a mystery that registers itself in the very happening (death) that makes it impossible for us to know for sure what the rhyme and reason of this mystery truly is. Heidegger never stops trying to interpret the rhyme of this reason and the way it plays itself out in our lives. He is more of a thinker than a poet who, in trying to speak the truth of what lies before him, offers a caring and thoughtful portrayal of something holy—the body in need. Indeed others are more absent than present in Heidegger's thought as he remains open to the call's silence so that he may tell us such things as this:

> *Being is the most said.* For it is said in every word of language, and nevertheless discourse and writing talk for the most part only about beings. This comes to articulation. Even where we actually say the "is" and thus name being, we say the "is" only to assert a being about a being. *Beings are said. Being is kept silent about.* But not by us and on purpose. For we are unable to discover any trace of an intention not to say being. Hence, the keeping silent must indeed come from being itself. Hence, being is a keeping silent about itself, and this is certainly the ground of the possibility of keeping silent and the origin of silence. In this realm of silence the word first arises each time. (BC 64–65)

Being, in other words, is never there to say such heartfelt things as "I'm sorry." Only the human being can be so kind.[18]

Perhaps Heidegger would have been more attentive to others if he had spent more time appreciating how the "interruption" of the call of conscience is made known by way of occurrences (for example, a loved one becoming seriously ill) that disrupt our typical involvements with things and with others. And perhaps he would not have continued to forget to offer this attention if he did not hold a certain belief about humankind's historical destiny. For this destiny, Heidegger maintains, is not rooted primarily in the efficacy of human praxis and thus in our sociopolitical ways of being-with-and-for-others, but in the play of Being itself, in the way that Being both reveals itself to us and holds itself back and withdraws at any moment in time (OTB 8–18; QT 33–34; LH 215). According to Heidegger, the present technological age is the latest result of Being's way of revealing itself to Western man—hence our propensity to be calculative thinkers who, at best, only serve to sustain technology's influence over humankind by abiding by its principles of control, power, speed, and efficiency.

So what is to be done in the face of our current destiny? Heidegger answers this question: "We are to do nothing but wait" (DT 62)—by which he means that we must learn to think and dwell poetically so as to be better prepared to answer a call whose revelation might indicate the coming of a "better" future. By opening ourselves to this revelation and giving expression to it, we can have something of a say in contributing to our destiny. We are not necessarily fated to continue our calculative and dominating ways. "Always the unconcealment of that which is goes upon a way of revealing," Heidegger writes. "Always the destining of revealing holds complete sway over man. But that destining is never a fate that compels. For man becomes truly free insofar as he belongs to the realm of destining and so becomes one who listens and hears . . . , and not one who is simply constrained to obey" (QT 25).

This passage is often evoked by those who emphasize that Heidegger's theory of "the destining of revealing" (or what he also refers to as "the destiny [Geschick] of Being") does not describe a fatalistic or deterministic worldview. In The Principle of Reason Heidegger lends support to this reading of his theory when he stresses that

> the Geschick of being is not only not a self-contained ongoing process, but it also is not something lying over against us. . . . The Geschick of being is, as an appeal and claim [or "a call"], the verdict on the basis of which all human speaking speaks. The Latin for Spruch [verdict] is fatum. But as the verdict of being in the sense of self-withdrawing Geschick, fate [Fatum] is not something fatalistic for the simple reason that it can never be any such thing. Why not? Because being, in proffering itself, brings about the free openness of the temporal play-space and, in so doing, first frees humans unto the openness of whatever fitting essential possibilities they happen to have. (PR 94)

Those like Jürgen Habermas, however, would have us believe that there is a significant deterministic element to Heidegger's theory and that it serves a particularly strategic function since it provides a way for him not only to revise the "decisionism" of Being and Time but also, and relatedly, to explain and rationalize his "personal decision" to associate himself with the movement of National Socialism in 1933. According to Habermas, the theory of the Geschick of Being enables Heidegger to interpret

> the untruth of the movement by which he had let himself be dragged along

not in terms of an existential fallenness into the "they" for which one is subjectively responsible, but as an objective withholding of the truth. That the eyes of the most resolute philosopher were only gradually opened up to the nature of the regime—for this astoundingly delayed reading of world history—the course of the world itself is supposed to assume authorship, not concrete history, indeed, but a sublimated history promoted to the lofty heights of ontology.[19]

My way of dealing with the controversy here at issue takes a somewhat different approach. When Heidegger, apparently after hearing the call of conscience, chose to speak of "the inner truth and greatness" of National Socialism, he added his voice to a movement whose rhetoric made it impossible to encourage, by way of "considerateness" and "forbearance," an authentic response from the non-Aryan Other. Hence, with what it tells us about the type of heroic rhetorical response that is required by the call of conscience, *Being and Time* provides one with a credible way of gauging Heidegger's tragic lack of judgment in 1933.[20] Seeking direction from Heidegger's thinking of the *Geschick* of Being (which I do not see as defining a totally deterministic worldview), one might argue that his most authentic course of "action" at the time should have been more in line with the ways of meditative and poetic thinking. Perhaps, but this "nonrhetorical" option is not without its problems. For example, when caught up in the midst of life's contingencies, of sociopolitical happenings that can bring us to our knees and perhaps send us to our graves, can we afford merely to sit back and wait and see what Being has in store for us? When the sufferings of others provoke us to hear the call of conscience, is it enough to release ourselves from the practical and ethical matters at hand so that we may properly stay attuned to the call of Being? Are there not times when the right and just thing to do is *at least* to speak up in a willful and deliberative way, to acknowledge and reach out to others, and thus to communicate and struggle with them? In short, should it not be the case that when conscience calls, rhetoric ought to answer, even if the word of the poet is yet to come and even if what one has to say is out of step with the party line?[21] A system of meaning (National Socialism, for example) that has been constructed in such a way so as to silence any critical, deconstructive impulses is not a system that lends itself to the ways of authentic Dasein.

Heidegger should have listened more carefully to what he wrote in *Being and Time;* he should have interrupted his ongoing thinking on the meaning and truth of Being and apologized *in no uncertain terms* for his tragic error of not speaking out against and interrupting the worldview of a murderous regime. Heidegger emphasizes the "courage" it takes to perform such a conscientious and rhetorically noble deed (BT 298, 310–11). To be sure, a well-formulated and appropriate rhetorical interruption often requires not only artistic skill but also the bravery that comes with the cultivation of this virtuous way of being-with-and-for-others. Offering a genuine response to the call of conscience is not an activity for the weak at heart.[22]

The call of conscience (Being) calls for, among other things, rhetorical interruptions. In his discussion of these interruptions, Thomas B. Farrell writes: "Rhetoric, despite its traditional and quite justifiable association with the preservation of cultural truisms, may also perform an act of *critical interruption* where the taken-for-granted practices of culture are concerned. . . . The phenomenon of rhetorical interruption juxtaposes the assumptions, norms, and practices of a people so as to prompt a reappraisal of where they are culturally, what they are doing, and where they are going."[23] What Farrell fails to realize, however, is that this phenomenon is always already at work before the orator steps in with his or her discourse. It is how the call of conscience embedded in the temporal structure of human existence calls us into question. Might it therefore be said that the call of conscience is a rhetorical interruption in its purest form?

Heidegger never speaks of the call of conscience as a rhetorical interruption. Perhaps he would have if, to repeat once again, he had given more thought to how the interruptive nature of the call makes itself known by way of breakdowns in our lives. Just like a tool that abruptly breaks in our hands, the practice of rhetoric can interrupt our habits of thinking and living and thereby encourage us to rethink the wisdom of our everyday behavior. As I hope to show later on, rhetorical interruptions are constantly at work in the euthanasia debate as people invent ways of getting others to see exactly what life, death, medical science and technology, and morality are supposedly all about. First, however, I want to supplement and extend what has so far been said about the call of conscience by turning to the work of Emmanuel Levinas. What this philosopher and Talmudic scholar has to say about the call not only enables one to clarify and advance Heidegger's thinking on the way in which the phenomenon functions to relate us to others, but it also helps one to realize that the call of conscience is itself a rhetorical interruption.

Chapter 3

Levinas and the Call of Conscience

A Question of the Other

> If at the beginning our reflections are in large measure inspired by the philosophy of Martin Heidegger, where we find the concept of ontology and of the relationship which man sustains with Being, they are also governed by a profound need to leave the climate of that philosophy, and by the conviction that we cannot leave it for a philosophy that would be pre-Heideggerian. (EE 19)

One can read and try to appreciate Heidegger's philosophy without ever referring to the works of Levinas. Coming to grips with Levinas' thinking, however, requires at the very least a basic understanding of Heidegger's phenomenological investigations of the meaning and truth of Being, of how "It gives" (*Es gibt*) and, in so doing, relates Itself to everyday existence and to the call of conscience that is heard there. Heidegger's thinking on these matters is consistently mentioned and very often challenged by Levinas as he conducts his own phenomenological inquiry into the meaning and truth of ethics.

For Levinas it is ethics, not ontology, that warrants the recognition of "first philosophy" (EFP): "Man's ethical relation to the other is ultimately prior to his ontological relation to himself (egology) or to the totality of things which we call the world (cosmology)" (EI 57). Hence, Levinas would have us never forget that "the Marvel of creation does not only consist in being a creation *ex nihilo,* but in that it results in a being capable of receiving a revelation, learning that it is created, and putting itself in question. The miracle of creation lies in creating a moral being" (TI 89), a being who is wise enough to care about justice, and caring enough to say "Here I am" to those in need of acknowledgment and assistance.

Levinas maintains that "Heideggerian ontology" subordinates this all-important relationship with others to the relation with Being in general. Hence, according to Levinas, Heidegger's thinking on the call of conscience leads us down the wrong path. For this call originates, not in "the temporality of Being," but rather in "the temporality of the interhuman," in the "face-to-face" encounter between the self and "the other."[1] This encounter, Levinas argues, defines the primordial domain of ethics—a domain where the self, existing as it does in constant "proximity" to the other, is always in the situation of trying to come to terms with the otherness or alterity of the other, with what the self can never totally be in mind and body, with a fundamental *differ-ence* embedded in life that forms the existential basis of all forms of social cri-tique because its mere presence "calls into question" the self's egoist tendencies and know-it-all-attitudes. Levinas equates this never-ending event of question-ing with the call of conscience—a call whose voice signifies "the revelation of a resistance to my powers" and to "my glorious spontaneity as a living being" (TI 84). The distinctiveness of the other, the sheerness of its "face," raises the issue of accountability and responsibility: Am I being just with my freedom to do and say what I will? It is this question, not the question of Being, that Lev-inas would have us constantly think about in order to be true to the miracle that we are.

Although Heidegger's philosophy does not focus on the moral character of human being, I hope it is clear from what was discussed in chapters 1 and 2 that the issue is not left unaddressed in what Heidegger reveals about Dasein's need to meet the challenge of the call of conscience whereby it must assume the eth-ical responsibility of affirming its freedom through resolute choice and at the same time remain open to the differences of others. Levinas' lack of hermeneu-tic charity toward Heidegger regarding the issue has not gone unnoticed by those like Jacques Derrida, who certainly would have us acknowledge the genius of both men—their all-important philosophical, political, and religious differences *and* how Levinas is more dependent on Heidegger than he admits.[2]

Yet despite his sometimes misleading reading of Heidegger, Levinas war-rants special attention—especially because he helps one to avoid Heidegger's mistake of not paying careful enough attention to how the otherness of others, like "Dasein itself," sounds a primordial call of conscience. Listening to this call coming from the Other, Levinas hears what he terms a "rhetoric without elo-quence." Although I take exception to Levinas' Platonic conception of the practice of rhetoric, I nevertheless find his characterization of the call's dis-course to be instructive for pointing out how there is indeed something rhetorical going on at the heart of existence, something that speaks against atti-tudes and outlooks that are close-minded, egotistical, brutally selective when it comes to caring for others, and unapologizing for this tragic lack of com-passion and wisdom.

As was the case with Heidegger, my discussion of Levinas' thinking on the call of conscience begins with some brief comments about his phenomeno-logical approach to the topic and then continues with an account of how he conceives of that realm of thought and action (that is, everyday existence) wherein the call is heard. Here too I will have some things to say about Lev-inas' take on the question of Being, for his understanding of what Being is plays a significant role in how he conceives of everyday existence. I next provide a detailed examination of how Levinas' specific understanding of the nature of the call both complements and extends Heidegger's appreciation of the matter. In the last two sections I bring together both philosophers' assessments of the call in order to emphasize the relationship it holds with rhetoric.

A Phenomenology

Summing up some of his major findings in his early work *Time and the Other,* Levinas writes: "I have attempted a 'phenomenology' of sociality starting from the face of the other person—from proximity—by understanding in its rectitude a voice that commands before all mimicry and verbal expression, in the mortality of the face, from the bottom of this weakness. It commands me to not remain indifferent to this death, to not let the Other die alone, that is to answer for the life of the other person, at the risk of becoming an accomplice in the person's death" (TO 109). This summary not only helps one keep in mind some of what Levinas has been doing so far in his text, but it also indicates some of the essential topics that will demand Levinas' attention as he further develops and fine-tunes his philosophy.

As a phenomenologist interested primarily in the question of ethics, of humankind's moral being, Levinas begins his investigations where he must— in the everyday social world where the presence of others (even when they are absent) is a given, a fact of life. Levinas terms this givenness "proximity," that primordial temporal and spatial relationship between the self and others that is always there before one even knows, for example, that for the last two minutes the person standing three feet to your left has been taken with your presence. Levinas' specific term for the presence of the other (and the self, who is also an other to other selves) is the *face,* or what he defines as "the expressive in the Other (and the whole human body is in this sense more or less face" (EI 97). Elsewhere he writes: "A face has a meaning not by virtue of the relationships in which it is found, but out of itself; that is what *expression* is. A face is the presentation of an entity as an entity, its personal presentation, . . . the existence of a substance, a thing in itself" (CPP 21).

Chapter 1 detailed how the empirical nature of phenomenological inquiry is associated with the generating of a discourse that is especially attuned to the "thing itself," to the way in which some phenomenon happens, to how it reveals and shows itself. The discourse of phenomenology assumes the task of disclosing a phenomenon's own disclosure, its being and truth. When Levinas speaks of the face, he is thus attending to something that comes before what someone like Erving Goffman means by the face. Without ever acknowledging that he is doing so, Goffman identifies and studies a sense of *face* that rhetorical theorists have long known as a person's "good character": "Face is an image of self delineated in terms of approved social attributes—albeit an image that others may share, as when a person makes a good showing for his profession or religion by making a good showing for himself." Goffman thus emphasizes a notion of "face" that goes no further than the "face-work" or learned behavior of "self-regulating participants in social encounters."[3] For Levinas, however, the face of the other in its simple "nakedness," its mere presence before it subscribes to the socially circumscribed rituals of self-presentation, is its own good showing—a showing that is good first and foremost because it "speaks" of the miracle and mystery of life.

So as not to get confused by the mixing of metaphors here (that is, showing and speaking), we must keep in mind again that this claim reflects a phenomenological appreciation of the face, of how its disclosing and showing of itself is a primordial "saying" (*logos*) that gives itself for understanding. Recall how Heidegger puts it when he speaks of how phenomenology requires one to engage in the thoughtful and respectful practice of "letting beings be": If we are to "listen" attentively to the call of Being (*Logos*), we must "follow the movement of showing"—the way the call presents itself as a disclosing of what is— so as to let whatever it is that concerns us speak for itself.[4] Levinas listens to a call that comes with the presence of the other's being, with his or her face. "Face and discourse are tied," writes Levinas. "The face speaks. It speaks, it is in this that it renders possible and begins all discourse" that we eventually express in oral and written form (EI 87). The saying power of language originates with the Other and before others ever open their mouths or write a single word.

But is it not the case, then, that in listening to the face, to its voice, to the call of the Other so as to come to terms with the question of ethics, Levinas is giving thought, albeit in a restricted way, to what Heidegger was totally taken with: the call of Being, which makes possible but is *other* than the being of any entity? I agree with Derrida's answer to this question:

> Thought—or at least the precomprehension of Being—*conditions* . . . the *recognition* of the essence of the existent (for example, someone, existent *as* other, *as* other self, etc.). It conditions the *respect* for the other as what it is: other. Without this acknowledgment, . . . or let us say without this "letting-be" of an existent . . . as something existing outside me in the essence of what it is (first in its alterity), no ethics would be possible. . . . To let the other be in its existence and essence as other means that what gains access to thought, or (*and*) what thought gains access to, is that which is essence and that which is existence; and that which is the Being which they both presuppose.[5]

Because Heidegger was too enthralled with a certain question, because his answer to the question was too neglectful of a source of otherness that for Levinas demands the utmost attention, given what it has to tell us about ethics and morality, and because of the horrendous political consequences that followed from such neglect, Levinas' philosophy is governed by a profound need to "leave the climate" of Heidegger's philosophy. Still, Levinas' philosophy presupposes much that is revealed by Heidegger's phenomenological investigations of the meaning and truth of Being. In saying this I in no way mean to diminish the importance of Levinas' work. As he conducts his phenomenology of the face-to-face encounter between the self and the other, Levinas offers many insights that both complement and extend Heidegger's "conscientious" thought. These insights start to take form as soon as Levinas begins his inquiry into that realm of common sense and common practice wherein the call makes itself known and that Heidegger termed "everydayness."

Our Everyday Way of Being-with-and-for-Others

"Everyday life," claims Levinas, "is a preoccupation with salvation" (TO 58). What we seek salvation from, according to Levinas, is the very thing that Heidegger associated with the ultimate source of anxiety but that he also claimed should elicit "unshakable joy" on our part: our own existence (Dasein), the givenness of Being, that which makes possible what we are but is Other than a human creation. As was briefly indicated above, and as will be discussed in more detail below, Levinas' take on Being is not as different from Heidegger's as he would have us believe. However, some important differences do exist and must first be accounted for in order to appreciate the full significance of Levinas' claim about everyday life.

At times Levinas speaks of Being much like Heidegger does. He notes, for example, "It is banal to say we never exist in the singular. We are surrounded by beings and things with which we maintain relationships. Through sight, touch, sympathy and cooperative work, we are with others. All these relationships are transitive: I touch an object, I see the other. But I *am* not the other. I am all alone. It is thus the being in me, the fact that I exist, my *existing,* that constitutes the absolutely intransitive element, something without intentionality or relationship. One can exchange everything between beings except existing. In this sense, to be is to be isolated by existing" (TO 42). Even though I am a social being by nature, a creature whose everyday life is always caught up in relationships with things and with others, there is still something here that I can truly call my own and that thereby is the source of what Heidegger defines as a human being's "authenticity." I exist, and in and through this existing it is I who, in a moment of great anxiety or immense joy, must constantly take on the *personal* challenge of affirming my freedom through resolute choice.

When Levinas speaks of existing (Being), however, he more often than not emphasizes its "darker" side. "Being," he writes, "is essentially alien and strikes against us. We undergo its suffocating embrace like the night, but it does not respond to us. There is a pain in Being" (EE 23). We experience this pain whenever we are forced to come face to face with what Levinas terms "the indissoluble unity between the existent and its existing" (TO 54). This unity, according to Levinas, defines the most primordial form of solitude or aloneness that can be experienced by human beings. "Solitude is the very unity of the existent, the fact that there is something in existing starting from which existence occurs. The subject is alone because it is one [with its Being] . . . it cannot detach itself from itself" and remain alive to be what it is (TO 55).

An example of one who is likely to experience the pain and solitude of Being would be a person suffering from a serious and incapacitating illness that, among other things, undercuts the person's "mastery over existing"; breeds despair and a feeling of abandonment; encourages a preoccupation with the person's own state of being; and thereby directs the person to wonder about life's meaning, purpose, and ultimate worth. In such suffering, writes Levinas, "there is an absence of all refuge. It is the fact of being directly exposed to being. It is made up of the impossibility of fleeing or retreating. The whole acuity of suffering lies in this impossibility of retreat. It is the fact of being backed up against life and being" (TO 69).

I see little difference between what Levinas is suggesting here and what Heidegger, as discussed in chapter 2, has to say about Dasein's coming to terms with its own "Being-unto-death"— a task that calls on one's authenticity and thus on one's ability to assume the personal responsibility of affirming her freedom through resolute choice. For Heidegger the awesomeness of Being is associated not only with its being a source of ontological anxiety but also with its "gift" of life, thought, freedom, and creativity. Being has a "dark" side, but it also is structured so as to allow us to be joyful about what we can do to improve our existence. Being is open to us—it grants us a future, another chance to get things right—and we can be open to Being, to the possibility of matters getting better; hence, for example, that far-away place that people "know" as "heaven."

But Levinas also perceives a "lighter" side to Being, for although he maintains that the solitude of Being brings about pain, he also admits that "a solitude is necessary in order for there to be a freedom of beginning, the existent's mastery over existing—that is, in brief, in order for there to be an existent. Solitude is thus not only a despair and an abandonment, but also a virility, a pride and a sovereignty" (TO 55). Heidegger would certainly agree. We are creatures who can take control of ourselves and, even in the face of death, display courage and resoluteness. For Levinas this "heroic" capacity should be understood as indicating that along with the pain, solitude, and suffering of Being, there comes "the love of life"—a love that is, in fact, presupposed by the darker side of Being. Here is how Levinas puts it: "At the origin there is a being gratified, a citizen of paradise. The 'emptiness' felt implies that the need which becomes aware of it abides already in the midst of an enjoyment—be it that of the air one breathes. It anticipates the joy of satisfaction, which is *better* than ataraxy. Far from putting the sensible life into question, pain takes place within its horizons and refers to the joy of living. Already and henceforth life is loved" (TI 144–45).

Heidegger speaks of the loving care that we owe to Being for "Its gift." Levinas stresses that "none of the generosity which the German term 'es gibt' is said to contain revealed itself between 1933 and 1945" (DF 292). Levinas thus does not want to be heard as merely echoing Heidegger's thinking on Being. "The love of life," writes Levinas, "does not resemble the care for Being, reducible to the comprehension of Being, or ontology. The love of life does not love Being, but loves the happiness of being. Life loved is the very enjoyment of life, contentment—already appreciated in the refusal I bear against it, where contentment is refused in the name of contentment itself" (TI 145) (as seen in those people who are content only when their lives are so busy that there is little or no time to relax, smell the roses, and enjoy life). The love of life that stirs in our being, or what Levinas terms "the primordial positivity of enjoyment," is what gives whatever value can be found in pain and suffering. Hence, Levinas tells us,

> In its opposition to being [that is, suffering pain], the I seeks refuge in being itself [that is, in the gift of life and the "goodness" that accompanies it]. Suicide is tragic, for death does not bring a resolution to all the problems to which birth gave rise, and is powerless to humiliate the values of the earth— whence Macbeth's final cry in confronting death, defeat because the universe is not destroyed at the same time as his life. Suffering at the same time despairs for being riveted to being—and loves the being to which it is riveted. It knows the impossibility of quitting life: what tragedy! what comedy. . . . The *taedium vitae* is steeped in the love of the life it rejects; despair does not break with the ideal of joy. (TI 146)

Indeed people who attempt suicide, by themselves or with the help of others, typically do so because circumstances have called this ideal into question and perhaps destroyed it altogether.

Is this to say that the "life" of a human being is less than it is—is essentially not itself—if the Being of this life is no longer capable of inspiring joy? Is such an abject state of being what "hell on earth" is all about? Levinas is a religious Jew who believes in the sanctity of life (Being) and who is thus taken with the person who takes seriously the fact that "prior to death there is always a last chance; this is what heroes seize, not death" (TO 73). Like Heidegger, Levinas champions such a person; hence, to Hamlet's famous question of conscience—"To be or not to be?"—he recommends throughout his philosophy the first alternative. But what if one's being has lost its capacity for joy, for hope, for one "last chance"? Levinas does not say. Unlike Heidegger, he is con-

tent to speak of life without spending too much time worrying about our way
of "Being-unto-death." In accordance with his religious worldview, Levinas is
much more concerned with what is happening now than with what is to come
in the future. "The now is the fact that I am master, master of the possible, master of grasping the possible. Death is never now. When death is here, I am no
longer here, not just because I am nothingness, but because I am unable to
grasp" (TO 72).

Levinas thinks of Being/life/death in a way that is both similar to, and different than, Heidegger's way of appreciating the matter. This difference has
much to do with where the thinking of these two philosophers is rooted. Heidegger's thought is steeped in the tradition made possible by the pre-Socratics
as well as by his staunch Catholic heritage. Levinas, on the other hand, interprets the matter with the help of a discourse that not only springs from the
wisdom of the ancient Greeks but also from an older tradition, the "Judaic" tradition, whose words, meanings, arguments, and stories comprise the teachings
of the Old Testament. "Are not we Westerners, from California to the Urals,
nourished by the Bible as much as by the Presocratics?" asks Levinas (CPP
148). The importance of the nourishment that Levinas receives from his religious roots cannot be overemphasized.

In the last paragraph of his influential *Man Is Not Alone,* Rabbi Abraham
Joshua Heschel summarizes one of the key aspects of his "philosophy of religion" when he notes: "The deepest wisdom man can attain is to know that his
destiny is to aid, to serve."[6] Heidegger spoke this way when defining the
"essence" of human being: Dasein's existence is where the call of Being is most
clearly heard and where this call must receive a most careful and respectful
response. We owe much to what gives us life but is always more and thus
"other" than any being there is. Heidegger praised the otherness (alterity) of
Being. As a Jew, Levinas is compelled to understand the matter differently. We
are here, first and foremost, to aid and to serve other human beings. Judaism
defines a way of being that, in name of the wholly Other (God), is awed by the
otherness of others and all that this otherness requires in order to maintain its
well-being (ITN 109–13, 167–83; NTR 12–29). Jews have been conditioned
to be especially sensitive to this requirement because for over three thousand
years they have been forced to know themselves not only as an "other," but as
an other whom others would marginalize, silence, and even exterminate
because of who they are. To be a Jew is to know of the tragedy and horror of
"anti-Semitism, which is in its essence hatred for a man who is other than oneself—that is to say, hatred for the other man" (DF 281). At the heart of
Judaism lies a keen awareness of what otherness is all about.

When Levinas proclaims that everyday life is a preoccupation with salvation and that what we seek salvation from is the pain, solitude, and suffering of
Being, he is guided by a worldview that would have us know that we *are* our

brothers' and sisters' keepers and that we should always remain open to the presence (the face) of others who, like the stranger, widow, or orphan referred to in the Old Testament, are in need of heartfelt acknowledgment. "I will give them a heart to know Me, that I am the Lord" (Jer. 24:7). This gift, as discussed in the introduction, is the capacity of conscience, which enables us to be awed by the happenings and mysteries of life. In moments of awe we are made to wonder; and wonder, we should recall, is the state of our being asked, that state where one is addressed and acknowledged and thereby given the opportunity to respond and be accountable. The self, one's ego, takes form in light of this opportunity, which comes to us from something that is wholly Other and whose presence, which can never be totally comprehended by a finite creature, still leaves a "trace" of Itself in what is other than one's self. From a Judaic and Levinasian perspective, "there is something more important than my life, and that is the life of the other" (PM 172). For here, in the otherness of other people, in the presence and difference of their sad and joyful faces, lies empirical evidence of what it is that challenges the selfish ways of egoism, that calls on us to recognize the importance of going beyond the limitations of our "personal" interpretations of the world, and that thereby indicates the value of "transcendence." Levinas writes: "It is as if God spoke through the face" (PM 169). A recognition of otherness is a moral act that "accomplishes human society" as it promotes "the miracle of moving out of oneself" (DF 9).

The self owes much to the other. Levinas emphasizes the point this way:

> I am defined as a subjectivity, as a particular person, as an "I," precisely because I am exposed to the other. It is my inescapable and incontrovertible answerability to the other that makes me an individual "I." So that I become a responsible or ethical "I" to the extent that I agree to depose or dethrone myself—to abdicate my position of centrality—in favor of the vulnerable other. . . . The ethical "I" is subjectivity precisely in so far as it kneels before the other, sacrificing its own liberty to the more primordial call of the other. . . . I can never escape the fact that the other has demanded a response from me before I affirm my freedom not to respond to his demand. (EOF 62–63; also see PN 72–74)

Standing exposed to the face of the Other, the self is called out of itself, out of its preoccupation with its personal wants and priorities, and toward what before anything else in this world really makes a difference. This difference (otherness, alterity), which is always already at work before we give it any thought, stimulates and informs who we are as beings gifted with moral potential. We are creatures whose well-being requires recognition from those who would have us return the favor. Indeed we are social beings—born from others and, right from the start, in need of family, friends, and even strangers who are willing to open themselves to and acknowledge our presence, be it joyful or desperate. "The social relation itself," writes Levinas, "is not just another relation, one among so many others that can be produced in being, but is its ultimate event" (TI 221).

Although this event sooner or later is likely to bring about discomfort (as when, for example, we become angry with others), it nevertheless is essential to our good health. Imagine what your life would be like if nobody cared enough to acknowledge your existence in a heartfelt way. There most likely would be the pain and suffering of solitude, of being alone with yourself for too long, of having no one you could trust and turn to for help. Marginalized, isolated, and abandoned, you would be left only with the givenness of Being, or what Levinas also terms the "there is" of existing, that "anonymous state of being" that, as noted above, "is essentially alien and strikes against us" and that at times can be so horrifying as to have one think that it would be a blessing "not to be" (EE 17–36). Everyday life is a preoccupation with salvation because it is here, in our being-with-others, that we are saved by what they, in the "goodness" of their presence, have to offer: considerateness, forbearance, companionship, trust, love, and other such things that might keep us from slipping back into a state of horror that, by itself, offers no escape.

Levinas speaks of our everydayness in a way that he perceives to be quite different than what one finds in Heidegger. Recall that when Heidegger discusses the phenomenon, he often associates it with the state of inauthenticity—a state wherein we allow ourselves to be ruled by the "dictatorship of the 'they,'" by routines, customs, and habits that make us forgetful of our own authenticity: that challenge we face every day whereby we must assume the personal and ethical responsibility of affirming our freedom through resolute choice. In our everyday way of being-with-others we are more likely to treat them like tools, as means to some ends, than as beings whose authenticity warrants the utmost respect. Here too human emotion becomes an instrument of manipulation, temporality is reduced to the workings of the clock, time is spaced and space is timed, and the revealing power of language is sapped of its strength by discursive routines designed to promote a ritualistic understanding of the world. For Heidegger too the everyday world is a preoccupation with salvation. Coming face to face with the Being that we are incites anxiety and guilt. Why not try to avoid the pain and suffering that goes along with these emotions? For Heidegger, of course, this avoidance of Being is a cowardly way to live; it lacks authenticity.

Levinas, on the other hand, would have us think differently about our everydayness. Here, for example, is a particular way he puts it during a critique of Heidegger:

> However much the entirety of preoccupations that fill our days and tear us away from solitude to throw us into contact with our peers are called "fall," "everyday life," "animality," "degradation," or "base materialism," these

preoccupations are in any case in no way frivolous. One can think that authentic time is originally an ecstasis, yet one buys oneself a watch; despite the nudity of existence, one must as far as possible be decently clothed. And when one writes a book on anxiety, one writes it for someone, one goes through all the steps that separate the draft from the publication, and one sometimes behaves like a merchant of anxiety. The man condemned to die straightens out his uniform before his last walk, accepts a final cigarette, and finds an eloquent word before the salvo. . . . There is something other than naïveté in the flat denial the masses oppose to the elites when they are worried more about bread than about anxiety. (TO 59–60)

Heidegger, I submit, would not disagree. Remember, Heidegger is critical of the world of the "they" because of how it supplies a breeding ground for the evils of conformism. But he never denies the existential importance of this domain of everydayness and being-with-others. "The world of Dasein is a *with-world* [*Mitwelt*]. Being-in[-the-world] is *Being-with* others" (BT 155). "So far as Dasein *is* at all, it has Being-with-one-another as its kind of Being" (BT 163). The common ways of structuring time and space, employing emotions, and using language are not simply degraded by Heidegger; they are also acknowledged as essential to the workings of Dasein's communal character.

What bothers Levinas about all of this, however, is Heidegger's failure to understand that it is not our being-with others, but rather our being-*for* others, that forms the basis of community building. That is, as discussed above, the self needs the other to move it out of itself and save it from the horror, the solitude, of its own Being. The salvation provided by everyday life presupposes this movement that maintains the integrity of what Levinas terms the "inter-human":

The inter-human lies in a non-indifference of one to another, in a responsibility of one for another. The inter-human is prior to the reciprocity of this responsibility, which inscribes itself in impersonal laws, and becomes superimposed on the pure altruism of this responsibility inscribed in the ethical position of the self as self. . . .

The inter-human lies also in the recourse that people have to one another for help, before the marvelous alterity of the Other has been banalized or dimmed in a simple exchange of courtesies which become established as an "inter-personal commerce" of customs. (US 165)

Being-with others would be nothing more than an adventure in power, violence, and survival of the fittest if it were not for the fact that, at its most primordial level, human existence is not only a temporal happening (a Being-unto-death), but something whose unfolding is directed toward the Other, toward what is not yet (the future), *and* toward who we are not and never will be (the Other). Having failed to appreciate the intricacies of this movement, Heidegger, according to Levinas, did not see how its direction of "one to another," of "one for another," defines a most primordial event, a "being-for others," out of which any particular act of moral acknowledgment (for example, considerateness, forbearance, compassion, love) is borne. The indelible communal character of human existence is made possible by an altruistic and thus moral impulse that lies at the heart of human being. Levinas thus claims that because of this impulse, "intersubjective space is initially asymmetrical" (EE 95). Human existence is so structured as to have the self move toward the other before the self can even raise the related issues of reciprocity and moral responsibility. Morality originates in a movement of being-for others (which is exactly what other *selves* are doing when they are responsible enough to acknowledge and assist *other* selves). Hence, Levinas would have us understand that, as in the case of Heideggerian ontology, a phenomenology of human being that fails to account for the primordial moral nature of its subject matter is missing something essential. Ontology without morality is heartless.

Yet here I must again express concern about Levinas' lack of hermeneutic charity. Recall that for Heidegger morality originates in the Being of Dasein, in its authenticity, in a human being's ability to remain open to the presencing of what is, so as to allow it to speak for itself. This is what it means to care lovingly for the truth, a caring that is desperately needed if human beings are to act wisely and justly as they go about assuming the personal and ethical responsibility of affirming their freedom through resolute choice. The challenge of this responsibility stares us in the face every day. It is the "call of conscience" that "comes from me and yet from beyond me and over me" (BT 320). The call of conscience is ultimately rooted in the Being of human being, which is other than a human creation.

In refusing to recognize how Heidegger's thinking on conscience entails a recognition of this primordial alterity that lies at the heart of human being, Levinas is able to say that Heidegger shows little appreciation for the essential structure of otherness that the presence (face) of the other always displays and from out of which, according to Levinas, the questioning call of conscience is first sounded. But Heidegger's philosophy of the call of conscience (Being) *does* acknowledge this essential structure. There is, of course, the alterity of Being itself, and there is also, as detailed in *Being and Time,* the otherness (Being) of others that must be treated with considerateness and forbearance so to ensure that all have a say in the telling of the truth and in the building of authentic community. Owing to the ontological structure of what and how we are, we exist in such a way that we are obliged to respect those who are other than ourselves. This is the obligation that Heidegger failed so miserably to meet when he began in 1933 to accommodate the immensely restricted rhetoric of National Socialism. Before Levinas has a chance to do it, Heidegger's own philosophy calls him into question.

In chapter 2 I noted that Heidegger might have been better prepared to avoid this problem if he had given more careful thought to how the interruptive nature of the call of conscience is actually heard in everyday life: it makes itself known only after something happens to disrupt the flow of our daily habits, activities, and ways of thinking. I also briefly suggested that such a disruption can be brought about by the practice of rhetoric. The discourse that sounds a rhetorical interruption, of course, comes to us from others—that is, from selves who hope that we (others) believe and accept what they have to say. Hence, if it is to be performed in both an ethical and effective way, the practice of rhetoric must be especially good at moving in the direction of "being for others." Rhetoric without the Other makes no sense, for as Calvin Schrag points out: "The distinctive stamp of rhetorical intentionality is that it reaches out toward, aims at, is directed to the other as hearer, reader, and audience. . . . In the rhetorical situation the other is not set at a distance. He is 'engaged,' brought into the space of praxial concerns. The rhetor seeks to evoke from the hearer a response to a particular situation. He calls for deliberative action and reasoned judgment."[7] This is certainly how rhetoric lends itself to being a voice of conscience for others and thus a voice that has a role to play in the establishing of community.

Like Heidegger's thinking on the question of Being, Levinas' thinking on the question of the Other has something to offer regarding the ethical nature of rhetoric. The movement of rhetoric, its intentionality, exhibits the same direction as that primordial movement of human existence (being-for) that forms the basis of morality. This perhaps simple observation is crucial to the present study because it will allow me to advance a position that neither Heidegger nor Levinas specifically admits: that the call of conscience is a rhetorical interruption in its purest form. In order to develop this position I must now spend more time discussing and critically assessing how Levinas understands the Other to be the source of the call.

The Other and the Call of Conscience

With Levinas we learn that everyday life is a preoccupation with salvation: we involve ourselves with things and with others and try to stay busy so as to avoid an isolating and painful confrontation with Being. In working and playing and socializing we find ways of making life livable, meaningful, worthwhile, and enjoyable. Levinas thus maintains that "the world is an ensemble of nourishments" (TO 63); it provides us with outlets for moving beyond the "evil" of suffering that is inextricably tied to Being (US 157–58). Levinas also maintains, however, that enjoyment can be quite immoral. This happens when enjoyment leads to "a withdrawal into oneself, an involution" whereby one's existence is "for itself": "It is for itself as in the expression 'each for himself'; for itself as

the 'famished stomach that has not ears,' capable of killing for a crust of bread,
. . .; for itself as the surfeited one who does not understand the starving and
approaches him as an alien species, as the philanthropist approaches the desti-
tute" (TI 118). Moreover, enjoyment can be so self-satisfying and addictive
that, as it nourishes our personal desires and egos, it makes us forgetful of others and of how our behavior might be adversely affecting them.

Recall that we first dealt with this problem of forgetfulness in chapter 1
when discussing how the world of everydayness manifests itself as a world of
"know-how," a world where forgetting others as well as ourselves is oftentimes
necessary in order for us to abide by the routines of the day in a competent
manner. In chapter 2 we returned to the problem in order to clarify how the
interruptive nature of the call of conscience makes itself known by way of disruptions that instigate breakdowns in our habits of living and thinking. The
example of computer usage was offered to illustrate how a sustained preoccupation with the routines of employing the computer to write a manuscript can
lead one to become too neglectful of others (such as family members) who
deserve to be treated in a more caring and respectful way. The forgetfulness at
work here is made apparent when the computer malfunctions and its user is
necessarily confronted with the personal challenge of critically assessing his
existence. He wonders: Should I be paying more attention to my family? Do
they understand that they are more important than my work and professional
ego? But what about my deadline? How am I going to balance these things for
the good of all concerned? In this situation the user must assume the responsibility of explicitly choosing a course of action; he must face the challenge of
responding to the call of conscience.

I do not think Levinas would object to this example as long as it was
understood on his terms. He maintains that we are made aware of the call by
way of a disruption that "interrupts" some self-satisfying state of enjoyment.
Moreover, like Heidegger, he would also have us understand that the genuine
nature of the call of conscience is itself an ongoing interruption, something
that, as long as we are alive, never stops calling us into question. For Levinas,
however, this call comes to us, not from the self's (Dasein's) existence, but
rather from the other's existence, that most valuable resource of alterity, of
something that is wholly other than the self witnessing it. Levinas writes: "The
Other as Other is not only an alter ego: the Other is what I myself am not.
This Other is this, not because of the Other's character, or physiognomy, or
psychology, but because of the Other's very alterity" (CPP 83).

With Heidegger one could say that the essence of alterity is what is otherwise known as Being—that which makes possible our existence but is not
itself a human creation. Given Levinas' restricted understanding of Being and
of Heidegger's understanding of Being, Levinas cannot admit as much. Alter-

ity, the otherness of others, is what calls the self to move out of itself. A computer, especially when it malfunctions, is an "other" to the self. Levinas, however, is not especially interested in how nonhuman things can incite our moral consciousness.[8] Rather, what most interests him is how other human beings, before they even know it, are themselves the most important source of the call of conscience—a call filled with and inciting wonder.

At any moment of the day or night a person's freedom can be called into question: Are you being just in all that you say and do? Compassionate and conscientious souls presumably ask this question of themselves as often as they can. The question interrupts, slows down, and perhaps brings to a halt the taken-for-granted routines and rituals that make up one's rule-governed everyday social encounters. Yet although the question directs one's concern toward the self and its possible improvement, it is raised initially because of what Levinas describes as "one's fear for the Other" (EFP 82), that is, a fear of how one's personal freedom can place a serious burden on others. Elaborating on this point, Levinas writes: "My being-in-the-world or my 'place in the sun' [Pascal] . . . , have these not also been the usurpation of spaces belonging to the other man whom I have already oppressed or starved, or driven out into a third world; are they not acts of repulsing, excluding, exiling, stripping, killing?" Indeed, says Levinas, as social creatures whose communal well-being is dependent on others, we owe it to them to feel a "fear for all the violence and murder [our] existing might generate, in spite of its conscious and intentional innocence" (EFP 82). We can pay this debt only by listening and responding to the other's call for recognition, respect, companionship, help, and perhaps love. For a finite being, however, the debt can never be paid in full; for as soon as one chooses to respond to the call of the other, a sacrifice must be made that increases the debt. What is sacrificed are the obligations the person also has to respond, in the same way, in the same instance, to all the others whose calls beg for acknowledgment. Still, something of the debt must be paid. Imagine what life would be like if nobody acknowledged your existence.

Levinas emphasizes the priority of the Other over the Self (Dasein); he would have us think otherwise than Heidegger. But does not the sacrifice we make of the Other presuppose what Heidegger termed the "Being-guilty" of Dasein? If an individual Dasein had not already personally experienced and learned something from the pain and suffering of Being, how would this self really "know" the other's plight, feel the other's pain, and understand what is owed to the other? Is not the other also a self, an individual Dasein? With these questions I am once again suggesting how Levinas' philosophy at times validates Heidegger's. The call of conscience is rooted in Dasein's existence, which is to say that this call can and does come from those who are other than oneself. The presence, the face of the other sounds an ongoing interruption of the activities of everyday life. There is nothing in Heidegger's philosophy that denies this occurrence. Compared to all that Levinas has to say about it, however, Heidegger can, at best, be credited with only offering hints about how the occurrence specifically takes place.

Are you being just in all that you say and do? This question, as noted above, arises because of what the self owes the other. The question, of course, is a moral one that raises the related questions of personal responsibility and accountability. Levinas often discusses the relevancy of all of these questions by recalling how they and their answers are recorded in the Old Testament. Here the story of moral consciousness unfolds as Adam, Abraham, Moses, Job, Jacob, and others are asked a question, "Where art thou?" and reply, "Here I am!" All of these souls are able to hear and respond to the question because they were given a "heart," the capacity of conscience, of being open to others—to their joys, fears, and needs. When we open our hearts to others, we make good our ability to be moral beings. The Lord demands nothing less, for even the Almighty is said to have cried and to have become angry when his/her call, need to be acknowledged, was ignored.

We finite beings share with an Infinite Mystery a fundamental need that we are reminded of whenever we stand face to face with others whose "simple" presence calls into question our freedom. We are creatures who know all too well what life would be like if nobody cared enough to acknowledge our existence. As creatures who can say "Here I am!" and really mean it, we stand in special relation to a Mystery that, when once asked to reveal its true identity, would only say "I am that I am." The Mystery remains, although not without a clue. The clue is empirical; it stares us in the face every day: we exist; each of us can say "I am." Each of us can "do unto others what [we] would have them do unto [us]." Acknowledgment is a life-giving event that is too often taken for granted and ignored. With the call of the Other that calls us into question, the self's situation becomes "religious" (not to be confused with the *institutions* of religion) (EI 85–122; OTB 144–65).

Levinas is a religious Jew. The greatness of his religion, he tells us, is that it knows itself for what it is: a way of being and thinking that recognizes how existence is a being-for others and thus how the good life is one that moves in a direction away from the self and toward the Other (DF 3–26). Before we can praise ourselves for being open-minded, we are already open to otherness. For Levinas this is how God, at least indirectly, shows God's face: by way of the face of the other, the human face that can speak without uttering a word as it moves us (beyond ourselves) with its sheer physical presence and its displays of joy and pain that signal that there is more going on than meets the eye. With the other there always comes a "surplus of meaning," of things not yet said, personal narratives that often tell complex stories that even the storyteller cannot fully understand. Moses spoke of a Supreme Presence, of something that offered only a "trace" of itself in a burning bush that did not consume itself, that was wholly Other than anything Moses had ever witnessed before, and that could not be described in words alone. The face of Moses, his being, was forever changed. He radiated otherness, the presence of difference, that which the face of the other places before us: alterity.

Levinas' phenomenology of the Other is drawn by this alterity, this sur-plus of meaning that always escapes in the otherness that it is, but that still shows a trace of itself when we stand in the presence of others and remain open to what they have to say, be it good or bad, supportive or critical. When we open ourselves to others and welcome their differences—what it is about them that calls into question our freedom—we provide the necessary space, the requisite dwelling place, that is needed to create and maintain the moral ecology of human fraternity. We must hear this call, and every day we are given the chance to do just that as we exist in constant proximity with others. The "face speaks," notes Levinas; and as it does, it calls for the life-giving gift of acknowledgment. "Where art thou?" "Here I am!" This exchange is considered by Levinas to be "miraculous" and "holy," for here it happens that the imperfect human being learns to set the grounds for "peace" by respecting the "plurality" of life that shows itself with every face in the crowd.

The "face speaks," repeats Levinas, and what it says can and does make a difference: Let there be peace, an openness to differences (EI 85–122; TO 109–86). In short, in carefully attending to the miracle of the face, Levinas hears a challenge, the ultimate call of conscience, which is both exhilarating and anxiety provoking. Levinas puts it this way: "Conscience welcomes the Other. It is the revelation of a resistance to my powers that does not counter them as a greater force, but calls in question the naive right of my powers, my glorious spontaneity as a living being. Morality begins when freedom, instead of being justified by itself, feels itself to be arbitrary and violent" (TI 84).

As a being gifted with a conscience, with a heart that can open itself to others, "I am he who finds the resources to respond to the call" (EI 89). That makes me and you and all others very special and very unique. We can be awestruck with what each of us, in our very differences, truly is: a self who is nothing without the other, whose face arouses the self's goodness as it speaks for justice and civic virtue, for "the miracle of moving out of oneself," out of egoism and know-it-all attitudes, both of which close us off to others (TO 25–44).

Certainly, human beings were not created to be so close-minded. We exist in a way that always opens us to the future, to what lies beyond the here and now, to a different time and place, to an otherness that is typically known by two different but related words: Infinity. God. In the Jewish religion it is said that if one could read the Holy Scriptures in one breath, he or she might then have a true understanding of what such absolute alterity is.[9] The task, of course, is impossible; nevertheless, it is always before us, always calling and challenging us to do the right thing, to be who we are—creatures who by nature are open to the otherness of others—so as to ensure that a conversation telling of compassion, respect, and the importance of acknowledgment will go on even after we die. And the moral discourse that is needed here begins with the "saying" of the face, with that which sounds the call of conscience as it interrupts our everyday ways of trying to live the good life. Providing a summary of his thinking on the entire matter, Levinas says this:

> The proximity of the other is the face's meaning, and it means from the very start in a way that goes beyond those plastic forms which forever try to cover the face like a mask of their presence to perception. But always the face shows through these forms. Prior to any particular expression and beneath all particular expressions, which cover over and protect with an immediately adopted face or countenance, there is the nakedness and destitution of the expression as such, that is to say extreme exposure, defenselessness, vulnerability itself. . . . The Other becomes my neighbor [in the most communal and moral sense of the term] precisely through the way the face summons me, calls for me, begs for me [with its interrupting call of conscience], and in so doing recalls my responsibility, and calls me into question. (EFP 82–83)

When asked to explain how one might construct an ethics in light of his thinking on such matters, Levinas, like Heidegger, made clear that his task "does not consist in constructing ethics; I only try to find its meaning. In fact I do not believe that all philosophy should be programmatic. . . . One can without doubt construct an ethics in function of what I have . . . said, but this is not my own theme" (EI 90). Indeed, with his hermeneutic assessment of the face of the Other, Levinas speaks of a phenomenon that the Pulitzer-prize-winning author Ernest Becker once described as "an awesome primary miracle" that "naturally paralyzes you by its splendor if you give in to it as the fantastic thing it is" and that carries "miracles again within it, deep in the mystery of the eyes that peer out—the eyes that gave even the dry Darwin a chill."[10] The ever-happening miracle of the face cautions against putting everything in order once and for all. Its meaning, as far as Levinas can tell, is the "transcendence" of unbounded alterity that heads us in the direction of the otherness of others, of "infinity" and thus "toward God." Is there no final system of ethics to be found at the end of the journey? What mortal being could say for sure? Even if one lived as long as Moses, he or she must still suffer the prophet's fate. Before you step into the "promised land," you must die!

So Levinas is true to what he perceives and thereby is not interested in taking the time to formalize his findings into a system of ethics. This makes Levinas something of a postmodern thinker. He writes: "If philosophy consists in knowing critically, that is, in seeking a foundation for its freedom, in justifying it, it begins with conscience, to which the other is presented as the Other, and where the movement of thematization is inverted" (TI 86). To invert the movement of thematization is to engage in the practice of deconstruction, of "unsaying" what has been said in the name of "truth" so that one might truly come to understand what the "truth" of the matter really is. Critics of deconstruction have delighted in making fun of this "endless" and "dangerous" way of doing criticism.[11] Endless because, as Levinas would have it, the Other—the "saying" of the face, the "call of conscience"—is always there calling the self into question, interrupting the "self-assurance" of people that makes them forget that matters could be different, that what is said can always be unsaid and stated differently by others, that with self-certainty comes the sacrificial acts of "repulsing, excluding, exiling, stripping, killing." Certainly it is good to expose such acts so that people's lives might enjoy a reprieve from the human suffering caused by these acts. People whose faces register pain, poverty, poor health care, and other hellish things need to be acknowledged in caring and helpful ways.

That exposure, to be sure, is the ethical goal of such postmodern thinkers as Michel Foucault, Jean-Francois Lyotard, and Jacques Derrida.[12] Yet what always seems to be missing in the discourses of these critics is a well-developed plan of reconstruction that would show exactly how people who are being sacrificed could improve their lot. Of course, such a plan, as Derrida readily admits, would be "incommensurate" with "the call" that inspires the "vocation" of deconstructive criticism.[13] The Other calls, "Where art thou?" and the deconstructionist responds, "Here I am!" But he or she shows up sans a positive plan of action; hence, the potential danger of allowing deconstructionism to be on the scene for too long. It is a devoted witness to evil happenings, admit its critics, but that in and of itself is not enough to prevent other evildoers from filling the gap left open by those who, when all is said and done, leave us only with self-interrogating words: Are you being just in all that you say and do?

As a Jew who survived the Holocaust, Levinas is certainly aware of the problem here. But as he witnesses the face and hears its call of conscience, Levinas maintains that there is a "positive" principle contained in its primordial and "silent" discourse, although this principle is presented negatively. The face speaks, and what it says first and foremost is "You shall not commit murder" (TI 197–201, 246, 262, 303). What has been said so far about "sacrificial acts" sheds some light on what Levinas considers to be the true meaning of this commandment. One must move further along with his thought, however, to grasp the meaning he has in mind.

The saying of the face—"You shall not commit murder"—means more than "Thou shalt not kill," the sixth commandment reported in the Old Testament. As should be obvious by now, Levinas' phenomenology of the face directs him beyond this phenomenon and toward the infinity of the "absolute alterity," the wholly Other whose words and actions are detailed throughout the Jewish Bible. The face speaks. "This first saying," writes Levinas, "is to be sure but a word. But the word is God" (TO 126), a word that commands acknowledgment, the responsible response of commitment whereby one says "Here I am!" and really means it. God speaks to us through the identity of the other as this identity is presented in the uniqueness, the sheer difference or alterity, of the other's face. "Thou shalt not kill" this presence, for to do so is to eliminate what the self needs to be itself: the other, that being who, as noted above, offers the life-giving gift of acknowledgment. Killing others begins a process that is actually suicidal in nature. The self could not exist without the Other. And this being so, Levinas hears the commandment of the face as being more than a prohibition, a "hortatory negative" that only speaks against the sin of intentionally stopping another's heart from beating. "Thou shalt not kill" is a saying whose true meaning speaks against any "murderous" deed that threatens the well-being of others. Death is something that not only is associated with physiological functioning but also happens in a "social" way.

Social death is a fate people suffer whenever they are marginalized, denied freedom of speech and educational opportunities, forced to live in abject poverty, refused decent medical care, or otherwise left to live a hellish existence that defaces the human spirit. The original saying of the face speaks against this "evil of suffering" and thereby poses "the inevitable and preemptory ethical problem of the medication which is my duty. . . . Wherever a moan, a cry, a groan or a sigh happen there is the original call for aid, for curative help from the other ego whose alterity . . . promises salvation." With the face comes a call of conscience whose interruption "is the original opening toward what is helpful, where the primordial, irreducible, and ethical, anthropological category of the medical comes to impose itself" (US 158). The face calls its witnesses to demonstrate a physicianship in their everyday dealings with others. The Hippocratic oath put it this way: "Do no harm"—which is to say that while attending those who seek the curing and caring ways of medicine, the physician must avoid having a hand in either the social or physical death of another. The same is true for any human being standing face to face with a presence that, without even opening its mouth, calls out, "Where art thou?"

For Levinas what all this means is that "the other must be closer to God than I. This is certainly not a philosopher's invention, but the first given of moral consciousness, which could be defined as the consciousness of the privilege the other has relative to me. Justice well ordered begins with the other" (TO 56) whose presence (face) interrupts consciousness and calls it into question. "What is at stake here is the calling of consciousness into question," Levinas notes, "and not a consciousness of a calling into question" (TO 97). The saying of the face that founds morality comes before any attempt by a human being to put it into words. The "realm" of the "inter-human relationship" (TO 56–57) does not originate with the "man-made" rules that regulate particular sociopolitical systems; rather the existence of such systems presupposes the workings of a more primordial discourse: the call of conscience that makes us care about the good health of others.

Levinas would have readers think of this primordial moral discourse as being the purest poetry there is, "a language without words or propositions, pure communication" (CPP 118–19). Phenomenologically speaking, the saying of the face is thus a "showing-forth" (*epideixis*) of a most fundamental truth, or what Levinas describes as an "epiphany" that discloses the "vulnerability" of the human body (TI 194–219). This primordial and moral "saying" is always already happening before it is reduced to what Levinas describes as the "said" of everyday discourse, with all its conventions, rules, customs, and laws (OB 34–59; OGCM 137–51). Levinas thus tells us that, in its most original form, "discourse conditions thought, for the first intelligible is not a concept, but an intelligence whose inviolable exteriority the face states in uttering the 'you shall not commit murder.' The essence of discourse is ethical," for it moves first and foremost in the asymmetrical direction of being-for others (TI 216). As the face speaks, writes Levinas, it "opens the primordial discourse whose first word is obligation. . . . It is that discourse that obliges the entering into discourse, the commencement of discourse rationalism prays for, a 'force' that convinces even 'the people who do not wish to listen' and thus founds the true universality of reason" (TI 201). Reason is borne of a discourse that is all about alterity and whose saying never tires of calling us into question. Before it is put to use by the expert (such as the scientist) or by the "average" person in everyday commerce, reason is first and foremost a moral happening: the call of conscience.

Levinas writes of a discourse that speaks before he does, that comes to him from outside his self, and whose truth always exceeds whatever can be said about it. Levinas is forever trying to say something truthful about this discourse. The face speaks; its saying is nonverbal: a silent but all-important call of conscience that questions the self on the basis of otherness, of alterity, of what the self is not and never can be but that, nevertheless, is essential to the self's moral being. The Other calls the self out of itself, away from selfishness and toward the responsibility and goodness of being-for others. This most authentic "fraternity with the neighbor," writes Levinas, "is a bond prior to every chosen bond" and is presupposed by such heartfelt emotions as "pity, compassion, [and] pardon" (CPP 123–24). In this primordial state of proximity, "the contact in which I approach the neighbor is not a manifestation or a knowledge, but the ethical event of communication which is presupposed by every transmission of messages, which establishes the universality in which words and propositions will be stated" (CCP 125).

A primordial state of proximity, fraternity with the neighbor, the ethical event of communication—all of this is essential to humanity. We *are* creatures, claims Levinas, that exist in a constant "caress" with others, a caress that holds us "hostage" to the needs of others, a state wherein we have been "chosen without assuming the choice" and thus where responsibility for the other is always antecedent to the self's freedom. Describing this responsibility that comes before choice, Levinas maintains that it is "a passivity more passive than all passivity, an exposure to the other without this exposure being assumed, an exposure without holding back, exposure of exposedness, expression, saying. This exposure is the frankness, sincerity, veracity of saying. Not saying dissimulating itself and protecting itself in the said, just giving out words in the face of the other, but saying uncovering itself, that is, denuding itself of its skin, . . . and thus wholly sign, signifying itself" (OTB 15). Put another way, one could say, following Levinas, that signification and the symbolic activities it makes possible presuppose the presence of alterity, of an otherness that catches our attention; can be put into words, named, and made meaningful; and, depending on the intelligence of what this otherness is (another person, for example), can engage us in communication. For Levinas, however, before anything is said in such communication, there is always a "saying" going on, a more original event of communication that comes about with our exposure to what is other than ourselves, and that poses the challenge of human responsibility. Standing face to face with any thing or any one that can be affected by our actions, we are always in the position of being obliged to hear and respond to an ongoing question: Am I being just in all that I think, say, and do? From the other there forever comes a call of conscience.

As he develops his understanding of this call, this primordial and ethical "saying," Levinas admits that he is involved in a phenomenological description of "the indescribable" (OTB 53), of something (alterity) whose essence is always beyond our grasp and whose presence is always there to "interrupt" and "call into question" whatever we think we "know" for sure. Hence, like Heidegger, Levinas would have us understand that the call of conscience is itself an "interruption," that which his own words (for example, "caress," "hostage") must interrupt in order to come to terms with "the thing itself" (OTB 170–71). Levinas' discourse is *a* call of conscience about *the* call of conscience; he is trying to educate us about an event that, as he perceives it, is first and foremost moral before it is understood to be anything else.

I noted earlier that Levinas does not want his call of conscience to be heard as an effort "in constructing ethics"; rather, he is primarily interested in finding "its meaning," although he admits that one "can without doubt construct an ethics in function of what [he has] said" (EI 90). In the final section of this chapter, I attempt to do just that. I begin with a brief case study of a woman (Jory Graham) who spent her final years of life helping others deal with the pain and suffering of disease. The study will allow me not only to illustrate in concrete terms what has been said so far about Levinas' thinking on the call of conscience but also to incorporate a topic that has yet to be stressed in my discussion of Levinas and that he deals with in an ambiguous manner. The topic is the practice of rhetoric—a practice that is crucial to those who would live their lives in accordance with the "meaning" of ethics offered by Levinas.

Speaking on Behalf of Others

Jory Graham was a journalist whose midlife years were complicated by serious illness: she was diagnosed as having cancer and had a bilateral mastectomy, and still her cancer metastasized. From 1977 until her death from cancer in 1983, she wrote about her situation in a column, "A Time for Living," which appeared in fifty American newspapers reaching five-and-a-half million readers weekly. She also detailed her experiences in her 1982 book, *In the Company of Others: Understanding the Human Needs of Cancer Patients,* which will be the basis for my discussion here.[14] She did all of this having learned from personal experience that "dying and its anguish are wholly individual" (128) and that "in truth, cancer comes with something worse than a death sentence: the denial of ourselves as individuals still able to manage our own affairs, direct our own lives, contribute to our households and the lives of others dependent upon us" (3–4). Moreover, her actions were warranted because, as she put it, "In accepting cancer as the probable cause of my death, I realize that I now have nothing but my life to lose. I am free to speak out, to crusade for the rights of cancer patients everywhere. . . . Yet my voice is nothing if it is not joined by yours" (23).

　　Graham's crusade was difficult. She was writing at a time when cancer patients were still being addressed by a dominating rhetoric that could be heard from both inside and outside the medical establishment. This rhetoric was deficient in hope and self-determination. Too often it spoke of cancer patients only in terms of mortality and morbidity statistics; it told them that they were "*doomed*" (12); it called them "victims" (5); it led others, through fear and mythology, to view them as "pariahs" (4); and it turned them against themselves by condemning them to a world of guilt, self-pity, and emotional isolation (1–15). "It is terrible enough when others write us off, but catastrophic when we discount ourselves," wrote Graham (117). And: "So help me God, I do not know whether the race is for man to conquer cancer or to conquer his feelings about it" (6).

Graham set out to help others conquer their feelings about cancer. She did this by speaking a rhetoric for the other, a rhetoric that interrupted the flow of an already-spoken and debilitating rhetoric. Her actions here were twofold: First, she assumed the ethical responsibility of affirming her freedom of choice by engaging in the deconstructive act of being what Susan Sontag terms "against interpretation."[15] That is, she sought to destabilize certain reified systems of meaning and "truth" that functioned to marginalize and silence the voice of the so-called "demoralized, pitiful cancer patient" (24). For example, as a way of challenging what Foucault terms "the *restraint* of clinical discourse,"[16] she cited a recent essay in gynecology and obstetrics wherein it is said that the "proper treatment [for cancer of the vulva] although disfiguring, is not mutilative" (102).[17] Second, after responding to this claim with the simple and startling question "*Not* mutilative?" and then going on to quote again from the textbook whereby the reader can see in a lengthy passage the sterilized language that is used to define a radical vulvectomy, Graham added her own voice to the discussion by noting: "The author is playing with words when he says that the procedure is not mutilative. It is massive amputation, but if it can be successfully denied through word magic, then the physician can dismiss the intensity of his patient's grief when she weeps over what has been done to her" (102).

Perhaps one can see from this quotation that Graham had more to say about her topic than what is *not* the case. Whenever she deconstructed a "truth," she also reconstructed a "truth"; and typically these reconstructed truths gave expression to the importance of rehabilitating the emotional life of cancer patients. Listen, for example, to what she tells her fellow cancer patients about developing a "healthy anger" toward their situations: "Healthy anger gives vitality. It is a glorious sign that we're far from dead. It makes us fight for our jobs—and pride makes us work twice as hard at them. Healthy anger gives us purpose, challenges us to make new decisions, encourages old ideas: to enroll in the courses we've always wanted to take; to embark on the trip we've always wanted to make; to create the journal that is our legacy to our children and our grandchildren" (26).

It was such a healthy anger that got Graham to speak her mind in the first place. And this makes perfect sense from a phenomenological point of view. The health of anger, its ability to function in a reasonable and rational manner, shows itself as the emotion gets people to distance themselves mentally from a debilitating situation and, with the advantage of this distance, to transform the situation's present meaning by interpreting it in a way that enhances their self-respect. Healthy anger (unlike self-pity, for example) is a "great equalizer": it enables us to take matters into our own hands instead of remaining subservient to the "inappropriate" behavior of others.[18] Moreover, healthy anger makes use of our authenticity, our ability to be more than what we are now because, as Graham points out in the above quotation, it "challenges us to make new decisions" and "encourages old ideas."

Graham enacted her authenticity by first using her anger for her own benefit and then sharing its disclosures with others. In so doing, she disclosed a truth that had much to do with the humanity of a class of people who had been conditioned by a currently spoken rhetoric to forget and forsake their authenticity, their freedom, their existentially sanctioned right to be more than lost members of some marginalized group. In using her anger to speak a rhetoric that addressed this right, she sought to fix responsibility, to be a voice of conscience for others, to change a certain set of societal moods, and to move cancer patients and their caretakers to action. Although her cancer unfortunately made it all too apparent that she was no longer "normal" and "healthy," her rhetoric was proof that she was also more than that.

Hans Blumenberg tells us that "rhetoric is a system not only of soliciting mandates for action but also of putting into effect and defending, both with oneself and before others, a self-conception that is in the process of formation or has been formed."[19] Owing to the success of her rhetoric (at least as indicated by the responses to her column and book), perhaps it can be said that Graham helped to create such a system. Or, borrowing a phrase from John Dewey, perhaps it can be said that she helped to "call a public into being."[20] This public was one that formed a system of meaning and truth that spoke (and still speaks) as directly as possible to the question of what it means to exist as a human being.

I cannot imagine that Levinas would take exception to how the case of Jory Graham serves as a concrete illustration of the "meaning" of ethics that he emphasizes—a meaning that speaks of the way in which a human being exists first and foremost as a moral creature, a being-for others. With Graham we have a person faced with the question that Levinas considers to be of primary importance: how to be just with one's freedom to do and say what she or he will. Graham enacts an answer to the question by speaking on behalf of people who tragically are too often thought of and treated as pariahs, and who are thereby forced to suffer the pain of solitude, of social death, of being marginalized and isolated because of their "different" nature. Graham devotes herself to aiding and serving these souls. She would have them (and others) realize that cancer patients can still experience the joy of living; that no matter how pitiful their "faces" appear to be, their presence speaks more of life than of death. Graham is acting heroically out of respect for others who are also capable of heroism; for they too can say, "Here I am!" to others whose needs call out a holy question: "Where art thou?" Graham is a "religious" soul who has come to understand that acknowledging (and being acknowledged by) others is a life-saving act. The face of the other speaks; it gives voice to the call of conscience that interrupts self-sufficiency, promotes fraternity, and thereby gives notice of how human existence defines a state of "caress" wherein being a "hostage" to the needs of others is more of a privilege than what it sometimes seems to be: a burden.

Levinas would not deny that in everyday life others can be such a thing. One must keep in mind, however, that Levinas, the phenomenologist, is describing the presuppositions of our everyday ways of being with others. Caress, hostage—these are terms meant to describe how we exist before social rules and routines take form and condition us to think and act in accordance with standards of "common sense." We are exposed to others before we understand their needs; we are hostage to a caress that chooses us before we decide to respond in any given case. Human being has a dimension to it that exists on "the hither side of freedom and non-freedom"—a life-giving dimension that is not a human creation and that, for Levinas, must therefore "have the meaning of a '*goodness despite itself*,' a goodness always older than the choice. Its value, that is, its excellence or goodness, the goodness of goodness, is alone able to counterbalance the violence of the choice (and, beyond counterbalancing, be for the better!)" (OTB 57).

"The Good is before being," writes Levinas; it is "my pre-originary *susceptiveness* [to the other] which chooses me before I welcome it" (OTB 122–23). Goodness is the way human existence is fundamentally structured as a being-for others, as a "saying" that calls the self out of itself and that thereby poses the challenge of responsibility. Goodness is the ongoing call of conscience that lies at the heart of human existence and that forever calls the self into question. "Goodness in the subject is anarchy itself" (OTB 138), a constant "interruption" that raises a moral issue: Are you being just in all that you say and do? The face speaks: "Where art thou?" Goodness makes it possible to say, "Here I am!" and thus to speak and to act on behalf of others.

The case of Jory Graham presents us with an illustration of goodness at work. She is a hero: an authentic and courageous soul who assumed the ethical responsibility of affirming her freedom of choice so that others might overcome the pain and suffering of social death. This description of Graham draws from the thinking of both Heidegger and Levinas. As discussed in chapter 2, Heidegger's understanding of the hero emphasizes one's authenticity—how an individual Dasein becomes true to his or her "Self" by taking on the responsibility of resolute choice. Recall too that Heidegger's hero also has an obligation to others: they warrant considerateness, forbearance, and respect so as to ensure that they are given the opportunity to enact their own authenticity. Levinas' consideration of the matter, however, places the emphasis, not on the Self, but rather on the Other's well-being. Interpersonal space is asymmetrical: existence is first and foremost a being-for others. In critiquing Heidegger's neglect of this "fact," Levinas develops a position throughout his works that extends beyond the explicit interests of Heidegger's philosophy. Otherness comes before the self; it is that which calls a person's attention away from egoism and toward the needy (the widow, orphan, and stranger).

But how does a self come to understand and appreciate the pain and suffering of others? Jory Graham's devotion to the plight of cancer patients was stimulated by a life-threatening interruption in her life. After this interruption Graham began the task of creating a rhetoric for others. This rhetoric offered a response to the call of conscience, a call that certainly could be heard coming from the life and death struggle of others. But Graham did not pay careful attention to this call until her own life suffered the ontological assault of a serious illness. With Heidegger, we have seen that such an interruption is likely to reveal how one's personal existence is itself a place of being from which the call of conscience makes itself known. Others had cancer before Graham. Her life-affirming rhetoric, however, was the result of *her* meeting a challenge that was no further away than her own body and personhood. Graham fully understood and appreciated a cancer patient's misery only after she became one herself, and thus only after she had to assume the personal and ethical responsibility that comes with living a life that is disabled by biological and social occurrences.

The point I am trying to make here is perhaps obvious, but it is nevertheless important for a project that is considering how Heidegger and Levinas educate us on the workings of the call of conscience. Even if one accepts Levinas' description of how human existence is structured as a being-for others, it is still the self, in a moment of authenticity, that must put this "goodness" into practice. Helping others presupposes the action of a self assuming the ethical responsibility of freedom of choice. Moreover, this action, as seen in the case of Jory Graham, can originate when the call of conscience is heard coming first from the self and then from the other.

Both Heidegger and Levinas have something truthful to say about the workings of the call. Still, I believe it is Levinas more than Heidegger who clarifies the authentic ethical nature of the self/other relationship and who thus has more to say about how we owe it to others to give them "the bread from our mouths" so that they will not starve. Levinas writes: "Dasein in Heidegger is never hungry" (TI 134). Indeed, Heidegger has more to tell us about the meaning and truth of Being than he does about how food brings "enjoyment" to those whose well-being is dependent on it. And for Levinas the danger of this bias must never be forgotten; for when we have more of a heart for the otherness of Being than we do for the otherness of other human beings, especially those who are suffering from the pain of Being, we may become too forgetful of what the human face demands of us. Heidegger would have us behold Being's generous "gift" (*es gibt*); Levinas would have us remember that "none of the generosity which the German term '*es gibt*' is said to contain revealed itself between 1933 and 1945" (DF 292).

While Heidegger fiddled away with the question of Being, the flesh of others was burning. And when Heidegger later took the time in 1949 to remark on this horrific moment of history, his words, conditioned as they were by his ontological investigations of the "language of Being," admitted but a cold-hearted and thus inappropriate understanding of the matter at hand: "Agriculture is today a motorized food industry, in essence the same as the blockage and starvation of countries, the same as the manufacture of atomic bombs."[21] Certainly Heidegger's rhetoric here displays a stunning lack of what lies at the heart of Levinas' philosophy and councils his use of language: moral sensitivity. Levinas writes to "interrupt" all those discourses that no longer work to remind us of how it is that the face speaks a primordial discourse that pleads for mercy and forbids murder (OTB 170; DF 291–95; AT 91–182). With Levinas, we hear a call of conscience that recommends the type of discourse that is happening, for example, with the rhetoric of Jory Graham—a rhetoric of the self and for the other; a deconstructive and reconstructive rhetoric dedicated to revealing the faces of others whose existential presence is being misrepresented and mistreated by the powers that be; an ethical rhetoric that speaks forcefully against the injustice of social death, of placing people on the margins of society where they tend to be seen more as "things" than as "faces." Levinas speaks of how such "art," in fulfilling its moral function, "seeks to give a face to things," thereby helping others to grasp something of the truth of some matter. At the same time, however, Levinas also warns of how art's construction of a face can display "deceit" (DF 8).

When Jory Graham found such deceit happening in medical discourse, she called it "word magic" and condemned it for its immoral manipulation and disregard of a cancer patient's emotional state. One might also use the phrase to describe Heidegger's handling of "the manufacture of corpses in gas chambers." In Levinas' philosophy such word magic is associated with the art of rhetoric; for this art, Levinas argues, aligns itself with "ruse, emprise, and exploitation," and exhibits too much "enthusiasm" for "eloquence," which gets in the way of our hearing the one true ethical and moral discourse that comes to us from the face of the Other. The pure "poetry" that the face speaks grants "access to the Other outside of rhetoric" (TI 70–72; DF 277–88). "Thou shalt not commit murder" is a saying that speaks the truth without the manipulative help of eloquence. Levinas thus tells us, "It is not by the degree of elevation achieved by the inevitable rhetoric of all speech that the essence of the 'life-word' and 'everyday language' can be defined; the latter are described by proximity to one's neighbor, which is stronger than that rhetoric and in relation to which rhetoric's effects are to be measured" (OS 142–43).

Before the practice of rhetoric ever comes on the scene, there exists a "proximity to one's neighbor." Much was made of this original existential state earlier in this chapter. It is associated with the "saying" of the face, that primordial "event of communication" that defines the purest "poetry" there is, and that discloses and exposes the "vulnerability" of the human body, the otherness (alterity) of others that holds us "hostage" to its "caress." In short, with proximity to one's neighbor comes the ethical discourse of the call of conscience that speaks "poetically" of our never-ending responsibility for others. With Levinas, then, one is encouraged to think of the practice of rhetoric as being, at best, but a way of employing and structuring one's words so that others might come to know the poetry, the truth, of which these words speak. Moreover, one is encouraged to think of rhetoric as being, for the most part, but a practice steeped in the immoral ways of deception and selfishness.

In Judaism, poetry is "the language of wonder." According to Heschel, "This is why poetry is to religion what analysis is to science, and it is certainly no accident that the Bible was not written *more geometrico* but in the language of poets."[22] I thus suspect that Levinas would be more comfortable being known as a poet-philosopher than as an orator-philosopher. His words are geared toward getting at the truth of a primordial discourse that makes possible all other discourses. When Socrates and Plato first began this task for philosophy, they sought direction by appropriating the empirical outlook of scientists (Hippocratic physicians). As a phenomenologist, Levinas also maintains such an outlook. But what he is after is much greater than the actual nature of the body and its diseases and, consequently, calls for a more robust and wondrous language to acknowledge something of its essence. Although this penchant for poetry distinguishes his approach from that of his Greek ancestors, Levinas' thinking on rhetoric is aligned quite well with what one reads about the practice in Plato's *Gorgias* and *Phaedrus*. Helping others to realize the true and the good may well require the orator's art, but this art is dangerous if it is not controlled by a disciplined passion for getting at the truth of all that can be thought and acted upon.

Levinas has a Platonist view of rhetoric; his appreciation of this practice, however, reflects more than an ancient Greek outlook. Levinas is a Jew who speaks of rhetoric in a way that is supported by the Hebrew Bible and that thus exhibits ambiguity in its stand on the matter. In concluding this chapter, I want to say a bit more about this ambiguity, for with it one finds an opening for developing an understanding of how the call of conscience is itself a rhetorical interruption. Everything discussed about Levinas in the present chapter has, in fact, been directed toward advancing this specific understanding of the call.

The Call's Rhetorical Eloquence

In her excellent study of how the related phenomena of rhetoric, persuasion, argumentation, and eloquence are treated in the Hebrew Bible, Margaret Zulick makes it clear that matters are not unambiguous when one listens to what this sacred text has to say about the phenomena.[23] For example, Zulick discusses how the Hebrew verb *pata* (persuade) "is never used in an unequivocally positive sense. Instead it connotes seduction, enticement and deceit"— things that, according to Levinas, are catered to by rhetorical eloquence. But such eloquence is also found happening with God's words. Zulick makes the point by noting that

> when in Hosea [2:16] YHWH [God] announces his intention to win back his straying bride Israel, *pata* is used in a way that echoes its seductive sense . . . "Therefore see, I will persuade her, lead her into the wilderness, and speak to her heart." The implication seems positive until we recall the negative connotations of wilderness in the Book of Hosea and indeed throughout most of the Hebrew Bible: a "howling desert waste," a place of exile and desolation (Deut 32:10). YHWH, in effect, entices Israel to a place she would never go on her own volition, a state of dire need where she will be forced once more to rely on YHWH alone.[24]

This is not to say, however, that YHWH acts in immoral ways. Rather, according to Zulick, "all the ambiguous connotations of *pata* are marshaled to create an image of the word of YHWH as an overpowering force."[25]

I believe that one can go further than Zulick in dealing with the matter here. Remember, YHWH led Israel into the "wilderness" to "speak to her heart," which is to say that God brought about a terrifying interruption in the life of Israel in order to open her heart (conscience) to his call. This call promotes a reconstruction of thought and circumstances by way of their deconstruction.

In the Jewish mystical tradition of Kabbalah, an interpretation of the story of Adam and Eve is offered that accounts for the origins of this creative process. According to Rabbi David A. Cooper, "The first Adam/Eve is called by Kabbalists *Adam ha-Rishon* (primeval human consciousness). This in no way resembled the human form as we know it. The Jewish sages spoke of it in hyperbole. It had stupendous proportions, reaching from earth to heaven; it stood astride earth from one end to the other. It could see to the far reaches of the universe, for the light at that time was *Ohr Ein Sof,* the Limitless Light, a metaphor for pure awareness." Hence, says Rabbi Cooper, "In many ways, the literal translation of the biblical stories of Adam, Eve, and the Garden of Eden in human proportions is a major disservice, for this invites comparisons, projections, and simplistic interpretations that frequently put us on a track of distorted images and wrongheaded deductions. The mystical perspective, however, imposes an altered frame of reference upon us from the start."[26] And with this perspective one is also provided with an interpretation of the Garden's serpent that is quite different than what has come down to us in the tradition of Christianity. Rabbi Cooper's remarks about this interpretation are worth quoting in full:

> The Torah says that there will be enmity between humans and serpents; humans will crush serpents' heads, and serpents will bite the heels of humans. In the Kabbalah, head and heel are code words for epochs in the unfolding of creation. The head represents the earliest part of an era, while the heel represents the end of an era.
>
> According to this way of looking at things, we are currently in the heel phase of a six-thousand-year cycle. When it ends, a messianic era begins. Crushing and biting suggest points of transition. The serpent biting at our heels indicates that we are moving closer to the realization of messianic consciousness. When we step on its head, we will finally enter the new era. . . . From this kabbalistic perspective, the serpent is the vehicle for messianic consciousness. Thus the serpent represents far more in mystical Judaism than is commonly known, and a deeper understanding of these teachings changes entirely our appreciation of the story of creation. Without the serpent, without the energizing of creation, we would never have the opportunity to follow a path returning us to our Divine Source.[27]

The story of creation is still unfolding; we are some of its characters—those beings whose temporal existence is always calling itself into question, always deconstructing itself, and in so doing, forever calling on us, for our own sake and the sake of others, to reconstruct our lives for the better after they have been interrupted by any of life's happenings. The story of creation is heard coming first and foremost from our own (and the other's) existence as it sounds its call of conscience and thereby reveals us to be creatures whose survival is dependent on how well we learn to think, question, and behave in order to be "just" and to live the "good" life.

For the sake of others and herself Jory Graham worked to achieve these goals. She heard the call and answered it. Despite his Greek and Hebrew biases toward the art, Levinas' phenomenology of the face allows for a assessment of rhetoric that, although ambiguous, is nevertheless favorable. In fact, in what I take to be his most explicit and far-reaching consideration of the topic, Levinas speaks of the saying of the face as being itself a rhetoric— albeit one that comes to us "without eloquence" (OS 135–43). As discussed earlier, the saying of the face is the original "showing-forth" (*epideixis*) of humanity's nakedness and vulnerability, that which is covered up by the make-up and fashion we put on to offer a "good showing" in our daily activities. Because Levinas thinks of eloquence as being primarily an exercise in the ornamentation of "everyday

language" (OS 138–40), it makes sense that he would speak of the saying of the
face as being a rhetoric without eloquence. It is the nakedness of the face, not
its manufactured look, that reveals its truth. Describing what eloquence does
to and for rhetoric, Levinas thus writes:

> Rhetoric brings into the meaning in which it culminates a certain
> beauty, a certain elevation, a certain nobility and an expressivity that
> imposes itself independently of its truth. Even more than verisimilitude,
> that beauty we call eloquence seduces the listener.
>
> Clearly in our time the effects of eloquence are everywhere, dominat-
> ing our entire lives. There is no need to go through the whole sociology of
> our industrialized society here. The media of information in all forms—
> written, spoken, visual—invade the home, keep people listening to an end-
> less discourse, submit them to the seduction of a rhetoric that is only
> possible if it is eloquent and persuasive in portraying ideas and things too
> beautiful to be true. (OS 138–39)

Eloquence seduces, dominates, and invades our lives. This is not an especially positive view of the phenomenon. Still, as in the case of Jory Graham,
"the rhetoric of the *Said* can absorb the ethics of proximity; but it is to the
degree that that proximity is maintained in the discourse that the circle within
which the 'life-word' signifies is drawn, with which *everyday exchanges* take
place, and from which eloquence is excluded under penalty of provoking
laughter" (OS 142). Following Levinas, then, would it be correct to say that
Graham's rhetoric is void of eloquence? Was Graham simply engaging in "word
magic" when, as noted above, she spoke eloquently of how "Healthy anger gives
us purpose, challenges us to make new decisions, encourages old ideas . . ."?

Clearly, not all rhetoric is eloquent in the best sense of the word. The
metaphorical structure of any discourse can be more confusing and inappropriate than it is revealing and fitting. Yet when some rhetor's discourse suc-
ceeds in avoiding the problem here so that what is heard or read is credited
with being truly moving, does it necessarily follow that those who acknowledge it as such have been duped?

Levinas' biased way of speaking about rhetorical eloquence is unfortunate.
He seems to forget what students of the orator's art have long understood: that
the true nature of this art "is made up of the methods which reflection and
experience have evolved to make a discourse such as to establish the truth and
to arouse a love for it in the hearts of [human beings]. Things which strike and
arouse the heart . . . eloquence is just that."[28] And if one appreciates "the heart"
in a strictly Jewish way—as the capacity of conscience—then rhetorical eloquence deserves to be praised as something that, as in the case of YHWH, can
serve the purpose of opening others to a truth that needs to be acknowledged
for the good of all concerned.

Levinas is right: "The face speaks." But the epideictic discourse that "silently" flows from its lips is not without eloquence. On the contrary, whether it is attractive or not, what the face expresses behind the masks that it might wear in public in order to put on a "good showing" is itself such a showing, a magnificent and moving discourse that reveals such an awe-inspiring truth that witnesses cannot help but be awestruck. The face speaks, interrupts, evokes a call of conscience. The "saying" going on here, I submit, is not a rhetoric without eloquence, especially if, as Levinas suggests, this saying speaks of something that is "closer to God than I." The other's face, in all its nudity, vulnerability, and alterity is a most revealing and fitting work of art—a rhetorical interruption *par excellence*.

Of course, not everyone sees it this way. People can be so good at putting on a face, at engaging in the socially circumscribed rituals of "face-work" so as to maintain for themselves and others a "positive self-image" that what they offer us is essentially nothing but a successful cover-up of who they really are and what they truly believe. To be sure, a person's public character can disguise horrid thoughts and forthcoming behavior that is downright unjust, if not totally evil. The rhetorical mechanics of face-work can be geared to ruse and exploitation. But again, this need not be the case. People can engage in face-work that is ethically motivated by what the human face, according to Levinas, was in truth meant to be: a most sacred and privileged rhetorical interruption, a call of conscience that speaks first and foremost of the goodness of life and how it ought to be respected.

The saying of the face; the call of conscience. Recall that Levinas thinks of this primordial epideictic discourse as being the purest poetry there is. I am arguing for another view of the matter. The discourse of the call also functions as a rhetorical interruption: it comes to us from something other than ourselves—Being, God, other people—something that speaks of the importance of authenticity, accountability, responsibility, and justice. The call commends a habit of thinking and acting that keeps us open to differences of opinion and lifestyles; it invites moral deliberation; it evokes in others a sense of wonder and awe for the matter at hand. Whenever discourse is working this way, it admits a rhetorical function, for as Henry Johnstone teaches: "*Rhetoric is the evocation and the maintenance of the consciousness required for communication.*"[29] And that is how Levinas describes what is going on as the "epiphany of the face" unfolds before us: the face evokes consciousness and conscientiousness; it offers discourse that makes us think and care about what we say and do (TI 197–209).

Raphael Demos offers a perceptive description of the process at work here: "Evocation," he writes,

> is the process by which vividness is conveyed; it is the presentation of a viewpoint in such a manner that it becomes real for the public. It is said that argument is a way by which an individual experience is made common

property; in fact, an argument has much less persuasive force than the vivid evocation of an experience. The enumeration of all the relevant points in favor of a theory and against its opposite can never be completed; far more effective is it to state a viewpoint in all its concreteness and in all its significant implication, and then stop; the arguments become relevant only after this state has been concluded.[30]

The process of evocation is a "showing-forth" of what is. The face speaks a truly epideictic discourse, the first there is. Writing about this phenomenon, Colin Davis maintains that, for Levinas, "the Other orders me not to kill, but has no means of persuading me to obey."[31] I take issue with the last part of this claim. The call of conscience that comes to us from the Other defines an emotional appeal that can fill us with anxiety and/or joy as it beckons us to meet the existential challenge of thinking and acting in morally responsible ways. The persuasiveness of this appeal has long been registered in what people do to avoid the discomfort of anxiety and to experience the joy that comes with the successful completion of the task. In the beginning was the word, and the word, no matter what else it was perceived to be, was rhetorical: it called for moral deliberation, action, and judgment. Aristotle long ago made clear how these are the means and end of rhetoric and how, as Heidegger puts it, the orator "must understand the possibilities of moods in order to rouse them and guide them in a right and just manner." Jory Graham did just that.

Levinas' thinking on the call of conscience ends where it begins: in the rhetorical and political realm of everyday existence where people must deal symbolically with particular matters that are recognized as pressing, and that require careful deliberation and judgment, but whose meaning and significance are presently ambiguous, uncertain, and contestable. Here, according to Levinas, the self must contend not only with a specific other but also with "the third party"—all those others who may be affected by what one says and does. And here too, writes Levinas, the self's ethical obligation to others doubles back on itself. "The relationship with the third party is an incessant correction of the asymmetry of proximity in which the face is looked at"; for in the company of others, the face of the self also demands attention and respect. Or, as Levinas would have it, "It is only thanks to God that, as a subject incomparable with the other, I am approached as an other by the others, that is, 'for myself.' 'Thanks to God' I am another for the others" (OB 158). The saying of the face, which speaks for otherness and its infinite and thus overwhelming presence, can be heard coming from the self who is other than other selves and who may at any moment take issue with their meanings, values, and sense of justice.

The relationship with the third party is ethical, rhetorical, and political. Ethics comes first for Levinas; it begins with the saying of the face. Matters become rhetorical and political as people struggle to do the right thing and thereby make sacrifices, limit or expand their own freedom, favor one person or group over another. "It is thus," writes Levinas, "that the neighbor becomes visible, and, looked at, presents himself, and there is also justice for me." And thus here too the ethical saying of the face "is fixed in a said, is written, becomes a book, law and science" (OB 159). In the name of "humanity" we owe it to ourselves and others to make sure that this rhetorical and political transformation of a primordial moral discourse is an ongoing event. People deserve acknowledgment and respect; their faces say as much, as their presence interrupts our everyday existence and utters a call of conscience: Where art thou? The question admits a "simple" rhetorical eloquence meant to speak to our hearts so that we might be good enough to put ourselves on the line as we give ourselves to others: Here I am! The call of conscience would have us think and act as beings who *are* their brother's and sister's keepers, who stand against the horror of social death and what it can lead to, and who thus, among other things, must cultivate their rhetorical competence in order to move people toward the good. A primordial event of rhetorical eloquence forever calls on us to become vehicles for its voice and teachings.

In suggesting how the call of conscience—or, if you will, the call of Being, the Other, God—defines an interruptive, epideictic, and rhetorically eloquent event, I have employed and gone beyond the teachings of both Heidegger and Levinas. For Heidegger the call originates in what makes possible, but is Other than, any human creation: Being, which has a deconstructive and reconstructive ring to it and whose happening is, at least for Heidegger, the best possible evidence for approaching the question of God's wholly other existence. Levinas' interest in the question, on the other hand, begins not with a phenomenology of Being's otherness, but rather with the otherness of other human beings. With Levinas we learn how the call of conscience functions as a primordial calling into question of the self by others. Heidegger never spoke of the call as a rhetorical phenomenon. Levinas, however, provides a way of understanding the call as being just that, although his biases toward rhetoric prevent him from appreciating how the call is itself an event of eloquence and thus a compelling disclosure or "showing-forth" of truth.

In developing this last point it was not my intention to produce an "unholy" doctrine of the call of conscience whereby it should be understood that the Absolute Other is as much of a rhetor as a poet. Both Heidegger and Levinas speak more highly of poetry than of rhetoric. Still, the call's disclosure is persuasive: it speaks to our hearts to encourage a critical questioning of who we are and how we might think and act for the better. Things that strike and arouse the heart—eloquence is just that. Is it immoral to say that in the beginning was the word and the word was rhetorical, that God is the master rhetorician who speaks through the human face and thereby makes it *the* master figure and trope? There is, I submit, nothing wrong in saying this if one recognizes rhetoric to be, despite all its human flaws, a noble calling—one that helps people to ask "Where art thou?" and to declare "Here I am!" in any number of evocative, eloquent, effective, and ethical ways.

One can construct an ethics from the related thought of Heidegger and Levinas. It is an ethics that recognizes the moral quality of rhetoric and calls for the development of rhetorical competence. Neither Heidegger nor Levinas has much to say about the specific workings of such competence, although both admit that it has a significant role to play in maintaining a community's moral character. The world of "the they," of the "third party," can be directed toward the good by the orator's art.[32] In a 1982 radio interview wherein he was asked to address the "ordeal of genocide" as it applies to both Jews and Palestinians, Levinas emphasized that in the everyday world "we are constantly faced with the problem of knowing who is right and who is wrong, who is just and who is unjust. There are people who are wrong" (EP 294). Indeed—and when helping people understand how this is so in a given situation, we oftentimes need to express ourselves in a rhetorically competent and eloquent way in order to move the hearts and minds of others in the right direction. Levinas was certainly attempting to do this in his interview. He had to understand the possibility of moods in order to rouse them and guide them in a right and just manner; he had to become a voice of conscience for others.

Influenced by Aristotle's *Rhetoric*—which he credited with being "the first systematic hermeneutic of the everydayness of Being with one another" (BT 178)—Heidegger spent more time than Levinas analyzing the ontological structure of this rhetorical domain and how it influences human communicative behavior. However, in drawing from his religious heritage, Levinas makes sure that we go further than Heidegger in understanding who this German philosopher would have us treat with considerateness and forbearance. Being-with others carries with it the obligation of *Being-for* others. It is a matter of hearing and responding to the call of conscience—a call that comes to us from the heart of existence, interrupts our daily routines, demands acknowledgment and action, and thereby directs us in what both Heidegger and Levinas recognize as the "heroic" struggle of trying to be authentic, caring, and just in all that we say and do.

These two philosophers offer us an ontological and metaphysical assessment of this struggle. We now have before us a theory that suggests that there is something fundamentally rhetorical about the call of conscience, something that speaks to us of the importance of questioning and cultivating the practical wisdom of human "know-how," of being-with-and-for others, and of using emotions in ways that structure the temporality and lived space of human existence such that even those who are less fortunate than any of us are given the opportunity to express themselves and to have their words be taken to heart. The call of conscience makes itself known in the everyday world of circumspective concern, where uncertainty and contingency are ever present and thus where there is a need to develop our rhetorical competence for the good of humankind. In the second part of this book, I intend to get more down-to-earth, practical, and specific about the entire matter.

Part II

Practice
Conscience, Rhetoric, and the Euthanasia Debate

My Father

In May 1980, at the age of fifty-eight, my father suffered complete kidney failure. For the rest of his life, he would have to live with the help of a dialysis machine. His life was sustained, but its quality was tragic: he lost his job, he lost his capacity to function sexually, he questioned his religious faith, he developed severe neurotic symptoms, and he was admitted to a psychiatric institute. Staring at his blood moving through a machine, he continued to ask: "What is going on here?" "What is happening to my life?" Alone in his house, he wrote in a diary that he kept to document personal responses to his deteriorating condition: "I can't die because I must stay to keep up with the 'Jones.' I can't die because I have traditions to carry on. I can't die because I am afraid to." In the next entry he wrote: "Everyone calls, the phone rings and rings with questions and professional advice. But it's too, too bad that they can't help—they don't know my pain—*nor do I.*" On February 20, 1984, owing to complications associated with his disease, my father went into cardiac arrest and died.

A success of medical science had enabled my father to live, but it was a living hell, evidencing how sophisticated medical care, despite the best of intentions, can increase levels of pain and suffering. Thousands of patients whose lives are sustained by the technological capabilities of medicine are experiencing this fate every day. The irony is discomforting, and never more so, perhaps, than when a patient gets to the point where he or she is compelled to ask: Is modern medicine prolonging my living or my dying? Is it worth going on? My father asked such questions. He had obligations. He was afraid to die. His pain and suffering became so great that he no longer had the words to describe and know his condition. He could not help but hear the call of conscience.

I thought I knew my father. I admitted as much to my mother when I arrived home for the funeral and was told by her that when my dad had his heart attack and was rushed unconscious into the operating room, she had given the physicians permission to install a pacemaker in his chest so that he might remain alive "to see his son one last time." The procedure failed, and in a way I was relieved. My father was a very proud and caring man. He would not want his son or wife or anyone else to suffer the pain of witnessing his final loss of dignity. He had a right to die before his days grew even worse than they had ever been in the last four years.

Although it went against his being a Jew, my father wanted to be cremated. He feared being buried alive. The fear was more powerful than the sin. He told me this in 1982 as he lay in an ICU bed because the dialysis treatments were not always as successful as one would hope. I made sure that his request was respected.

My father never spoke to me, however, about how he wanted to die. Certainly he would have wanted it to be with dignity. Would there have been any dignity remaining if his final operation had been successful? If I had been in my mother's place when my father died (instead of thousands of miles away attending a professional conference), would I have been so quick to say "Enough already!"? I must admit that I do not know for sure if these would have been my father's words. Theory is easier than practice.

Nietzsche once wrote:

> One may well ask why, aside from the demands of religion, it is more praiseworthy for a man grown old, who feels his powers decrease, to await his slow exhaustion and disintegration, rather than to put a term to his life with complete consciousness. In this case, suicide is quite natural, obvious, and should by rights awaken respect for the triumph of reason. This it did in those times when the leading Greek philosophers and the doughtiest Roman patriots used to die by suicide. Conversely, the compulsion to prolong life from day to day, anxiously consulting doctors and accepting the most painful, humiliating conditions, without the strength to come nearer the actual goal of one's life: this is far less worthy of respect. . . .
>
> . . . There is a justice according to which we take a man's life, but no justice according to which we take his death: that is nothing but cruelty.[1]

My father's illness weakened his body, mind, and spirit. He was willing to sin when it came time to deal with his remains. But he never confided in me regarding his thinking on suicide, which, to be sure, is against the "Law" for the religious Jew. If he had, maybe he would have said something like: "You know, son, Nietzsche has a point!"

Given what I said to my mother about the pacemaker—that Dad would not have wanted it—I like to think that my father would have offered some such declaration. I was willing, at least in theory, to help my father die a "dignified" death. "Enough already! No more cruelty!" If my father had believed in the "morality" of suicide, and if he had requested that this belief be respected when the time came, then in refusing additional medical treatment I would have been acting, albeit "passively," to help my father die. Such an act of passive euthanasia is not against the law in any of this country's fifty states. One can engage in the act and still have a "good conscience."

But the thought of the matter not going so smoothly continues to haunt me. How well did I know my father? He never took the time to construct a living will. What if he took great exception to Nietzsche's position? And what if he then went on to recall something that Nietzsche wrote in the latter half of 1888, the year before this "yea-sayer" to life, to its magnificence and awesome "will to power," became "officially" insane? When offering "A moral code for physicians" in *Twilight of the Idols,* Nietzsche proclaimed:

The invalid is a parasite on society. In a certain state it is indecent to go on living. To vegetate on in cowardly dependence on physicians and medicaments after the meaning of life, the *right* to life, has been lost ought to entail the profound contempt of society. Physicians, in their turn, ought to be the communicators of this contempt—not prescriptions, but every day a fresh dose of *disgust* with their patients. . . . To create a new responsibility, that of the physician, in all cases in which the highest interest of life, of *ascending* life, demands the most ruthless suppression and sequestration of degenerating life—for example in determining the right to reproduce, the right to be born, the right to live. . . . To die proudly when it is no longer possible to live proudly. Death of one's own free choice, death at the proper time, with a clear head and with joyfulness, consummated in the midst of children and witnesses: so that an actual leave-taking is possible while he who is leaving *is still there*, . . . We have no power to prevent ourselves being born: but we can rectify this error—for it is sometimes an error. When one *does away with* oneself one does the most estimable thing possible: one thereby almost deserves to live. . . . Society—what am I saying! *life* itself derives more advantage from that than from any sort of "life" spent in renunciation, greensickness and other virtues—one has freed others from having to endure one's sight, one has removed an *objection* from life.[2]

My father was an "invalid" by medical definition. He felt slighted when his physicians treated him more as a body than as a person and when their communications grew a bit hollow in light of his no longer "ascending life." My father was afraid to die; still, he was too great a man not to have wanted "to die proudly," to be *there,* at least with his wife and son, so he could say goodbye in person and with much love. My father was not an "objection" to be silenced or otherwise disposed of. But was he a man who, if possible, would have wanted medical science and technology to intervene further into his life so that he might have a bit more "quality" time with family and friends?

I did not know enough important things about my father   a man who certainly would have taken exception to what he would have understood to be "fascist ideology" coming from a philosopher. I can imagine him saying: "Good grief, what Nietzsche advocated came true with the Nazi program of 'involuntary euthanasia.' Certainly I want to die as proudly as I have lived. And I don't want to be a burden to you and your mother. But what's wrong with spending a few more days, hours, minutes with loved ones, especially when you know that this is likely the last time the opportunity will present itself?"

"OK, Dad, but does this mean that, no matter what, you want your physicians to do *everything* they can to keep you alive?"

Did I say the right thing to my mother when she told me about the pacemaker? Would I have acted as she did as she responded to the call of conscience? I can no longer say for sure.

My father's tragic situation came to reveal itself to me as one raising such related issues as a person's "right to life" and "right to die"—issues that lie at the heart of the debate over the justifiability and social acceptability of euthanasia and physician-assisted suicide. The remainder of this book deals with this debate, especially as it has developed with unprecedented intensity over the past ten years or so. What I have to say about the topic reflects some of the things that have been on my mind for the last nineteen years as I have tried, out of love for my father and mother, to answer a host of questions.

Please keep in mind, however, that this is not a book about the euthanasia debate per se; rather, as discussed here, the debate serves as but a case study for understanding how the relationship between the call of conscience and the practice of rhetoric shows itself in our everyday existence. I am interested in how the debate "means" and thus in how it functions rhetorically to sound a call of conscience to beings who sooner or later will have to deal with at least some of the factors that contribute to the debate's significance. For indeed, as Martin Marty and Ron Hamel point out, "Anyone may someday encounter a loved one pleading for relief of pain and suffering. Even more fundamentally, everyone has to die, and everyone knows that today the many ways to prolong life [medically] can make the end of life something even more dreaded than it used to be. When people today talk about euthanasia, they are in some sense talking about themselves."[3]

My discussion of the debate is organized around three topics that, as should be clear by now, have much to do with the call of conscience and that I believe help one to see what good is happening with the debate: (1) how the deconstructive/reconstructive nature of the call functions as a rhetorical inter-ruption that speaks of the importance of authenticity, accountability, responsi-bility, and justice; (2) how one's answering the call tests one's rhetorical competence; and (3) how the call involves its listener in a "heroic" adventure. When approached with these topics in mind, the euthanasia debate, no matter how sad it often is, can still be a source of inspiration and hope. Heidegger's and Levinas' thoughts on the call of conscience are both affirmed and chal-lenged by what is going on with the debate.

In turning first to a consideration of how the call's deconstructive/recon-structive nature is at work in the debate, I focus my attention primarily on an artifact that, as I read it, is designed first and foremost as a call of conscience weighted heavily on the side of deconstruction. Like human existence itself, the artifact never ceases to call its readers into question; whatever reconstruc-tion takes place is totally up to them. Helping to enhance its questioning ten-dency is the place where it was published: the field of medicine—whose Hippocratic ancestors long ago conditioned physicians to feel ill at ease not only with the topic of euthanasia but also with the art of rhetoric. The brief history I first offer to clarify this point will establish the necessary background for reading the chosen artifact, which actually calls on the reader to appreciate something of medicine's historical stance on the topics of euthanasia and rhetoric. Moreover, the artifact's way of being rhetorical helps to promote at least a general understanding of the circumstances and key terms that surround and inform the euthanasia debate. I thus hope that my way of getting into this national controversy will allow those readers who are not as familiar with the debate as they would like to be the opportunity to form, right at the start, a more knowledgeable opinion of a specific matter involving the good life and the good death.

Chapter 4

The Call of Conscience/
Rhetoric/Medicine

In the Platonic dialogue that bears his name, Gorgias has this to say when responding to Socrates' puzzlement about the "almost superhuman importance" that Gorgias attributes to "the scope of rhetoric":

> Ah, if only you knew all, Socrates, and realized that rhetoric includes practically all other faculties under her control. And I will give you good proof of this. I have often, along with my brother and with other physicians, visited one of their patients who refused to drink his medicine or submit to the surgeon's knife or cautery, and when the doctor was unable to persuade them, I did so, by no other art but rhetoric. And I claim too that, if a rhetorician and a doctor visited any city you like to name and they had to contend in argument before the Assembly or any other gathering as to which of the two should be chosen as doctor, the doctor would be nowhere, but the man who could speak would be chosen, if he so wished.[1]

For Socrates, all that Gorgias is saying here merely suggests that one who does not know the truth of medicine but who is skilled in the "routine" of rhetoric can be more persuasive than the physician (the "expert") before those who share the same ignorance about this healing art. As initially set forth in the *Gorgias* and then later developed in the *Phaedrus* (where he makes explicit reference to Hippocrates, the father of scientific medicine), Socrates' prescription for remedying this situation is clear: rhetoric is not well; in performing its principal function of influencing men's souls, it is suffering from the malady of sophistry, of granting priority to opinion, appearance, and probability over science, knowledge, and truth. And the prescription that Socrates offers to remedy this malady is equally clear: as medicine is currently developing a rational understanding of the body and its diseases, so must rhetoric develop a rational understanding of the soul and of any topic that is discussed to influence it.[2] In short, if rhetoric is to be cured of its ill-mannered behavior such that it will no longer insult the intelligence of those who "know the truth about things" or further infect those who do not, it must acquire the healthy status of a *techne*. It must become scientific in scope and function; it must know itself to be a true medicament of the soul.

When this prescription is handed over to Aristotle, however, it is judged to be too harsh a remedy for rhetoric; hence, he does not refill it but instead rewrites it. And he does this so as not to destroy rhetoric's "true nature" (*physis*).[3] For unlike medicine, rhetoric is not a science; it has no definite subject matter to call its own. Rather, it makes its living by dealing "with what is in the main contingent" (1357a15). Rhetoric is there to help human beings deliberate about the certainty of their uncertain existence. It stands ready to answer the call of those who find themselves in situations where definitive evidence that can guide moral action is lacking, but where such action, nevertheless, is required.

The prescription that Aristotle writes for rhetoric is based on all this and more, but on no more than what he observes this mode of discourse to be, in truth. The prescription marks the mean between the overly unscientific leanings of those like Gorgias and the overly scientific leanings of Socrates and Plato. With this prescription, rhetoric is still encouraged to function as a medicament for the soul, and Aristotle assumes that physicians will use it in this way when deliberating about the "good" of their patients. But again, rhetoric is not a science. To live a healthy life it need only strive to become the best that it can be: a *techne* of the probable. That is Aristotle's prescription.

Hippocratic physicians made use of the orator's art. Whether in spoken or written form, it enabled these first men of scientific medicine to define and defend their *techne* during public debates and while treating patients in the patients' homes or in the physicians' workshops. It thus served the important purpose of calling into being a "medical public" that, owing to its new scientific education, could stand with the Hippocratic physicians in their initial fight against traveling sophistic lecturers and those quack doctors whose practice still admitted the use of magical charms.[4] Plato commended this rhetoric of science in his *Laws*.[5] Hippocratic physicians employed it, however, so as to be done with it. The author of the Hippocratic *and rhetorical* treatise, *The Art*, gives testimony to this fact when, in concluding his defense of scientific medicine, he willingly discredits what he has been engaged in by noting with approval that "the multitude find it more natural to believe what they have seen than what they have heard."[6]

Hippocratic physicians turned to rhetoric in order to solidify their reputation and social standing, both of which were predicated on a scientific understanding of the body and on the definitive evidence about disease that such understanding makes possible in the form of a "true" *techne,* a true realm of technical knowledge that can be used to cure the body of what ails it. Once this understanding demonstrates itself, not in words but in action, rhetoric becomes superfluous for the Hippocratics, or at best something that must be uttered to patients whose opinions and fears bespeak their ignorance about the truth of medicine and about the trust they should have in their healers' diagnostic and prognostic abilities.[7] The wisdom that these healers possess and that they must constantly seek as their first priority makes them "the equal of a god. Between wisdom and medicine there is no gulf fixed."[8]

As dictated by both the Hippocratic oath and law, this sacred wisdom or technical knowledge is the private property of the physician (and his students), to be shared only through the silence of action (treating patients) but never through the noise of words (communicating with patients): "The profane may not learn . . . [of this wisdom] until they have been initiated into the mysteries of [medical] science."[9] Moreover, the profane must not expect the physician to go beyond the rational boundaries of his private property, his wisdom, when being asked to help "those who are overmastered by their diseases"; for here "medicine is powerless" and, if practiced, deserving of ridicule and contempt.[10] Medicine is a science and must remain a science by continuing to give witness and proven remedy to the body. For the good of the patient, life must be *protected and prolonged* (scientifically), and in the process *no harm* should be committed against the one who is seeking health.[11]

All of this is the prescription that Hippocratic physicians offer to medicine. Rhetoric is an ingredient in this prescription, but one designed to self-destruct; for as one reads in the Hippocratic law: "There are in fact two things, science and opinion; the former begets knowledge, the latter ignorance."[12] From the time of the Hippocratics until the sixteenth century, the full effect of this prescription on the body politic of medicine was inhibited in great part by religious and social prohibitions against dissecting human corpses. Beginning in the sixteenth century, however, the rhetoric that informed these prohibitions and thereby restricted the prescription's scientific calling was dismantled as anatomists, true to this calling, opened up the human body to the gaze of the physician. They thus revealed through careful observation physiological structures and happenings that had been greatly misjudged by the Hippocratics and by those medievalists who knew only how to respond to the letter and not to the scientific spirit of their Hippocratic texts.[13] Extending into the eighteenth century, these innovative experiments in dissection enabled physicians to behold a wealth of evidence about illness. Physicians could now understand their patients and their bodies from the inside out; they could now correlate illness with places in the body and could begin telling the "true" story of disease, its pathophysiology.

Medicine's privileged and private technical knowledge was growing. Real scientific progress was at hand. The Hippocratics were right: there is science, and there is opinion; there is knowledge, and there is ignorance. Dissection proved this point. It helped medicine to cut to the quick, to the meat of the matter, and thereby to cut out more of medicine's rhetorical flab, or what one physician-researcher I know terms "humshi"— "humanistic shit."[14]

Standing at the gate of the nineteenth century, medicine was now ready to begin an unprecedented journey of scientific progress. Along the way it would acquire a battery of diagnostic technologies and surgical procedures to combat disease and death; it would establish the causal role between bacteria and disease; it would ready itself to leave its patients' homes so that it could find legitimate sanctuary in hospitals and university-based research centers; it would enhance its professional sovereignty with the help of corporate capitalism; it would proliferate its technical knowledge through the process of specialization; it would facilitate a drug revolution and acquire the outright capacity to prevent or cure a host of life-threatening illnesses. With all of this, it would eventually revolutionize its scientific and technological capabilities and be able to sustain the lives of even the most critically ill patients.[15] Having reached this end by the 1970s, medicine became "miraculous"; its practitioners were now more "godlike" then ever before. With newly developed life-support systems by their side, they had the power to prevent "nature from taking its course," a power that so broadened their Hippocratic and moral obligation to protect and prolong life that, for all practical purposes, they no longer needed to refuse to treat any patients who were seeking help.

Through science, medicine had further released itself from the burdens of rhetoric, though it still had a role to play in medicine's "art." Persuading a patient to comply with a medical decision is more of an art than a science. Yet in cultivating the life-saving addiction of scientific wisdom, medicine had conditioned itself to see its dependence on its art as a sign of "defeat."[16] Science and technology, not rhetoric (or "humshi"), are what protect and prolong life. In the current practice of medicine, however, this attitude must still admit that its realization remains incomplete.

For example, what are physicians to do when, in treating critically ill patients, they find themselves performing necessary life-sustaining activities that fail miserably to pass the long-honored test of doing no harm? Phrasing the question somewhat differently, how should physicians react to the medically created situation wherein a second chance at life turns out to be only a second and prolonged chance at death, a chance that this time around accentuates and contributes to a patient's suffering and offers little or no "rational" hope for improving the patient's "quality of life"?

This situation sounds a call of conscience and compels action. For example, should life-support systems and medications (except for those that can relieve pain) be withdrawn so that nature can take its course and so that no further harm is committed to the patient? But then the physician would not be abiding by the obligation to preserve life. If, however, the sanctity of the patient's life is protected and prolonged, then the physician breaks the promise to do no harm. Moral conflict is inevitable in this situation. Yet the physician must act. To the extent that this action is in any way directed toward relieving the patient's pain and suffering—or, to put it more blatantly and realistically, toward helping the patient to end his or her life in an easier, more expedient and humane manner than that allowed for by life-support systems—the physician is set on a course for performing an act of euthanasia.[17]

This act is typically labeled "passive" when it is confined to the withholding or withdrawing of life-prolonging and life-sustaining technologies. Death is brought about by the underlying disease or assault to the body. If, on the other hand, the patient's merciful death is the result of some "direct intervention" (injecting the patient with potassium chloride, for example), we would have a case of "active" euthanasia. Notwithstanding the efforts of those associated with the "right to life" movement, patients have a constitutional right to opt for passive euthanasia.[18] This right, however, does not extend to a voluntary request for active euthanasia. The "intentional" termination of life by a physician, even when performed in response to a patient begging for mercy and in accordance with proposed legal and medical guidelines, constitutes "murder." But should it? Is there truly a moral difference between passive and active euthanasia, between "letting die" and "killing"? Are not both acts directed toward bringing about a merciful and peaceful end? If so, then should not patients have the right, and physicians the license, to make use of the ways and means of active euthanasia? Public and medical opinion do seem to be moving in that direction.[19]

The present-day controversy about the justifiability and social acceptability of active voluntary euthanasia places medicine in a rather difficult situation. For what is at stake here is medicine's very "moral center," its Hippocratic tradition. The performance of passive euthanasia can be rationalized in terms of this tradition. The Hippocratic treatise, *The Art,* states that the purpose of medicine is "to do away with the sufferings of the sick, to lessen the violence of their diseases, and *to refuse to treat those who are overmastered by their diseases*" (emphasis added).[20] Active euthanasia, however, violates a crucial element of the physicians' oath: Do no harm![21] Responding to the potential of allowing this violation to occur, Dr. Willard Gaylin and colleagues emphasize that "if this moral center collapses, if physicians become killers or are even merely licensed to kill, the profession—and, therewith, each physician—will never again be worthy of trust and respect as healer and comforter and protector of life in all its frailty."[22] Agreeing with this line of reasoning, Dr. Robert Moss points out, however, that physicians cannot ignore their "responsibility to address growing public sentiment and the unmet needs of suffering patients who are the victims of . . . [medical] interventions. To do so could further erode the trust that patients have in their doctors and even promote the proliferation of less scrupulous physicians who would be willing to perform euthanasia more indiscriminately."[23]

Indeed medical euthanasia has become a major public concern, and the profession of medicine is being called upon more than ever before to address this concern. What is needed here, of course, is the very art that medicine's Hippocratic ancestors instructed it to marginalize for the sake of the growth of scientific wisdom: rhetoric. Yes, there *is* science, and there *is* opinion. But medical science so far has proven incapable of providing the "definitive evidence" for answering the question about the morality and/or immorality of euthanasia, and the ethic of "do no harm" has been called into question by the profession's own technological progress. Medicine thus finds itself in the midst of a life-and-death situation demanding the ways and means of rhetorical invention. Conscience calls!

A Case Study

In 1988 medicine answered this call when the *Journal of the American Medical Association* (*JAMA*) published an essay in "A Piece of My Mind," that section of the journal where contributions need not be strictly "scientific" in nature.[24] The essay is titled "It's Over, Debbie." The story told there was the first of its kind to appear in a U.S. medical journal.

> The call came in the middle of the night. As a gynecology resident rotating through a large, private hospital, I had come to detest telephone calls, because invariably I would be up for several hours and would not feel good the next day. However, duty called, so I answered the phone. A nurse informed me that a patient was having difficulty getting rest, could I please see her. She was on 3 North. That was the gynecologic-oncology unit, not my usual duty station. As I trudged along, bumping sleepily against walls and corners and not believing I was up again, I tried to imagine what I might find at the end of my walk. Maybe an elderly woman with an anxiety reaction, or perhaps something particularly horrible.
>
> I grabbed the chart from the nurses station on my way to the patient's room, and the nurse gave me some hurried details: a 20-year-old girl named Debbie was dying of ovarian cancer. She was having unrelenting vomiting apparently as the result of an alcohol drip administered for sedation. Hmmm, I thought. Very sad. As I approached the room I could hear loud, labored breathing. I entered and saw an emaciated, dark-haired woman who appeared much older than 20. She was receiving nasal oxygen, had an IV, and was sitting in bed suffering from what was obviously severe air hunger. The chart noted her weight at 80 pounds. A second woman, also dark-haired but of middle age, stood at her right, holding her hand. Both looked up as I entered. The room seemed filled with the patient's desperate effort to survive. Her eyes were hollow, and she had suprasternal and intercostal retractions with her rapid inspirations. She had not eaten or slept in two

days. She had not responded to chemotherapy and was being given supportive care only. It was a gallows scene, a cruel mockery of her youth and unfulfilled potential. Her only words to me were, "Let's get this over with."

I retreated with my thoughts to the nurses station. The patient was tired and needed rest. I could not give her health, but I could give her rest. I asked the nurse to draw 20 mg of morphine sulfate into a syringe. Enough, I thought, to do the job. I took the syringe into the room and told the two women I was going to give Debbie something that would let her rest and to say good-bye. Debbie looked at the syringe, then laid her head on the pillow with her eyes open, watching what was left of the world. I injected the morphine intravenously and watched to see if my calculations on its effects would be correct. Within seconds her breathing slowed to a normal rate, her eyes closed, and her features softened as she seemed restful at last. The older woman stroked the hair of the now-sleeping patient. I waited for the inevitable next effect of depressing the respiratory drive. With clocklike certainty, within four minutes the breathing rate slowed even more, then became irregular, then ceased. The dark-haired woman stood erect and seemed relieved.

It's over Debbie.

Name Withheld by Request

It would seem that what we have before us is a firsthand account of how a physician engaged in the practice of active euthanasia, or "mercy killing." Dr. George Lundberg, the editor of *JAMA,* abided by the author's request to withhold his/her name. He also refrained from publishing an editorial comment at the time because he felt such comment would interfere with readers' interpretations of the narrative.[25]

Although he believed the story to be true, Lundberg admitted that no attempt was made to verify its factual basis before, during, or after it was sent out for "peer review." He argued, however, that whether the essay is true or not is at best a secondary matter, for the controversial issue the essay brings to light is, in fact, real. Writing in an editorial that eventually appeared in *JAMA,* Lundberg further defended his actions when noting that he published the essay "to provoke responsible debate within the medical profession and by the public about euthanasia."[26]

Publication of the "Debbie" case in one of the most widely read medical journals in the world led to intense media coverage of the story and generated many reactions.[27] Some of these reactions were positive, supporting the physician-author's compassionate actions.[28] Some, like those written by officials from the Hemlock Society of Illinois and from the National Hemlock Society and the World Federation of Right to Die Societies, were more "middle of the road" in nature—praising *JAMA* for contributing "substantially to the dialogue on the important and unresolved issue of physician aid-in-dying," condemning "the Debbie case as both illegal and unethical," and offering clarification about what "requirements" ought to be followed for assisting patients who want to die a humane and dignified death.[29]

Many of the reactions, however, were negative. For example, a grand jury in Chicago, where *JAMA* is published, delivered a subpoena to the American Medical Association (AMA), demanding the disclosure of the author's ("murderer's") name.[30] Dr. Eugene F. Diamond, a representative for the AMA Medical Staff Section, called for Lundberg's firing and emphasized that "the American public needs to be reassured that, despite the scandalous publication of 'It's Over, Debbie' in . . . [*JAMA*], the rank-and-file membership of our once-proud organization finds direct euthanasia to be totally abhorrent and unacceptable."[31] Other readers, pointing to what they believed were "omissions" and medical inaccuracies in the story, dismissed "Debbie" as a "hoax."[32] And one group of esteemed physician-ethicists, who assumed a more literal-minded reading of the case, went so far as to say that "decent folk do not deliberately stir discussion of outrageous practices, like slavery, incest, or killing those in our care."[33]

What these and many other physicians feared was that the "rhetoric" of the essay would bring the medical community and those whom it is obliged to serve one step closer to adopting a comprehensive policy on active euthanasia. Dr. Mark Siegler, a leading medical ethicist in the United States and a major critic of Lundberg, also added this in one of his responses to the publication: "Medical killing is regarded by some as a quick fix to the dual problems of dying and dependence and, further, as a way to control the power of physicians. But this quick fix will fix nothing and will cost plenty. If killing by physicians is legalized, everyone will lose. All patients will be endangered by such a policy but particularly those who are old, physically disabled, mentally impaired, poor and uninsured."[34]

With all this in mind, one might think of the rhetoric in question as being nothing less than deplorable and hence an easy mark for the critic. "Medicine bashing" is not my goal here, however. On the contrary, I have chosen the "Debbie" case because as a rhetorical artifact concerned with the issue of euthanasia it is, I believe, highly original and deceptively instructive. Despite its short, simple, and straightforward appearance, there is more to this case than meets the eye that would read it, for example, only as an account of compassion, an admission of murder, a scandalous publication, a hoax, something written and published by indecent folk, a call for legalizing medical killing—or, as Dr. Harold Jenson put it, an "intolerable" attempt by "an AMA employee [that is, Lundberg] to impugn physicians and residents publicly, in the official AMA journal."[35]

As a way of supporting the contention I am making here, I want to offer a reading of "Debbie" that pays particular attention to what the text is doing *rhetorically*—that is, *how* it means, not just *what* it means. Such a reading will enable me to suggest how the text, in the specific ways it addresses both its topic and its readers, is functioning primarily as a call of conscience. Drawing direction from key observations made by both Heidegger and Levinas regarding the workings of the call and their relationship with the spatiotemporal, emotional, interpersonal, and discursive realm of our everydayness, what I thus intend to emphasize about the narrative is this:

The story of "Debbie" is a rhetorical experiment in uncertainty and ambiguity—an experiment that "presents the unpresentable" to its readers and thereby disrupts their expectations; an experiment that deconstructs and thus undermines its own "apparent" meaning; an experiment that subverts a modernist sensibility by bringing together powerful but incommensurable truths; an experiment that is always "other," always different than what it is taken to be. "Debbie" favors heterogeneity, not homogeneity. Defined in and between the lines of the story's unfolding narrative is a text whose multiple and competing voices speak to us of a history of medical progress that is currently mired in what the story is essentially about—the uncertainty and ambiguity marking the debate over the morality and/or immorality of euthanasia.

This text gives evidence of itself in and through the plurality of interpretations that it inspires.[36] The presence of this plurality exists as a necessary supplement to the text because it not only accentuates issues pertaining to euthanasia that are raised by "Debbie," but it also grants further expression to something that the story, in its own "postmodern" and conscientious way, encourages us to take seriously: namely, that we lack definitive evidence upon which to gauge the "truth" of the morality and/or immorality of euthanasia, and that only by way of sustained public moral argument do we stand a *rational* chance of determining how right and good our *opinions* might be regarding a situation of life and death. In short, "Debbie" is a story that at one and the same time calls into question both itself and its readers, and that thereby sounds the ongoing rhetorical interruption of the call of conscience that we tend not to hear until something important in our lives breaks down. A discussion of how all of this "is the case" will now be offered.[37]

Presenting the Unpresentable: A Rhetorical Interruption

"It's Over, Debbie" is a story "ahead of its time." By telling us what it does (at least on the surface), this narrative is sanctioning an act that is beyond the present (modern) limits of the law. The story of "Debbie" is postmodern; it ends up presenting what is supposed to be totally *un*-presentable, totally not allowed *now*.[38] Doctors are not supposed to engage in mercy killing; they are not supposed to react against the often life-giving, death-prolonging capabilities of medical science and technology by forsaking the tradition of the Hippocratic oath and sliding down that "slippery slope" that leads from passive to active euthanasia.[39]

Adding to the unpresentability of the presentation is the unprofessional and unethical way Debbie's storyteller descended the slope. No time was lost by entering into consultations with the patient, her family, or her attending physician. The tired resident witnessed the patient's pain and suffering, heard her say "Let's get this over with," made no attempt to clarify what these words actually meant, decided that "I could not give her health, but I could give her rest," ordered and administered an injection of morphine sulfate, and then, without any indication of remorse, watched her stop breathing.[40] A middle-aged woman who had been holding the patient's hand and stroking her hair "seemed relieved" with this outcome. Presumably, this woman (a relative? a friend?) and the physician thought alike: because of Debbie's excruciating condition, giving her "rest" was a merciful thing to do.

This need not necessarily be the case, however. For example, perhaps the woman "seemed relieved" because, like the physician, she was tired from being awakened in the middle of the night to attend to a "particularly horrible situation." Now that Debbie was dead, the woman would no longer have to be bothered by a "duty" that was currently disrupting *her* life. Without additional information regarding the identity of this woman, why she was present in Debbie's room, and what she knew about the patient's wishes, this sad scenario of selfishness cannot be discounted.[41] As for the physician, his/her motivations can likewise be questioned. If this physician was indeed a caring and compassionate individual, why did he/she not take the time to determine the whole truth behind Debbie's last request? What if the "rest" she apparently wanted was not immediate death but, at least for now, only a drug that could stop her from vomiting and enable her to get some sleep? Again, more information is needed if one is to resolve these additional uncertainties.

Even if the physician is credited with guessing right, uncertainty still prevails, for the "rest" given to Debbie could have been achieved by way of a legal form of passive euthanasia—"allowing" the patient to die (stopping all aggressive treatment) while still keeping her "comfortable" with constant sedation. Was this less radical option of mercy avoided because the physician was genuinely motivated by the argument that there is no moral difference between passive and active euthanasia? Would the patient have agreed? Given her condition, would she have been "competent" enough to do so?[42]

In telling the story of "Debbie," the author is not only presenting something that is supposed to be totally unpresentable, but is presenting it in a way filled with uncertainty. Absent from the story is information that can help answer important questions about a purported (albeit illegal) act of mercy that was executed in a very unprofessional and unethical manner. With the discovery of this particular presence/absence phenomenon happening with "Debbie," we have before us what I take to be an essential rhetorical ingredient in what the story is doing—how it means.

How "Debbie" *means* is by presenting the unpresentable in an uncertain way. The presentation works to disrupt readers' expectations about what they should be reading in a prestigious medical journal. "Debbie" is a rhetorical interruption that will not quit. This being the case, certain questions arise: Why would an author publicly sanction an illegal act, performed in an unprofessional and unethical manner, by telling a story whose uncertainty casts doubt on the author's motivation of mercy? Did the author not realize that, as written, the story is "deconstructing" itself by making ambiguous the only "favorable" meaning that can be given to it? Despite details included in the story that beg to be recognized as describing a life that most "rational" people would not want to endure, are we not to believe that the doctor "could not give her health" but "could give her rest"? Those who support the "right to life" would surely know how to answer this question.[43] But "Debbie" is a story that is far to the left of this "right." So what's the story here?

The author, of course, has no intention of answering these questions because, as is all too clear, he/she has taken a version of "the Fifth" and so cannot be called forth "to tell the truth, the whole truth, and nothing but the truth." Indeed the author of "Debbie" haunts us with an uncertainty that, as with existence itself, is always there to interrupt and challenge our desire to know for sure "what it all means," to stimulate anxiety, and thus to make us feel *unheimlich* (not at home).

Still, the author's presentation does carry with it some degree of believability. "Debbie" took on this feature of "the truth" as soon as the editor of *JAMA* read and then responded to the story by publishing it *without editorial rebuke or comment*. Such an act of silence says a lot, especially when heard in a journal like *JAMA*—a journal whose professional calling is to publish pieces that presumably are telling the truth. This presumption forms a bond of trust between those who publish in *JAMA*, its editor, and its readers. One way that the editor acknowledges this trust and the truth it presupposes is by allowing a publication to speak for itself. That is what the AMA had long done with Lundberg, and that is what Lundberg did with "Debbie." He presented this unconventional story to his readership in a way that said: Trust me! What you have here is an account that is supposedly telling the truth.[44]

This is not to say that Lundberg is an advocate of medical euthanasia, for "Publication does not constitute endorsement."[45] Still, there is no "Debbie" in *JAMA* without Lundberg's decision to present this unpresentable text.[46] This decision could only go so far, however. "Debbie" must rest on the margins of *JAMA*, at a site called "A Piece of My Mind," a site left over by medical science for its rhetorical remains, for "opinion pieces." We pay our respects to the "art" of medicine when we visit this site and read its inscriptions. In the rush to learn about the latest findings of medical science, it is easy to skip over and ignore these inscriptions or to perceive them only as would a tourist on the run to more exciting and important places. The media, for example, initially reacted this way. Jon Van, the medical science writer who then reviewed contributions in *JAMA* and who first broke the story about Debbie's death, did so only after being notified that Lundberg allowed "Debbie" to rest in ". . . Piece. . . ."[47] And allow it he did. He placed a certain story, a piece of rhetoric, within the body politic of medicine—a body that, like the body human, is "mined" with "explosive devices" for fighting off "invaders," things alien to the body's well-being.[48] With this action, the rhetorical workings of "Debbie" (how it means) took on the additional feature of believability. But can a story that is so unpresentable and so unconventional really be true?

Truth/Fiction

What "Debbie" *is doing* in *JAMA* encourages one to ask a question that further enhances the rhetorical interruption at work here. This question was posed time and again by many outraged readers. One such reader was Eugene Kennedy, a prominent Chicago-based writer and professor of psychology. He noted, for example, "One would have to travel into the heart of darkness itself to find a physician whose experience matched even roughly that of the author of this piece. For where, even in the relativistic shambles of American culture, could you find another physician willing to end a patient's life with less information than the average hit man gets about the life and habits of an intended target?"[49] Kennedy next expressed his outrage over Lundberg's decision to publish the unverified story and suggested that "perhaps Lundberg is not acquainted with the journalistic ethical code that prevents any of his editorial peers from employing fictitious incidents in order to initiate debates on serious subjects." He then asked, "How does editor Lundberg deal with the problem of accurately representing and perceiving what Joyce called 'all that is grave and constant' in our human condition?" Kennedy secured an answer to the question during a phone conversation with Lundberg, which is included in his article. Given the reading of "Debbie" that I am attempting to develop here, part of that conversation is important enough to warrant our attention:

> "You," Lundberg responded to one of my questions, "apparently think you can only take this article one way."
>
> "It was presented," I said, "as many other articles in that section [A Piece of My Mind] have been, without any warnings that it might not be true. The reader would presumably accept this as an accurate account of a true incident."

"Well, that's reader-response theory."

"What exactly do you mean by reader-response theory?"

"That is the theory of literary criticism that delves into finding out why the reader reads something the way he does, what he takes out of it, and why. It has to do with different readers getting different messages."

"As in deconstructionist literary theory?"

"Yes, something like that. The reader is responsible for making the judgment about what the article means. I agree with that theory."

"But that's a literary theory. You're editing a scientific journal."

"It appeared outside the well of strict scientific articles."

"Then you believe it is the reader's obligation to decide whether this happened or not?"

"I would agree with that."[50]

Kennedy's reading and appreciation of the story is certainly different than Lundberg's. Unlike the editor, Kennedy is not what is termed in the politics of postmodernist thought "a champion of readers' rights." He is not willing to put the truth up for grabs by appealing to "reader-response theory," "deconstructionist literary theory," or "something like that."[51] Kennedy maintains instead a traditional modernist outlook; as noted in his article, he wants the perception and reception of texts to be built on a conception of "the truth observed keenly." He wants what the author of "Debbie" makes unclear and what another reader, whose ultimate response to the story was to publish it, fails to clarify, at least beyond saying, as reported above, that "the reader is responsible for making the judgment about what the article means." "Debbie's" authenticity (what and how it truly is) calls on the reader's authenticity (his or her responsibility to assume the burden of decision and choice). For Kennedy this was totally unacceptable. "The purpose of scientific journals," he declared, is not to "blur the issues" but "to communicate the truth as clearly as possible."[52]

The lawyers Francis H. Miller and George J. Annas believed the story to be true: "'It's Over, Debbie' constitutes a textbook example of medical arrogance, ignorance, and criminal conduct. . . . Truth can indeed be more frightening than fiction. Thank you, Debbie, for reminding us."[53] If "Debbie" is a truthful story, it must be functioning *to disclose and show forth* a real honest-to-goodness "thing in itself"; for that, as Heidegger reminds us, is how "truth" happens, how it comes about in this world (BT 256–73). A fiction, however, can also perform this epideictic function.[54] Perhaps "Debbie" is both a "truth" and a "fiction."

I would submit that there is something of the truth at work in "Debbie," something that not only is quite dear to medicine but that also has a role to play in how the text means. This truth is reflected in the style of the presentation, in the way the author's prose is simple, direct, and fast paced, presenting itself in sentences that tell about facts and events in a very economical manner. This style makes an effort in trying to be effortless, in trying to efface itself, to say that it has no style, that it is only a report, without arguments and questions that might betray a lack of self-assurance on the author's part and that might slow down the presentation and its reception. Throughout their training, physicians are conditioned to acquire an appreciation for the way in which the speed and efficiency of this style provides the most fitting and thus "eloquent" mode of expression for the scientifically oriented "voice of medicine."[55] Such conditioning takes place whenever students of medicine are schooled in the "proper" practice of writing up and reciting a patient's "medical case history." One is reminded of the stylistic nature of such a case history when reading "Debbie."[56] More must be said about what we are being reminded of here, however, if the truth at work in "Debbie" is to be fully appreciated as something contributing to how this narrative means.

As first noted in chapter 1 when clarifying Heidegger's assessment of the fundamental nature of everyday discourse, medical case histories are rooted in the "illness stories" of patients—stories that almost always have at least two characters to whom things happen: a *person* and that person's *body*. Patients are under no professional obligation to make this distinction when telling the story of their illnesses, when trying to remember all that has been happening to them because of some bodily disorder that they believe is indicative of some disease. Physicians, on the other hand, do have a professional obligation to make the distinction, for only then can they properly diagnose and perhaps cure the diseases afflicting their patients. Thus, of the two characters that motivate the patient's illness story, it is the body, the place where a disease unfolds, that must assume priority as a matter of interest to the physician. Levinas aside, the patient's "face" is essentially flesh and blood and bone.

Directed by this priority, the physician can now begin constructing a story that, as expected by his or her peers, cuts like a scalpel through the personhood, the life and times, of a patient, thereby leaving intact only those portions of the patient's history that can be used to make a good case about some disease. Although such an effort in dissection is directed toward offering a *depersonalized* perception of the patient—a perception that, recall, thrives on what Heidegger terms the "leveling tendency" of discourse—it nevertheless helps to guarantee that a much-needed style (speed and efficiency) will facilitate the telling of a vital body story.[57]

There is something of all of this going on with "Debbie." Contained in the body of this account is a story about a diseased body. With the words of a nurse in mind and with a medical chart in hand, a physician tells us that a twenty-year-old girl, "who appeared much older than 20," was dying of ovarian cancer. She "was having unrelenting vomiting" because of her sedation. Her breathing was "labored." She was "emaciated." "She was receiving nasal oxygen, had an IV," and was "suffering" from "severe air hunger." She weighed "80 pounds." "Her eyes were hollow, and she had suprasternal and intercostal retractions with her rapid inspirations. She had not eaten or slept in two days." Her chemotherapy was unsuccessful. She "was being given supportive care only." She spoke but five words to her storyteller: "Let's get this over with." Beyond these words, we know nothing about the patient's personal assessment of her history. The patient's voice has faded. Body stories do that. Being quick, clean, and clinical, they de-personalize their subjects.

There is, of course, a "subjective" dimension to the story. It is rooted in how a gynecology resident, "not believing I was up again," came to think about Debbie's situation. Notice, however, that the way in which this thinking is expressed also admits the style of a well-told body story. We are informed quite briskly and economically that Debbie's situation was "very sad"; that her "room seemed filled with the patient's desperate effort to survive"; that "it was a gallows scene, a cruel mockery of her youth and unfulfilled potential"; that Debbie "was tired and needed rest"; that "I could not give her health, but I could give her rest." With these admissions, the existential character of Debbie's face begins to take form.

Such "rhetoric," as one distraught reader of the story disparagingly described it,[58] is uncalled for when telling a body story. It is too personal, too subjective, too telling of what a body story is not supposed to be: a story about a person who is ill, a "person story," if you will. From the standpoint of medical science, these two stories are not meant to go together. They employ different "language games"; their respective "characters" are incommensurate; the opinionated subjectivity of one gets in the way of the scientific objectivity of the other. When this happens, the medical matter at hand may become too time-consuming, too existential, *too uncertain and ambiguous.* Remember again what is written in the Hippocratic law: "There are in fact two things, science and opinion; the former begets knowledge, the latter ignorance." Thus, there are body stories, and there are person stories. Each has its place. In "Debbie," however, these stories are conflated; hence, her physician has broken the law, albeit in a law-like way: with speed and efficiency.

Perhaps this injustice was committed because the physician is neither a good teller of body stories nor a good teller of person stories. Perhaps this deficiency in narrative ability becomes especially apparent whenever the physician is forced to write up a case about someone like Debbie, someone whose personhood is being destroyed by a diseased body that is well beyond the curative means of medical science. What words are appropriate for telling us about such a patient/body/person? How are they best expressed to reveal the "truth" about the matter at hand?[59] Physicians have the responsibility of being rhetorically competent when using stories to share their wisdom with those who they are obliged to serve.

The author of "Debbie" could have said more about this patient. In her letter to Dr. Lundberg, Dr. Bernadine Paulshock suggested as much when she asked, for example: "Was [Debbie] not already getting morphine, and if not, why? Why did [the physician] have to resort to a deliberate overdose to give her the surcease that was her right? What were this patient's daytime therapists doing about the failure of their regimen to control her pain and suffering? Why weren't they doing enough?"[60] Answers to questions about morphine doses for relieving the unrelenting pain and suffering of a hopelessly ill patient ought to be a part of a patient's medical case history, for they definitely have a role to play in the telling of a body story. Yet such questions arise not only because of some *body* but also because of some *person* whose experience of pain and suffering result in a request for help. Debbie made such a request when she said, "Let's get this over with." Did she make similar requests in the past? Perhaps her physician was at a loss for words when considering this historical matter because answers to questions such as those raised by Dr. Paulshock were omitted from Debbie's chart. According to Dr. Paulshock, this omission makes the "dramatic account" of Debbie "ring less true." Perhaps she is wrong. In their summary of medical practices affecting the care of dying patients at the time, Dr. Sidney H. Wanzer and eleven of his fellow physicians point out that "physicians have a responsibility to consider timely discussions with patients about life-sustaining treatment and terminal care. Only a minority of physicians now do so consistently."[61] Thus, perhaps Debbie's physician is telling the truth by omitting what was truly not there in Debbie's medical case history.

With its appearance in *JAMA,* "Debbie" is presenting the unpresentable in an uncertain but believable way. The story is doing this by making use of a discursive style that medicine employs when telling body stories. The economical and clinical nature of such stories have the effect of de-personalizing and thus de-facing patients. There is a truth at work in "Debbie"; it has a role to play in how the text means, in how a narrative on euthanasia, which takes place in a journal where the truth is supposed to happen, is making things ambiguous and undecidable. This is not the way the "voice of medicine," dedicated as it is to telling the truth about diseased bodies, is meant to be used. But this is what "Debbie" *is doing.* The story is turning medicine against itself by using one of its truths in a confusing and thus inappropriate manner. With this disruptive act of "deconstruction," the story raises additional questions about itself and its topic but leaves it up to readers to provide the answers, or at least to raise more questions.[62] "Debbie" mimics our temporal existence; it sounds a call of conscience. Looking back at the narrative one final time, it is possible to find further evidence of this act's occurrence; there is still more uncertainty and

ambiguity at work in the narrative than has been noted so far. "Debbie's" call
of conscience is made known by way of a *robust* rhetorical interruption.

Other Than What It Appears to Be

When reading "Debbie," one ought to recognize that, up to a certain point in
the story, there is not a clue that a "mercy killing" is underway. On the contrary, most of what is being reported to us with speed and efficiency suggests
that a tired yet compassionate physician was merely doing his/her "job." Right
after telling us that Debbie "was having unrelenting vomiting apparently as the
result of an alcohol drip administered for sedation," the physician confides:
"Hmmm, I thought. Very sad." Such compassion speaks to Debbie's situation. It
thereby might also be referring to the fact that the patient's treatment regimen
included the use of an outdated therapy (that is, an alcohol drip for sedation).[63]
Nothing specific is said about this occurrence of medical incompetence. But,
"sad" to say, the incompetence was there. Along with the knowledge of proper
medical procedure, compassion demands that this problem be remedied *immediately.* A patient was in dire straits. She made a request for help. Her physician
knew what to do. "I could not give her health, but I could give her rest." This
was done: 20 mg of morphine sulfate injected intravenously. Perhaps as any
caring and competent doctor would do, the physician stood by to make sure
that his/her "calculations on its effects would be correct." They were. "Within
seconds her breathing slowed to a normal rate, her eyes closed, and her features softened as she seemed restful at last." Debbie was now asleep. Good pain
management prevailed.

Then, suddenly and unexpectedly, the plot shifts. "I waited for the
inevitable next effect of depressing the respiratory drive. With clocklike certainty, within four minutes the breathing rate slowed even more, then became
irregular, then ceased. . . . It's over, Debbie." In a startling moment of recognition, we now know that what we have been reading all along *is* a story detailing a mercy killing that was performed in the same way as the story that recalls
its occurrence: with speed and efficiency.[64] A patient's life and death are
acknowledged in but a moment of a very short story. Is that fair, right, just?
We ask these questions of a physician and author whose professional, moral,
and rhetorical competence are in question. We ask these questions of what
seems all too clear to be a strange story.

There is indeed something strange going on here, something that does not
make sense. According to Dr. Verne Marshall, "The alleged 20 mg dose of
morphine, even if administered intravenously, should be inadequate to do
more than induce a deep coma, death might have occurred in hours, not four
minutes."[65] Keying on this point, the medical ethicist Kenneth Vaux offered the
following reading of the story:

Morphine is not normally a poison but an analgesic drug, and 20 mg is scarcely a murderous dose. The physician could not possibly have known with the brash confidence that his narrative displays that his injection would kill. More likely, he sought to provide relief and rest to this dying young woman, knowing that it would speed her death. In the pursuit of a legitimate, indeed obligatory, purpose of relieving suffering, he shortened the remaining hours of her life. If this is a true rendition of Debbie's case, it represents an instance of morally acceptable double-effect euthanasia (or what is technically called *agathanasia,* a better death). The side effect is unfortunate, indeed grievous, but it is not unethical.[66]

Vaux's reading is important since it suggests that owing to an enigma (the morphine dosage) contained in what presumably "is a true rendition of Debbie's case," the story of her death must be *other than what it appears to be.* With this reading, the morphine dosage obviously no longer poses a problem because it is now associated with the physician's merciful "pursuit of a legitimate, indeed obligatory, purpose of relieving suffering." The compassion and competence displayed by this physician—who "could not possibly have known . . . that his injection would kill"—is thus crucial to Vaux's informative interpretation of the story.[67]

Yet things are not that simple with "Debbie." If what her physician is telling us does constitute "a true rendition" of her case, then a reading that sees it to be an instance of double-effect euthanasia must prove incorrect. In such a case the "primary intent" of a physician can only be that of wanting to make a patient more comfortable by using some therapy to relieve the patient's pain. This seems to be the case throughout the majority of the story, but not at the end. When we learn that the physician's "calculations" were directed toward "depressing the respiratory drive," we have before us a confession that signifies a clear intent to terminate the patient's life. Such intent disqualifies the suggestion of death being a "side effect."[68] Hence, based on the physician's own admission, the deed in question here must go by the name of active euthanasia, not double-effect euthanasia. Now, however, the alleged morphine dosage once again becomes a problem, something that contributes to the story's uncertainty by raising the possibility that "Debbie" is other than what it appears to be. With this possibility at hand, the story's call of conscience becomes more forceful; for as we have learned with both Heidegger and Levinas, "otherness" and the call of conscience are fundamentally related.

Like everything else that makes the story uncertain, this specific contribution to how the story *means* has a deconstructive ring to it: "20 mg of morphine sulfate" *calls for* a reading of the story that the story itself denies. But as soon as this denial is registered, the call is repeated. This call would have us affirm that "Debbie" cannot be what it is; the denial would have us affirm that

"Debbie" cannot be what it isn't. The story, to be sure, haunts us with uncertainty. What the morphine dosage *is doing* in the story makes certain of that.

Confronted by the totality of the story's uncertainty, one might conclude, as did certain medical experts, that "Debbie" is simply a "hoax." It "doesn't make sense"; it lacks "the ring of truth." At best, then, the story is a "fiction," and a "poor" one at that.[69] Recalling that the narrative was presented in a context where the truth is supposed to happen, and having learned from experience that truth is stranger than fiction at times, one might nevertheless be tempted to grant authenticity to the narrative. Yes, this *is* a genuine account of a mercy killing! Accepting this interpretation, one might share the sentiments of readers like Eileen Moran who would have us believe that "the author of the essay is a brave, caring, and progressive member of his profession. His actions were those of one who values an individual's right of choice—Debbie's choice, my choice, the choices of many who refuse to suffer when hope of recovery is nil."[70]

Of course, the way in which Debbie's death was managed with such speed and efficiency might call forth an opposite response: "This is not mercy killing. This is existential murder, Meursault dressed in surgical gown and a pretense of compassion."[71] Such an assessment might then lead one to wonder about how much of the physician's "cold-blooded" behavior was but a consequence of his/her being trained to offer "technical responses" to human suffering. Wasn't Debbie "dispatched" by way of such a response?[72] Going one step further with this line of thought, one might even come to the shocking conclusion that history is repeating itself—for the worse: "Our civilization had an experience with simplistic and institutionalized medical killing earlier in this century; many of us naively thought that this experience was permanently behind us. Apparently, the killing of patients by physicians is no longer inconceivable to the medical public or American society."[73] Yet what about the morphine dosage? Double-effect euthanasia? It can't be; the story says so. But this doesn't make sense. Maybe the story is a hoax. Then again, maybe it isn't.

Postmodern Wisdom

So what is one to conclude about the story? No answer to this question can avoid having about it some degree of speculation. Only the anonymous author of the story knows how truthful "Debbie" is, and the one person (Dr. Lundberg) who made the decision to publish the story and who knows the author's name is willing and able to keep everyone else in suspense. All we have to go on, then, is a text whose uncertainty undermines and calls into question its own "definitive" account of a situation of life and death. This act of deconstruction coincides with what the text is doing or how it means. As written, the story casts doubt on the author's motivation of mercy by omitting information that could help clarify why the author acted as he/she did. The story also employs a discursive style that, although dear to medicine, only serves to enhance the narrative's ambiguity and undecidability. Moreover, owing to an enigma (the alleged morphine dosage) contained in what presumably is a true account of Debbie's case, the story, when all is said and done, fails to make sense.

With "Debbie," consequently, we have a narrative that denies itself and thus its readers a sense of closure. "It's Over, Debbie" is never over. It is *too* unpresentable, *too* unconventional, *too* uncertain and ambiguous. It continually goes around and around, raising questions about itself and its topic: Is "Debbie" a truth? A fiction? Should euthanasia be legalized? Will society be endangered by such a policy? What about the Hippocratic oath? What about the sanctity of life? What about a patient's quality of life? Don't competent patients have the right to die a dignified death? Is there truly a moral difference between active and passive euthanasia? Is the fast-paced world of high tech medicine conditioning physicians to become ever more insensitive to the needs of those whom they are obliged to serve? How common is double-effect euthanasia? One could go on. "Debbie" is a perpetual rhetorical interruption.

What "Debbie" is doing is *inviting*. With the questions that it raises by way of its uncertainty and ambiguity, the story opens up a space for deliberation and calls for a response, for the production of other texts that perhaps can educate people about matters that inform and motivate the debate on euthanasia but that remain unclear in a story whose "truth" might in fact be a fiction. Could it be that "Debbie" was designed by its author to perform this civic and moral function? Could it be that the story's uncertainty and ambiguity are there on purpose, as they are with existence itself? If this is the case, then what we have with "Debbie" is a type of rhetorical experiment intended to produce, with the help of others, a wide-ranging understanding of the issue of euthanasia. Given all that this understanding entails, one might further characterize "Debbie" as a narrative meant to refine "our sensitivity to differences," to reinforce "our ability to tolerate the incommensurable," and thus to have us display "considerateness" and "forbearance" toward others.[74] This "postmodern" characterization of the narrative heads us in the direction of thinking about it as being an "invention" of some imaginative author.[75] Is this to suggest, then, that "Debbie" is, in truth, a fiction? Well, yes and no.

Having tried so far to be more merciful than murderous in my reading of the text, and still wanting to continue with this approach, I would grant the author the benefit of the doubt and maintain that "Debbie" is at least a fictionalized version of something that may have happened. What this story is doing, how it means, is too unconventional, too uncertain and ambiguous to be only a simple statement of fact. Yet in suggesting that "Debbie" is a fiction, I would not follow those readers who would dismiss this fiction as a "hoax." The story is more truthful than that. Recall, for example, how the discursive style of the story bespeaks a truth of medicine (the telling, with speed and efficiency, of body stories). Having coded this truth into the narrative, the author helps to educate readers about how the values informing this truth can instill in physicians a "technofix" mentality that may inhibit them from "treating their patients as persons." This real and present "danger" is far from being a hoax, and is certainly an issue in the ongoing euthanasia debate.[76]

There is, however, another and related reason why I would not dismiss the author's story as a hoax. Recall that the truth found happening in "Debbie" assumes a deconstructive purpose: the style of the narrative has a role to play in how the text means, in how a "tale" about euthanasia is making things ambiguous and undecidable, and in doing so, is opening up a space for deliberation and inviting a response. Those who accepted this invitation by producing their own texts offer clear evidence that the question of euthanasia is a very controversial matter, that the controversy defines a situation wherein a moral and rhetorical crisis is at hand, and that this crisis, like the story itself, is one filled with uncertainty regarding the issue in question.

With "Debbie," then, we have a narrative whose *way of meaning* speaks to us of something that is really taking place in society. It may thus be said that although this story is offering us an account of a mercy killing, it is also educating us about the uncertainty and ambiguity marking the debate over whether or not euthanasia is a morally justifiable action. This educational process is rooted in what the text is doing, in how it means, in how it sounds a call of conscience. The process is "designed" to have readers give back what is being given to them: controversy, crisis, rhetoric, uncertainty, emotion. "Debbie" calls upon readers to sound its call for the benefit of others. Where art thou? This call is not a hoax; on the contrary, the call has a truthful ring to it. Responses to the story testify to this fact. Here I am!

I am suggesting that "Debbie" is both a fiction and a truth. Its truthfulness is embedded in the very thing that I believe makes it a fiction: what the story is doing rhetorically. How postmodern![77] And this being so, I feel obligated to address a question that was asked of Dr. Lundberg by some of his harshest critics: Was publishing "Debbie" a "responsible way for the prestigious voice of . . . [medicine] to address the subject of medical killing?"[78] The question forced Lundberg's hand. It does the same thing to the rhetorical critic. Lundberg believed the story would "stimulate debate" and thus serve "the greater public good."[79] With this reply in mind, one might think of "Debbie" as being a *pharmakon*. Indeed sustaining the vitality and good judgment of a democratic society requires that its members constantly seek out the "remedy" of collaborative deliberation whenever controversial matters are at hand. A *pharmakon,* however, can also be a poisonous drug.[80] Lundberg's critics saw "Debbie" to be just that. Although I take exception to this diagnosis, I do not believe that it should be summarily dismissed.

"Debbie" is a strange story, if not a potentially dangerous one. As demonstrated in some reader responses, the narrative can be read without seeing anything "wrong" with it.[81] That, I think, is a sign of danger. Even if one believes in the morality of euthanasia, the unprofessional and unethical conduct depicted in the story should not go unnoticed. Lundberg's critics definitely have something going for them here. Fortunately, however, even those individuals who applauded the physician without blinking an eye still offered "good" reasons for doing so. Hence, like those who would silence their voices, or those who would deny Lundberg the right to publish "Debbie," or those who took a position but only after struggling with the dilemmas posed by the text, these particular advocates of euthanasia did contribute something to a debate that *was stimulated* by a strange story.

Dr. Lundberg guessed right. For "the greater public good"? It has been said that the issue of euthanasia calls for as much public moral argument as possible, especially since this issue "goes to the very core of how we will eventually understand what we mean by life and death."[82] To the extent that one adheres to this viewpoint, it would be hard not to offer something of an affirmative response to the question. "It's Over, Debbie" is designed to get readers personally involved in the rhetorical process of public moral argument; answering the many questions raised by the narrative is left to us. There is nothing "wrong" with that. So yes, "Debbie" is a strange and potentially dangerous story, but it is also a good one. Keeping the discussion going about a highly complex and controversial issue is a responsible thing to do. In Heidegger's and Levinas' terms, it is a way to get people to affirm their authenticity and to demonstrate the ethic of being-with-and-for-others.

Yet one might ask: How much controversy is too much controversy? Is there such a thing as a public that is too rhetorically vibrant? Instead of publishing "Debbie," perhaps Lundberg should have presented an essay that was less unpresentable, less threatening to medical authority, and more in line with his profession's claims to veridical communication. This could have added closure to the debate, thereby curtailing controversy.[83] When curtailing controversy, however, authorities run the risk of marginalizing and disempowering voices that, if given the time and space to air their differences, might provide an enriching rhetorical take on a matter of importance. One can only wonder about how much controversy would have been generated had Lundberg decided to assume this risk. As this controversy unfolded, maybe some disempowered rhetor might have had the chance to say something like this: "When discourse is responsible for reality and not merely a reflection of it, then whose discourse prevails makes all the difference."[84] Perhaps Lundberg had this very point in mind when, thinking about all of the discourse that is associated with the "good" life and the "good" death, he chose to publish "Debbie." One might therefore credit Lundberg with possessing what Zygmunt Bauman describes as "postmodern wisdom":

> What the postmodern mind is aware of is that there are problems in human and social life with no good solutions, twisted trajectories that cannot be straightened up, ambivalences that are more than linguistic blunders yelling to be corrected, doubts which cannot be legislated out of existence, moral agonies which no reason-dictated recipes can soothe, let alone cure. The postmodern mind does not expect anymore to find the all-embracing, total and ultimate formula of life without ambiguity, risk, danger and error, and is deeply suspicious of any voice that promises otherwise. . . . The postmodern mind is reconciled to the idea that the messiness of the human predicament is here to stay. This is, in the broadest of outlines, what can be called postmodern wisdom.[85]

Rhetoric with Eloquence

The wisdom spoken of here comes with existence itself, with the way it calls us into question with its call of conscience and thereby challenges us to assume the ethical responsibility of affirming our freedom through resolute choice while at the same time remaining open to the otherness of others. "Debbie" exposes us to this challenging call that, although present in the story, is nevertheless essentially other than a human creation. Both Heidegger and Levinas instruct us about this dimension of otherness that informs our lives. Guided by this instruction, I have argued that the call that comes to us from this dimension is properly heard as being a rhetorical interruption whose epideictic nature and eloquence moves us with its emotional (anxious and joyful) appeal. Is this to suggest, then, that the story of "Debbie" must also contain at least a modicum of eloquent prose?

As can be seen in the responses to the story reported above, readers of "Debbie" felt anxiety and joy over the way a young woman was given rest. What showed forth in the story was for some simply a tragedy and for others a tragedy that still had a decent ending. "Debbie" certainly possesses enough epideictic energy to strike and arouse the hearts of others. Still, "Debbie" is a story that is not "well told": its uncertainty, ambiguity, and lack of carefully formulated arguments make it a "read" that is too simplistic and too unbelievable. At its best, eloquence dedicates itself to revealing the "truth" of something that has yet to be understood and genuinely appreciated for what it is. I have argued that, with respect to the vast number of variables informing the euthanasia debate, there nevertheless is something of the truth to be

found in "Debbie." Is there such a thing as eloquence that is not especially eloquent?

Kenneth Burke tells us that "the great danger in eloquence resides in the
fact that it tends to . . . confine itself to certain usages traditionally ceremoni-
ous;" it thereby derives its "Symbolic charges from the Symbolic charges of . . .
poetic forbears" and, in so doing, risks forfeiting the originality of expression
that is needed to reveal and convey the "new elements" of currently pressing
situations "to which the tradition is not accurately adapted." In short, says
Burke, the eloquent speaker avoids the temptation to rely solely on language
that is familiar and revered and instead seeks to make sure that her observations, arguments, and overall prose are firmly grounded in the situation at
hand. The primary purpose of eloquence is to "covert life" to its "most thorough verbal equivalent."[86]

"Debbie," I think it is fair to say, avoids the danger of which Burke speaks.
The story's rhetoric does not confine itself to certain usages traditionally cer-
emonious. On the contrary, the rhetoric marks out an adventure in breaking
the rules, in being nondecorous, as it obscures a body story with a person story
and a person story with a body story and thereby leaves us guessing about the
genuine presence (face) of a person who is about to die. Who was this person?
What was her whole story? These and the many other questions that are raised
by the story call on the reader to listen carefully to and wonder about a host of
matters. For example, how should people talk with a person who, like Debbie, knows that her or his life "is over"? What is the right thing to say to a person who, perhaps in a day or two, will have "passed on"? I think Bauman is
correct when he notes:

> We do not know what to tell the dying, though we gladly and easily
> conversed with them before. Yes, we feel embarrassed, and to avoid feeling
> ashamed we prefer not to find ourselves in the presence of the dying, though
> before they came to be dying we avidly sought their company and enjoyed
> every moment of togetherness. . . . Indeed, we have nothing to say to a per-
> son who has no further use for the language of survival. . . . We may offer
> the dying only the language of survival; but this is precisely the one language
> which cannot grasp the condition from which they (not unlike us, who may
> still desert them and look the other way) can hide no more.[87]

The face of a dying person speaks to us of a fact of life that most people
would rather forget. In avoiding being in their presence, we deny them the
respect of acknowledgment and thereby run the risk of contributing to the
pain and suffering of their social death, their being further abandoned by loved
ones and friends. If, on the other hand, we do pay them respect with our presence but do not know, beyond uttering the language of survival, what to say to
them, we still may promote their social death by not providing them with an

environment where their voice can be heard and responded to in a genuine way. A person who is dying and for her "peace of mind" wants to talk about her death, funeral arrangements, and perhaps how she is going to miss the presence of others is not being authentically acknowledged if all that is afforded her are words of dispirited encouragement: "Think positive!" "Things are going to be OK!" "As long as you are sick, I'm stuck eating your daughter's cooking!"[88] The language of survival can facilitate social death. And if one agrees with Levinas that the primordial discourse of the face commands "Thou shall not commit murder," then one must admit to committing a crime if one fails to at least alleviate somewhat the social death of a dying person. We are beings who have an obligation to be for others.

Death itself has no sense of decorum; it can come at any time, unexpectedly, and make a real mess of things before it finally has its way. Humankind long ago began dealing with this mess and its accompanying sadness by developing the "art of dying," an art whose rules of right action (decorum) are meant to bring compassion, comfort, and care to those who are about to leave us and to their family members and friends who are already mourning the loss.[89] I read "Debbie" as offering a strange version of this art—one that would have us think about the "good" death by way of a narrative that calls into question its own "appropriateness" and thereby makes us wonder, for example, about the right way in which we should treat those who are dying. In other words, as I have been trying to suggest, "Debbie" functions as a call of conscience whose rhetorical interruption is meant to cause a break in one's thinking about the sanctity of life and the right to die. With this break comes the need to rethink about what, for example, is truly going on in hospitals where patients' rooms are filled with what Debbie's doctor described as "a desperate effort to survive" and where patients are begging for acknowledgment when they say such things as "Let's get this over with."

"Debbie" is artistic in a deconstructionist sort of way. Is this an appropriate way to be when engaging in the euthanasia debate? Indecorously decorous? Crediting such a rhetorical stance with being eloquent may offend those who want to associate eloquence first and foremost with the use of discourse to move the heart toward the truth and who might instead declare: "Debbie" is deceptive, not eloquent! Receiving direction from its Hippocratic colleagues, philosophy has long trained its students to disparage this sophistic strategy.[90] Heidegger certainly carried on the tradition with his characterization of the "inauthentic discourse" (*Gerede*) that conceals the truth of things. And Levinas, as we have seen, goes so far as to equate rhetorical eloquence with deceptiveness.

I, on the other hand, want to say that although the story's deceptiveness is what makes it eloquent, this way of being is not necessarily unethical and immoral. "Debbie" speaks of the truth in a way that encourages others to join the conversation and the debate. The story calls on the potential of their authenticity and their being for others. The rhetoric of "Debbie" is not without eloquence, not without a way of being given over to the saying of truth—a saying that the story calls on others to contribute to and thereby to "convert life" to its "most thorough verbal equivalent." The rhetorical eloquence of "Debbie" sounds this call with what it does and does not say about a controversy that is at least as old as the teachings of Hippocrates and that, even as I now write, continues to be as intense as it has ever been. "Debbie" tells the story of this controversy with a narrative whose uncertainty, ambiguity, and deconstructive thrust inform the story's own controversial admission. The story speaks of an emotional controversy by way of an emotional controversy.

Recall that Heidegger, when commending Aristotle's *Rhetoric*, emphasizes how the orator "must understand the possibilities of moods in order to rouse them and guide them in a right and just manner" (BT 178). Rhetoric, in other words, is not merely a tool for cultivating "idle talk." Recall also Levinas' observation that "art seeks to give a face to things, and in this its greatness and its deceit simultaneously reside" (DF 8). "Debbie" is a story whose rhetoric is meant to operate in what Heidegger termed the "everydayness" of existence (see chapter 1)—that realm of daily life wherein we display the "know-how" of practical wisdom. As it becomes more understandable with the responses it calls for, the eloquence of this rhetoric shows forth something of the "face," the controversy, of the euthanasia debate. With this display comes "deceit," but for a "good" reason: to uncover in a moving way the truth about a matter of life and death.

The euthanasia debate is filled with stories that span the range from being gut wrenching and tragic to being loving and hopeful. In my study of this debate I have yet, however, to come across a story that is as strange as "Debbie." This strangeness, as I have tried to suggest, is rooted in the story's never-ending capacity to be deconstructive in its sounding of the call of conscience. Like existence itself, "Debbie" presents us with the challenge of being called into question, and of having to respond so as to maintain some sense of order in our lives. When the well-known advocate of euthanasia, Dr. Jack Kevorkian (a.k.a. "Dr. Death") chose to comment on the story, he called it a "farce" and accused the AMA of "trying—much too late and too ineptly—to pretend that it had been a champion of, or at least sympathetic to, free dialogue all along."[91] Although I do not find Kevorkian's reading to be especially elucidating, his response does make me a bit paranoid. The AMA has long stood against the euthanasia movement. What if the author of "Debbie" is a conscientious member of the AMA, or at least someone who supports the organization's thinking on "mercy killing," and who submitted the story with the sole purpose of discrediting the integrity of those who believe in, and would write about, the importance of dying a dignified death? Is "Debbie" the product of a conspiracy? Leave it to Kevorkian, who will be dealt with in greater detail later on, to enhance the potential strangeness of the narrative.

Or perhaps the author of "Debbie" is, in fact, a staunch member of the right-to-die movement who hoped all along that his/her story would eventually be read as a piece that points to one of the supposedly unethical ways that the right-to-life movement conducts its business. The conspiracy thickens, and the deconstructive, rhetorical eloquence of "Debbie" does nothing to prevent a reader from thinking about the story in such a mind-boggling manner. Indeed "Debbie" would have its readers do most of the talking about the controversy at hand. It is our right. Existence calls us into question and thereby also calls us to respond, to rethink, and perhaps to reconstruct our everyday way of being who we are and of being with and for others. "Debbie" commends the process by offering itself as a "well-written" narrative lacking clear definitions and carefully formulated arguments.

But the call of conscience that comes from existence and its otherness and that calls us into question challenges us to produce such rhetorical creations so that we might build and rebuild traditions that are sensible, good, and just. Deconstruction is only half of the story when it comes to hearing and responding to the call of conscience. Reconstruction must also go on if human beings are to counter the dis-ease and anxiety that are there to be felt when our lives break down and when we must then confront the freedom and responsibility that comes with our finitude and thus with who we are as beings who owe something special (acknowledgment) to others. The call that asks "Where art thou?" needs to be addressed in a positive manner: "Here I am!" The next three chapters offer a closer look at how such reconstruction takes form in the euthanasia debate.

Chapter 5

Reconstruction

Emotions, Definitions, Arguments, and Stories

Heidegger tells us that "The ultimate business of philosophy is to preserve *the force of the most elemental words* in which Dasein expresses itself, and to keep common understanding from levelling them off to that unintelligibility which functions in turn as a source of pseudo-problems" (BT 262). I think it is fair to say that *Being and Time* and the many other works that Heidegger produced as he continued his investigation of the question of Being were devoted to carrying out his profession's ultimate business. Life, death, time, truth, conscience, language: these are but some of the most elemental words that demanded Heidegger's attention. Levinas too showed great respect for such words and, in so doing, struggled to make sure, for example, that the "otherness of others" (alterity) received more genuine acknowledgment than that given to it by Heidegger.

The ultimate business of philosophy is present in the euthanasia debate. Those who want to contribute to the debate have an obligation to know at least something about that which they would speak: life, death, time, truth, conscience, ... Within the euthanasia debate these and related topics are commonly coded as the "right to life," the "right to die," "mercy killing," "death with dignity," the "good life," and the "good death." The story of "Debbie" is about the codes at work here; it seeks to uncover what they are and thereby encourages a question: Do we truly know what we mean when we employ the rhetoric of these codes to clarify our stance on the morality or immorality of euthanasia?

In his award-winning book, *How We Die: Reflections on Life's Final Chapter,* the physician Sherwin B. Nuland reads "Debbie" as being a true story that shames the medical profession.[1] In going on to discuss how Debbie's physician was engaged in a "misconceived mission of mercy," Nuland has occasion to emphasize how important it is to keep the conversation going about the practice of euthanasia. He writes: "In the United States and democratic countries in general, the importance of airing differing viewpoints rests not in the probability that a stable consensus will ever be reached but in the recognition that it will not. It is by studying the shades of opinion expressed in such discussions that we become aware of considerations in decision-making that may never have weighed in our soul-searching." Nuland maintains, however, that "Unlike

the debates, which certainly belong in the public arena, the decisions themselves will always properly be made in the tiny, impenetrable sphere of personal conscience. And this is exactly as it should be."[2]

Although I find Nuland's book to be worthy of all the praise it received, I
must admit that on certain matters he seems a bit confused. "Debbie" *is* a story
given over to soul-searching and to having people speak their minds such that
they too may have a say in the matter at hand. Moreover, as Hans Zbinden
reminds us, in the United States and democratic countries in general, this is
how citizens contribute to the moral ecology or "collective conscience" of their
communities; the workings of conscience are not confined to an "impenetrable sphere" inside the person.[3] On the contrary, notes Zbinden, although it
may be said that conscience "expresses the personal makeup of the individual,
mirroring in weakness or in victory that which is unique in his nature," it also
"bears the features of the society, the epoch, and the tradition, as well as the
environment, in which a man lives." The language of conscience is not simply
derived from the "intrapersonal" realm of one's existence. In emphasizing the
importance of this point, Zbinden writes: "Conscience has a language. It
speaks. At times it whispers, at other times it cries out. What it says is influenced by the everyday, as well as by the artistic, language of the times. Whenever language loses its clarity, conscience also forfeits some of its power. Flat,
worn-out words are blunt weapons for its use. This is why reverence for the
word and education for a wide-awake and keen-eared sense of language are
prerequisites for the formation of conscience."[4]

What Zbinden is saying here about the relationship between conscience
and language certainly receives ontological and metaphysical support in the
writings of both Heidegger and Levinas. The call of conscience comes to us
from our temporal existence and beyond and it is heard and responded to
under the influence of our everyday way of being with and for others. Granting that the ultimate business of philosophy includes preserving the force of
those most elemental words that define most clearly what is going on when
conscience calls, I think it is fair to say that both Heidegger and Levinas would
thus applaud Zbinden's claim that "whenever language loses its clarity, conscience also forfeits some of its power"; hence, philosophy's obligation "to keep
common understanding from levelling" and thus degrading the true meaning
of the call of conscience and all that goes with it.

In the introduction I discussed how philosophy's long-standing conflict
with rhetoric is rooted in its unhesitating commitment to this obligation.
There too, with the help of Cicero and his civic republican outlook, I noted
how the rhetorical tradition not only acknowledges the importance of this but,
in so doing, also directs philosophy toward the recognition of another essential moral obligation: if the wisdom of philosophy is to have any practical appli-

cation to the everyday dealings of human beings, it must remain open to the teachings of the "art of eloquence" (*oratio*) concerning how to equip (*ornare*) knowledge of a subject in such a way that it can assume a publicly accessible form and function effectively in the sociopolitical arena. To be sure, even if they are only talking to their fellow "experts" and students, philosophers still need rhetorical competence if they are to make known in an understandable and persuasive way what is on their minds regarding some matter of importance.[5]

With what I have said so far about Heidegger's and Levinas' respective thinking on the call of conscience, it should be clear that this call, in its very way of functioning, demands responsible thought and action and the rhetorical competence that can bring the two together and move them in the right direction. The call of conscience and the practice of rhetoric go hand in hand—so much so, in fact, that, as I have argued, the call shows itself as a rhetorical happening. The call of conscience calls for what it, itself, is: a saying/speaking that discloses the truth of something and does so in a compelling and thus moving way. With the call of conscience there comes the most primordial form of epideictic and eloquent discourse that there is.

Although both Heidegger and Levinas help one to grasp the intricate nature of the relationship between the call of conscience and the practice of rhetoric, neither expend much effort illustrating how this relationship manifests itself in the everydayness of our lives and thus in that realm of sociopolitical practice where, by way of collaborative moral deliberation, the self must learn to come to terms with others, the "they," the "third." The story of "Debbie" exemplifies how this process can be carried out in a most deconstructive way. But let us not forget that when it comes to the call of conscience, deconstruction is only one half of the story; for this call also summons us to engage in the process of reconstruction, of building and rebuilding worlds of meaning, morality, and justice. For a being whose lived body is not everlasting, deconstruction without reconstruction is but the anxiety of Being-unto-death with no way out.

In the euthanasia debate the rhetorical process of reconstruction centers around a life-threatening act of deconstruction: the physiological and psychological well-being of a person is breaking (or already has broken) down because of some illness or accident. Difficult, if not heart-breaking, existential questions thereby present themselves. "Debbie" acquaints us with many of these questions. Allow me now, however, to have you think once again about some of these questions by placing you in a factually based set of circumstances that should make matters more personal. Like most things going on in the world, the euthanasia debate really becomes meaningful only when, as they say, "it hits close to home."

Suppose that your physician has just received some laboratory findings on tests that were taken during your annual medical checkup. The findings are definitive; they show that you have contracted an incurable and fatal disease. Your life expectancy, at best, is two to five years. Sometime during the next twelve months, as your central nervous system begins to degenerate, you will become noticeably lethargic and your motor skills will decline. Then, during the following year, you will become blind, experience petite mal seizures lasting for several seconds, be unable to eat because of the deterioration of your respiratory and digestive systems, and suffer mental retardation and complete paralysis. Your physician informs you of these findings; there is nothing more she can do at the present time beyond compassionately explaining what sorts of medical, psychological, and social service care can be made available to you and your family as the disease progresses. The cost of this care will be substantial. Now the questions: Has the awareness of your disease and its prognosis presently put an end to your "good life"? If not now, then might this end present itself during the course of the disease? If so, would your life still be worth living? If you decided that your life was no longer worth living, what would you do?

It is important that you formulate answers to these questions before reading on; so please do so. Commit your thoughts to paper. Once this is done you should have before you "sensible" discourse that offers a reconstructive reply to an event of deconstruction. You will have occasion to refer to your reconstruction as this chapter progresses.

The illness I have given you is real, although anyone who can read what I have been writing need not fear its actual affliction on your body. The illness is known as Tay-Sachs disease, a hereditary disorder which occurs primarily in Jewish infants of eastern European ancestry. Medical authorities have acknowledged that for Tay-Sachs, with its well-demonstrated early mortality and with science's technological ability to verify its presence in the fetus, the decision to terminate pregnancy "is a relatively easy one."[6] And in accordance with the landmark case of Roe v. Wade ([1973] 410 U.S. 113, 93 S. Ct. 705, 35 L. Ed.2d 147), the infant's mother would have the right to enact this decision.

If you and your partner conceived a child stricken with Tay-Sachs disease, what would you do? Would you answer for the child as you did just a minute or so ago when thinking about your good life? The most altruistic reason for aborting the fetus would be that no one deserves to live and die in such a horrible way. Here, abortion would become an act of involuntary euthanasia since the fetus is unable to speak for itself. Unlike abortion, however, involuntary euthanasia is not protected by the law. And consider this: A child born with Tay-Sachs may experience nearly a year of "normal" life before things take a noticeable turn for the worse. During that time do you think you could help your child experience pleasure, joy, love? Would it thus be worth keeping the child alive? Could you then afford all that was yet to come?

I asked you to think about yourself. I then asked you to think about the other. Especially when read together, Heidegger and Levinas emphasize the importance of such related thinking. The self and the other are topics that are forever being raised in the euthanasia debate. Are your thoughts the same in both cases? What if the other was not your child but rather the child of a stranger? Should that make a difference? If taken to heart and thought about seriously, all of the questions I am asking here should provoke some type of emotional response. Dealing with death can be handled with all forms of institutionalized rhetoric (scientific, religious, for example), but at bottom the issue is fundamentally existential and thus emotional. The call of conscience that comes with the breakdown of our lived bodies makes clear that we are beings who are "blessed" with the ability to experience and be overwhelmed by our finitude. The emotion that is most likely to be at work here is anxiety. Should we rejoice over the fact that this most disquieting of emotions can be easily dealt with if we are allowed and helped to die a "dignified" death? When the breakdown of our bodies sounds a call of conscience—"Where art thou?"—what is the best way of saying "Here I am!"

Those who believe in the morality of euthanasia have at their disposal a long-cultivated rhetoric for offering an affirmative answer to the question. Those who believe in the immorality of the act also have a rich rhetorical tradition from which to counter such an answer. Both rhetorics are meant to deal with a situation arising from an event of deconstruction; both rhetorics are filled with what it takes to reconstruct the broken lives in question here by acknowledging their plight and providing them with "reasonable" solutions. Hence, like any debate conducted by passionate, committed, and rational people, the euthanasia debate is composed of "precise" definitions, "logically sound" arguments, and "well-told stories," all of which are put forth to tell the truth and to help others judge correctly about the good life and the good death.

In the rest of this chapter, I discuss how such a rhetoric of reconstruction is at work in the euthanasia debate. The rhetorical artifacts emphasized here represent what I have found to be the three major genres of discourse that inform the debate: religious, analytic/scientific, and existential.[7] Moreover, I chose these specific artifacts because of how they exemplify, especially when read together, the emotional, definitional, argumentative, and narrational nature of reconstructive rhetoric at work in the euthanasia debate. In order to add a degree of manageability to my inquiry, attention is focused primarily on a specific matter that no one involved in the debate can afford to leave unattended and undefined: "human dignity." To control the discourse that is used to clarify and demonstrate what this matter is all about is to maintain an advantage of power in the debate; for as should become clear as this chapter continues to unfold, "dignity" is something that is essential to humankind's well-being and spiritual welfare.

The Dignity of Human Being: An Emotional Matter

In its spring 1988 newsletter, the Hemlock Society of Illinois featured a contribution from the Reverend Robert Fraser titled "A Plea for the Right to Die with Dignity":

> Medical Science is my shepherd:
> I shall not want.
> It maketh me to lie down in hospital beds;
> It leadeth me beside the marvels of technology;
> It restoreth my brain waves.
> It maintains me in a persistent vegetative state for its name sake.
> Yea, though I walk through the valley of the shadow of death,
> I shall find no end to life;
> For thou art with me:
> Thy respirator and thy heart machine, they sustain me.
> Thou preparest intravenous feeding for me
> In the presence of irreversible disability;
> Thou anointest my head with oil;
> My cup runneth on and on and on and on and on.
> Surely coma and unconsciousness shall follow me all the days of my continued breathing,
> And I will dwell in the intensive-care unit forever.[8]

What we have here, of course, is a rhetorical transformation of the Twenty-third Psalm—a psalm of King David's confidence in the grace of God that was not intended to be an effort in tragic irony, as in Fraser's presentation. Rabbi David J. Wolpe provides some background that will be helpful for what I have to say about the particular rhetorical artifact before us:

> The Jewish tradition teaches that most of the Psalms were written by King David. The attribution adds poignancy to those remarkable poems. They are not the product of someone removed from the rough-and-tumble of life. These songs are not ornaments of a quiet soul contemplating the world distant from the hum of the marketplace. The Psalms are steeped in the real world of human beings. Their texture is the coarse-grained substance of lessons wrung from experience, from struggle and survival.[9]

With his use of the Twenty-third Psalm, Reverend Fraser sounds a plea echoing the Hemlock Society's supportive stance on active voluntary euthanasia for the terminally ill. People who can no longer bear the pain and suffering that accompanies the deconstruction of their bodies have "the right to die with dignity." But what exactly does this mean? (Do your answers to the earlier questions answer this last one?)

Fraser offers no formal and explicit definition of what he calls for; rather, his plea is more of an evocation than a well-defined argument. The difference between these two rhetorical processes was noted in chapter 3 when quoting Raphael Demos on the matter. Recall that evocation "is the process by which vividness is conveyed; it is the presentation of a viewpoint in such a manner that it becomes real for the public." Recall too that "an argument has much less persuasive force than the vivid evocation of an experience. The enumeration of all the relevant points in favor of a theory and against its opposite can never be completed; far more effective is it to state a viewpoint in all its concreteness and in all its significant implication, and then stop." According to Demos, "arguments become relevant only after this state has been concluded."[10]

Fraser's discourse, I suspect, is meant to evoke an emotional response—one that is quite common and simple to say, despite all that it entails: "God forbid!" The Twenty-third Psalm expresses confidence in God, the "shepherd" who, in King David's words, "restoreth my soul," protects me from my "enemies," and allows "goodness and mercy" to "follow me all the days of my life." In the euthanasia debate one is more likely to hear how God is on the side of those who advocate God's greatest gift—the sanctity of life—than on the side of those extolling the rhetoric of the right to die: God gave us the gift of life, and only God has the right to take it away. Euthanasia is a sin because the act allows *us* to "play God." But is not such a sin also at work when, for example, we intervene in the ways of the Almighty in an attempt to cure a disease and save a life? David Hume was the first to make this point over two hundred years ago: "Were the disposal of human life so much reserved as the peculiar providence of the almighty that it were an encroachment on his right, for men to dispose of their own lives; it would be equally criminal to act for the preservation of life as for its destruction. If I turn aside a stone which is falling upon my head, I disturb this course of nature, and I invade the peculiar providence of the almighty by lengthening out my life beyond the period which by the general laws of matter and motion he had assigned to it."[11]

Hume co-opts the position he opposes by using its own logic against it. The contradiction surfaces as soon as one who is against "playing God" admits, for example, that he or she ever sought assistance from medicine when plagued by some illness, thereby interfering with providence by allowing people who are playing God to "invade" his or her existence. To remedy this contradiction, we would have to abolish the practice of medicine. With the possible exception of those who adhere strictly to such doctrinal teachings as Christian Science, I think most people would consider such a remedy to be absurd. Certainly many of them would not be around to make the argument that only God has the right to determine how long a life shall last. Hence, for Hume it is best to "thank providence, both for the good, which I have already enjoyed, and for the power, with which I am endowed, of escaping the ill that threatens me."[12]

And what is this power? I think it is fair to say that it is nothing if it is not at least that (God-given?) ability that both Heidegger and Levinas analyzed in great detail: the ability to assume the ethical responsibility of affirming one's freedom through resolute choice. Fraser addresses the issue by employing a holy text that is, as Rabbi Wolpe put it, "steeped in the real world of human beings" and whose "texture is the coarse-grained substance of lessons wrung from experience, from struggle and survival," and thus from an author's (King David's) ongoing challenge of having to assume the ethical responsibility of his freedom of choice (having confidence in God's ways). Human dignity presupposes the ability to meet this challenge. From a religious perspective, dignity is the "good" that we can display as we struggle to do what we will with all that God has given and keeps giving us. It is a matter of hearing and responding to the Almighty's call of conscience.

Fraser writes about the tragic loss of human dignity that can accompany the miraculous use of medical science and technology. Medicine can sustain a patient even if his "irreversible disability" places him "in a persistent vegetative state." A person in this state, however, has run out of choices. For him freedom is not even "another word for nothing left to lose." He has no freedom, for he has no temporal existence to speak of. The related challenges of authenticity and moral responsibility, and all the emotions that can accompany them, are gone; they began to vanish as soon as the person started to lose the ability to think about himself, about his thoughts and actions and how they affect others. In short, a patient who is forced to "exist" in a persistent vegetative state no longer qualifies as being that particular being (Dasein) who can hear and respond to the call of conscience. One might therefore conclude, as I certainly think Fraser would have us do, that in such a case the patient in question has lost that which the author pleads for: freedom of choice, authenticity, moral responsibility, being with and for others—basic aspects of human being that make possible human dignity and that are no longer at work for one who is fated to "dwell in the intensive-care unit forever" because he is "a vegetable."

Fraser speaks indirectly of dignity and of the sin of playing God at one and the same time. He supplies us with a rhetorical artifact whose religious tone helps to call into question certain consequences of health care that can result when medicine goes too far in its attempt to prolong life rather than death. As noted in previous chapters, medicine, given its scientific capabilities to save lives, was taught by its Hippocratic ancestors to think of itself as being "god-like." Yet as also previously noted, medicine's Hippocratic ancestors produced an "oath" emphasizing how physicians must "do no harm." This injunction is not an invention of science; rather, it is rooted in Pythagorean religious beliefs that emphasize, among other things, that assisted suicide, as well as an unrestricted zeal to keep people alive even when their plight is hopeless, are sacrilegious and thus immoral acts. The Reverend Fraser writes in such a way that a reader might think about how medical science, which has long prided itself on its progressive movement away from religious superstitions, still must be mindful of religion in order to do the right thing. Like Hume before him, Fraser uses religion to call into question its fanatic use by those who, in its name, would rather err on the side of "life" than on the side of death, and who thus would risk sacrificing a patient's dignity.

There is, to be sure, something deconstructive about Fraser's maneuver here. He is calling into question the momentum and consistency of a worldview that proves to be unclear about how life and dignity ought to go together. The author of "Debbie" did the same thing. In Fraser's case, however, the deconstructive workings of his rhetoric are not without a vital reconstructive component. By way of an effort in rhetorical ingenuity, Fraser is making a point about dignity, about what it is *and* is not. Dignity is associated with the fundamental way that we dwell on earth, as beings gifted with the capacity to be awed and moved by what nature and other beings have to offer us. The dignity of human being comes with this being's struggle to survive in the everyday world, even if this world is no larger than the close confines of a patient's room in an intensive care unit. With Heidegger, we learn that this struggle is never without some emotion to sustain its energy. With Levinas, we learn how essential the "other" is to the entire process. Fraser would have us get caught up in the emotional debate over what we owe to others (and ourselves) when the issue of "the right to die with dignity" is before us. Although he supplies us with no explicit definition of his topic, the rhetorical workings of his discourse help to make clear that he knows where to draw the line when it comes to deciding the issue.

This, of course, is how definitions are created: by using symbols "to draw a line around" (*definire*) something so to mark its meaningful borders.[13] Fraser's definition of dignity has ontology, metaphysics, and religion on its side. And as he develops this definition, he simultaneously puts forth an argument for the need to respect what makes us the moral beings that we are: we have a right to live and die with dignity—a right that comes with the gift of existence, a gift that opens us to ourselves, to others, to the not yet, and thereby grants us the opportunity and power of freedom of choice, of being responsible, of acting in ways that build moral character (*ethos*) and thereby warrant being called dignified.[14]

Perhaps this reading of Fraser's rhetorical endeavor squares with the answers I asked you to formulate earlier. Or perhaps your answers have changed along the way? In any case, let us be clear that Fraser is answering the call of conscience with a rhetorical interruption that deconstructs and reconstructs a way for acknowledging the dignity of human being. He has designed a discourse that takes advantage of one's "knowledge" of a psalm that, like the scene he constructs with his discourse, is steeped in the rough and tumble of life. He offers neither a well-defined and rigorous philosophical argument nor a scholarly religious assessment of what his appropriated psalm means. Rather, the rhetorical function of his language is evocative, epideictic, emotional, and enthymematic. I include this last rhetorical attribute in order to made a certain point. The use of *enthymematic* reasoning allows a rhetor to employ a way of thinking that invites audience participation. The deconstructive workings of Fraser's discourse promote this invitation, but they do so in order to have his audience become open to his plea for the right to die with dignity. The enthymeme correlates with the Greek term *enthumeisthai* or "taking something to heart [to the *thumos*]." Fraser is sounding a call of conscience designed to be effective in the everyday world. In Heidegger's words, he is an orator who, having tried to understand the "possibility of moods" associated with a specific issue, is now trying "to rouse them and guide them in a right and just manner" (SZ 138–39).[15]

Although he sounds his call so as to have readers understand that God is on his side, one does not have to be religious to accept Fraser's sense of things. The "empirical" evidence supporting his position is certainly there to be found in the very presence, the authenticity, of human being (Dasein)—its temporality, emotional makeup, freedom, responsibility—and the alterity that always accompanies this intricate presence. Take away religion and it is still possible to conceive of dignity. Heidegger certainly teaches us as much. But does not the marvel of our *even being able to recognize* human dignity point to something that both transcends and makes possible its existence? Heidegger allows for this possibility, and Levinas is quite willing to encourage an affirmative answer to the question.

From Emotion to a Well-Defined Argument

So is it the case that we have a right to die with dignity (and with God's blessing)? The physician and highly regarded bioethicist Leon R. Kass would have us think about this question in light of a more well-defined argument than that offered by the Reverend Fraser. In one of his many (and what I take to be the most important and specific) essays on the topic, Kass sets up his position in the following way: "Although many look forward to further triumphs in [medicine's] war against mortality, others want here and now to exercise greater control over the end of life, by electing death to avoid the burdens of lingering on. The failures resulting from the fight against fate are to be resolved by taking fate still further into our own hands." Kass then goes on to emphasize that "this is no joking matter. Nor are the questions it raises academic."[16] Moreover, the situation is not as straightforward as those like Fraser, with his depiction of a brain-dead patient, make it out to be.

> Shall I allow the doctors to put a feeding tube into my eighty-five-year-old mother, who is unable to swallow as a result of a stroke? Now that it is inserted and she is not recovering, may I have it removed? When would it be right to remove a respirator, forgo renal dialysis, bypass life-saving surgery, or omit giving antibiotics for pneumonia? When in the course of my own progressive dementia will it be right for my children to put me into a home or for me to ask my doctor or my wife or my daughter for a lethal injection? When, if ever, should I as a physician or husband or son accede to—or be forgiven for acceding to—such a request? (117–18)

Kass stresses that these dilemmas and "their human significance" are "hard to capture in words." For "speech does not begin to convey the anguish and heartache felt by those who concretely confront such terrible decisions, nor can it do much to aid and comfort them. . . . No amount of philosophizing is going to substitute for discernment, compassion, courage, sobriety, tact, thoughtfulness, or prudence—all needed on the spot." Still, Kass admits that "the attitudes, sentiments, and judgments of human agents on the spot are influenced, often unwittingly, by speech and opinion and by the terms in which we formulate our concerns" (118). Another way of making this admission is to say what I have been stressing all along: the call of conscience admits the influence of rhetoric. Commenting on this influence, Kass notes:

> Some speech may illuminate, other speech may distort; some terms may be more or less appropriate to the matter at hand. About death and dying, once subjects treated with decorous or superstitious silence, there is today an abundance of talk—not to say indecorous chatter. Moreover, this talk frequently proceeds under the aegis of certain increasingly accepted terminologies, which are, in my view, both questionable in themselves and dangerous in their influence. As a result, we are producing a recipe for disaster: urgent difficulties, great human anguish, and high emotions, stirred up with inadequate thinking. We have no choice but to reflect on our speech and our terminology. (118)

Indecorous chatter (*Gerede,* or "idle talk") that is questionable, dangerous, a recipe for disaster, and that is emotionally stirred up with inadequate thinking. Plato spoke this way of the rhetoric of the Sophists—those teachers of oratory who, unlike the genuine Socratic soul, were more concerned with taking advantage of the way the meanings of words "fluctuate" than with getting at the "truth" about some subject by first isolating it in a precise definition (*Phaedrus* 263b,

277b). Socrates taught Plato and others about this matter by referring them to the "scientific" practice of speech advocated by Hippocrates and his students. Instead of being taken with the rhetorical wordplay of those like the Reverend Fraser, Kass would have us carry on this tradition of philosophical/medical thought as we involve ourselves in the euthanasia debate. And for Kass, the proper way to begin this task is to become clear about the nature of human dignity, especially as it concerns the "right to die" and what, according to Kass, is typically and erroneously defined in the euthanasia debate as its polar opposite: the "sanctity of life."

As he works out this entire matter Kass shows himself to be an exceptionally caring and learned thinker involved in the scientific practice of speech. He takes us beyond Fraser's emotional depiction of an undignified life/death by offering an intricate yet compelling argument whose call of conscience is meant to put an end to at least some of the "indecorous chatter" that is contaminating the moral climate of the euthanasia debate. For Kass "death with dignity, understood as living dignifiedly in the face of death, is not a matter of pulling plugs or taking poison. To speak this way . . . is to shrink still further the notion of human dignity, and thus heap still greater indignity upon the dying, beyond all the insults of illness and the medicalized bureaucratization of the end of life." Hence, Kass argues: "If it is really death with dignity we are after, we must think in human and not technical terms" (135).

In continuing to discuss and critically assess how Kass performs this act of rhetorical reconstruction below, I do not attempt to include every one of the many rich insights he has to share as he lays out an intricate argument that is, of course, meant to be persuasive. Kass's unfolding position is consistently thought-provoking and at times mesmerizing, and he ends up drawing a rather large line around those subjects that he confidently defines. But the wisdom and rhetorical competence that makes this all possible are not beyond question, especially when one is able to step back from the momentum of his argument and see what is being symbolically manipulated and marginalized with his definitions. My reading of Kass is intended to do just that.

This is not to suggest, however, that I perceive Kass to be an unethical scientific practitioner of speech. On the contrary, for me Kass is a philosophical and rhetorical touchstone who provides valuable guidance for the reconstruction that is needed in the euthanasia debate. But when one takes on the task of constructing a well-defined argument, manipulation and marginalization are necessarily at hand, no matter how perfect one attempts to be. For as Kenneth Burke so often reminds us, although definitions constitute vocabularies intended to be "reflections" of reality, they also at the same time are "selections" of reality. And any selection of reality must function as a "deflection" of reality, whereby the beginnings of manipulation and marginalization begin to take form.[17] Kass sees such a process going on in much of the rhetoric of the euthanasia debate, "though seldom with any regard . . . for the meaning and ground" of the related powerful notions of death with dignity and the sanctity of life (120). Kass intends to solve this problem. I intend to expose something of the way in which he goes about doing this as he involves himself in a rhetorical process that he wants to improve. I also intend to make generous use of Kass's discourse in order to give readers a decent and fair sense of his argument and rhetorical competence.[18]

The Meaning and Ground of Human Dignity

Kass is perfectly clear about where he stands: "Proponents of euthanasia do not understand human dignity, which, at best, they confuse with humaneness." This confusion, according to Kass, shows itself in one of the proponents' favorite arguments: "Why, they say, do we put animals out of their misery but insist on compelling fellow human beings to suffer to the bitter end? Why, if it is not a contradiction for the veterinarian, does the medical ethic absolutely rule out mercy killing? Is this not simply inhumane?" "Perhaps inhumane," admits Kass, "but not thereby inhuman." Kass's elaboration of this point is worth noting: "On the contrary, it is precisely because animals are not human that we must treat them (merely) humanely. We put dumb animals to sleep because they do not know that they are dying, because they can make nothing of their misery or mortality, and therefore, because they cannot live deliberately—that is, humanly—in the face of their own suffering or dying. They cannot live out a fitting end" (138). For Kass, human dignity shows itself as people struggle to reach such an end, and euthanasia has no role to play in this struggle. Human dignity calls for "the bolstering of the human," not its elimination; for such dignity, as its Latin root *dignitas* suggests, speaks to us of "worthiness, elevation, honor, nobility, height—in short, of excellence or virtue" (133).

When Kass first introduces readers to how he specifically intends to lay out his argument about human dignity and thereby move them toward a well-grounded understanding of the matter, he readily admits that he has no illusions about the ability of his reflections to resolve the "horrible dilemmas" involved with the euthanasia debate. "In fact," he writes, "I have no intention here even to try to resolve them. On the contrary, I want rather to increase the difficulty by showing the dangers in sloppy and simplistic thinking" (119), especially as such thinking characterizes the rhetoric of those who demand the right to die a dignified death.

People who make their living as "deconstructionist" critics are in the business of increasing the difficulty of whatever matters are at hand. But Kass is no deconstructionist, and he loathes the type of "postmodern" philosophy that such a critical stance supports.[19] Yes, Kass is quite adept at making things difficult for advocates of euthanasia; but when all is said and done, one realizes that, to the contrary, Kass has every intention of trying to resolve certain dilemmas associated with the euthanasia debate. He keeps our expectations low by first sounding like a deconstructionist. This sets up readers to be perhaps pleasantly surprised as they receive the "positive" direction that was never promised. The rhetorical competence at work here draws energy and influence from the ontological dynamics of human existence: we are always being challenged by our *own* existence to hear and respond to the call of conscience—which calls us into question with deconstructive force and summons us to reconstruct our lives by assuming the ethical burden of freedom of choice. We thus are always in the position to be pleasantly surprised and to feel relieved and good as we find some success in answering this summons. Human being has something fundamentally deconstructive and reconstructive about it. Kass takes advantage of this fact by putting it to "good" use throughout his discourse. As he deconstructs, he also reconstructs. He has something "positive" to offer readers, something that grants them hope—the very thing we all need in order to live through major disruptions in our lives, especially when these disruptions get us to think about our final moments.

Kass is no supporter of the "right to die." Listen to some of what he has to say about this so-called right, which he deconstructs during a discussion of the right to refuse life-prolonging treatment:

> Roughly two decades ago, faced with the unwelcome fact of excessive medical efforts to forestall death, people asserted and won a right to refuse life-prolonging treatment found to be useless or burdensome. This was, in fact, a reaffirmation of the rights to liberty and pursuit of happiness, even in the face of imminent death. It enabled dying patients to live as they wished, free of unwelcome intrusions, and to let death come when it would. Today, the demand has been raised: we find people asserting not just a right to refuse burdensome treatment but a positive "right to die," grounded not in objective conditions regarding prognosis or the uselessness of treatment, but in the supremacy of choice itself. In the name of choice, people claim the right to choose to cease to be choosing beings. From such a right to refuse not only treatment but life itself—from a right to become dead—it is then a small step to the right to be *made* dead: from my right to die will follow your duty to assist me in dying, that is, to become the agent of my death, if I am not able, or do not wish, to kill myself.

This "small step," of course, places one on the "slippery slope" leading from passive to active euthanasia. Kass argues that in addition to endangering the moral well-being of society, the step itself is illogical: "Since *all* of our so-called natural or human rights presuppose our self-interested and self-loving *attachment* to our own *lives*—the foundational right, after all, is the right of self-

preservation—attempts to derive therefrom any 'right to die' or a right to be made dead are not only groundless but self-contradictory" (119).

With all that he is saying here, Kass is setting up his major move to define human dignity. His deconstruction of the "right to die" is designed to pay off later on (as he surprises our expectations) as well as right now. That is, with his rhetorical interruption of the "rallying cry" of the pro-euthanasia movement, he discredits a "well-known" understanding of "right" and "freedom of choice" and their relationship that is crucial to the movement's integrity and that has religion (at least when understood in a certain way) and philosophy (for example, existentialism, phenomenology, hermeneutics, deconstructionism) to support it. For Kass the freedom and right to choose, or what he also describes as "human will," is not the "supreme principle" on which to determine the morality or immorality of euthanasia. Rather, this principle presupposes another more fundamental one. Kass puts it this way: "Individuals strive to stay alive, both consciously and unconsciously. The living body, quite on its own, bends every effort to maintain its living existence. The built-in impulses toward self-preservation and individual well-being that penetrate our consciousness, say, as hunger or fear of death, are manifestations of a deep-seated and powerful will to live. . . . Beneath the human will, indeed, the *ground* of human will, is [*this* will to live—] something that commands respect and restraint, willy-nilly" (124–25).

Kass contends that it is the "will to live" that defines the most essential and thus "sacred" aspect of human being (hence "the sanctity of life") and that makes possible human dignity and thus "the possibilities for human excellence," *dignitas*. "*Full* dignity, or dignity properly so called, would depend on the *realization* of these possibilities" (133). Kass points out that this realization has long been associated with "man's divine-like status"; for human beings are capable of demonstrating dignity by way of those "divine *activities* and *powers*" that, as recorded in Genesis 1, are at work as God calls life into being: "(1) God speaks, commands, names, and blesses; (2) God makes and makes freely; (3) God looks at and beholds the world; (4) God is concerned with the goodness or perfection of things; (5) God addresses solicitously other living creatures. In short, God exercises speech and reason; freedom in doing and making; and the powers of contemplation, judgment, and care" (127–28).

As one who believes that "if it is really death with dignity we are after, we must think in human and not technical terms," Kass stresses that the association he recalls here between God and human beings is not absolutely needed for him to make his point: "Please note that the *truth* of the Bible's assertion does *not* rest on biblical authority: Man's more-than-animal status [his being godlike] is in fact performatively proved whenever human beings quit the state of nature and set up life under . . . a law . . . which exacts just punishment for shedding human (that is, more-than-animal) blood. The law that establishes that men are to be law-abiding both insists on, and thereby demonstrates the truth of, the superiority of man" (127). Kass offers additional examples of this superiority throughout his argument. He would have us wonder, for example, if there is not "something 'protoreligious' in the joyous experience of birth, in the horror of extinction, and in many of the astonishing appearances and doings of all living things, before which the proper response is wondering awe" (122). Moreover, the existential and empirical evidence that speaks so highly of human being can also be found "in the valiant efforts ordinary people make to meet necessity, to combat adversity and disappointment, to provide for their children, to care for their parents, to help their neighbors, to serve their country" (134). Elaborating further on this point, Kass makes clear what, for him, is the only reasonable way to conceive of a dignified death: "Life provides numerous hard occasions that call for endurance and equanimity, generosity and kindness, courage and self-command. Adversity sometimes brings out the best in a man, and often shows best what he is made of. Confronting our own death—or the deaths of our beloved ones—provides an opportunity for the exercise of our humanity, for the great and small alike. Death with dignity, in its most important sense, would mean a dignified attitude and virtuous conduct in the face of death" (134).

Without saying it explicitly, Kass is expressing here a position made famous by an orthodox understanding of the Judeo-Christian tradition: adversity and the pain and suffering that can accompany it are a part of God's plan for us. God permits suffering so that human beings may rise to a height of dignity that would otherwise be beyond their scope. Those who display the courage to withstand suffering at the same time provide others with the opportunity for charity, for a giving of oneself in a much-needed moment of acknowledgment and love. In the face of suffering we can be creatures of immense dignity—heroes.[20]

Before going on to examine more closely Kass's rhetorical handling of this "religious" matter, it will be helpful first to take stock of where we are so far with his argument on dignity. In doing this I will also be offering a critical assessment of certain aspects of Kass's argument that, at least from a rhetorical perspective, are significant.

With his deconstruction of the related notions of the "right to die" and "freedom of choice," Kass emphasizes that the true ground of the possibilities for human excellence (*dignitas*) is a human being's "will to live." Human dignity manifests itself with the "realization of these possibilities." Granting this to be the case, one would also have to grant that freedom of choice must play a crucial role in the life of this will. Assuming the ethical responsibility that comes with this freedom is, of course, a prerequisite for actualizing one's excellence. Following Kass, then, one must understand the definition of human dignity as designating at least a three-stage process: first there is the will to live, followed by the potential for human excellence, and then resolute choice.

With the wisdom of Socrates and the dissecting skill of a physician, Kass exposes the insufficiency of choice as a ground for truth. But is there not still a problem with this way of thinking? Kass's sense of things allows for a precise definition of human dignity, but, I submit, it does this by distorting and simplifying the ontological structure of freedom. As I tried to show in my discussions of Heidegger and Levinas, this phenomenon is inextricably tied to many other phenomena (temporality, everydayness, responsibility, being with and for others) that, like "freedom itself," do not come *after* the will to live, but rather come *with* it as part of its being. In Heidegger's terms one would say these phenomena are "equiprimordial," not simply sequenced. The entire matter is far more complex than Kass's thinking produces. His take on the "right to die" has something of a straw-man character about it.

This last point, it must be emphasized, should not simply be taken to mean that Kass is wrong and euthanasia advocates are right in their appreciation of freedom, autonomy, or the human will. Listening to the everyday discourse of these advocates, one rarely hears a careful analysis being offered of how freedom and dignity are ontologically related; hence, it is often difficult to determine if the rhetoric of the right to die reflects a genuine philosophical appreciation of its own "ground."[21] Nevertheless, I submit that this ground is as necessary for Kass as it is for his counterparts; that is, putting biblical authority aside, Kass's argument presupposes at least an ontology of human being (Dasein) that calls into question his way of discriminating between the will to live and human will. Freedom comes with the openness of our temporal/finite existence, with a future whose final moment is death. Remember, Dasein *is* a Being-unto-death, and as such, it is at the same time a being who is fated to forever confront the challenge of having to assume the ethical responsibility of affirming its freedom through resolute choice. Human beings, in other words, are those creatures who can hear and respond to the call of conscience.

Kass has nothing to say specifically about this call and about how its functioning in life makes no sense without the possibility of death showing its face at any moment. Life is in part what it is because of its ending. Admittedly, a person's will to live shows itself at a fundamental physiological level. Hearts beat, blood flows, lungs breathe, and the synapses of the brain fire without our giving them a second thought. But life, as Kass readily admits, defines something that entails more than this. "For life is to be revered not only as manifested in physiological powers, but also as these powers are organized in the form of *a* life, with its beginning, middle, and end" (136). Putting this in terms introduced earlier, one could say that *a* life is at one and the same time a "body story" *and* a "person story."

Kass omits any detailed discussion of how human existence displays a "narrative" structure: a person's life, from beginning through the middle to the end, is a story in the making.[22] Such a story speaks most fundamentally of the relationship that exists between the value of a person's life and the life of that person's values. To lead the "good life," one that is "worth living," requires that the relationship itself be kept alive to some extent. As will be discussed in greater depth later on in this and following chapters, stories told in the euthanasia debate about people whose existence has become a "living death" offer accounts detailing the demise of this relationship—of how the body's physiological will to live and the aid it receives from medical science and technology are oftentimes not enough to overcome the pain and suffering of an illness or accident. Euthanasia advocates make much of how such an existential state is more often than not a *horror* story for patients and their loved ones. If a patient wants to end this story because it "only is going to get worse" for all concerned, why not help him conclude the final chapter with whatever human dignity he has left?

Considering this question in light of Kass's argument about dignity, Ronald M. Green tells us that one's decision to die, the choice to "cease being a choosing being," is *not* patently absurd or irrational. "Life involves many choices that have the effect of foreclosing future choices of the same kind, and the choice of death or a course leading to death is only the most extreme of these. . . . We must not forget," Green argues, "that for some persons 'dignity' does have the meaning of not spending their last days being treated like an infant or a noisome inanimate object, or of not being subjected to conditions that disempower them and alter their personality so as to render them unrecognizable to their loved ones."[23]

In making this point Green does not merely marginalize or dismiss the importance of the "sanctity of life." The rhetoric of the right to die must value this notion, at least as it defines it as being a life that unfolds as a story, that records the particular history of a person's Being-unto-death, and whose sanctity can be greatly if not totally destroyed by an illness or accident that results in unbearable heartbreak for all concerned. The way a person dies certainly affects how loved ones remember and tell the person's tale. My mother, for example, has taught me how terribly sad it is for a widow to remember her *dying* husband instead of remembering her *living* husband. For euthanasia advocates, however, when the dying are able to demonstrate whatever is left of their dignity (for example, freedom of choice), they may help combat the "endless" suffering that their loved ones are often sentenced to after the dying process.

Dying with dignity does not merely put an end to dignity; it also may demonstrate and serve as a reminder of its own essential worth. Being the ultimate sacrifice, dying with dignity can define a holy act (*sacer facere,* 'to make holy')—one that not only allows a patient (before it is too late) a last chance for taking some control over the final chapter of her life, but also one that pays homage to the "good life" of others and their need for stories that, as much as possible, have a good ending. Martin Foss puts the matter well: "Sacrifice, even it if is a sacrificial death, is not an end but a transition to a new beginning. It is an offering which in its passing way is somehow preserved because it integrates and intensifies that for which it was an offering. In the sacrificial deed, that which is seemingly destroyed is made to live on and is thus not only preserved, but—more than that—it is elevated [*dignitas*] and plays a role in a higher sphere of meaning. Here is a destruction which turns into a creation; it is an end which converts into a beginning and has meaning beyond mere destruction."[24]

What Foss is saying here finds philosophical support in Levinas' understanding of how the call of conscience and the Other are related. This call, remember, summons the self from out of itself and toward the Other; it commands self-sacrifice, a being-for others. Sacrificing oneself for others is a noble deed, a mark of human excellence. A patient who needs help to do this calls on others for a similar, although less severe, deed. Recall what Levinas had to say about the origins of such a request: "[The call of conscience] commands before all mimicry and verbal expression, in the mortality of the face, from the bottom of this weakness. It commands me to not remain indifferent to this death, to not let the other die alone, that is, to answer for the life of the other person, at the risk of becoming an accomplice in that person's death" (Levinas, TO 109).

Kass rejects this way of thinking about suicide and voluntary euthanasia: "One can *sympathize* with such a motive, out of compassion, but can one admire it, out of respect? Is it really dignified to seek to escape from troubles for oneself? Is there . . . not more dignity in courage than in its absence? . . . How can I honor myself by making myself nothing?" (137). But is the issue here simply that of honoring oneself? What about others? Kass addresses this last question with a series of additional questions:

> Is it dignified to ask or demand that someone else become my killer? It may be sad that one is unable to end one's own life, but can it conduce to either party's dignity to make the request? Consider its double meaning if made to a son or daughter: Do you love me so little as to force me to live on? Do you love me so little as to want me dead? What person in full possession of their own dignity would inflict such a duty on anyone they loved? (137).

How about a self whose relationship with loved ones is informed by a knowing-together (*con-scientia*) that values the acknowledgment and love that comes with the sacrifice of being for others?

Kass does not recognize the possibility of such a relationship being cultivated between the dying and their loved ones. Perhaps this omission is due to
his failure to consider more carefully how the self (Dasein) is a story in the
making, a narrative that offers an account of various ways of responding to the
challenge of existence, with its call of conscience, which speaks to us of life
and its Being-unto-death. Human dignity is rooted in the intricate association
of such ontological matters, which form a "ground" more complex than the
body's will to live. When this particular mode of will ceases to exist, so too
does a particular person story. Yet without such a story to give it a life that is
more than a living death, a body lacks a necessary ingredient for maintaining
its "good" existence.

Although what I am suggesting here calls into question Kass's definition of
dignity, I am, nevertheless, still abiding by his desire to define the phenomenon in "human" rather than in "technical" or even "religious" terms. Recall that,
for Kass, the will to live and all that it makes possible can be traced back to our
physiological functioning. Physicians are expected to be experts when it comes
to the biochemistry of this level of existence. Empiricism and science, not biblical authority, must be the guiding forces at work here if medicine is to carry
on the tradition of its Hippocratic ancestors. Indeed, Kass continually reminds
readers that his unfolding definition of dignity draws its truth primarily from
humankind's physiological and existential reality. Hence he tells us: "Never
mind for now where . . . [the] powers [that inform our dignity] came from;
their presence, and the difference they make for human life, is indisputable.
Human beings, alone among the earthly creatures, speak, plan, create, contemplate, and judge. Human beings, alone among the creatures, can articulate
a future goal and bring it into being by their own purposiveness conduct.
Human beings, alone among the creatures, can think about the whole, marvel
at its articulated order, and feel awe in beholding its grandeur and in ponder-
ing the mystery of its source" (128).

Yet from beginning to end, Kass associates the reality of human being with
its "divine-like status," or what he also terms "human godliness" (129). Is one
therefore to believe that even though he does not ask for it, Kass still feels that
God is on his side? (I have yet to meet an anti-euthanasia advocate who admits
that his or her "fundamental" support comes only from a "protoreligious" perspective.) In the euthanasia debate, having God on your side is never depicted
as a weakness. You may be critiqued for a misunderstanding of what God is all
about, but it is not God who is meant to take the beating with the counterar-
gument. Like the Reverend Fraser with his rhetorical use of the Twenty-third
Psalm, Kass writes in such a way that God is never far from what he has to say.
This certainly makes his rhetoric more powerful, even though he sets aside
biblical authority. Moreover, Kass's strategy here allows him to deal with a vex-
ing problem that I promised to return to: the value of suffering.

Dignity, Suffering, and God

The medical scientist makes his or her living by being empirical. Hence, it is no surprise to hear Kass say:

> Everything high about human life—thinking, judging, loving, willing, acting—depends absolutely on everything low—metabolism, digestion, circulation, respiration, excretion. In the case of human beings, "divinity" needs blood—or "mere" life—to sustain itself. And because of what it holds up, human blood—that is, human life—deserves special respect, beyond what is owed to life as such: The low ceases to be the low. (Modern physiological evidence could be adduced in support of this thesis: In human beings, posture, gestalt, respiration, sexuality, and fetal and infant development, among other things—all show the marks of the copresence of rationality). (128–29)

Right after he says this, however, Kass once again returns to religion for support: "The biblical text elegantly mirrors this truth about its subject, subtly merging both high and low: . . . Respect the god-like; don't shed its blood!" (129). Granting that Kass did not *really* have to make this last point (or other ones that he also associates with biblical authority) in order to establish the validity of his argument, is it fair to align (as I did above) Kass's stance on the worth of "adversity" with the Judeo-Christian doctrine on the value of suffering? Putting aside the psychology, politics, and economics of things like "just" wars and capital punishment, how else is one to justify suffering if not without the help of God?

Kass recognizes how his explicit instructions for appreciating his argument can lead one to raise this question. Yet in raising additional and related questions that make clear his awareness of the difficulty here, he cannot avoid speaking in "religious" terms: "What are we to think when the continuing circulation of human blood no longer holds up anything high, when it holds up little more—or even *no more*—than metabolism, digestion, circulation, respiration, and excretion? What if human godliness appears to be humiliated by the degradation of Alzheimer's disease or paraplegia or rampant malignancy? And what if it is the well-considered aspiration of the 'god-like' to put an end to the humiliation of that very godliness, to halt the mockery that various severe debilities make of a *human* life?" (129–30). Kass never relates such questions to the problem of "playing God." When addressing these questions he does, however, appeal to his fellow "god-like" creatures. Hence, in what I take to be one of the most crucial passages in his essay, Kass stresses this:

> Who we are to ourselves is largely inseparable from who we are to and for others; thus, our own exercise of dignified humanity will depend crucially on continuing to receive respectful treatment from others. The

manner in which we are addressed, what is said to us in our presence, how
our bodies are tended or our feelings regarded—in all these ways, our dignity in dying can be nourished and sustained. Dying people are all too easily reduced ahead of time to "thinghood" by those who cannot bear to deal
with the suffering or disability of those they love. Objectification and
detachment are understanding defenses. Yet this withdrawal of contact,
affection, and care is probably the greatest single cause of the dehumanization of dying. Death with dignity requires absolutely that the survivors treat
the human being at all times as if full god-like-ness remains, up to the very
end. (135)

Is this to say, then, that when facing the pain and suffering of death, and in
the name of dignity, of human excellence, we have an obligation to enact *our*
"divine" powers and abilities so that our loved ones who are dying will perhaps
gain the courage to hang in there for as long as possible? Indeed, for Kass, the
"conclusions of life require courage, they [thus] call for our encouragement . . .
and for the many small speeches and deeds that shore up the human spirit against
despair and defeat" (139). Learning to deal with, instead of giving in to, suffering has value: it is a dignified thing to do; it speaks well of our "god-like" status. Does God value suffering? Kass does not say. But he does believe that
suffering has value. It is a matter of *human* dignity. "Thus," writes Kass, "when
the advocates for euthanasia press us with the most heart-rending cases, we
should be sympathetic but firm. Our response should be neither 'Yes, for
mercy's sake' nor 'Murder! Unthinkable!' but 'Sorry. No.' Above all, we must
not allow ourselves to become self-deceived: We must never seek to relieve
our own frustrations and bitterness over the lingering deaths of others by pretending that we can kill them to sustain *their dignity*" (140).

Kass puts the burden of suffering, not on God, but rather on us "god-like"
creatures. His argument is meant to offer us what Kenneth Burke terms
"equipment for living," as opposed to what might be termed the discursive
"equipment for dying" advanced by advocates of euthanasia.[25] Addressing these
advocates at the end of his essay, Kass writes: "People who care for autonomy
and human dignity should try . . . to reverse [the] dehumanization of the last
stages of life, instead of giving dehumanization its final triumph by welcoming
the desperate goodbye-to-all-that is contained in one final plea for poison"
(141). And what about the patient that the Reverend Fraser writes about—the
poor soul who exists only in a persistent vegetative state? Kass admits that "one
faces here the hardest case for the argument I am advancing." Still, he maintains
he would nevertheless "be restrained by the human form, by *human blood,* and
by what I owe [as a creature of dignity] to the full human life that this particular instance of humanity once lived." Hence, Kass admits that "I would gladly
stand aside and let die, say in the advent of pneumonia; I would do little

beyond the minimum to sustain life; but I would not countenance the giving of lethal injections nor the taking of other actions deliberately intending the patient's death. Between only undignified courses of action, this strikes me as the least undignified—especially for myself" (140).

Kass's position here is aligned with the teachings of his Hippocratic ancestors, which, one should recall, are steeped in religion and in the belief that active euthanasia constitutes a sin against God. Passive euthanasia (letting nature take its course without medical intervention), on the other hand, is allowed, because this "action" exhibits the necessary restraint that medical science must perform in cases where a patient's illness exceeds the boundaries of medicine's curing and caring reach. Kass makes no reference to his ancestors' adherence to God's will; he wants his position to be defined "only" in human terms.

The key for Kass is "dignity," which is phenomenologically and thus empirically verifiable, and whose "true" meaning happens to be associated with a human being's "god-like" status here on earth. This status, among other things, entails the power of freedom of choice. Kass ridicules this power as it is emphasized in the discourse and actions of the "right-to-die" proponents. Still, he would have us employ this power in *choosing* as a last resort the least "undignified" option of passive euthanasia. Unlike those he counters in the euthanasia debate, Kass sees a significant moral difference between "letting die" and assisting in the death of a patient who, even after much rational deliberation with others, remains convinced that with all the pain and suffering at hand the time has come to die with whatever dignity one has left. But that is impossible, claims Kass: "There is nothing of human dignity in the process of dying itself—only in the way we face it: At its best, death with complete dignity will always be compromised by the extinction of dignified humanity" (132).

Kass associates dignity with the will to live and the courage to face death, not choose it. Although he never puts it this way, I think it is fair to say that he wants us to be heroic as we deal with our own pain and suffering and that of others. Hence, with Kass, one must hold that a person is not a hero if he or she begs for a merciful death that will put an end not only to the unbearable suffering of the person but also to the immense suffering of family and friends whose hearts are being broken by what they are witnessing as they stare at the face and listen to the words of a loved one who continues to say, "It's time!"

Suffering calls for courage, not surrender. Courage helps us face death with dignity to the very end—when the last bit of the will to live operating in our physiology vanishes. Displaying courage in the face of death is the most profound way that human beings instruct each other about the respect that is owed to others. Kass puts it this way: "Humanity is owed humanity"; that is, it "is owed the bolstering of the human, even or especially in its dying moments, in resistance to the temptation to ignore its presence in the sight of suffering"

(138). Kass further explicates this point when he notes: "What humanity needs most in the face of evils is courage, the ability to stand against fear and pain and thoughts of nothingness. The deaths we most admire are those of people who, knowing that they are dying, face the fact frontally and act accordingly: They set their affairs in order; they arrange what could be final meetings with their loved ones, and yet with strength of soul and a small reservoir of hope, they continue to live and work and love as much as they can for as long as they can" (138–39).

The heroes being referred to here are examples of what Heidegger referred to as "authentic" Dasein: human beings who, especially in the face of death, are still courageous enough to assume the ethical responsibility of free-dom of choice such that they can maintain some degree of control and dignity in their lives. With Heidegger, however, such authenticity is also at work when the suffering hero eventually decides that "enough is enough," that an alterna-tive form of sacrifice is needed, and therefore requests from others assistance in dying. Kass, we have seen, will have nothing of such a sacrificial act. When it comes to human dignity, the only genuine sacrifice is that made by people (patients, loved ones, medical personnel) who struggle to encourage and bol-ster the will to live of humankind. I suspect, then, that Kass would feel more comfortable being associated with Levinas, who, as noted earlier, emphasizes that "prior to death there is always a last chance; this is what heroes seize, not death" (TO 73). Put another way while still following Levinas, one could also say that heroes pay homage to the fundamental way in which we exist with and especially for others: in a constant state of "caress" wherein responsibility for others is always antecedent to the self's freedom.

Yet with this point in mind, I would ask: Are there not moments in everyday life where one's caring and devotional caress of others can become burdensome and suffocating? This question, I think it is fair to say, is one that is forever being asked, for example, by loving parents who want their children to be strong, independent, and responsible citizens. Out of respect for who they are as human beings, it is often necessary that we ease our caress of loved ones so that they are free to be themselves and to make their own mark on the world. Life without the caress would be torture. We are creatures who thrive on the gift of acknowledgment. Where art thou? Here I am! The ques-tion, however, is sometimes asked by people whose lives, because of illness or accident, are doomed to a state of unrelenting pain and suffering and who, in turn, have decided that the caress of family, friends, and medicine is no longer worth the cost. In such cases the caress, despite the best of intentions, is seen by patients as contributing to their "living death." And this too is a horrible way to go.

In his highly acclaimed book, *Toward a More Natural Science,* Kass tells us that "Liberal and democratic regimes cannot be indifferent to the attitudes and postures of their citizens regarding the dignity of human life and its place in the larger whole."[26] Kass, to be sure, is not indifferent to advocates of euthanasia. Still, he would have us say "No" to their "most heart-rending cases"; for, as quoted earlier, he insists that "we must never seek to relieve *our own* frustrations and bitterness over the lingering deaths of others by pretending that we can kill them to sustain *their dignity*" (140). Given the way he speaks about God when making this point, it is hard not to believe that Kass feels secure in thinking that God is on his side. For who can justify suffering without making some (albeit indirect) appeal to a higher and more perfect Judge? Certainly not one who, like Kass, would have us believe that "we stand most upright when we gladly bow our heads."[27]

I am taken with the eloquence of this last remark. I trust it is clear, however, that I am not totally comfortable with the definition of human dignity that complements it. For this definition, when considered in light of Heidegger's and Levinas' thinking on the call of conscience, proves to be too limited in what it has to say about the matter. I do believe that the definition offers a reflection of reality. But I also find that the corresponding deflection of reality that attends Kass's attempt to speak the truth promotes a misunderstanding of what the rallying cry of the right to die— "death with dignity"—is all about. Death with dignity is something that requires thinking about a number of other matters (the self, sacrifice, courage) that Kass omits or defines too narrowly as he goes about constructing an argument intended to remedy the "indecorous chatter" and thus the rhetorical confusion that surrounds one of the most prominent and powerful terms operating in the euthanasia debate.

I want to emphasize again, however, that despite this problem with his definition of human dignity, I still find his argument to be valuable. Not content to leave matters where they stand after rhetors like the Reverend Fraser have had their say, Kass interrupts and takes us beyond an evocative and emotional account of how human dignity is threatened by the technological zeal of the medical profession. He does this so that we might first get our terms straight before we condemn his colleagues. With this rhetorical interruption, Kass sounds a call of conscience that first deconstructs than reconstructs the meaning of death with dignity. He is a physician/philosopher with a vision of how to improve the moral nature of health care. And he is a rhetor who, like his Hippocratic ancestors, is well aware of the importance of calling into being a public that is equipped with the requisite knowledge for making truth-based, and therefore good, healthcare decisions.[28]

But there is something missing in Kass's rhetoric—something that would make its reconstructive intent more instructive and persuasive; something that speaks to the ontological nature of human beings; something seen going on in the Reverend Fraser's presentation; something that Kass wants us to say "No" to when we enter the debate: those concrete and "heart-rending cases" or *sto-*

ries about pain and suffering. To be sure, such stories play a large and crucial role in the rhetoric of the right to die. But they can also be found in the rhetoric of the right to life. In the final section of this chapter, I use a case study to elaborate on the rhetorical importance of stories in the euthanasia debate. The case presented here is one that Kass could use to his advantage. But it is also a case that could be employed by euthanasia advocates in order to clarify the meaning of their conscientious rallying cry: "Death with dignity."

The Rhetorical Workings of Stories

Woody Allen—that great teller of existential, humorous, and sometimes dark stories—once informed his audience about his life by declaring: "It's not that I am afraid to die, I just don't want to be there when it happens."[29] I take it that Allen is referring here to his fear of a time when his life might become the oxymoronic "living death" that is so often publicized by euthanasia advocates. I suspect that for a writer and filmmaker like Allen, such an existence would be particularly sorrowful because the ending of its story would be so bad, humorless, indecorous, and thus lacking in character, style, and overall aesthetic quality. Even in his most serious and *angst*-filled work, Allen is a much better storyteller than that.

So too is the late Anatole Broyard, the book critic and editor of *The New York Times Book Review* who was diagnosed with metastatic prostate cancer in August 1989 and died from the disease in October 1990. Broyard wrote about his illness up to the very end; it was his way of taking control and going out with "dignity" and "style." Here, for example, is one of the many ways in which he made the point:

> I'm not a doctor, and even as a patient I'm a mere beginner. Yet I *am* a critic, and being critically ill, I thought I might accept the pun and turn it on my condition. My initial experience of illness was a series of disconnected shocks, and my first instinct was to try to bring it under control by turning it into a narrative. Always in emergencies we invent narratives. We describe what is happening, as if to confine the catastrophe. When people heard that I was ill, they inundated me with stories of their own illnesses, as well as the cases of friends. Storytelling seems to be a natural reaction to illness. People bleed stories, and I've become a blood bank of them. . . . Stories are antibodies against illness and pain. . . . Anything is better than an awful silent suffering.[30]

Elaborating on the therapeutic value of his poetical and rhetorical medicament, Broyard goes on to note: "Writing is a counterpoint to my illness. It forces the cancer to go through my character before it can get to me" (23). This particular route of cancer is especially important to Broyard because it allows him to temper his illness with "style": "It seems to me that every seriously ill person needs to develop a style for his illness. I think that only by insisting on your style can you keep from falling out of love with yourself as the illness attempts to diminish or disfigure you" (25).

Although he appreciates how important it is to have a physician who is an expert in deciphering and telling the story of a patient's disease, its pathophysiology, or what I termed earlier a body story, Broyard makes clear that he longs for a doctor whose range for appreciating and telling stories transcends the boundary of the body's biology and chemistry. Such a physician, according to Broyard, would be a master in treating both the "body and soul." He or she thus would be not only an excellent reader and teller of stories but also "a bit of a metaphysician, too." Here is how Broyard explains it: "There's a physical self who's ill, and there's a metaphysical self who's ill. When you die, your philosophy dies along with you. So I want a metaphysical [doctor] to keep me company. To get to my body, my doctor has to get to my character. He has to go through my soul. He doesn't only have to go through my anus. That's the back door to my personality" (40). Broyard, in other words, is calling for a physician whose talents include being open to, and respectful of, the person story that contextualizes and humanizes his ongoing battle with cancer. "I would . . . like a doctor who *enjoyed* me. I want to be a good story for him, to give him some of my art in exchange for his. If a patient expects a doctor to be interested in him, he ought to try to *be* interesting" (45). For Broyard the effort needed here is worth the cost. Many doctors, he tells us, "look at you panoramically. They don't see you in focus. They look all around you, and you are a figure in the ground. You are like one of those lonely figures in early landscape painting, a figure in the distance only to give scale. If he could gaze directly at the patient, the doctor's work would be more gratifying. Why bother with sick people, why try to save them, if they're not worth acknowledging? When a doctor refuses to acknowledge a patient, he is, in effect, abandoning him to his illness" (50).

Exactly! Acknowledgment, as I have suggested throughout this book so far, is a life-giving phenomenon. What would life be like if nobody acknowledged your existence, if nobody was willing to say "Here I am!" when, for whatever reason, you called out "Where art thou?" The call of conscience sounded here is an interruption steeped in the ontological and metaphysical nature of human being. This interruption is like the cough or the tap on the shoulder that immediately precedes the moment of gaining another's attention.[31] Like Woody Allen, Broyard has the artistic and rhetorical competence that it takes to be humorous and eloquent when writing about his predicament. Indeed when suffering from the torment of some disease, who wants to be treated only "like one of those lonely figures in early landscape painting, a figure in the distance only to give scale"? That, to be sure, would be inhumane and undignified—an act of social death, of extreme marginalization, of symbolic murder. Our lives are stories that, whether we admit it or not, beg for acknowledgment. We are creatures who are fated to hear and respond to the call of conscience. The deconstruction of our bodies by illness or accident is the most dramatic way in which we become aware of this fate and the challenge it poses.

"I would like to die in my own way. It's my house, my life, my death, my friends. Why not?" asks Broyard. "A critically ill person ought to be entitled to anything that affords him relief" (64). These words are as close as Broyard comes to admitting where he stands on the euthanasia debate. His way of avoiding a living death was to write about how he was "intoxicated" by his illness and how this intoxication added to his storytelling ability. "My body, which in the last decade or two had become a familiar, no-longer-thrilling old flame, was reborn as a brand-new infatuation. I realize of course that this elation I feel is just a phase, just a rush of consciousness, a splash of perspective, a hot flash of ontological alertness. But I'll take it, I'll use it. I'll use everything I can while I wait for the next phase. Illness is primarily a drama, and it should be possible to enjoy it as well as to suffer it. I see now why the Romantics were so fond of illness—the sick man sees everything as metaphor. In this phase I'm infatuated with my cancer. It stinks of revelation" (7). Revelation, a sudden and memorable "showing-forth" (*epideixis*) of what is. The deconstructive nature of illness evokes a truth about existence—that we are fallible and finite and thus always faced with the challenge of trying to get things right before it is too late. Broyard was able to meet this challenge: he heard and answered the call of conscience; he hung in there and told stories; he was the kind of patient that Kass admires.

The call of conscience, the euthanasia debate, and stories go hand in hand. Broyard is but one of many writers who helps us appreciate the relationship. A student once told me that, in her opinion, the euthanasia debate will be decided by those who end up telling "the best" stories. Perhaps she is right. She certainly has support from authors such as Rabbi David Wolpe, who reminds us that "at times the dramatic story of a single life can bring truth home more powerfully than any abstract description."[32] The story that will direct my attention in the rest of this chapter is a case in point. It brings the truth home, not with a well-defined argument, but rather with a vivid tale that performs a fundamental function of storytelling—what I term here the rhetorical construction of the face.

A Story That Both Moves and Educates

In the March 1996 issue of *Harper's Magazine,* B. J. Nelson wrote about his "Mother's Last Request," which he subtitled "A Not So Fond Farewell."[33] With his opening paragraph, Nelson gives us a sense of why this subtitle is appropriate:

Marie wanted to die. She'd been wanting to for most of her life, I think, and wasn't it time? She was asking me. She'd been thinking about how to kill herself for months, years, especially the last few weeks. Now she knew how she would do it and was simply focusing on when. She was eighty and a couple of her teeth had recently fallen out, her stomach was swollen, food made her sick; she was in pain all over, the worst pain she'd ever had, she said, though every pain throughout her whole life was always the worst. Over the years, the hundreds of times she was sick, each time she was "deathly sick." Each pain for decades had been "the most horrible pain" she'd ever felt. You never knew. She'd turn the least matter into melodrama, managing her life neurotically, even from the beginning, I've come to believe, by pretending, by living in a world of pretense. (35)

Have you ever known a person like Marie, someone whose very presence is discomforting and whose typical behavior makes this presence all the more irritating if not maddening? Have you ever wondered why people act this way? Have you ever tried to "reason" with such people in an attempt to have them see what is "wrong" with them? Did they finally see their problem and realize that by being more presentable and genuine they perhaps could receive more positive acknowledgment from others? Did you feel good about what you had accomplished? Did you tell the story to friends and acquaintances in an attempt to be the recipient of such acknowledgment? Wouldn't it be a bit depressing to find out that some of the good people who listened to your story were irritated and much annoyed by having to listen to what you had to say about yourself?

Sometimes what goes around comes around. Nelson's story about his mother—who is only referred to as Marie throughout the narrative—is, among other things, a tale that illustrates the often tragic reality of this existential way of being. Broyard deals with, and writes about, death and dying by putting the best face possible on the entire matter. Nelson's story, however, is dark, sad, tragic, and, according to one reader, "repugnant."[34] When all is said and done, we know that Marie is dead and that her son assisted her in committing suicide. The way in which Nelson reveals this state of affairs is, from beginning to end, evocative. Nearly every line is given over to producing a vivid picture of Marie's horrible life, and thus the story lacks any well-defined, philosophical argument that justifies the author's action. Nelson, it seems, is of the school that believes that an argument, no matter how intellectually rigorous it is, has much less persuasive force than the vivid evocation of an experience, and that such an argument becomes relevant only after this emotional stage of storytelling has been completed.[35]

Marie's son admits that he told her that suicide "had to be up to her, no one else" and that she would ask: "But didn't I think she might as well? What

did she have to live for?" (35). Continuing with a description of Marie's existence, Nelson immediately notes: "She had terrible noise in her ears and
couldn't hear, she'd disconnected her phone, no one called anyway, she had no
friends. She had lived for fifteen years as an almost total recluse, and other than
a sister she hated and another son she hadn't heard from in thirty years, there
was only me. She couldn't see her soap operas except as a blur, she was shak-
ing, trembling, she got out of breath walking from her room to the front of the
house, so before being too helpless, while she could still manage, wasn't it
time?" (35).

   We are being told about a woman who is bothersome, who lives in a
world of pretense, who seems quite ill, and who is certainly alone, although
there is still Nelson, the son who has to hear Marie ask for a reality check,
given what she wants to do. When those who are suicidal make such a request,
they present a classic example of people in need of what I have been describing here as the life-giving gift of acknowledgment—a gift given by a self
answering the call of the other, the call of conscience. Where art thou? Here I
am! We are being told a story about this call, about an other (a mother) who
sounds it, and a self (a son) who hears it. The son reports what his mother has
told him: "You don't know how many times I've prayed I wouldn't wake up.
Every night I go to sleep praying, dear God, please, just let me die and not wake
up. So I'm going to do it. But I can't by myself. You'll have to help me" (36).

   A request for assisted suicide made by a mother to a son—two people
who share a "blood bond" that is greater (at least biologically) than any other
bond that can form between human beings. The plan was simple. Marie had
saved a stash of one hundred Xanax, a sedative. The pills would put her right
to sleep, then all Nelson would "have to do was slip a bag over her head and
wrap it airtight around her neck with a scarf. No rubber bands. They might
leave telltale lines." Nelson explains how Marie had "already tried the bag on
to be sure it wasn't too big. She said it wasn't. A large bag would retain too
much air and take longer. She'd read that in a book from the Hemlock Society." Marie would call Nelson later that night when she was ready. Another
admission is made: "Was there anything I needed to consider? Feelings, emotions? No. My feelings for Marie were fairly reconciled. I came into this world
out of her body, or the physical me did, . . . but I didn't like her as a person. I
was ashamed of her as a mother. I wouldn't miss her" (36).

   The scene is as chilling as Nelson is cold-hearted. He feared that "Marie
would struggle, even zonked on Xanax, and she would be clawing the thing to
get free, to breathe. The Hemlock Society book said that this was common. I
could see myself trying to hold her hands down or, frozen, just standing there,
watching" (36). The event would take place in a room in Nelson's house, the
room were Marie had lived for the past two-and-a-half years. In all of that time

she had never left the house. Nelson shopped for her and secured whatever medicine she needed. The two never had a good conversation. Rather, as Nelson details, Marie typically took charge by airing one complaint after another. "The arthritis in my hand is so bad, I took four of those pain pills, they didn't help a bit, I don't know what I am going to do. . . . Those ratty kids next door were playing so loud, hollering and carrying on, I couldn't hear myself think. I wish that family'd move away, they're nothing but white trash. I saw the woman out in her yard yesterday wearing shorts, with big ol' fat legs, I'd be ashamed" (37).

Nelson is remembering Marie, a woman who "didn't like herself," probably "hated herself, and the way it showed was depressing" (37). The illness that she had "was probably a consumptive heart condition," although this fact is never clarified by the author beyond his telling us that, according to Marie, her condition, as described in her "medical book," would lead to serious lung, stomach, kidney, and liver problems. Eventually one becomes "bedridden," unable to "go to the bathroom or feed yourself—you couldn't eat anything anyway—and you'd just lie there in agony and finally die" (37). We also learn that Marie knew that she had "messed up" her kids because of her reckless lifestyle. She left her children, married several times, was trying "to have fun" and, at the same time, find a home for her kids, "but it never turned out, she never got what she wanted, which was just to be happy and for us kids to be happy, but she couldn't help any of that now, she couldn't go back" (37).

Nelson has no good memories of Marie. Let us take a moment to consider how tragic this is. I imagine that most of you have given some thought to your own death—how you might die, how it would feel, who would be around at the end, and who would attend the funeral. Perhaps you even have gone further with your thinking as you pictured those folks who "should" have but did not attend your funeral and thereby warranted your anger. Why would a "rational" person conceive of such a bitter situation? Why not be more optimistic or at least more relaxed about it? Why not leave well enough alone and rest in peace?

Although answers to these questions might lead one to conclude that the person in question is somewhat neurotic, I submit that there is something more positive going on when we think this way. We are creatures who need the acknowledgment of others, and even after death we want to be remembered as someone who was worthwhile and who will be missed. The acknowledgment that comes with fond memories at least keeps our "spirit" alive; it thereby provides a way to satisfy what Becker terms a human being's "urge to immortality." This urge "is not a simple reflex of the death-anxiety but a reaching out by one's whole being toward life . . . , a reaching-out for a plenitude of meaning. . . . It seems that the life force reaches naturally even beyond the earth itself, which is one reason why man has always placed God in the heavens."[36] Indeed—and here is where we can seek help when no one else will acknowledge our existence. It is a wonderful and awesome (symbolic) construction—the perfect place to find One who, at least according to the Bible, is also in need of the acknowledgment that we pray for. What would your life be like if no one acknowledged your existence? Without acknowledgment, even being immortal would not mean much.

At the heart of the case before us lies an existential paradox. Marie asked Nelson for the gift of life, of acknowledgment: Say "here I am!" and help me to die. This paradox is a staple of the euthanasia debate. It comes about when people whose final chapter of life has become a living death do not want to be remembered for dying this way. Yet Marie's request was not always straightforward. It sometimes included a question: Didn't Nelson think that she was right in wanting to die? As he shares his memories with readers, Nelson tells a story of a presence, a face, a person whom he took in when nobody else would and whom he would not miss when she died. Marie's life was becoming ever more a living death for both her and her son. Marie spoke of God; Nelson did not. Marie wanted a second opinion about the worth of suicide, and all that Nelson had to go on were horrible memories of a woman who inspired no compassion or love. So when for the last time she said, "I can't think about it anymore, . . . I want to just go on and do it, is that all right with you?" Nelson would only say, "If you're ready" (39).

Was Marie hoping for more acknowledgment than this? If she was, neither she nor Nelson would admit it. Instead, Nelson goes on to discuss in great detail how he assisted Marie with the pills, the bag, and the scarf. During this discussion Nelson admits, "A terrible feeling came over me, a weight of darkness. Here was this old, lonely woman actually going to die, killing herself. This was the last moment she would ever know, a worthless, measly last moment in a dismal, cluttered room in central Texas. She would never again see the two squirrels in the tree outside her window. Or the sky, the sun, the rain. This earth, this great beautiful earth around her would be no more. She was going to die and nothing would be all. I had no words for what I felt, except pity. Poor old woman" (39). Nelson hugged Marie and she patted his arm. He told her he loved her. "I love you, too," she said. The words were "perfunctory." There was "no clutch of emotion." The pills began to take effect. The bag and scarf were at hand. "Poor Marie, I thought, your whole life so damned unhappy. I felt sorry for her. I snugged at the scarf to be sure it was trapping the air." After approximately two-thirds of his story is completed, Nelson reports Marie "died at 7:25 in the evening, April 19, 1995" (40).

A sentence from Levinas needs repeating here: The "mortality of the face . . . commands me to not remain indifferent to this death, to not let the other die alone, that is, to answer for the life of the other person, at the risk of becoming an accomplice in that person's death" (TO 109). In the euthanasia debate, this way of thinking comes into play when arguing about whether an assisted suicide was an act of murder or mercy. I suspect that Levinas would allow the point to be made *only after* a patient's loving "caress" of the other was no longer of any use to the other because, owing to physiological complications, he or she had gone beyond the point of ever being able to experience its heartfelt emotion. This certainly was not the case with Marie. Nelson, however, is not yet done telling Marie's story. He continues to remember:

> Marie had been a dirt-poor country girl, her parents sharecroppers from Alabama who moved to Texas. She claimed she graduated from high school, I think maybe she got to the tenth grade. . . . Growing up, she'd worked in the fields like a man. . . . She married Charlie, she said, to get away from home. She had my brother and me by the time she was nineteen. . . . She married six times, well, seven, if you count the one she married twice, the one who regularly beat her. . . . Marie's most articulate aspiration was "just to be happy, that's all I ever wanted." This was her litany. She never learned that happiness is a matter of degree, not a permanent condition. . . . To hear her tell it, most of her life was occupied with "getting a man." . . . If she could attract a man, get a man to want her, this had to mean that she had some value, didn't it? On the other hand, by being so easy that any man could screw her and did—"screwing" is what she called it—didn't that really prove she was of the least value, a throwaway? Being little more than a fuck is being little more than faceless. (40–41)

Nelson continues to tell a story about a person who long ago lost what for someone like Levinas is an essential existential feature of life: a face whose presence sounds a call of conscience. Marie was but a "throwaway," a disposable creature of little if any value. Recalling what the Reverend Fraser had to say about the poor soul who exists in a persistent vegetative state, we learn that even in this horrendous situation a person still has a face whose presence calls out for relief from a living death. Nelson's memories of Marie made it impossible for him to see such a face beyond *his* rhetorical construction of its miserable existence. "After all," writes Nelson, "when you have children of your own, you find out that you don't just up and leave them after a few years and make an X for them in your life, not if you care. You don't leave your kids with a hole in their heart" (43).

Nelson concludes his story by telling how he cleaned up the scene, had a drink to calm his nerves, and called the police. "I told the coroner my mother had deteriorated rapidly in the last week. . . . He took a cursory look at her, pronounced her dead from natural causes, and called the mortuary." Nelson told the "mortuary man" that he wanted Marie cremated. "How about a service? No, none of that, I said, just the simplest, quickest way." And finally he remarks: "My mother, I thought, the one person I'd known my whole life, she'd given me life. But I always only knew her as Marie. I never called her mother and she never called me son" (43). Sad words, to be sure, but no sadder than the ones that reveal what perhaps is the most telling admission by the author: He is a person whose mother left her "kids with a hole in their heart."

The ailment being noted here, especially when considered in light of what I had to say in the introduction about the Old Testament, warrants the diagnosis of being a severely impaired conscience. This is an illness that attacks the person more than the body, for it makes one uncaring and unreceptive to a call that sometimes, as in the case of Marie, can only be heard as an irritating question concerning the worthiness of one's life. Marie transmitted this illness to Nelson, who returned the favor. What was left of his conscience allowed him to remember nothing good about his mother, nothing that deserved being acknowledged as inspiring and worthy of continuation. One reader of Nelson's story saw this to be its primary "message": "[When it comes to] the achievement of some sort of understanding between a difficult mother and her son," we need merely "put on a 'clinical' face, write about it in a matter-of-fact style, relate the facts of death without any reference to loss, and generally let loose the little Kevorkian in us before the real emotional work is done."[37] I must disagree with this interpretation, for it is philosophically and rhetorically naive.

Unlike the Reverend Fraser, Nelson is not witty with his discourse; and unlike Dr. Kass, he opts to tell an evocative story that avoids the strain of intellectual abstraction. The story is not written by one who has "put on a clinical face"; rather, it comes to us from a son whose mother never called him by his name and whose fate it was to struggle with an emotional and moral ailment that took hold when he was only a child. The euthanasia debate is not just about the problem of medical and technological zeal that may be counseled by well-defined, intellectual arguments. "Mother's Last Request" helps to make that clear. The debate over the morality or immorality of assisted suicide is rooted in the lives of people, in personal stories whose characters have many different histories, lifestyles, dreams, and nightmares—all of which come into play as the characters assume the burden of having to face up to the challenge of freedom of choice and ethical responsibility.

Marie and Nelson took on this challenge that calls upon the authenticity and dignity of human being (Dasein) and that Heidegger stressed so well. What is missing from their story, however, is the same thing that is missing in Heidegger: a more nuanced appreciation of how Dasein exists not only "with" but also "for" others. One reader made the point this way: "New glasses, a home health aide, and antidepressant medication might have made [Marie's] last months far less miserable. . . . A phone call to the doctor by her son, stating her problems and asking for exclusively home-based care, may have been all that was necessary. After all, she was depressed, not terminal."[38] Yes, but again I must stress that the case is not that simple.

Nelson's story offers an account of conscience: how it calls through sickness and misery, how it may itself become ill, and how such an illness can affect one's memory and acknowledgment of others. The story is tragic; its characters bear faces that are repugnant and that perhaps remind us of others whose hearts are cold and crippled because of life's circumstances. Perhaps we are even reminded of ourselves—creatures who, like Broyard, tell stories in order to bring some coherence to what illness or accident has made incoherent. The activity is therapeutic and rhetorical. Isn't Nelson engaged in this activity? Hasn't he reconstructed from memory a scene that is as educational as it is horrible? Doesn't Nelson's story sound a call of conscience that is heard as a confession about his illness? Doesn't "Mother's Last Request" speak to us of things that, for the sake of humanity, we cannot afford to forsake? Nelson's story is a reconstruction of events of deconstruction; of heartbreak; of choices gone wrong, bad memories, illness, and death. He offers readers a picture of persons whose faces, I suspect, are not for most people objects of envy. Who would want to be remembered like Marie? Who would want a son like Nelson? But it wasn't all his fault! Does that matter?

What if Marie wanted the type of acknowledgment that Nelson was incapable of giving? What if Nelson proved capable of giving this gift? What if mother and son eventually healed each other's hearts through loving conversation and understanding? Would Marie still have wanted to die? Would her son still have been willing to assist her? Would that have been death with dignity? It certainly would have been a better way to end the story: two people being with and for each other; two people making a sacrifice for the other. Marie would no longer be a burden and would leave her son with some good memories. Nelson would be able to say that he finally gave back to his mother a gift that she desperately wanted, that granted her reprieve from a living death, and that both she and her son knew was given and received with much love. If such a story were told in as evocative a way as "Mother's Last Request," one might read it as a story of heroism as well. The rhetoric of the right to die is filled with such stories—the type that Kass and others would have us say "No" to.[39]

As it stands now, Nelson's story is not about heroes. His remembrance of Marie constitutes a rhetorical construction of a "faceless fuck." His confession of assisting in a suicide makes him out to be, for the most part, a creature without much of a conscience. But still there is a call of conscience at work in this confession. If you don't have a big hole in your heart, you should be well enough to notice it. My interpretation of this call has emphasized how it speaks to us (albeit at times indirectly, but still forcefully) of matters that play an important role in the euthanasia debate: acknowledgment, personal histories, fond memories, faceless souls, and why it is so important to cultivate caring relationships with family, friends, and neighbors (who presently are still strangers). The particular way that Nelson treats these concerns in his story may be nothing more than an attempt to clear his conscience. No matter, though; the story still functions as a rhetorical interruption of our moral consciousness.

Nelson's reconstruction of Marie's and his own face presents a story that, as depressing and repugnant as it is, begs for deconstruction. "Marie's Last Request," like "It's Over, Debbie," was made to remind us of how certain things that are at work in the euthanasia debate need to be called into question. Unlike Debbie's physician, Nelson tells a story that is far more straightforward and much less ambiguous and deconstructive. The story is in no way an argument for the right to die; it is too anti-heroic. Hence, Kass could use it in support of his definition of, and argument about, human dignity. Fraser too could use it as an example of what euthanasia advocates would also have us avoid.[40] Death with dignity requires more than what Nelson and Marie had to give. Their story, I would argue, is more evocative and effective than what either Fraser or Kass have to offer.

Throughout this chapter I have been concerned with how discourse is used in a reconstructive way to clarify a major theme in the euthanasia debate: the meaning of human dignity. Four ingredients of reconstructive rhetoric were identified as being crucial to this task: emotions, definitions, arguments, and stories. In the discussion of how these ingredients are at work in discourses aimed at fostering judgment about the morality or immorality of assisted suicide, additional matters also warranted consideration—matters that were first introduced when discussing Heidegger's and Levinas' respective theories of the call of conscience. We thus had occasion to talk about such ontological and metaphysical concerns as freedom of choice, the authenticity of human being, community, God, suffering, the presence or face of ourselves and others, acknowledgment, memory, sacrifice, and heroism.

In the next two chapters I intend to take a much closer look at this last concern. More specifically, I will be discussing and assessing what I believe is the most *positive* rhetorical event of the euthanasia debate: the symbolic construction of heroes. All the rhetorical, philosophical, and religious matters that were considered in this chapter will also be present in the next two. When my discussion of heroes comes to an end, I will then be able to conclude this study as I make clear my personal stance on the question of euthanasia.

Chapter 6

The Rhetorical Construction of Heroes

Among their many attributes, heroes are people who act in such a way as to "stand out" from the crowd and who are admired for doing so. Both the act and the admiration are rooted, however, in a more primordial process than what they themselves define. With Heidegger, we understand this process to be the ecstatic workings of temporality—the way the no-longer, the not-yet, and the here-and-now interpenetrate each other such that human existence is always in the state of "standing outside and beyond itself" (Gk. *ek-stasis*), at every moment opening out toward the future, toward the world of possibilities, and thus toward the unknown, that *awesome* place of uncertainty, anxiety, hope, and joy. The ontological structure of human being has something heroic about it, and thus the potential is there for all of us to be heroes.

As many myths would have it, those who actualize this potential are understood to have begun a "journey" or "struggle" by answering a "call to adventure"—a call that summons the hero and transfers "his spiritual center of gravity from within the pale of his society to a zone unknown."[1] We have seen, however, that from an ontological point of view this call is continually being voiced by the ecstatic temporality of human being; it challenges us to assume the ethical responsibility of affirming our freedom through resolute choice. Any act of heroism presupposes the answering of this call of conscience. Heroes and conscience go hand in hand, and as they do, they provide the material that directs a society's moral compass. Ernest Becker puts the matter this way:

> Society is and always has been . . . a symbolic action system, a structure of statuses and roles, customs and rules for behavior, designed to serve as a vehicle for earthly heroism. Each script is somewhat unique, each culture has a different hero system. . . . But each cultural system is a dramatization of earthly heroics; each system cuts out rules for performances of various degrees of heroism: from the "high" heroism of a Churchill, a Mao, or a Buddha, to the "low" heroism of the coal miner, the peasant, the simple priest; the plain, everyday, earthy heroism wrought by gnarled working hands guiding a family through hunger and disease.[2]

A hero system records and directs courageous and virtuous behavior; it provides instructions for understanding what human greatness is and thereby what it takes for a finite being to live on after death in the hearts and minds of others. A hero system, in other words, speaks of the possibility of being immortal and thus "god-like"; hence, its great attraction to humankind. Again, Becker puts it well: "Man will lay down his life for his country, his society, his family. He will choose to throw himself on a grenade to save his comrades; he is capable of the highest generosity and self-sacrifice. But he has to feel and believe that what he is doing is truly heroic, timeless, and supremely mean-ingful."[3] Like the beings they surpass, heroes need the gift of acknowledgment in order to be remembered beyond the moment of their accomplishments.

This, of course, is not to say that heroes only do what they do in order to gain attention and recognition. The stranger who risks his life to save a child from drowning would not be thought of that highly if it were learned that his primary motivation was to become famous for a courageous deed. The gen-uine hero answers the call of conscience, not for egotistical reasons, but rather for the sake of something other than the self, something that is in need of acknowledgment but that is not necessarily expected to return the favor. Cer-tainly, a heartfelt thank-you would be nice, but this is not what true heroism is all about. For as Levinas reminds us, such heroism reflects a truth of existence: how it is that human being is structured as a "being-for others." Remember, "I am defined as a subjectivity, as a particular person, as an 'I,' precisely because I am exposed to the other. It is my inescapable and incontrovertible answer-ability to the other that makes me an individual 'I.'. . . I can never escape the fact that the other has demanded a response from me before I affirm my free-dom not to respond to his demand" (EOF 62–63).

With Levinas in mind, I am encouraged to think of one of Judaism's most famous heroes who, when called on to lead his people out of slavery, first answered his Caller by declaring his unworthiness and lack of ability. I speak, of course, of Moses, a man who knew himself to be "slow of speech" and "slow of tongue" and who therefore was not "eloquent" enough to preach and proph-esy to Israel and her enemies (Exod. 4:11). Moses, in short, lacked the requi-site rhetorical competence to spread the word of God in a moving and truthful way. Remedying this problem was part of Moses' heroic struggle, and the One who called him to it made sure that the task was fraught with difficulties. For example, when Moses is told to confront Pharaoh, God not only gives him "the words" (*devarim*) to speak but also "harden[s] Pharaoh's heart" (conscience) so that he will not "listen" to what Moses has to say (Exod. 7:3–4, 13).

Words meant to move people toward the truth are at a great disadvantage when one's audience does not have that awesome "gift" of heart/conscience that enables people to remain open to points of view that are not their own. Moses always seems to find himself in difficult, if not tortuous, rhetorical sit-uations. Rabbi David Wolpe makes much of this plight in his telling of the story of Moses:

Moses has to wrench words from inside himself. He cannot simply summon the phrase that would placate and please. Rather than the gentle comfort of rolling phrases and smooth oratory, God's leader has to prove by his inner struggle that he shares the people's plight. The leader must also have a catch in his throat, not spread ready rhetoric like a salve over all wounds. Moses cannot lead by means of the easy fluency of the demagogue. His is a hard-earned eloquence. His is less the mastery of the word than the heroism of the word.[4]

Hard-earned eloquence: I understand this to mean a form of rhetorical competence that one acquires, not simply by knowing and talking theory, but instead by being open and devoted to the call of conscience and the effort that it takes to spread the word in a convincing and honest way. Moses is set on a path where the acquisition of rhetorical competence must take place in the muck and mire of everyday existence. Before there was a Socrates, Plato, Aristotle, and Cicero, there was a young Hebrew who was commanded to perform a monumental task that entailed learning how to speak wisely and effectively in the everyday world.

With Moses, I think it is fair to say, we have an example of a hero whose story is not without significance to a project concerned with understanding the fundamental relationship that exists between the call of conscience and the practice of rhetoric. The example also can be used to point to one additional topic that needs introduction before I return to the issue of euthanasia: Moses died and is remembered as a hero, not as a celebrity. Although it has been said that twentieth-century American culture has reduced the first to the second, the differences between the two are significant. Daniel J. Boorstin's classic discussion of "celebrity-worship" and "hero-worship" identifies some of the more important of these differences, which he maintains must be taken seriously lest "we lose sight of the men and women who do not simply seem great because they are famous [celebrities] but who are famous because they are great [heroes]."[5]

A hero, argues Boorstin, is one who has shown greatness in some achievement and who possesses praiseworthy character. A celebrity, on the other hand, is primarily known for his or her "well-knownness," which displays much more form than substance. Boorstin writes that the celebrity

is neither good nor bad, great nor petty. He is the human pseudo-event. He has been fabricated on purpose to satisfy our exaggerated expectations of human greatness. He is morally neutral. The product of no conspiracy, of no group promoting vice or emptiness, he is made by honest, industrious men of high professional ethics doing their job, 'informing' and educating us. He is made by all of us who willingly read about him, who like to see him on television, who buy recordings of his voice, and talk about him to our friends.[6]

Moreover, the "passage of time, which creates and establishes the hero, destroys the celebrity. One is made, the other unmade, by repetition. The celebrity is born in the daily papers and never loses the mark of his fleeting origin."[7] Celebrities prosper in a world where the limelight is the rage, where the tempo of our high-tech times is fast, strong, and clear, and where "big names" need managers and agents to ensure constant exposure. But even in such a vacuous world, Boorstin admits, heroes still exist, although in an "unsung" way:

> In our world of big names, curiously, our true heroes tend to be anonymous. In this life of illusion and quasi-illusion the person with solid virtues who can be admired for something more substantial than his well-knownness often proves to be the unsung hero: the teacher, the nurse, the mother, the honest cop, the hard worker at lonely, underpaid, unglamorous, unpublicized jobs. Topsy-turvily, these can remain heroes precisely because they remain unsung. *Their* virtues are not the product of our effort to fill our void. Their very anonymity protects them from the flashy ephemeral celebrity life.[8]

I believe all that Boorstin said about heroes and the world of celebrity still rings true today. Fueled by the computer revolution, the media can now make and expose us to "big names" like never before. Heroes are being outnumbered by celebrities at an incredible rate. To borrow words from Joshua Meyrowitz, it almost seems that the hero's predicament today is that of having "no sense of place"; for "greatness," Meyrowitz tells us, "is an abstraction, and it fades as the image of distant leaders comes to resemble an encounter with an intimate acquaintance."[9] The more we know about a person, the greater the chance that we will discover the imperfections that mark their character and that reveal them to be "only human." In today's ever-growing media and computer age, where perhaps nothing about a person's life is safe from exposure, a hero's "god-like" presence is easily called into question because of its all-too-apparent fallibility. Yet as Joseph Campbell reminds us, all is not lost for the modern hero. If we take the time to open ourselves to "the wonderful modulations of the face of man," it is still possible to recognize greatness—something *outstanding,* ecstatic; something that Campbell, like Levinas, associates with "the lineaments of God."[10]

It is literally impossible *not* to bring God into the picture sooner or later when trying to come to terms with a phenomenon—heroism—that has forever been associated with a Supreme Being. There is a good reason for this: with their achievements, heroes speak to who we are as beings whose very existence is ontologically structured to do what heroes are expected to do— to offer a performance that stands out and that allows others to gain some sense of their potential to do good and hence to be godlike. Is this to say that the structure of existence is *meant* to have us think about and remember God?

Who can say for sure? I simply take the matter as a given, something that an ontological appreciation of existence reveals: we *are* beings of heroic potential who must therefore face the fact that our fate is to listen to a constant calling that challenges us with the task of being ethical and moral. And this is so even when "celebrity life" is thriving, as it certainly is doing today.

In the remainder of this chapter, I focus on how rhetoric plays a role in the construction of heroes in the euthanasia debate. These heroes arise on both sides of the debate as well as in between the extreme discourses of the hard-core right-to-die and right-to-life movements. The role played by rhetoric here is to show forth the heroic character of people caught up in the debate. We learn of this character as rhetoric is employed to portray the presence or "face" of people whose lives have suffered the ontological assault of serious illness or accident. The heroes of the euthanasia debate are both dead and alive; they are patients, family members, healthcare professionals, and others who would have us understand what it is *really* like to hear and respond to the call of conscience when staring death in the face. Becoming a celebrity is not a respected goal here, for such an achievement gets in the way of the real work that needs to be done in the debate: creating a society that possesses an abundance of practical wisdom and displays strong moral character.

The heroes who capture my attention include such people as Nancy Cruzan and her family, certain justices of the Supreme Court, members of the disability civil rights group "Not Dead Yet!," anti-euthanasia advocate Joni Eareckson Tada, the physician and comfort-care advocate Timothy Quill, and, at least to some extent, even the famous and infamous Jack Kevorkian. Because of all the publicity they receive, such people, whether they like it or not, have had to contend with the privileges and perils of celebrity life. Some have handled this challenge better than others. The first case I discuss—that of Nancy Cruzan—exemplifies just how difficult the challenge can be.

The Face of Nancy Cruzan

Nancy Cruzan became a major figure in the euthanasia debate in 1988, when her right-to-die case first went to trial court.[11] In the winter of 1983 the twenty-five-year-old Cruzan was driving alone when her car went off a Missouri country road and she was hurled face down into a ditch. When she was found, paramedics were called immediately. After about ten minutes of CPR, Nancy's spontaneous respiration was restored, but she never regained consciousness. Instead, at the hospital she was eventually diagnosed to be in a persistent vegetative state; hence, her existence was such that she was oblivious to her environment except for reflexive responses to sound and perhaps to painful stimuli. She could no longer move her body or swallow, and her cerebral cortical atrophy was irreversible and progressive. With gastrostomy feeding she was expected to live for another thirty years.

After three years of witnessing their daughter's existence deteriorate into a living death, her parents, who were also her appointed guardians, requested hospital authorities to withdraw the gastrostomy feedings. These authorities agreed to do so, but only after they received a court order in which the state of Missouri was named as a party. In 1988 the trial court authorized Nancy's parents to exercise her constitutionally guaranteed liberty to request the withholding of nutrition and hydration. The state's attorney general and the guardian *ad litem* (Nancy's court-appointed attorney) appealed the decision. The Missouri Supreme Court overturned the trial court's decision, arguing instead that the state has a primary and unqualified interest in safeguarding and sustaining the life of its citizens. This new decision was based on, among other things, the state's newly amended (1986) abortion act, wherein the life of an "unborn child" is understood to begin with "the moment of conception," and its "viability" is defined in terms of when the child's life may be sustained indefinitely outside the womb by natural or artificial life-support systems. According to George Annas, "*Cruzan* was thus transformed into an abortion opinion." In his critical assessment of the case, Annas writes:

> The court seemed to say that it would be difficult to explain why the state could permit parents to withdraw artificial life support from their adult daughter, but not from an extracorporeal embryo. Instead of appreciating the distinctions between these cases, the court concluded simply that if life can be supported "indefinitely . . . by natural or artificial life-support systems" then it *must* be because of Missouri's unlimited interest in "the right to life of all humans." Thus, the court, allegedly protecting Nancy Cruzan, transformed her not just to the status of a child, but to the status of an embryo.[12]

Nancy's parents appealed to the United States Supreme Court, which granted them a hearing on December 6, 1989. The Court's decision came on June 25, 1990, its first ever on the issue of the right to die. The Cruzan family lost the case on a five to four vote. The majority opinion emphasized that a state has a constitutional right to set any evidentiary standard it wishes and that this standard must be met before a guardian can instruct an institution to discontinue the provision of artificial hydration and nutrition. Missouri's standard was "clear and convincing evidence" of a patient's desire to stop all treatment. Nancy, however, never composed in writing an "advance directive." Hence, although the majority found (1) that artificially provided nutrition and hydration are "medical treatment" and thus no different from any other form of artificial treatment, (2) that a competent person has a constitutional right to accept or reject life-sustaining treatment, and (3) that a person who has enacted an advance directive while competent also might have a constitutional right to have it implemented, Nancy's case fell outside the letter of the law and she was therefore left by the Court to continue her living death in Missouri.

But of course the matter was not yet finished. Nancy's father told it this way: "Because of the publicity of Nancy's case, a young woman teacher who had known Nancy as Nancy Hayes, her married name, and not as Nancy Cruzan, the name associated with the picture of Nancy used in the media, realized who the 'Nancy' was when she recognized the picture and contacted us. She stated that she and Nancy had had a conversation regarding quality of life and that she was willing to testify in court about what was said in the discussion."[13] This testimony, along with the decision of Missouri's attorney general to remove his state as a party to the action, eventually led to a series of further legal and hospital actions that would allow the removal of Nancy's gastrostomy tube. She was then moved from the chronic care ward to the hospice unit where, according to her father, she received "excellent treatment" up until the day (December 26, 1990) she died.[14]

Right outside the hospital, however, it was a different story. During the last six days of Nancy's life, right-to-life protesters accused her parents of being murderers who were willing to starve their daughter to death. One protestor's sign read: "Nancy's Gift at Christmas from her Parents and Doctors—Death." Nancy's father jotted down a response that he would later share with the press: "Today, as the protester's sign says, we give Nancy the gift of death, an unconditional death that sets her free from this twisted body that no longer serves her, a gift I know she will treasure above all others, the gift of freedom. So run free, Nan, we'll catch up later."[15]

Nancy Cruzan and her family were in the national media spotlight for over two years, and all of the publicity certainly contributed to their becoming "well-known" to the American public. This celebrity status played a role in persuading state and medical authorities to allow Nancy to die. Sadly, however, it also brought with it years of depression for the Cruzan family as they continued to be condemned as murderers by anti-euthanasia advocates. The Cruzans were a religious family; they prayed to God to help "release" their daughter from a living death. But in 1996, when he was no longer capable of withstanding the onslaught of his accusers, Nancy's father, Joe, chose to "catch up" to his daughter by committing suicide. It was a tragic end for a human being who never wanted his daughter to be a celebrity, who hated having to assume this status himself, and who had received much public support for his courage, stamina, and faith over the years. In a letter that arrived at the Cruzan home soon after Nancy's death, one supporter put it simply: "I pray to God that someone would love me enough to fight to let me die."[16]

Perhaps it would be fair to call Joe Cruzan a hero. He certainly demonstrated authenticity and resoluteness as he continually responded to a call of conscience coming from an "other" whom he dearly loved and who was in much need of acknowledgment. For Joe Cruzan, however, the only thing that really mattered was his daughter's "legacy"—how she would be remembered for what she had to go through to rest in peace and to thereby help others whose final chapter in life might resemble her concluding years. Nancy's father wanted *her* story to be told by her loved ones and by others who were open to the argument that keeping Nancy alive constituted a heartless act. Such story-telling was the only way for Nancy to have a "voice" in the debate.

The two Supreme Court Justices who articulated the minority opinion in the *Cruzan* case (Brennan and Stevens) helped to make sure that Nancy's story would forever be on the record of our nation's highest court. In fact, as I hope to show, Justices Brennan and Stevens actually made Nancy into a hero by doing what the five justices comprising the majority refused to do: bring her back to life so that we could see and feel her presence. With the discourse of Brennan and Stevens, we have before us an effort in the rhetorical construction of the face of a hero. A brief look first at how the majority talked out its opinion will help readers better appreciate the rhetorical competence of the dissenting view.

The Supreme Court's "impersonal" opinion. Chief Justice Rehnquist delivered the majority opinion of the Court, in which Justices White, O'Connor, Scalia, and Kennedy joined. O'Connor and Scalia also filed concurring opinions.[17] Rehnquist made clear the cautious attitude that guided the majority: "This is the first case in which we have been squarely presented with the issue whether the United States Constitution grants what is in common parlance referred to as a 'right to die.' We follow the judicious counsel of our decision in *Twin City Bank v. Nebeker,* 167 U.S. 196, 202 (1897), where we said that in deciding 'a question of such magnitude and importance . . . it is the [better] part of wisdom not to attempt, by any general statement, to cover every possible phase of the subject'" (277–78). With Scalia, however, we find that at least one of the justices wanted to be even more conservative in handling the case:

> I would have preferred that we announce, clearly and promptly, that the federal courts have no business in this field; that American law has always accorded the State the power to prevent, by force if necessary, suicide—including suicide by refusing to take appropriate measures necessary to preserve one's life; that the point at which life becomes "worthless," and the point at which the means necessary to preserve it become "extraordinary" or "inappropriate," are neither set forth in the Constitution nor known to the nine Justices of this Court any better than they are known to nine people picked at random from the Kansas City telephone directory; and hence, that even when it *is* demonstrated by clear and convincing evidence that a patient no longer wishes certain measures to be taken to preserve his or her life, it is up to the citizens of Missouri to decide, through their elected representatives, whether that wish will be honored. (293)

Scalia concluded his opinion with a reminder and a warning: "This Court need not, and has no authority to, inject itself into every field of human activity where irrationality and oppression may theoretically occur, and if it tries to do so it will destroy itself" (300–301).

The warning here sounds as if Scalia was worried about the Court's committing suicide if it chose to play with such a "loaded gun" as the *Cruzan* case. To be sure, the case was loaded with a host of related and complicated issues (for example, patient competency; a person's liberty interest versus state interests; the ethical use of medical technology; the constitutionality of parents' right of "substituted judgment"; the "true" distinction between active and passive euthanasia). Such issues were acknowledged by the majority as they narrowed their judgment to what they decided to be the most salient and manageable issue at hand; hence, Justice O'Connor's concluding remark: "Today we decide only that one State's practice does not violate the Constitution; the more challenging task of crafting appropriate procedures for safe-guarding incompetents' liberty interests is entrusted to the 'laboratory' of the States" (292).

Yet as they went about employing language that abided by a certain way of interpreting the Constitution and that would lead them to their final decision, neither Rehnquist nor Scalia nor O'Connor offered any detailed account of who Nancy Cruzan was beyond her current physiological status. These three justices spoke of a young woman as would a conscientious physician presenting a patient's *medical* history. The most intimate take on the case was offered by Rehnquist when he concluded:

> No doubt is engendered by anything in this record but that Nancy Cruzan's mother and father are loving and caring parents. If the State were required by the United States Constitution to repose a right of "substituted judgment" with anyone, the Cruzans would surely qualify. But we do not think the Due Process Clause requires the State to repose judgment on these matters with anyone but the patient herself. Close family members may have a strong feeling—a feeling not at all ignoble or unworthy, but not entirely disinterested, either—that they do not wish to witness the continuation of the life of a loved one which they regard as hopeless, meaningless, and even degrading. But there is no automatic assurance that the view of close family members will necessarily be the same as the patient's would have been had she been confronted with the prospect of her situation while competent. (286)

If a more *telling* "person story" were to be offered regarding the Cruzan family, it would have to be concocted and experimented with in the "laboratory" of the states. Rehnquist and some of his colleagues did not feel obligated to take to heart everything concerning the Cruzan's predicament. The face that is put on this family by these justices is thus one whose historical features begin with a car crash and end with a gastrostomy tube still inserted in an incompetent patient. Constructed with discourse that abided entirely by the letter of the law, this face lacked spirit, emotion, and personality. The minority's take on the matter, however, granted this face a much more real-to-life expression.

The Supreme Court's "personal" opinion.   Justice Brennan filed a dissenting opinion in which Justices Marshall and Blackmun joined. Justice Stevens also filed a dissenting opinion. As stated by Brennan, these justices maintained that "Nancy Cruzan is entitled to choose to die with dignity" (302). And as soon as Brennan begins to share his thinking on the matter, a sense of *personal suffering* is described that is nowhere found in the majority's opinion. Appropriating language from the trial court decision and from related cases, Brennan emphasizes that Nancy Cruzan "has dwelt in [a] twilight zone of suspended animation" for six years. "Her body twitches only reflexively, without consciousness. The areas of her brain that once thought, felt, and experienced sensations have degenerated badly and are continuing to do so. The cavities remaining are filling with cerebro-spinal fluid. . . . 'Nancy will never interact meaningfully with her environment again.'" She will, however, "remain a passive prisoner of medical technology" for as long as she is kept alive (301–2). And while she remains alive, her surgically implanted gastrostomy tube "may obstruct the intestinal tract, erode and pierce the stomach wall, or cause leakage of the stomach's contents into the abdominal cavity." Additionally, "the tube can cause pneumonia from reflux of the stomach's contents into the lung" (307).

Brennan's vivid description of Nancy Cruzan's "dwelling place" (*ethos*) and her corresponding mental and physical state is as discomfiting as it is factual. The description interrupts the impersonal discourse of the majority; the interruption sounds a call of conscience; the call grants acknowledgment. Brennan speaks of a body whose personhood has been lost but whose broken (deconstructive) presence still admits its own call of conscience—a call that, as Brennan interprets it, requires us to take exception to how "Missouri and this Court have displaced Nancy's own assessment of the processes associated with dying. They have discarded evidence of her will, ignored her values, and deprived her of the right to a decision as closely approximating her own choice as humanly possible." With this interpretation of the call in mind, Brennan also is reminded of a "warning" first articulated by "one of our most prominent jurists," Louis Brandeis: "Experience should teach us to be most on our guard to protect liberty when the government's purposes are beneficent. . . . The greatest dangers to liberty lurk in insidious encroachment by men of zeal, well meaning but without understanding" (330).

Brennan offers here an emotionally powerful indictment of both the State and some of his colleagues. As his opinion unfolds, we learn that the lack of understanding displayed by these official parties concerns their limited reading of the Constitution and their refusal to acknowledge the particular situation of Nancy and her family—a situation that, with the Court's decision, continues to be unjust and shameful because it allows a patient and her loved ones no escape from a system that has gone wrong. Brennan puts it this way: "The 80% of Americans who die in hospitals are 'likely to meet their end . . . in a sedated or comatose state; betubed nasally, abdominally and intravenously; and far more like manipulated objects than like moral subjects'" (329).

Brennan, to be sure, is opposed to such mistreatment; hence, throughout his opinion he speaks on behalf of moral subjects whose certain inalienable rights are guaranteed by the Constitution and who thereby should not suffer the pain and humiliation of becoming part of an experiment that supposedly is best conducted in the "laboratory" of the States. Appropriating language that is humanistic in spirit from past Supreme Court decisions, Brennan writes: "The right to be free from medical attention without consent, to determine what shall be done with one's own body, *is* deeply rooted in this Nation's traditions, . . . 'The inviolability of the person' has been held as 'sacred' and 'carefully guarded' as any common-law right. . . . Thus, freedom from unwanted medical attention is unquestionably among those principles 'so rooted in the traditions and conscience of our people as to be ranked as fundamental'" (305).

Noting that the majority acknowledges this last point, Brennan finds it unsettling that they did not take the next logical and existential step toward a more careful consideration of the *actual* people involved in the case. The real and most fundamental issue before the court, insists Brennan, is not that of "States' rights" but rather of "individuals' rights." What, asks Brennan, makes the State think that it "is *more* likely to make the choice that the patient would have made than someone who knew the patient intimately?" (326). Yes, the State does have a "general" and "legitimate" interest in the preservation of its citizens' lives. "But the State has no legitimate general interest in someone's life, completely abstracted from the interest of the person living that life, that could outweigh the person's choice to avoid medical treatment" (313). Hence, for Brennan, the case of Nancy Cruzan is just that: it's *her* particular case, *her* life and death, *her* personal story that needs to be listened to with the utmost respect. And when it comes to attending to such a story, we must keep in mind, writes Brennan, that "dying is personal. And it is profound. For many the thought of an ignoble end, steeped in decay, is abhorrent. A quiet, proud death, bodily integrity intact, is a matter of extreme importance." Moreover, he continues, "A long, drawn-out death can have a debilitating effect on family members." And for some patients and their loved ones, "the idea of being remembered in their persistent vegetative states rather than as they were before their illness or accident may be very disturbing" (311–12). Indeed a living death makes a tragedy out of a person's story. Who has the right to demand that a person's life end this way? Not the State, argues Brennan: "Whatever a State's possible interests in mandating life-support treatment under other circumstances, there is no good to be obtained here by Missouri's insistence that

Nancy Cruzan remain on life-support systems if it is indeed her wish not to do so. Missouri does not claim, nor could it, that society as a whole will be benefited by Nancy's receiving medical treatment" (312).

This last point can be contested. Certainly Missouri *could* have claimed that society as a whole would be benefited by Nancy's receiving medical treatment. The rationale supporting this claim, as we have seen, is provided by Kass when he emphasizes how "life provides numerous hard occasions that call for endurance and equanimity, generosity and kindness, courage and self-command. Adversity sometimes brings out the best in a man, and often shows best what he is made of." Displaying courage and perseverance in the face of death "provides an opportunity for the exercise of our humanity," and it is this exercise that defines the "most importance sense" of what it means to die a dignified death.[18] Hence, if only they could have hung in there, Nancy Cruzan and her family would have performed a "heroic" and thus "godlike" deed, an awesome act of sacrifice whereby, in order to be a model of morality for others, they would accept the suffering associated with one's living death for perhaps another thirty years. Here, then, would have been a classic case illustrating how, as Levinas would have it, human beings are capable of going to extremes in order make good their "being-for others."

But how many of us could and would make such a sacrifice, even if guaranteed by others the status of becoming a hero of mythic proportions? The difficulty of saying "yes" to the challenge here is rooted in knowing all that we do about the Cruzans' story. Brennan accused the Missouri court of showing disregard for the "personal" details of this story—details that were down-played by some of his Supreme Court colleagues as they concerned themselves more with the abstractions of legal theory than with the facts and circumstances of the particular case at hand (325). With Brennan, however, one is called on to stand face to face with the existential horror of these details and to pay witness to their deconstructive reality. Unlike Kass and others, Brennan would not have us say "Sorry. No" to the Cruzans' story.[19] On the contrary, he insists that we see Nancy as a particular other in need of help, sounding a call of conscience, crying out "Where art thou?" He insists that we see her parents as people of good conscience who are willing to answer this heartrending call. Yet what about Nancy's "right to life"? Indeed. But her story need not end in "sin." For in the Judeo-Christian tradition:

> Our greatest problem is not how to continue but how to return. "How can I repay unto the Lord all his bountiful dealings with me?" (Psalm 116:12). When life is an answer, death is a home-coming.
>
> The deepest wisdom man can attain is to know that his destiny is to aid, to serve [, to be for others]. . . .

This is the meaning of death: the ultimate self-dedication to the divine.
Death so understood will not be distorted by the craving for immortality,
for this act of giving away is reciprocity on man's part for God's gift of life.
For the pious man it is a privilege to die.[20]

Perhaps because he wants to keep the Court free of "religious" matters,
Brennan never appeals to any theological doctrine to support his position and
to thereby counter the right-to-life philosophy undergirding Missouri's assessment of the matter. Still, there is something of a "David vs. Goliath" story going
on throughout his opinion: the Cruzan family is being forced to live in the
shadow and submit to the power of the State, with its standard of "clear and
convincing" evidence. Yet under this standard, the members of the Cruzan
family have no voice. Brennan makes much of this point when, for example,
he shares certain facts that the State, with its "heightened evidentiary standard,"
must deem unreliable: "Nancy's sister Christy, Nancy's mother, and another of
Nancy's friends testified that Nancy would want to discontinue the hydration
and nutrition. Christy said that 'Nancy would be horrified at the state she is in.'
. . . She would also 'want to take that burden away from [her family].' . . . Based
on 'a lifetime of experience [I know Nancy's wishes] are to discontinue the
hydration and the nutrition.' . . . Nancy's mother testified: 'Nancy would not
want to be like she is now. If it were me up there or Christy or any of us, she
would be doing for us what we are trying to do for her. I know she would, . . .
as her mother'" (322). As Brennan continues to emphasize all that the State
would dismiss as being irrelevant to the case, he drives home the point that,
unlike her loved ones, the State is refusing to "treat the patient as a person" and
is instead acting selfishly by making Nancy into "a symbol of a cause." The
State, Brennan argues, "is a stranger to the patient" and thereby must admit that
its "knowledge" of Nancy is nowhere near that of her family and close friends
(327–28).

Brennan would have us know something of what the Cruzan family knows
and feels about Nancy. Hence, his way of telling their story is informed not
only by legal theory and precedent, but first and foremost by the personhood
of people whose suffering warrants acknowledgment and with whom others
can identify. Brennan believes that he has the Constitution on his side; his rhetoric also makes clear, however, that the case before him is rooted both in "the
traditions and conscience" of a nation whose citizens have long sacrificed their
lives to protect their freedom of choice, and in the personal histories of members of the Cruzan family. These histories, and especially Nancy's, were transformed by an auto accident and by medical and legal procedures such that they
became a source from which to hear the call of conscience. Brennan's rhetoric gives notice of this call as his words interrupt an official discourse that

would have us listen only to itself. Earlier I associated the selfishness of such an egotistic discourse with what I termed *social death*—the marginalizing and disempowering of people that leads to their unjust suffering. With Brennan's rhetoric we thus have before us an emotional story that sounds its own call of conscience against the performance of such an action. Brennan's opinion is evocative of a suffering presence—the "face" of Nancy Cruzan—that demands acknowledgment. Keeping in mind all that both Heidegger and Levinas reveal about such a demand, I think it is fair to say that failure to respond to it constitutes a form of immoral behavior.

When Justice Stevens adds his dissenting opinion to that of Brennan, the face of Nancy Cruzan is further enhanced. According to Stevens, this young woman's "liberty to be free from medical treatment must be understood in light of the facts and circumstances *particular to her*" (331, emphasis added). Like Brennan, Stevens details the horror of Nancy's condition so as to make clear what is missing in the State's and the majority's respective opinions. Hence, Stevens maintains that the Cruzan case speaks to us of how continuing developments in medical science and technology have "transformed the political and social conditions of death: People are less likely to die at home, and more likely to die in relatively public places, such as hospitals or nursing homes" (339). With this transformation, "ultimate questions that might once have been dealt with in intimacy by a family and its physician have now become the concern of institutions" (340). Moreover, "When the institution is a state hospital, as it is in this case, the government itself becomes involved" (340–41). For Stevens, however, "Dying nonetheless remains a part of 'the life which characteristically has its place in the home.'. . . The physical boundaries of the home [not only] remain crucial guarantors of the life within it but also mark out a 'private realm of family life which the state cannot enter'" (341).

To speak of Nancy Cruzan's "home" is to associate her existence with a family that loves and knows her and who are thus in a better position to deal appropriately with a matter of "individual conscience": "Choices about death touch the core of liberty. Our duty, and the concomitant freedom to come to terms with the conditions of our own mortality are undoubtedly 'so rooted in the traditions and conscience of our people as to be ranked as fundamental' . . . and indeed are essential incidents of the unalienable rights to life and liberty endowed us by our Creator" (343). The Cruzans are a religious family; they maintain a close-knit and righteous home. It is not uncommon for people to become uncomfortable and perhaps even quite anxious when they "do not feel at home" (*unheimlich*) in a given environment. Stevens would thus have us question the treatment of Nancy Cruzan: Why make a young woman and her loved ones prisoners of technology? Why force her and her family to suffer further emotional turmoil by permitting the State to invade the privacy of their most cherished dwelling place? Why not grant Nancy the gift of a loving and final homecoming? Stevens never hesitates in offering answers to these questions. Like Brennan, he sounds a call of conscience whose eloquence is meant to interrupt a misguided way of thinking and acting: "However commendable may be the State's interest in human life, it cannot pursue that interest by appropriating Nancy Cruzan's life as a symbol for its own purposes. Lives do not exist in abstraction from persons, and to pretend otherwise is not to honor but to desecrate the State's responsibility for protecting life" (356–57).

Stevens speaks to us of persons, not abstractions. He wants us to move closer to a reality of pain and suffering, a reality of living death; his epideictic discourse works to transform everyday space and time. Although he admits that "not much may be said with confidence about death unless it is said from faith," he nevertheless maintains that we may "justly assume that death is not life's simple opposite, or its necessary terminus, but rather its completion. It may, in fact, be impossible to live for anything without being prepared to die for something" (343). Such existential insights receive much philosophical and religious support from the traditions that inform and are informed by the work of Heidegger and Levinas. Stevens, however, turns another way in order to develop his point and its specific relevance to Nancy Cruzan's personhood: "Certainly there was not disdain for life in Nathan Hale's most famous declaration or in Patrick Henry's; their words instead bespeak a passion for life that forever preserves their own lives in the memories of their countrymen." Quoting from Lincoln's Gettysburg Address, Stevens notes: "From such 'honored dead we take increased devotion to that cause for which they gave the last full measure of devotion'" (343–44).

Nathan Hale, Patrick Henry, Abraham Lincoln, . . . Nancy Cruzan: Stevens associates this last person with individuals known for their courage, commitment, and willingness to make personal sacrifices for the good of others. Stevens thus places Nancy in the context of American heroes whose actions helped to secure some of the very "rights" that the State would deny her. This denial, one might argue, is un-American. Nancy Cruzan is a person who in her own heroic way speaks of sacred matters that are meant to be remembered by "we, the people."

Although Stevens certainly maneuvers readers so that they will see Nancy in a very positive and patriotic light, he nevertheless admits that "Nancy Cruzan's death, when it comes, cannot be an historic act of heroism"; rather, "it will inevitably be the consequence of her tragic accident" (344). Indeed a person who is in a persistent vegetative state is incapable of acting in an authentic, resolute, and heroic manner. This is not to say, however, that heroism has nothing to do with the case at hand. Think of it, once again, this way: Have you ever thought about your own death? When doing so, have you ever become upset with those who, you imagined, failed to pay their proper respect to you and yours by attending your funeral? Even when we see ourselves as dead, we are still in need of the life-giving gift of acknowledgment. Where art thou? Here I am!—and, yes, you are missed and mourned and remembered. To be thought of in this way is to be granted some association with the ranks of the honored dead, of people whose stories stand out from the crowd, and who thereby display in a particular form the ecstatic and heroic workings of human existence.

Stevens concludes his opinion by emphasizing that "insofar as Nancy Cruzan has an interest in being remembered for how she lived rather than how she died, the damage done to those memories by the prolongation of her death is irreversible" (353). Nancy, sadly, is incapable of undoing this damage on her own. Still, Stevens would have us remember that there are people who can and will aid her in the heroic struggle at hand:

> Each of us has an interest in the kind of memories that will survive after death. To that end, individual decisions are often motivated by their impact on others. A member of the kind of family identified in the trial court's findings in this case would likely have not only a normal interest in minimizing the burden that her own illness imposes on others, but also an interest in having their memories of her filled predominantly with thoughts about her past vitality rather than her current condition. The meaning and completion of her life should be controlled by persons who have her best interests at heart—not by a state legislature concerned only with the "preservation of human life." (356)

Stevens speaks of a woman whose story suggests that, if capable, she would act authentically by assuming the ethical responsibility of affirming her freedom of choice so that she could die with dignity. She would do this out of self-respect *and* out of loving concern for others. The story of Nancy Cruzan, if allowed to come to a peaceful and good end, would exemplify the most fundamental aspects of Heidegger's and Levinas' respective thinking on the call of conscience. Nancy could thereby be remembered in as positive a way as possible and thereby differently from how right-to-life advocates would have it. *She gave her life for the welfare of others who,* at the same time, *acted with her welfare in mind.* Although their memories would always hold tortuous thoughts, the Cruzan family could honor one of their own as a wonderful and cherished daughter and sister whose vitality and loving ways warranted the utmost respect and served to inspire others. Nancy's family appreciated this inspiration coming from one who was more than a mere celebrity. The face of Nancy Cruzan displayed a heroic presence that called on her family to return the favor.

When recalling some of the horror of his daughter's situation, Joe Cruzan told of how his relationship with some of Nancy's nurses became "strained" right after the family initiated legal proceedings: "The nurses began to report seeing Nancy cry or laugh or smile. One nurse said she had read a valentine that was sent to Nan and when she turned around she saw tears in Nancy's eyes. I'm not saying she didn't see it; I really don't know. But I can tell you this: We literally cried over her body and never did we see a response."[21] This snippet of Nancy's story says much about the strong emotions that informed her circumstances and that Justices Brennan and Stevens would have us understand in order to appreciate all the relevant facts in the Cruzan case. The Cruzan's were not zealots but only what I would term "reluctant heroes" whose pain, suffering, and sacrifice told a heartbreaking tale that in the end was not without some degree of redemption. For when all was said and done, calls had been answered and gifts had been given. Where art thou? Here I am! Brennan and Stevens helped to give voice to these calls and to facilitate the exchange of gifts. Nancy and her family were acknowledged for being persons who knew the importance of hearing and answering the call of conscience—a call that came from one who was once a model of love and joy but whose body was currently in such a sorrowful state of deconstruction that her goodness could only be reconstructed and sustained by the fond memories of others. The case is about mercy, not murder.

Brennan and Stevens admitted as much. They told emotional stories and developed well-defined arguments about the meaning of life and death and related legal matters. And as they also recalled certain memories throughout their opinions, they at the same time performed an amazing rhetorical deed that Rehnquist, Scalia, and O'Connor could not perform, given their interpretation of the case: Brennan and Stevens brought Nancy Cruzan "back to life" so that she could die in peace, with dignity, and as an honored and heroic soul. In the Supreme Court case of *Cruzan vs. Director, Missouri Department of Health,* one can hear a call of conscience sounded by two men who saw fit to acknowledge the suffering of others and thereby to remedy an injustice that had been going on for years. Perhaps these men warrant acclaim as heroes, too.

Reinhold Niebuhr may be correct: "The ending of our life would not threaten us if we had not falsely made ourselves the center of life's meaning."[22] The issue here often takes center stage whenever postmodern philosophers and critics take exception to the egocentric worldview that they associate with their modernist counterparts. Heidegger, with his appreciation of the otherness of Being, and Levinas, with his appreciation of the otherness of others, helped to make sure that twentieth-century philosophy was well informed about certain sociopolitical and technological dangers that are born of this worldview. Indeed one might even go so far as to argue that Nancy Cruzan, members of her family, and certain justices are guilty of promoting this view's egocentric bias: Does not the Cruzan case center around a single family fixated on the welfare of *its* members? As the Cruzans and their supporters advocated their constitutional rights, did they not also have a duty to recognize how their behavior might adversely affect others outside of their family circle? Moreover, as those like Kass remind us, is not the hero one who is willing to sacrifice his or her personal welfare for the benefit of the community?

I, however, have little trouble thinking of the heroism of the Cruzan family. Their story warrants heartfelt recollection; it has something important to teach us about the "good life" and the "good death" and the virtues that are related to such goodness. The case of Nancy Cruzan sounds a call of conscience that echoes in the rhetoric of those who detailed this person's emotional story—who she and her loved ones were before and after her accident. This rhetoric is interruptive, evocative, eloquent at times; it works to transform everyday space and time so as to move us closer to matters that are truly awesome; it offers us more than idle talk; it speaks to us of the importance of being-for others. The heroes that speak such rhetoric, however, are not only those who advocate the right to die. The next case study should make this clear.

The Faces of Those Who Are "Not Dead Yet!"

The specific rhetorical transaction that concerns me now occurred in cyberspace and lasted from October 1996 to February 1997. During this five-month period members of a disability civil rights group known as "Not Dead Yet!" (NDY)—a group that opposes the rhetoric of the right to die—conducted what their opponents described as an "invasion" of an electronic mailing list operated by the Euthanasia Research and Guidance Organization (ERGO). I will argue that this invasion actually operated as a call of conscience, a call that, among other things, had to work as an interruption given over to the rhetorical task of constructing a "real" and moving image or "face" of NDY's membership. Performing this task enabled NDY advocates to present something of their true and heroic character to those who seemed to forget their plight.

This presentation was essential because of what happens to the flesh and expression of the human face in cyberspace. As Michael Heim, for example, notes: "Today's computer communication cuts the physical face out of the communication process. Computers stick the windows of the soul behind monitors, headsets, and datasuits. Even video conferencing adds only a simulation of face-to-face meeting, only a presentation or an appearance of real meaning." What is lost in computer-mediated communication, according to Heim, is "the primal interface" whose "physical eyes are the windows that establish the neighborhood of trust. Without the direct experience of the human face, ethical awareness shrinks and rudeness enters."[23] Heim provides no evidence to support this claim. We have seen, however, that with his phenomenological description of the "epiphany of the face" that presents itself in our everyday social and political encounters and from which is heard the interruptive voice of the call of conscience, Levinas does provide such evidence.

Recall that the "face speaks" and in a "primordial" way: "Prior to any particular expression and beneath all particular expressions, which cover over and protect with an immediately adopted face or countenance, there is the nakedness and destitution of the expression as such, that is to say extreme exposure, defenselessness, vulnerability itself" (EFP 83). Owing to this epideictic event, "the Other becomes my neighbor [in the most communal and moral sense of the term] precisely through the way the face summons me, calls for me, begs for me [with an interrupting call of conscience], and in so doing recalls my responsibility, and calls me into question" (EFP 83). This call sounds a command, a primordial rhetorical interruption—"Thou shalt not commit murder"—that speaks against any deed that threatens the well-being of others with physical and social death. Where art thou? Here I am! At the heart of existence lies a need for acknowledgment.

The Cruzan case says as much; yet so do the stories of persons whose physical disabilities might encourage others to think and say, "I wouldn't want to exist that way," but whose desire to live on enables them to cope with these disabilities. One of the added burdens that goes with these disabilities is having to deal with the way advocates of the right to die often advance arguments by telling stories of pain and suffering that the disabled know all too well but that now are being employed for the specific purpose of having people realize that they have the right *not* to live that way. This added burden is ethically and rhetorically significant. The disabled who want to live on are made to listen to discourse that uses the material of their lives to justify why people who suffer as they do need not, and should not be forced to, live on. The disabled thus find themselves in a situation where their own existence, which has already been marginalized by society, is now actually being turned against them by people whose stories and arguments, ironically, are meant to help the pain and suffering of disabled individuals.[24]

One might even state the problem more forcefully. As the euthanasia controversy unfolds, the disabled, who are not yet ready to die, are nevertheless being de-faced, dehumanized, and demoted to a class of people whose presence is represented in society as a living death sentence, as death staring others in the face and reminding them of a future that too often comes to a painful end. People who have "only" been disabled by their race or gender or religion or sexual orientation or age certainly know something of the social death that is happening here. Of course, one of the most gut-wrenching and heartbreaking episodes of this occurred with the Holocaust. Here, being put to social death was but an indication of worse things to come: total extinction. "That couldn't happen in this country!" claim advocates of the right to die.[25] Members of disability civil rights groups like NDY, however, are not so sure, for they are already on a slope that feels too slippery, a slope where calls for help— Where art thou?—are being answered by a growing number of citizens and medical personnel who are willing to say, "Here I am to assist in your suicide!"[26] The face speaks: "In the name of mercy, thou shall commit murder." With the euthanasia controversy, the primordial saying of the face that operates as a call of conscience, a rhetorical interruption that calls us into question, is now heard to say something more about the goodness of life: when such a life is no longer possible, a good death should follow.

On October 5, 1996, members of NDY chose to express their fears about such "mercy killing" by beginning a five-month "invasion" of an electronic mailing list of a group of right-to-die advocates, the Euthanasia Research and Guidance Organization (ERGO), whose founder and list manager is Derek Humphry, author of the best-selling book *Final Exit: The Practicalities of Self-Deliverance and Assisted Suicide for the Dying*. By October 7, members of ERGO were somewhat upset. Jesse Ledgerwood, for example, had this to say: "I am disgusted by the influx of right to life stuff on this list, but instead of giving them any attention, trying to reason with them, etc., I have decided to just delete there [sic] messages as soon as I see what they are without reading the whole thing, and recommend the rest of us do the same thing. If any of them expect to convert me by wasting my precious time, dream on."[27] In cyberspace social death is no further away than a quick keystroke. And five months later the act was still being strongly recommended. Said a certain Harry Brickman: "The invasion of this list by NDY has become intolerable. We are sorry for these people but, inasmuch as they are totally immune to both evidence and logic, debating with them is a complete waste of precious time. I propose that we RTD people ALL REFUSE TO RESPOND TO THEIR POSTS. . . . Here is an alphabetical list of recent NDY posters. When you see any of these names in the list of posted messages, simply delete the message unread. . . . If other NDY people invade us, add their names to the list."

Being characterized as invaders who are "totally immune to both evidence and logic" and whose messages only warrant the most negative acknowledgment (deletion) must have been a rather unpleasant "final solution" for NDY members. They were made out to be creatures who, like viruses that are immune to the body's defenses, pose a serious threat to the health of a body politic. As far as I can tell, however, this was not NDY's goal. Rather, its members were fighting for their lives in a place where the ruling discourse hardly ever recognized their presence, their faces, their humanity. They wanted positive acknowledgment, for they, to be sure, were not dead yet.

What faced NDY members who chose to occupy for as long as they could a dwelling place where their true character was shown little respect was, in fact, a rhetorical challenge. In a place where faces are seen only as they are put into words, NDY members had to make an especially "good showing" of themselves, one that was awe-inspiring enough to interrupt and call into question a way of thinking and speaking that unintentionally gave support to a climate of social death. How well they met this challenge is best illustrated by way of a more detailed discussion and assessment of how the NDY's call of conscience came and went in cyberspace.

Sounding the call: a rhetorical interruption for the sake of acknowledgment. The invasion came with no warning and was performed with ease on what at the time was ERGO's open, unmoderated listserv.[28] The first to speak was Stephen N. Drake: "Not Dead Yet! is a group of disability activists who are opposed to the legalization of assisted suicide. We have invited ourselves to your forum for a number of reasons." The first two reasons dealt with how Derek Humphry and his associate, John Hofsess—acknowledged "experts on the topics of assisted suicide and euthanasia"—had yet to make available on their listserv "materials and news items that reflect opposition based in the disability community." Stating the third reason, Drake wrote:

> We believe this pattern of omission is intentional. Promoters of assisted suicide and other related agenda have been successful in presenting the issue as an argument between the religiously-based "right to life" movement and advocates of "choice." There is a third voice in this debate, an opposition based in a civil rights perspective. In growing numbers members of the disability community are alarmed by the stereotypes and discrimination widespread in the medical community and reflected in the language and stories used to promote the legalization of the right, putting it bluntly, to be killed.

The fourth and final reason contained a warning: "We do not expect to be welcome participants in your ongoing *discussion,* as it is currently framed on this list. Accordingly, we will be posting materials that will probably be unfamiliar to most of you and then leave. However, unless we see an acknowledgment of our voice in this debate, as evidenced by distribution of news stories related to Not Dead Yet! actions as well as other disability-based material, we *will* be back."

Drake's words interrupted an ongoing flow of discourse given over to such things as the activities of the right-to-die movement in and outside of the United States, the trials and tribulations of Jack Kevorkian, and discussion of pertinent news stories, new and forthcoming books, and essays found in medical journals. The interruption called this discourse into question. It was missing something: a "third voice" that was not simply the re-presented voice of the right to life being constantly critiqued by supporters of ERGO. Drake sought "acknowledgment" of what this third voice was saying: he issued a call of conscience. The call warned of future interruptions. The warning had something of an Arnold Schwarzenegger ring to it: "we *will* be back." But of course Drake's words were not meant to end on a humorous note. On the contrary, his call of conscience was dead serious, for it functioned to open a space for other "wounded storytellers" like himself, who were engaged in the "authentic" act of speaking for their particular "personhoods" so as to ensure that their disabled existence would not be misunderstood, misrepresented, or in the worst case, effaced entirely.[29]

Derek Humphry, emphasizing that he was the "list manager" of ERGO's Web page, was the first to respond to Drake's call. The response was a bit defensive. Not only did Humphry ignore Drake's claim about the NDY being a "third voice" and thereby continue to associate this voice with the religiously based right-to-life movement, but he also felt it necessary to raise a question that further branded his opposition: "Why should this 'right to die' list burden itself with the news of opposing groups when that is available to all elsewhere with a few clicks?" The voice of NDY is a "burden." Humphry followed this slight the next day (October 6) with a post that was more conciliatory but that also added insult to injury: "After consultation and consideration of many different viewpoints, I've decided that this right to die mailing will continue in its present form—warts and all. Freedom of speech has its price." In the name of this freedom ERGO was willing to put up with the burden of having "warts" blemish its cyberface.

Countering social death.   NDY members are human beings, not warts, even though by commonsense definition these beings are not "pictures of health." It is this definition that NDY members seek to change. Their integrity, self-respect, and psychological well-being depend on it. "The human body, for all its resilience, is fragile; breakdown is built into it."[30] Stephen Drake and his colleagues are quite aware of this fact of life. They live it every day to an extreme. When one's body breaks down or is otherwise disabled, it sounds its own call of conscience. The broken body is an interruption to itself as well as to others; it presents discomfort to those who must live with it and to those who witness its dysfunction. Witness, for example, the physical disabilities of people whose arms and legs no longer work or are gone completely and whose existence depends on such things as hard-to-take drugs (such as chemotherapy), wheelchairs, ventilators, respirators, dialysis machines, and similar types of medical technology. Can I live on? Would I want to live on? These are the basic questions that are typically raised as illness or accident wreak havoc with our bodies and thereby show the world a face that can tell with much practical wisdom a story of life and death.

In his analysis of how the narratives of wounded storytellers work, Arthur Frank notes that "ill people's storytelling is informed by a sense of responsibility to the commonsense world and represents one way of living *for* others. People tell stories not just to work out their own changing identities, but also to guide others who will follow them."[31] Storytelling is thus a moral activity that seeks to turn "suffering into testimony" and that thereby offers itself as a response—a Here I am!—to anyone whose illness or disability makes them cry out: "Where art thou?" Adhering as he does to some of Levinas' teachings, Frank also notes, however, that "one of our most difficult duties as human beings is to listen to the voices of those who suffer. The voices of the ill are easy to ignore, because these voices are often faltering in tone and mixed in message, particularly . . . before some editor has rendered them fit for reading by the healthy. These voices bespeak conditions of embodiment that most of us would rather forget our own vulnerability to." Franks admits that listening carefully to these voices is hard, but like the telling of stories, it too is "a fundamental moral act."[32]

The stories told by NDY members were hard to listen to, for they often spoke at length of very discomfiting things. For example, during the five-month debate, one NDY member, Cal, made clear why he and his associates oppose the legalization of physician-assisted suicide, especially "in the current atmosphere." He began by expressing some common fears of the disabled that constantly arise because, in this atmosphere, they are pushed to "complete despair" by poorly run healthcare facilities, physicians who lack good communication and listening skills, inadequate educational and vocational opportunities, and the loss of health insurance. "In other words," wrote Cal:

> I have a pretty good idea of what it takes to push me to complete despair, and these circumstances occur on a regular basis. And they don't need to. It is not my disability that is causing this despair; it is a combination of my disability and the environment I live in—an environment which could be changed. And while I support having as wide a range of choices for people as are possible without harming other people, I do not think that setting it up so that large numbers of people with disabilities are likely to perceive their only choices as death or the financial ruin of their families, or death or uncontrolled (but not uncontrollable) pain, or death or incarceration in a nursing home or other institution, or death or the exhaustion of loved ones and the increasing straining of relationships between them. In theory it should never come down to options like these. In practice it does. As a society increasingly sees death as the dignified option in each of these pairs, the balance is tipped. There is pressure to die. There is *already* pressure to die. If we legalize PAS [physician-assisted suicide] in the current situation, it can only increase.

Cal then took some time to offer a narrative that was a bit more personal. Despite the length of this narrative, which as presented here is less than half of his full posting, the discourse warrants attention:

> If the choices were going to be death or supports so that I could work and contribute to my family's financial situation, death or the best pain management medicine can reasonably offer, death or adequate assistant services in my own home, or death or a family life as harmonious as it would be were I not disabled, then I would trust myself to make an autonomous choice. Until then, the risk of coercion disguised as self-determination is too high.
>
> As far as good will, there are two problems. First, I only need to encounter a small number of doctors without good will in order to be dead. Secondly, even if I only encounter doctors with good will, that isn't enough. On several occasions I have said to a doctor that I was tired and had that misinterpreted as "I want to die." . . . On several occasions I've requested that a doctor explain the purpose and the likely side effects of a drug he wanted to prescribe and had that misinterpreted as "I don't want any treatment at all." . . . Beyond that, a lot of doctors in my life have thought I would be better off in a "facility." I disagree. (I have tried out that life, and I do not want ever to go back.) Many of these doctors have been people of good will who've honestly thought I'd have a "better life" if I were thus protected. And some of them have managed to get me put into the institution of their choice. Where would I be if they thought I'd be better off dead? And this is not idle rhetoric; when people ask me what's "wrong" with me, and I tell them, the response is more frequently than not, "That's awful!" or "But how do you get through life?" Those who know me tend to assume I have a relatively high quality of life (and, most days, I would agree). Those who know only my symptoms tend to assume I have a fairly low quality of life. And the days of the general practitioner who knows you well are coming to an end. I can assume that any doctor I encounter will *at most* know my symptoms.

Cal shared these words three months into the debate. He thus had not been deterred by being called an invader, a burden, a wart—someone who is "totally immune to both evidence and logic" and whose presence warrants no more of a response than the striking of a deletion key. Like those NDY members who logged on before and after him, Cal seemed intent on putting a face on matters so that others could recognize and acknowledge the plight of people whose call of conscience was not receiving an adequate response from society or on ERGO's Web page.

Following Levinas, one would have to admit that the situation here was, to say the least, unethical. "The other calls . . . with a vocation that wounds, calls upon an irrevocable responsibility, and thus [addresses] the very identity of a subject" (OTB 77). This call is already taking place before it is put into words by those like the members of the NDY. Arising from the a priori condition of human sociality, the call poses "the inevitable and preemptory ethical problem of the medication which is my duty" (US 158). For the members of the NDY or any other person suffering the consequences of social death, this principle must not be confined to hospital rooms and physicians' offices. The never-ending call of the other makes us all doctors—beings whose existence is fundamentally and ethically structured such that we exist not only *with* others but also *for* others.

Thou shalt not commit murder.   Why is it so difficult for all those people mentioned by Cal to open themselves fully to the disabled? Cal certainly points to one reason when he tells of how his physical symptoms are too easily and shallowly read as indications of "a fairly low quality of life." Standing face to face with one whose body speaks so readily of wounded humanity, we must acknowledge and come to terms with our finitude. As soon as we are born, we are old enough to die. Being reminded of this fact of life, of how our bodies are fated to break down, we are likely to undergo the experience of "annihilation anxiety," whereby the future is known primarily by a sorrowful if not terrifying name: death. NDY members are not yet ready to die, but reactions to their presence can often make them feel that their life "is not worth living."[33] Not being totally opened to the disabled not only helps people avoid offering such impolite reactions (which promote social death), but it also makes it easier for them to ignore their own mortality and to avoid the anxiety that can accompany thinking about the end of life.

There is something strange going on here. People are being polite to others by closing themselves off to the pains, sufferings, and needs of these others. Where art thou? The response of Here I am! in this situation is too half-hearted, too selfish, too protective of the self rather than the other. The disabled lack genuine acknowledgment from those who can hear their call—"Thou shalt not commit murder"—and who thereby have a responsibility to respond to it. Levinas writes: "Evil shows itself to be a sin, that is, a responsibility, despite itself, for the refusal of responsibilities" (CPP 137). Reactions to the disabled can be disgraceful, unethical, murderous. But in the case of the debate between the NDY and advocates of the "right to die" (RTD), these advocates did not blame themselves for this sorry state. On the contrary, they felt it ethical to turn the tables.

Consider, for example, how Paula Marceau did exactly that: "I am dying and have the pain to go with it. Please don't make it harder than it already is. I have been ill for eighteen years and have finally entered the terminal state. I am tired, Mr. Drake. . . . I am sorry, but I feel violated by you barging in. . . . The tears are real, and I thank you for the personal despair that is setting in."

And as the debate continued, Ms. Marceau's despair was expressed by her fellow RTD members with greater hostility. Here, for example, is how "Rose" put it:

> I am also a woman who is disabled. However, unlike the "Not Dead Yet," I am fighting for the right to die of my own choosing. . . . What I want is the right to end my life . . . before the pain becomes my sole experience. I want to end my life while joy and love can still be felt. I want the right to say "This is MY body, & MY life.". . . I am not asking to give this right to another human being . . . in whose values I may not agree. . . . I am saying that I, as a 39-year-old adult, want the right to say . . . "I have lived enough. . . . I have survived enough. . . . I have fought to rebuild my life enough." . . . I say enough is enough. Let me die. For it is not you who must live in this body. It is not you who must fight every day to make a future of nothing. It is not you who live with the horror of what I live with every minute of the day. So it is not you who should [have] the right to tell me that I must continue to live this life, in this body, . . . in this condition. . . . It is my body. Keep your values, your hopes and dreams off of it. . . . Let me go.

Like the members of the NDY, the members of RTD also fear death and the pain and suffering that accompany its process. Unlike the members of the NDY, however, the members of the RTD are more fearful of death's accompaniments than they are of death itself; hence, their countercharge of guilt: The evil going on here is not the fault of those who want to "die with dignity" but rather the fault of those who are described by "Geedel" in the following way: "I find it interesting that the able disabled—that is, those who can get around, manage for themselves more or less, make choices—want to deprive the unable disabled—the bedridden and extremely feeble—of assistance to do what every other living human is free to do. I find it interesting that they are apparently so afraid for their own lives that they are willing to see people much worse off suffer for their sakes. Much of their opposition to [physician-assisted suicide] is tinged with this readiness to see others suffer as living human sacrifices to anxiety about death."

Members of the RTD emphasize a crucial difference between themselves and their NDY counterparts. The NDY are made up of the "able disabled," who are guilty of increasing the pain and suffering of the "unable disabled." The able disabled are sacrificing those who are worse off than they are. Here too, then, is a murderous refusal of responsibilities and thus the presence of evil and sin. The call of conscience comes not only from people who, despite their disabilities, are not yet ready to die, but also from those whose disabilities make them long for a "good death." In both cases it is a question of human dignity. "Help us to die in peace," plead the members of the RTD. "Help us to live in peace," cry the members of the NDY. The pleas and cries are intended to interrupt any complacency and misunderstanding on the part of others. An open-hearted way of "being-for-others" is needed *now*. Listening to their voices, to their requests for acknowledgment, is a fundamentally moral act.

Rhetorical eloquence. Both the NDY and the RTD sound calls of conscience that speak of the misery of wounded humanity. It is hard not to be moved, as least emotionally, by these calls. The discourse at work here is a "showing forth" (*epideixis*) of vulnerability. Such epideictic discourse begins with the presence of the ill body that, as Frank notes, "is certainly not mute— it speaks *eloquently* in pains and symptoms—but it is inarticulate."[34] Indeed eloquence, especially as expressed on the face of one suffering from the ontological assault of disease or physical injury, is heard even before the poor soul opens his or her mouth. This silent and moving discourse interrupts the everyday status quo with a call of conscience that asks: Where art thou?

As the five-month debate between the NDY and the RTD neared its end, the responses to the question that were made by each side continued to be more of a war of words than anything else. For example, John Hofsess wrote on February 2:

> It is an abuse of this mailing list to turn it into a place of interminable sophomoric debate. There already exists a forum on the Internet [talk.euthanasia] for such Hyde Park posturing. . . . Those of us who respect choice do NOT invade the private or public mailing lists of "pro-lifers"; but those for whom moral certitude is the only text of certainty apparently feel free to engage in any kind of disruptive behavior. They also seem to assume that disrupting the ERGO mailing list is an objective worthy of grown-up individuals. Such people do not belong here. . . . But since they lack all decency in respecting the views of others, it will be left to Derek [Humphry] to alter the manner in which this list functions to minimize future abuses.

And NDY members like Michael Volkman continued giving lengthy and determined replies:

> I am a thirty-one-year-old man. I have a bachelor's degree from a respected university. I have long, dark brown hair. I am nearsighted. I weigh fifty pounds. My legs are contracted at the ankles, knees, and hips, and the nerves which carry signals to the muscles do not work. My arms are contracted at the wrists, elbows, and shoulders and also have very limited strength and range of motion. My back has no support of its own; it curves at an arc that was reduced to 89 degrees in 1981 by a surgical procedure that implanted three stainless-steel rods and fused the vertebrae.
>
> . . . I need assistance with almost every single activity I perform. . . . That includes being lifted to my bed, my chair, the toilet. That includes

mopping my kitchen floor. That includes getting a roll of quarters to do the laundry. That includes washing my penis.

It would be very undignified if none of these things were done. Especially if I were to come to a job interview looking like a slob. Especially if I were to get on a city bus smelling like a compost heap. . . . Especially if I could never go to an interview or travel on business because there were no means for me to leave my house. Especially if it never occurred to me that I have a right to want and to pursue these objectives. . . .

I oppose any action or inaction that will result in my death. . . . I acknowledge that everything within my awareness will become irrelevant with the first nanosecond of necrosis, but I vehemently deny permission to engage in any act, or to fail to engage in any act, that will bring about the only result that cannot be changed.

I deny any judgement of my state of mind. I deny any assessment of the degree of my "disability.". . . I proclaim that the use of choice is an abusive justification for paternalism, prejudice, and bigotry that is practiced routinely in the name of compassion; such practices are repugnant. . . .

Every day there will be a risk, and there will be attacks on my body from forces beyond it. I will let none of them defeat me. I will not surrender. I denounce any person who will disavow or betray my declaration.

Volkman provides one of the best examples of rhetorical eloquence that I found in the debate. At first his call of conscience sounded like something one could read in the "personal ad" section of a newspaper or magazine: "I am a thirty-one-year-old man. I have a bachelor's degree from a respected university. I have long, dark brown hair. I am nearsighted." This last admission may be a bit strange for a personal ad, but it sets readers up for stranger and sadder things to come: "I weigh fifty pounds. My legs are contracted at the ankles, knees, and hips, and the nerves which carry signals to the muscles do not work." Volkman uses a formulaic way of presenting oneself and then interrupts it with a starker and more shocking story of his body that, by the second paragraph, also takes on the qualities of a "person story"; that is, a story that emphasizes existential rather than physical or physiological aspects of a person's "lived body." This combination of stories allows the author in the next paragraph to talk about how "very undignified" his life would be if others did not help him with certain basic needs. Despite all of his disabilities, Volkman nevertheless desires to live on. He refuses to be thought of as an illustration of a life not worth living. His continued insistence on his existential worth culminates with some concluding words of heroic defiance: "Every day there will be a risk, and there will be attacks on my body from forces beyond it. I will let none of them defeat me. I will not surrender. I denounce any person who will disavow or betray my declaration."

Volkman transformed the eloquent silence of his body with both sorrowful and joyous words. The face he presented in cyberspace was that of a person whose severely disabled body maintains an undeniable air of dignity. The NDY calls its proactive campaign against the right to die "The National Heroes Campaign"—not a campaign in search of celebrity. As can be seen in Volkman's "heroic" rhetoric, members of the NDY have no intention of giving up the good fight. But neither do the members of ERGO's right-to-die mailing list. Hence, on February 5, Derek Humphry began moderating the listserv, and the NDY's "third voice" was no longer a "disruption." Just before this happened, however, a prominent member of the RTD, Peggy Battin, took exception to her colleagues' "plan not to listen to disability-rights activists or right-to-lifers on the [ERGO] list":

> I actually welcome their discussion. . . . I think it is crucial that each of us who supports the legalization of physician assisted suicide . . . listen carefully to what opponents have to say, to what fears they express, and to the insight about human insensitivity, callousness, and cruelty they have gained in their contacts with medicine. I do not think this undercuts the strength of the argument in favor of legalization—indeed, because legalization makes possible stronger protections than anybody now has, it should be something that people in vulnerable positions most want. Nevertheless, it certainly should force us supporters to think more clearly about how our protections are devised.

Battin's post speaks to the importance of acknowledgment, of being-for others. Sylvia Gerhard, another longtime ERGO list member and ardent right-to-die supporter, was also able to chime in before the plug was pulled on the NDY. She admitted that the NDY's criticism of the-right-to-die movement "makes points that deserve thought. . . . I feel we have common interests." The NDY and the RTD need to work "together toward legislation which will improve care for the dying and disabled." Although I cannot be sure of how much of Battin's and Gerhard's openness toward the NDY was a product of this civil rights group's presentation in cyberspace, both women obviously were attentive to what they were hearing as they listened to the group's rhetorical interruptions and call of conscience. It was a very ethical thing to do; for indeed, says Levinas, "To be an I means . . . not to be able to escape responsibility, as though the whole edifice of creation rested on my shoulders. . . . The uniqueness of the I is the fact that no one can answer for me" when it comes to responding to the other, to his face, to her interrupting call (CPP 97).

At the heart of human existence lies an ever-present difference: the alterity of the other person. Human existence is fundamentally pluralistic. Levinas makes much of this fact of life. Standing exposed to the face of the other, the self is called out of itself, out of its preoccupation with its personal wants and priorities and toward that which before anything else in this world really makes a difference. Sociality and the morality that maintains its just ways presuppose the constant calling out of the self toward the other. The question is always being raised: Where art thou? A heartfelt reply is needed: Here I am! Egoism becomes altruism with the reply to a call of conscience that "commands before all mimicry and verbal expression, in the mortality of the face, from the bottom of this weakness. It commands me to not remain indifferent to this death, to not let the other die alone, that is, to answer for the life of the other person, at the risk of becoming an accomplice in that person's death" (TO 109).

The rhetoric of the RTD that speaks for the morality of euthanasia and physician-assisted suicide gives voice to this call of conscience. The call also informs the rhetoric of the NDY that stands against the immorality of social death and that thereby would have us remember a holy commandment: Thou shalt not commit murder. Is this to say, however, that the face of the other speaks a contradiction? Please help me to die in peace! Please help me to live in peace! How can these two commands be uttered at the same time by the same voice? Levinas, whose appreciation of the face informs the present case study, does not say.[35] The debate between the NDY and the RTD nevertheless encourages one to search for an answer. Human beings are suffering great pain and mental distress; their bodies as well as their words tell the story.

The NDY's invasion of ERGO's electronic mailing list was intended to make known the full range of this story. Life can be a living hell not only for those who believe with all of their hearts that their quality of life has come to an end, but also for those who know that despite their handicaps the end need not be so near as long as something is done to alleviate their ongoing social death. Although spoken with the best of intentions, the rhetoric of the RTD is nevertheless heard by the NDY as legitimating this form of demise. The NDY are not necessarily against the right of individuals to choose a dignified death. What they *are* against is a rhetoric that, in the name of the "good death," ends up promoting a discursive realm of social death and the pain and suffering that go with it.

As is seen in the present case, the NDY's "heroic" rebuttal to this rhetoric can also be a threatening and thus intimidating source of distress. Is one not a "hero" if he or she begs for a merciful death that will put an end not only to the unbearable suffering of oneself but also to the immense suffering of family and friends whose hearts are being broken by what they are witnessing as they stare at the face and listen to the words of a loved one who continues to say "It's time"? The case of Nancy Cruzan offers an answer to the question—one that I suspect the heroes of the NDY would accept, even though it took five months for members of the RTD who subscribe to ERGO's mailing list to begin offering an open-minded and open-hearted response to the NDY's call of conscience.

Perhaps the NDY would not have been so unwelcome if they had not begun their invasion the way they did—with a rhetorical interruption from Stephen Drake that demanded acknowledgment but refused to give any: "We will be posting materials . . . and then leave." This is a one-sided way to conduct a constructive debate, and it certainly set the tone of much of what was to follow. Members of the NDY made a "good showing" in cyberspace by constructing a face that was hard to look at and listen to, that made members of the RTD "feel violated," that aroused their anxiety and hostility, and that encouraged them to respond in kind. During a five-month debate there was an abundance of Where art thou's? and a dearth of Here I am's! The discourse at work was more of an epideictic display of vulnerability than it was an effort in compassion—a being-for others who, on one side, are the able disabled and, on the other side, the unabled disabled. The body may speak eloquently in pains and symptoms, but when this eloquence found its way into the rhetoric of the NDY and the RTD, it was often dressed in embitterment. So much for *perfect* heroes of flesh and bones and blood and "high-level" cognition.[36] Still, both the NDY and the RTD are engaged in the heroic struggle for human dignity. Even in a war of words this topic can inspire eloquent discourse, for as Leon Kass reminds us, the goodness of human dignity points people in the direction of such all-important virtues as courage, compassion, and generosity—things that are likely to strike and arouse the heart and thus one's moral consciousness.

The moderating of the listserv silenced it as a context for debate, eloquent or not. But that did little to quell the discussion. At the time that the NDY was sounding their rhetorical interruption, lawyers on both sides of the debate were hammering out varied legal interpretations of a right to die. Two cases, *Washington v. Glucksberg* (117 S. CT. 2258 [1997]) and *Vacco v. Quill* (117 S. CT. 2293 [1997]), were on their way to the Supreme Court of the United States, where it would be determined if there was a legal basis for protecting physician-assisted suicide. Before the Court were appeals from pro-euthanasia advocates offering differing reasons why the Constitution protects a legalized right to die.[37] In defense of the status quo were government attorneys upholding the laws of their state and amici curiae briefs from those opposed to assisted suicide, including the NDY, who argued that assisted suicide is the most lethal form of the pervasive prejudice and social devaluation faced by individuals with disabilities.[38]

With their brief, the NDY again constructed a "face" through text. For example, they wrote of people like Elizabeth Bouvia, who fought through cerebral palsy and emotional duress to win the right to starve herself to death, only to decide not to exercise that "right." Kenneth Bergstadt was a quadriple-gic who required both a ventilator and the assistance of his father to function. Depressed about the burden he placed on his family and his future in a nurs-ing home, he won the right to die and used it. The Nevada Supreme Court later "recognized that he had not been properly informed and had not made a free and intelligent life-and-death decision." David Rivlin was paralyzed in a surfing accident and placed on a ventilator. He won the right to die after being confined to a nursing home because of a lack of adequate in-home care. These person stories caution against the right to die as the only appropriate response to the other, to one who unfortunately is an "invalid" but is in no way invalid. Larry McAfee, a quadriplegic who was quoted in the NDY's brief, put it this way: "[A disabled individual is] looked upon as a second-rate citizen. People say, 'You're using my taxes. You don't deserve to be here. You should hurry up and leave.' You reach a point where you just can't take anymore."[39]

The Supreme Court, in a 9-0 decision, held that the Constitution does not protect a legal right to physician-assisted suicide. Was the Court responding to a call? Amidst a sea of legalese, Chief Justice Rehnquist noted in *Glucksberg* that the "State's interest here goes beyond protecting the vulnerable from coercion; it extends to protecting the disabled and terminally ill people from prejudice, negative and inaccurate stereotypes, and 'societal indifference'" (2273). Justice Stevens, concurring, nevertheless concluded by undermining the authority of the Court's unanimous decision. When noting that the State's "unqualified interest in the preservation of human life is not itself sufficient to outweigh the interest in liberty that may justify the only possible means of preserving a dying patient's dignity and alleviating her intolerable suffering," Stevens remained consistent with his thinking in the Cruzan case and stressed the importance of the "face" of the individual: "There remains room for vigorous debate about the outcome of *particular* cases that are not necessarily resolved by the opinions announced today. How such cases may be decided will depend on their *specific* facts" (2275, emphasis added). And Rehnquist concluded the majority opinion by noting: "Throughout the Nation, Americans are engaged in an earnest and profound debate about the morality, legality, and practicality of physician assisted suicide. Our holding permits this debate to continue, as it should in a democratic society" (2275).

With this debate, we are bound to hear calls of conscience from those who are in desperate need of acknowledgment, who simply want to live in peace and to die in peace, and whose cries for help are intended, at the very least, to interrupt what are perceived to be unjust and thus immoral ways of thinking and acting. Such rhetorical interruptions will perhaps continue to cultivate the moral ecology of the nation as they raise questions about the good life and the good death and about how, in the name of humanity, we have an obligation to be there for others.

Being-for others means taking responsibility for their well-being. Having recently passed the "Death With Dignity Initiative," the citizens of Oregon put into law their understanding of what that responsibility and well-being demand.[40] Moreover, physicians continue to acknowledge that they will help their patients end their lives if a similar law is passed in their states.[41] The faces of people favoring the right to die are receiving ever more attention. There is nothing wrong with that as long as we also remain open and attentive to the presence of others whose rhetoric has much to teach us about the horrors of social death and thereby warrants recognition as being more than idle talk and indecorous chatter.

With this rhetoric (and the one from the right to die that inspires it), one reads stories that construct faces whose presence calls us into question, whose pain and suffering is, to various degrees, eloquently displayed, and whose character can be quite heroic. What I have said so far about the rhetorical construction of such faces was based on how they were presented as a call of conscience—a call that comes from you and me and others who are in need of acknowledgment and who, in our "goodness," are capable of returning the favor. Rabbi Abraham Heschel has a wonderful way of describing this needful character of human being:

> Man insists not only on being satisfied but also on being able to satisfy, on *being a need* not only on *having needs*. Personal needs come and go, but one anxiety remains: *Am I needed?* There is no man who has not been moved by that anxiety. . . .
>
> Sophisticated thinking may enable man to feign his being sufficient to himself. The feeling of futility that comes with the sense of being useless, of not being needed in the world, is the most common cause of psychoneurosis. The only way to avoid despair is *to be a need* rather than an end. *Happiness,* in fact, may be defined as the *certainty of being needed.*[42]

In the next chapter I continue my investigation of the rhetorical construction of heroes in the euthanasia debate by focusing on three people whose contributions to the debate are steeped in the need to be needed.

Chapter 7

The Face of the Needed Caregiver

In his book on the history of the science of immunology, the physician Ronald Glasser emphasizes how, when it comes to battling disease, it is the human body with its immune system, not medicine, that is the true "hero":

> We live today as we always have, at the bottom of a sea of bacteria and viruses. They have evolved with us every step of the way. They swam beside us even before we could breathe. As cells, we fought them for bits of food, and then, a billion years later, for our very lives. No matter how we may wish to view ourselves, despite all our fantasies of grandeur and dominion, all our fragile human successes, the real struggle once chemical evolution ended has always been against bacteria and viruses, against adversaries never more than seven microns wide. In the battle for species survival it has been our immune system, more than all of our other strengths and assets, more than our hands, our speed and agility, even more than our minds, that has sustained us and allows us to endure for whatever ends.[1]

Heroes are often praised as "lifesavers," or at least as persons who, in a given situation, went "beyond the call of duty" in attempting to right a wrong and to ease, if not eliminate, the pain and suffering of others. Without their immune systems, human beings are goners. Glasser admits that the human body's heroics in sustaining life are complicated by psychological and existential factors that warrant careful attention by healthcare professionals. "We know that a man coming home from a coronary care unit and labeled by his physician as cured of his heart attack, yet fearful of walking too fast or going on a plane, terrified of every increase in his heart rate, of the strain of sexual activity, can hardly be viewed by anyone, except maybe his doctor, as being healed of his illness." Still, Glasser ends his book by emphasizing some Hippocratic wisdom: "The task of the physician today is what it has always been, to help the body do what it has learned so well to do on its own during its unending struggle for survival—to heal itself. To accomplish this we must remember what doctors have always had to remember, to 'look and observe, go back to the bedside, be suspicious of eloquence, ignore ceremony.' It is the body, not medicine, that is the hero."[2]

Okay. But when this specific hero is no longer capable of undoing the damage caused by some illness or accident, physicians and members of other health-related professions are still called upon to be heroic, to "stand out" from the crowd, and to assist those whose bodies, minds, and spirits are not in good health. Such heroism is certainly a noble way to fulfill the human need to be needed—a need that requires people to put into practice, for the benefit of others, their "authenticity," their ability to assume the personal and ethical responsibility of affirming their freedom through resolute choice. In the words of both Heidegger and Levinas, one might say that the dedicated healthcare professional is a self (Dasein) who takes seriously how human existence is structured as a being with and for others.

The rhetoric of the euthanasia debate is continually being informed by this type of hero who, in an effort to satisfy his or her need to be needed, takes on the additional task of educating the public about what is actually going on in the debate and what needs to be done in order to direct matters toward an appropriate and just conclusion. Of course, assuming this task brings with it the risks associated with any attempt of trying to make a "good showing" in front of others. One such risk that is especially noticeable in today's media-influenced society is that of getting caught up in the flashy world of celebrity life—a world where so-called heroes are a dime a dozen, where the actions of these heroes are more the product of staged events than of any authentic concern for others, and where, according to career advisor Laura Berman Fortgang, "it really doesn't matter if you're good famous or bad famous" as long as you can become a well-recognized "face" and a source of entertainment.[3] In this chapter I discuss the rhetorical activities of two individuals who, because of all the publicity they have received, could be called "celebrities," but who I take to be much more authentic than that. Whether they intended it or not, these two caregivers—a right-to-life activist and a physician and comfort-care advocate—show themselves to be heroes. I then turn to the case of Dr. Jack Kevorkian, whose activities provide perhaps the most celebrated spectacle of the world of celebrity life going on in the euthanasia debate. Kevorkian sees himself as a needed caregiver and hero. As I hope to show, however, this self-appraisal is somewhat deceptive.

Case One: Joni Eareckson Tada

Joni Eareckson Tada was only seventeen when a diving accident left her totally paralyzed from the neck down. In the preface to her 1976 autobiography, she writes: "What happened on July 30, 1967, was the beginning of an incredible adventure which I feel compelled to share because of what I have learned."[4] Her story would make her "famous": a media personality, quadriplegic, and devout Christian whose years of suffering were not without purpose. For her paralysis and depression and hope and courage and artistic skills were a way for the "Holy Spirit" to use her presence, her face, to call people to God. That is what the richly detailed book *Joni* is all about.

With her 1992 book, *When Is It Right to Die?* Tada employed her continuing story to construct an argument against suicide and euthanasia. This is how Tada begins her book: "I've never been one for dissertations. . . . I barely squeezed by [philosophy 101]. . . . Oratory was for others, especially if it was dispensed in the language of computers, manuals, or big, heavy textbooks. 'Don't give me the *War and Peace* version. Just answer my questions.' And as far as . . . philosophy was concerned, seriously now, did anybody really care that 'I think, therefore I am'? . . . Whether moralistic codes were situational or rigorously rigid was of little use to me. Just state the plain facts: Was it immoral? Illegal? Unethical? Just tell me."[5]

In this beginning, Tada offers clues to a self-selecting audience interested in having their own interests addressed. If one wants to read about the "ethics" of suicide and euthanasia, the book might be made to order, but don't expect a scholarly, well-documented treatment of these related topics. Rather, what the author is about to share with readers is how the academic questions that once bored her were made real only as she had to deal with medical crises in her life that called into question her ability to want to live on, even as she stared death in the face.

Tada had long been challenged by the call of conscience that can be heard when one's existence is interrupted and broken down by accident and illness, and that demands an answer. Every day the author presents a face to others that, in a most concrete way, asks them a question that they too must ask in their just being present to one another: Where art thou? With her book, Tada offers readers a way of saying "Here I am!" She certainly has the existential credentials to make such an offering: she "had been there . . . as a severely depressed disabled person, as a family member, as a national advocate, and as a political activist" (20); she had experienced her own "personal holocaust" (25); and she was living proof that "where there is a will there is a way." A rather good-looking picture of the author seated in her wheelchair is found on the back jacket of her book.[6]

Both the "will" and the "way" are, for Tada, inextricably tied to Christian doctrine. Yet it is not until the second half of her book that she begins to make explicit use of this doctrine's rhetoric. In the first half of the book, one finds instead an account of how the ongoing plight of a quadriplegic led her to take a serious interest in the euthanasia debate. After twenty-five years of living in a wheelchair, Tada's paralyzed body was beginning to break down. "I shouldn't complain," she writes. "I haven't suffered through the usual lung and kidney infections that accompany quadriplegia. I've enjoyed miraculously good health for years." But in 1991 all of that changed: "It was a year of blood pressure problems, drastic weight loss, infections and worst of all, pressure sores on my sides and back. For three long weeks during that summer, two stubborn pressure sores forced me to bed. . . . My last stint in bed with sores lasted two months!" (23).

Tada's husband and friends helped to keep up her spirits. She also wrote articles and letters, listened to cassette tapes, and "watched a little television" to maintain an "active heart." Still, the depression became overwhelming at times:

> Like the day I began to feel claustrophobic, so hedged in. Being para-lyzed, I couldn't stretch or toss and turn. It's not like I could hop out of bed for a few minutes, visit the refridge, stop by the bathroom and run a brush through my hair, then climb back under the sheets with a good book. Grav-ity was my enemy in bed. The only movement I could manage was to turn my head on the pillow. And after several weeks of lying stiff and still, I felt at that point I couldn't take any more. I had gone through enough.
>
> . . . *I am tired, just plain worn out from living life with hands that don't work and feet that don't walk. I'm not pitying poor me, I'm just weary and ready to let go.* . . .
>
> . . . I spent the rest of the afternoon staring at the ceiling . . . and lis-tening . . . to the drip-drip of the urine that flowed from my tubing into the bedside bucket. (24–25)

Tada is a good writer; her discourse is clear, straightforward, and eloquent ("Gravity was my enemy in bed"). If it were not for the depressing and heart-breaking stories that she tells about herself, and later on about others, one might even feel comfortable characterizing Tada's book as an "easy read"—one whose prose is sometimes a bit sappy and sophomoric. Students often make this accusation, and I agree. But then I ask them to remember who the author is. Could they accuse her of rhetorical incompetence while staring her in the face? I have yet to meet a healthy student who did not pause and stumble when considering this question. Pity has a role to play in this reaction, but more often than not the students recognize with this question that the person they are criticizing is one who has survived an ordeal that might be too hard for them to overcome. Only a coldhearted individual would not be open to the call of conscience that comes with Tada's condition and the words that describe and evoke its presence, its face.

As she continues to introduce the reader to her story, Tada recalls watch-ing *The Today Show* when host Bryant Gumbel was interviewing Derek Humphry (the author of *Final Exit*) and Dr. Robert McAfee (a surgeon from the American Medical Association). According to Tada, "Mr. Humphry argued dispassionately, almost serenely, that he was not promoting suicide, but that dying individuals who wish to achieve a painless death ought to be allowed to plan for it"; hence, they "should study suicide options, including different kinds of pills and their dosage, self-starvation, and the implications an act of suicide might have on an insurance policy" (27). Recalling Dr. McAfee's reaction dur-ing the interview, Tada noted that he commented on the problems every physi-

cian faces when his or her patient is near death, and then he concluded: "When
there's a situation of significant suffering, then appropriate medication to control pain, to hasten the end . . . may occur." Gumbel's reaction to the interview
was this: "Gentlemen, I don't think we have so much disagreement as we do
varying viewpoints" (28).

Tada was shocked:

> No disagreement? Just varying viewpoints?
>
> Did the three men understand what they had just done? Or said? Or
> suggested to someone like me? . . . I fixed my gaze on my lifeless legs being
> stretched this way and that. Another hour of a tiresome routine. Each morn-
> ing the same, day in and day out, year after year. At best, boring. At worst,
> especially on days like this, depressing.
>
> My mind began to play more games. . . . *When you're back up in your
> chair, all it will take will be a quick jerk of the steering mechanism on your handicap
> van, and you'll be over the side of the freeway. Nobody would even know that you com-
> mitted suicide, and you'll be free of that paralyzed body.*
>
> I shivered and shook the thought out of my head. Yet I couldn't escape
> the cool, calm rationale of Mr. Humphry telling me in his relaxed tone that
> certain people in certain circumstances should end it all. (28–29)

As far as I can tell from reading Humphry's *Final Exit,* nowhere in the book
does he argue that "certain people in certain circumstances should end it all."
Rather, his basic point is that people have the right to die a "dignified death" and
that "self-deliverance" is a viable and "humane" option.[7] This is not to say, however, that Tada's selective perception of this author of a best-selling "suicide
manual" should be summarily dismissed. Her perception is grounded in the
same fear as the NDY's: a fear of language being used in a way that is detri-
mental to the well-being of others who, like herself, are too easily seen as
examples of a life not worth living and who must therefore be quite attentive
to a movement whose rhetoric does not function to call this view into question. Commenting on this rhetoric and those who speak it, Tada writes:

> One no longer commits suicide, one performs self-deliverance. A
> physician under a right-to-die law would not give a lethal injection, he
> would administer an aid-in-dying measure. . . .
>
> Why the semantic gymnastics? Why the subtle attempt to clap
> respectability and sterility around a cold, hard reality? . . . Maybe they feel
> it's better to drain the horror from certain words.
>
> . . . The dry discourse I saw on television lessened the debate to an
> anesthetized conversation about varying viewpoints. It made me wonder if
> somewhere professionals are sitting around open dictionaries trying to
> invent more euphemisms like "aid-in-dying measure" or "self-deliverance."

And if they are, is their motive really to dismantle the long-held ethics that have guided people for centuries? (31)

I think it would be fair to say that for Tada the rhetoric in question here—a rhetoric that "drain[s] the horror from certain words"—has too much of a dulling effect on the call of conscience that these words could otherwise evoke before they were replaced by euphemisms for the purpose of facilitating what Tada describes as "pleasant-sounding persuasion" (32). Throughout the rest of her book, and primarily through the use of person stories, Tada attempts to debunk this persuasion, to call it into question so that, by way of her rhetoric, readers will once again be able to hear the "true" summoning of conscience.

Most of the stories Tada tells in the next forty pages of her book stress how people who were severely disabled lost their battle with depression and ended their lives. Tada admits being in touch with some of these people and trying "to argue with reason and objectivity a case for 'life worth living.'" She also admits how a "huge chasm" could form between their "topsy-turvy emotions" and her "right-side-up reasoning," their "frayed feelings" and her "cool-headed statements," their "insensibilities" and her "sensibilities." "True," says Tada, "people ready to check out of life . . . can occasionally be talked down off the ledge. But many times the rational appeals don't reach their target" (44–45). Hence, the reader is told about one of Tada's dear friends (Ada) who was also a quadriplegic but who had given up hope and who thereby "dispassionately believed" that life "was not worth living." Ada died of a lung infection caused, in part, by increased cigarette smoking which, Tada informs us, was Ada's way of committing "methodical suicide." According to the author, "Ada's story is bittersweet. Bitter in that she . . . purposefully abused her body in order to engineer an early death. Sweet in that perhaps a year or so before her death, Ada finally crossed that huge chasm between despair and hope and found life worth living." Now she was "buoyant," "inspiring," and "encouraging" in her relationships with others. Tada does not detail how this transformation took place, except to tell us that Ada's "topsy turvy emotions turned right side up" (47–48). Presumably, Tada's "rational appeals" did some good.

The reader is given some indication of what these appeals entailed as Tada moves on to consider the question that names her book: When is it right to die? Tada considers how the reality of pain, expense, and indignity can direct answers to the question. "There is for each of us a time to die," writes Tada, "and when that time comes, we should be prepared to go." For Tada, however, the key problem still remains: "Exactly when is it time?" (50). When all hope is gone? When pain becomes excessive and personal dignity is shattered? When medical costs become prohibitive? Tada tells the story of "Arlene" to help clarify the matter. Arlene damaged her spinal cord and became "severely paralyzed" when she fell during a hiking trip in the coastal mountains of California. Less than a year into her disability, and unwilling to face life as a quad-riplegic, Arlene decided to starve herself to death. Her husband and family supported the decision. They did so because, as Tada puts it, Arlene was a "self-directed young woman" who "knew whose life it was—her own. It wasn't her husband's and it wasn't her two children's. Her life was not owned by the doc-tors and nurses she left behind at the hospital. And the life-and-death choices she was contemplating certainly weren't the business of her rabbi or even the pastor who ran the little support group in her community" (51).

Learning of Arlene's condition and decision, Tada wrote her a letter wherein she talked about the similarities of their situations and pleaded with her to reconsider her choice. The plea failed. Why? Tada writes:

> Arlene's death was her own business. That's what she believed. . . . I can't help but picture Arlene's life before her accident. It's easy to imagine her climbing the cliffs of Big Sur, blazing a trail into the wilderness, or pow-ering ahead on her bicycle, leaving the pack in the dust. And in a way her choice to die fits her do-it-yourself profile. After all, Arlene was obviously a first-class individual, a born and bred American who gripped onto her individualism as a highly prized value. Her brand of private initiative found its logical and ultimate expression in her decision to die. (53)

Tada's "right-side-up reasoning" failed with Arlene because this young woman's worldview was steeped in a different rhetoric—one that is known for the way it champions freedom and individual rights. One thus wonders once again what Tada's reasoning is all about; apparently she is devoted to its logic. She sheds some light on this logic as she addresses a question: Was Arlene's demise *really* her business and hers alone? "To make a decision before life involuntarily leaves us," writes Tada, "is a decision we have the power to make. But is it pos-sible such a choice is the ultimate expression of selfishness?" (53).

The question is rhetorical; Tada raises it to open the reader to what, at least for her, is obvious: as creatures whose existence is marked with an indeli-bly communal character, we have an obligation to judge how our thoughts and actions might adversely affect others. Tada, it seems, is a communitarian, an advocate of civic republicanism, someone who recognizes that "it's good to yank euthanasia out of the closet and expose it to the open air of public debate because people need to understand and be able to make informed decisions" (63). But civic republicanism presupposes an outlook that values individual rights and freedom. So why did Tada's reasoning fail with Arlene? Why was the author's call of conscience not enough to save another? Because Arlene, Tada suggests, was already too far gone on a slippery slope that is leading us ever faster through a "Brave New World" where *the character of a helping society is beginning to disintegrate.* In this world "it's easier to kill than cure, or even care.

Society is now assigning no positive value to suffering and is becoming more oriented toward a culture of comfort" (77).

This last point is made in a section of the book titled "God's Laws Make for a Better Society and Vice Versa." Although Tada does not mention God in this section, she certainly has said enough up to this point about community and society that a reader might easily associate "God's Laws" with what Tada is emphasizing when she notes: "Your gutsy choice to face suffering head-on forces others around you to sit up and take notice. It's called strengthening the character of a helping society. When people observe perseverance, endurance, and courage, their moral fiber is reinforced" (71). Certainly, both Heidegger's and Levinas' theories of conscience lend ontological and metaphysical support to this viewpoint. With his "religious" thinking on human dignity, Leon Kass too should find the viewpoint acceptable and commendable.

If a reader did not know it beforehand, he or she is now aware that Tada is giving voice to a religious calling. We learn the specific nature of this calling as Tada first writes about the importance of *Man's Search for Meaning,* a book authored by the Jewish psychiatrist and Holocaust survivor, Viktor Frankl. Tada reads this book about Frankl's surviving the concentration camps as a lesson in how "no thinking person chooses suffering. But we can choose our attitude in the midst of suffering" (82).[8] The attitude Tada adopts is now made clear and expanded throughout the rest of her book: suffering is a major way that God educates us about goodness. Tada, in fact, tells us that "the longer [she] hung in there through the process of suffering," the more she realized how rewarding the education can be. In Tada's case her friendships deepened and became "more honest"; she learned that "what's important in life is people," that "God is real" and can be experienced when one is "alone at night," and that "there are others who are hurting a lot more than me and I'm beginning to care, honestly care, about them." The "fabric of meaning" behind her suffering "was beginning to take shape. Life, [she] was discovering, was worth living" (85–86)—thanks to her close-knit community of family and friends and "He" who made it all possible.

Tada's face—the way she shows herself to *be* throughout her book—speaks of the way one's relationship with God is weakened when a civic-republican outlook becomes too infatuated with individual rights and freedom. Tada, of course, would not have us dispose of these rights, but she would have us temper them in light of the "Source of Life." Another story is offered to clarify the point: Larry McAfee[9] was paralyzed from the neck down by a motorcycle accident and sustained on a ventilator. He wanted to "pull the plug" because, as noted in a court petition, he "has no control over his person and receives no enjoyment out of life." The petition was granted. Tada wrote a letter to Larry telling him how he was not alone: "As I wrote, I wished there were no pages between Larry and me. I would have given anything to wheel into his room and angle my chair close to this bed so he could see me through the tubes and machines. If we were together, I'd confess how I, too, at one time wanted to leapfrog the process of pain. . . . [Moreover, Larry should remember that God suffered, too, and] that Jesus' decision to face the cross squarely secured a deeper meaning for the suffering in us all. More meaning than we could possibly imagine" (89).

Larry did not pull the plug. In a conversation Tada had with him several years later, he explained that he changed his mind once he learned that he would not be forced to live in an institution or hospital anymore but could instead share "a little independent living house with two other guys in wheelchairs." Life here was "a lot more enjoyable" and "less rigid. You can set your own schedule. As long as I'm not forced to live under the conditions of the state, then I consider life worth living" (91). Larry stressed that this worth had much to do with the opportunity of being free to forge friendships and thus "to feel more human." According to Tada, Larry "learned what every hurting person who chooses life discovers: *Answers most often come in the form of people rather than sentences*" (93). But Larry still held on to a belief: "I'll be honest. If a person, after years of trying, feels like he can't go on, then I feel it's within his right to . . . well you know" (92). Tada admits that her "spirits sagged a little" when she heard this, but they were renewed when Larry went on to say that, besides friends and family, God too had a role to play in his right and freedom to choose life.

A strong community of family, friends, and God: this is the prescription that Tada continually writes as she adds to her stories about the disabled, suicide, and euthanasia. For readers lacking any religious bent these stories can become, as my students often say, a "turn-off." But let us not forget who it is that stares us in the face with her book: a quadriplegic, a survivor, a civil rights activist, a person who is so dedicated to helping others that she wishes there "were no pages" between them and her. Where art thou? Tada is a stand-out when it comes to answering this question. Her book tells the story: Here I am! "Your Creator never intended that you should shoulder a load of suffering by yourself. That's the whole purpose of spiritual community—God deliberately designed people to need each other" (99). Tada sounds a bit like Rabbi Heschel, who pointed out that human beings insist not only on being satisfied but also on being able to satisfy, on *being a need,* not only on having needs. By having needs we set the ground for earthly heroism, for the wondrous deeds of heroes who stand out in their generosity with the life-giving gift of acknowledgment. Heroes hear and answer the call of conscience not only for their own sake but also, and primarily, for the sake of others. Tada is such a person: a Christian hero.

Tada would not want us to forget that she is this particular type of hero. The last half of her book is filled with Scripture and with religious anecdotes that emphasize how readers can feel just like her— "significant" and "noticed" (178) if they choose to open themselves to God and receive the life-giving gift that is always present: acknowledgment. God does not abandon us; rather, we abandon God. For Tada this sin becomes especially unfortunate when it is committed by those (such as the disabled) who are often most in need of God's gift. Tada shows herself to be a person who is needed to rectify the sin. For the sake of herself, others, and most important, God, Tada must spread the word about acts of courage, sacrifice, and kindness. She must sound a call of conscience. She does this in a strategic way: emotional stories direct readers along a path of argument that eventually shows its "true" nature as it directs us toward a specific religious outlook on the meaning of life and death. As indicated in the first half of her book, Tada would have us see this outlook as being "rational," a genuine illustration of "right-side-up reasoning"—the type of reasoning that a person like Arlene was unable to grasp and accept. With Tada, however, we are encouraged to think that the journey of such a person is not yet over.

As a devout Christian, Tada believes in "heaven" *and* "hell." She thus speaks to us at length of the "devil," whose "goal is to destroy your life, either by making your existence a living nightmare, or by pushing you into an early grave" (97). Tada illustrates the point by sharing the story of her friend, Dan. This "young man in his early twenties" was born with and disabled by a neuromuscular disease that confined him to a wheelchair, led to a heart attack, and eventually required him to be on permanent life-support technology (an "iron lung"). Given Dan's disease, this technological solution was bound to fail, and he would thus have only one medical option left: "a respirator requiring a tracheotomy." Dan did not want to accept such "extraordinary" care because, given all his other physical problems, life would now be too difficult. Tada admits that she respected Dan's decision for five reasons: (1) he is "*mentally competent,*" not "suicidal," and thus "has the *legal right* to decline treatment"; (2) "his *motive* in refusing the trach is not to hurry his death, but [to] safeguard his best chances for life"; (3) "he's conferred with his doctor, a disability expert, and is *totally informed* about his condition"; (4) "he has *specifically expressed* his wishes, underscoring that further treatment would be extraordinary and burdensome"; and most important, (5) he "understands Scripture," is "a *Christian,*" knows that life is "a gift" and that "dying is a part of the given," and thus "is heading for heaven" (143–44, 153).

Is this to say, then, that for Tada anyone who does not meet these standards is going to hell? Given the progression of Tada's argument, the question begs to be raised and answered. Tada, however, does neither; hence, at best, she leaves people like Arlene in what might be described as rhetorical purgatory. Perhaps because it would be rhetorically inappropriate and cruel to describe such a place to those who supposedly are "fated" to journey there, Tada also keeps quiet about this matter. Displaying courage in the face of "the enemy," death, is the only message that needs repeating for our and for "His" sake. She thus concludes her work with an inspirational message confirmed by Psalm 49:15: "Be patient. Don't give up. This life's not over yet, It will get better. One day you will enjoy the most perfect final exit. . . . [For indeed] 'God will redeem my life from the grave; he will surely take me to himself'" (180).

Holiness or hogwash? Answering this question need not concern us here. My interest in the life of Joni Eareckson Tada is directed by how she exemplifies one of the major ways that people in the euthanasia debate engage in the rhetorical construction of heroes. With Tada's book before me, I can see a caring and supportive face that would be nice to have around when experiencing some personal crisis. What would a person's life be like if nobody acknowledged his or her existence? Heroes answer the question with action that is needed by humankind and that, for better or for worse, is "attractive" to the world of celebrity. I get the feeling after reading Tada's book that in no way is such a world attractive to her. Her rhetoric is not an effort in exhibitionism. She has more important things to do: heroic things. In the euthanasia debate, however, not all heroes have hell and salvation on their minds.

Case Two: Timothy Quill

Three years and two months after the *Journal of the American Medical Association* published "It's Over, Debbie," the *New England Journal of Medicine* (NEJM) published an essay titled "Death and Dignity: A Case of Individualized Decision Making." Here Dr. Timothy Quill shares the story of one of his patients, Diane.[10]

Like "Debbie," this story rocked the medical profession. It too tells of a case of euthanasia; it too sounds a call of conscience. Unlike "Debbie," however, the story of Diane is not primarily a rhetorical exercise in deconstruction. On the contrary, Quill's account of his patient's life and of her death, which he helped to secure, offers a reconstruction of the deconstruction that is going on in the euthanasia debate. That is, Quill attempts to bring some order to the debate by offering a carefully constructed and unambiguous narrative that enables readers to understand how physician-assisted suicide can be an act that is far more merciful than murderous. For someone like Tada, death is the "enemy"; however, for Quill, this is not always the case. As he explains in his 1993 book *Death and Dignity*—which opens with a reprint and elaboration of his NEMJ essay—when a patient's medical condition becomes "a meaningless existence with no escape . . . , death can be a welcome friend."[11]

A grand jury eventually decided that Quill's assistance in Diane's suicide did not warrant prosecution. This decision, according to Quill, was influenced in part by the fact that Diane was alone at her death. She requested that the end be this way "to protect her family and [Quill] from potential prosecution should her act be discovered." Quill goes on to note that although Diane "was a brave person who faced death squarely," it nevertheless "violates every principle of human care of the dying if she felt she had to be alone at the end because of our laws." As a physician who was a hospice medical director for eight years, Quill knows the importance of a certain "promise" that is owed to dying patients: doctors will not "abandon them no matter where their illness may take them." Perhaps more than any other profession, medicine, with its bottom line of life and death, must take to heart how human beings need to be acknowledged. "Ironically, had I been with Diane at her death," Quill notes, "the outcome of the grand jury hearing might have been different" (22).

Dr. Quill is "a hero—a physician with a head and a heart"; he is "a real doctor who writes eloquently and compellingly about real patients"; his is "a book of wisdom and compassion," "a landmark event in the right to die movement." These are some of the things that are said by Quill's medical colleagues and other professional associates on the back cover of his book. With my assessment of the "face" that the author presents in this and related writings, I do not have a difficult time accepting such opinions of the man and his work. Having had the pleasure of being a respondent to one of his university presentations, I would also say that the author's face is consistent with the one he shows in public. Quill appears to be both a master storyteller who has achieved celebrity status and a good soul. Yet, as with Tada, after reading his accounts of wounded humanity, one gets the feeling that if the euthanasia debate is ever settled, the result will be determined, at least to some extent, by those who tell the "best" stories about the heroic deeds of people who, like themselves, have to stare death in the face on a regular basis.[12]

The story of Diane begins with a paragraph wherein we are told that she "was feeling tired and had a rash. Her hematocrit was 22, and the white-cell count was 4.3 with some metamyelocytes and unusual white cells. I wanted it to be viral, trying to deny what was staring me in the face." When Diane was told she might have leukemia, her initial reply was simple: "Oh, shit! . . . Don't tell me that" (9).

The rest of Diane's story (fourteen more paragraphs) is given over to a recounting of her personhood rather than the pathophysiology of her disease. Diane "was raised in an alcoholic family and had felt alone for much of her life. She had vaginal cancer as a young woman. Through much of her adult life, she had struggled with depression and her own alcoholism" (9–10). Quill goes on to tell us that Diane was "an incredibly clear, at times brutally honest, thinker and communicator"; although when her leukemia was confirmed, she was "terrified, angry, and sad." Moreover, she was "enraged" at an oncologist's "presumption that she would want treatment, and devastated by the finality of the diagnosis. All she wanted to do was go home and be with her family" (10).

With Diane, Quill "lamented her tragedy and the unfairness of life"; he also asked her to reconsider her decision. Her mind, however, was set. "[Diane] was convinced she would die during the period of treatment and would suffer unspeakably in the process (from hospitalization, from lack of control over her body, from the side effects of chemotherapy, and from pain and anguish)." Looking into the face of a woman who, he admits, "had a remarkable grasp of the options and implications," Quill notes that: "although I could offer support and my best effort to minimize her suffering if she chose treatment, there was no way I could say any of this would not occur. . . . Her family wished she would choose treatment but sadly accepted her decision. She articulated very clearly that it was she who would be experiencing all of the side effects of treatment" (11–12).

Having "seen Diane fight and use her considerable inner resources to over-come alcoholism and depression," Quill still thought she might change her mind as they continued to meet over the next several days and as they "talked at length about the meaning and implications of treatment and nontreatment." Diane consulted a psychologist. Nothing changed. Quill "gradually understood the decision from her perspective and became convinced that it was the right decision for her. We arranged for home hospice care . . . , left the door open for her to change her mind, and tried to anticipate how to keep her comfort-able in the time she had left" (12).

Repeating how "extraordinarily important [it was] to Diane to maintain control of herself and her own dignity during the time remaining to her," Quill then shares how Diane introduced the topic of how, when the time came, "she wanted to take her life in the least painful way possible." Quill notes: "Know-ing of her desire for independence and her decision to stay in control, I thought this request made perfect sense. I acknowledged and explored this wish but also thought that it was out of the realm of currently accepted medical prac-tice and that it was more than I could offer or promise." But still Quill "feared the effects of a violent death on her family, the consequences of an ineffective suicide that would leave her lingering in precisely the state she dreaded so much, and the possibility that a family member would be forced to assist her, with all the legal and personal repercussions that would follow." Diane's hus-band and son believed that they should respect her choice. With this in mind, Quill "told Diane that information was available from the Hemlock Society that might be helpful to her" (13).

Diane followed his advice and one week later requested a prescription from Quill for "barbiturates for sleep." He invited Diane to come to the office so that he might "be sure that she was not in despair or overwhelmed in a way that might color her judgment." Quill writes: "It was apparent that she was hav-ing trouble sleeping, but it was also evident that the security of having enough barbiturates available to commit suicide when and if the time came would leave her secure enough to live fully and concentrate on the present." Moreover, Quill also admits that it "was clear that she was not despondent and that in fact she was making deep, personal connections with her family and close friends. I made sure that she knew how to use the barbiturates for sleep and also that she knew the amount needed to commit suicide." Diane agreed to meet regularly with Quill and promised that she would meet with him before taking her life, for this was the only way that Quill could "ensure that all other avenues had been exhausted." Quill then "wrote the prescription with an uneasy feeling about the boundaries I was exploring—spiritual, legal, professional, and personal. Yet I also felt strongly that I was setting her free to get the most out of the time she had left, and to maintain dignity and control on her own terms until her death" (13–14).

Quill clarifies in his book the "comfort care" philosophy that governs his treatment of people like Diane: "Caring humanely for the dying and trying to help them find a dignified death is a fundamentally vital role for physicians. It has little of the surface appeal of life-saving medical technology, and it is certainly not reimbursed at a fraction of the rate of an invasive medical procedure. Yet if judicious use of medicine's potential is central to our mission as physicians, then its personal and professional reward are unparalleled" (52). Medical "heroics" are typically associated with saving lives. For Quill, however, caring humanely for the dying is no less of an honorable deed for the physician. The story he tells of Diane illustrates the point. We learn that throughout the next several months of her illness she experienced some joyful moments with her family and friends, but for the most part her existence consisted of episodes of physiological and psychological pain and suffering. According to Quill, "Diane's immediate future held what she feared the most—increasing discomfort, dependence, and hard choices between pain and sedation." She knew "she would be leaving soon," so she called her closest friends so that they could visit and say goodbye. She also kept her promise to Quill, who recalls that "when we met, it was clear that she knew what she was doing, that she was sad and frightened to be leaving, but that she would be even more terrified to stay and suffer. In our tearful goodbye she promised a reunion in the future at her favorite spot on the edge of Lake Geneva, with dragons swimming in the sunset" (14–15).

Diane died two days later. Quill was notified by her husband, who explained how his wife had said her final good-byes that morning and then asked him and their son to leave her alone for an hour. (Dying "alone" was part of the procedure recommended by the Hemlock Society as a way for family and friends to guard against being accused of assisting in a suicide.) Once he arrived at the family's house, he called the medical examiner and informed him that a hospice patient had died of "acute leukemia." That, of course, was not the entire story, but it was the one that would protect all concerned. Diane's husband, son, and trusted doctor would not be subject to criminal prosecution; and Diane would be protected "from an invasion into her past and her body" that would come with the required autopsy.

Quill ends the story by emphasizing how Diane "taught" him "about life, death, and honesty and about taking charge and facing tragedy squarely when it strikes." She also taught him more about the importance of being open to the needs of patients and how he can "take small risks" for people he "really" knows and cares about. Indeed, Quill assisted in Diane's suicide—a case of "passive" euthanasia. He believed in the justice of his actions. But still he wondered about many things, especially "why Diane, who gave so much to so many of us, had to be alone for the last hour of her life." The practice is cruel. The dying must not be "abandoned," for then they too easily might die in despair. Quill's last thought is more hopeful: "I wonder whether I will see Diane again, on the shore of Lake Geneva at sunset, with dragons swimming on the horizon" (16).

Quill received "thousands of phone calls and inquiries" once the story of Diane was published. He admits publishing the story because medical ethicists too often minimize the anguish faced by many dying patients and their families, and he wanted "to challenge the medical profession to take a more personal, in-depth look at end-of-life suffering" (20). Moreover, he also knew "that other physicians have secretly assisted patients of their own to die under similar circumstances. . . . Given the compelling nature of Diane's request, I felt that the article illustrated as much about careful, patient-centered decision making as it did about the physician's potential role in compassionately assisting death" (21). Quill risked his career by sounding a "challenge," a call of conscience intended to interrupt a medical practice that was not sensitive enough to the problem of "abandoning" patients. Quill would have his colleagues go further when answering their patients' call: Where art thou? The miracles of medicine entail more than technological know-how; physicians are also in the business of dispensing generous doses of acknowledgment to those they are obliged to serve. The story of Diane is meant to tell it like it is; for as Quill admits, "if change is to occur, it will be driven by the stories and passions" of those who have "firsthand experience" of how it sometimes makes good sense to see death as a friend (22–23).

Tada, I suspect, would have a hard time with this last point. Death is the "enemy," at best a "friend" of the devil. Remember the Bible! Beyond wondering whether he will see Diane again— "on the shore of Lake Geneva at sunset, with dragons swimming on the horizon"—Quill gives no indication that his moral and ethical way of being is somehow connected to this holy text. Still, a "heavenly" scene is included in his story. As Diane did for him, so Quill does for us: he leaves us with a sense of hope that grants some relief; he allows us to wonder about how death may not simply be the end of life.

Telling a story about death that lacks any sense of hope is, by definition, a morbid task. Yes, we are finite, mortal creatures; but human existence is also structured so as to open us to a call that is other than ourselves; that evokes our moral capacity; that makes us wonder about the tragedies, joys, and mysteries of life; and that thereby inspires awe. Remember the words of Rabbi Heschel: "The beginning of our happiness lies in the understanding that life without wonder is not worth living." The story of Diane is not a religious story in any "institutionalized" sense; rather, its sense of hope remains unnamed beyond "wonder" and thus beyond that experience that founds all religious doctrines. Is that not good enough? Perhaps not for someone like Tada who still might insist that Quill committed a "sin": by assisting in ending a life, he "played God." Diane didn't have to be abandoned. Her family, friends, and physician should have helped her stay alive for as long as possible; she and they could then use their suffering to educate others about its worth.

I personally am not comfortable with this idea, for I do not see Diane, her family, or Quill as being agents of the devil. True, Quill felt obliged to *confess* to what he had done. This too, of course, adds to the religious quality of his story. But the showing-forth or epideictic nature of this confession entails and emphasizes thoughts and actions of earthly heroism, of things being done in the name of mercy, of being-for others who are terrified about losing their dignity and thus having their life's story end only in a tragic way. Much has been said so far about how such heroism need not merely define an unholy deed. I do not believe that Quill told his story to preach a worldview stripped of goodness. On the contrary, Diane was a women who, despite some serious health problems, was strong enough to be a "teacher" to Quill and to others. She was honest and forthright, courageous and caring; and she valued her freedom, knew her limitations, and kept her promises. At least as described by Quill, Diane was a good soul, a scared but still *outstanding* patient and person, one whose presence, face, and life story revealed heroism.

Because of her health problems, Diane's story includes the character of Quill. Her body was deconstructing, sounding a call of conscience that was heard and responded to by a compassionate physician, a careful listener and sensitive communicator, respectful of others and exceptionally conscientious when it comes to making sure that patients and family members really know what they are doing as they deal with their tragic circumstances. We see this same physician in the many other stories that he tells—stories that make clear that "[facing the] unknown with dying patients is one of the richest, most rewarding challenges in medicine. Our dying patients have no choice about facing death; perhaps the greatest gift of comfort care is that they don't have to face it alone" (84). Quill's commitment to acknowledging others whose lives have become living deaths is praiseworthy. As he tells the story of Diane, a hero, Quill also tells another story of heroism: his own. Quill is a person who has long been taught the importance of "person-centered care," of being heroic in one's being-for others.[13] The widow, orphan, stranger, sick, and dying must never be abandoned as their presence sounds a call: Where art thou?

By his own admission, however, Quill's "Here I am!" was not generous enough: "Diane was a thoughtful, challenging, loving, very generous person, who had the courage to take charge of her own destiny. She should not have had to pay for taking charge by feeling forced to die alone" (216). Although one could blame the "law" for this horrible fate, Quill still failed Diane when she perhaps needed him most. Dying alone can only add to what some consider to be the root of death anxiety: "Since human life is a transaction, a communion, human death is the end of transaction or a failure of communion. The being which is annihilated by death is a *being with,* a coexistence, a fellowmanhood." Anxiety about death "is not anxiety about the loss of being as such, but anxiety about the absence from the company of these fellows."[14] Quill did indeed sin. He played a role in allowing something to happen, something that some might consider a fate worse than death: dying alone.

Still, Quill would certainly have us believe that his sin pales in comparison to the one committed by those who would err on the side of prolonging suffering and death. With what he confesses in the story of Diane, Quill uncovers something worse at work in the care of the dying: abandonment and lack of acknowledgment. In the final paragraph of his book, he addresses the problem in personal terms:

> I cherish life and do not want to die. At this point in my life, I would be willing to fight substantial medical battles to continue living. But for me, continued living must always have a purpose. I hope that I will be willing to struggle to find enough new meaning and direction to keep going should I become severely ill and debilitated in the future. But if and when that struggle comes to an end and no meaning can be found or recovered, take the bed to the window and let me fly as quickly and painlessly as possible. If there is a next life, I hope it is as challenging, interesting, and filled with love and heartache as this one has been. If not, then at least there will be peace and relief. (216)

Quill's last words are not without a heartfelt respect for life. He cherishes it; he will fight to maintain it; he even envisions its possible next stage, one that perhaps he can enter if and when his bed is taken to the window so that he can "fly as quickly and painlessly as possible." There is more to death than utter decay. When the moment comes, one might still experience what was once only a dream: the ability to fly to a better place, even if it is only a place of simple peace and relief. Like Quill's book on death and dignity, a life doomed to abject pain and suffering can end in a positive way, but others who care have to be there to aid and witness this moment of flight.

The "happy" endings that mark Quill's stories are steeped in sadness, in circumstances in which the call of conscience is heard for what, at least in part, it is: a call that comes to a creature whose existence is at the same time a being-unto-death and a being-for others. Being this way challenges human beings to display resolute generosity, a decisiveness in their own lives that includes a well-maintained openness and responsiveness to others. Quill faces us in exactly this manner. He presents himself as one who stands out, albeit imperfectly, and who possesses a host of virtues that make him praiseworthy and that make possible the good life and the good death. Looking into the face of such a person, it is hard for me not to see something that appears heroic.

In Quill's case, the rhetorical construction of his face displays traces of another one—a face that, in the end, did not hesitate to seek and find release. Although Quill might have hesitated a bit, he certainly was not reluctant enough to keep quiet about his time with a certain hero. Quill sought and found release with a public confession about an illegal act that he believed with all his heart was merciful. The media frenzy incited by this confession made him into an overnight celebrity of the right-to-die movement. But being a celebrity does not necessarily disqualify one from also being a hero. The deciding factor lies in how the person's "true" character is perceived. Quill is not a fanatic when it comes to helping others die a dignified death. On the contrary, as displayed in the story of Diane, his commitment to treating people who are in desperate need of help and who want to die is counseled by a conscience that speaks with reluctance about what in the name of humanity ought to be done for these people. Quill tells stories whose morals always have something to say about how physician-assisted suicide must never be a quick and easy option but, instead, must always be a heartbreaking last-ditch stand against the horrifying presence of a life that has become a living death. Quill shows himself to be a reluctant hero who is unreluctant to write and speak about his and others' struggles. Yet he is not a braggart and show-off. Rather, like Tada, he has better things to do with his rhetoric: he feels compelled to utter a call of conscience that may instruct others about what it means to live a good life and to die a good death.

In his award-winning book, *How We Die: Reflections on Life's Final Chapter,* Dr. Sherwin Nuland maintains: "The process by which [Quill] gradually recognized that he should help speed [Diane's] death is exemplary of the human bond that can exist and be enhanced between a doctor and a competent terminally ill patient who rationally chooses and with consultation confirms that it is the right way to make her quietus." And two pages later, as he continues to write about the moral uncertainty of euthanasia and assisted suicide, Nuland also concedes that until a better decision-making procedure is invented, "Dr. Quill's way—of empathy, unhurried discussion, consultation, questioning, and challenged assumptions—will do just fine."[15] Beyond this, however, Nuland's call of conscience, which also unfolds primarily by way of moving stories, never advocates in a straightforward way the justness of physician-assisted suicide. Instead, Nuland is content to tell stories that primarily emphasize this: "The dignity that we seek in dying must be found in the dignity with which we have lived our lives. *Ars moriendi* is *ars vivendi:* The art of dying is the art of living. The honesty and grace of the years of life that are ending is the real measure of how we die. It is not in the last weeks or days that we compose the message that will be remembered, but in all the decades that preceded them. Who has lived in dignity, dies in dignity."[16]

The "final chapter" of one's life should seek direction from the most honorable and heroic moments of the person story that comes before it. Quill agrees, but he also goes further than Nuland with the stories he tells about his involvement in the right-to-die movement. Quill is not the least bit ambiguous in admitting how he has actively helped people to die a dignified death. Such a straightforward and candid way of telling stories is also seen in Lonny Shavelson's *A Chosen Death*.[17] Shavelson is an emergency room physician, an author, and a photojournalist. Hence, as Shavelson employs stories to argue for the morality of physician-assisted suicide, he complements his rhetoric with pictures of patients whose once bright and lively faces now offer only a view of agony, despair, and hopelessness. These pictures enhance the evocative and epideictic quality of Shavelson's stories; they help to put a realistic face on death that makes it even more personal and striking than Quill's and Nuland's remarkably moving rhetoric.

There is, however, another physician who has gone even further than Shavelson in presenting a picture of death that is meant to promote the morality of euthanasia. This physician is Jack Kevorkian, a would-be hero who perhaps has the most well-known face to be found in the euthanasia debate.

Case Three: Jack Kevorkian

Jack Kevorkian is a pathologist, researcher, and author; a musician and painter of macabre works of art; the inventor of a suicide machine; and a staunch advocate of the right to die who—beginning in 1990 and before he went to jail in 1999—assisted in over one hundred and thirty suicides.[18] His supporters see him as what he made himself out to be during this time: a "hero." His detractors, on the other hand, typically see him as being nothing more than an extremely eccentric individual whose actions are more appropriately described as "murderous" than "merciful." Kevorkian has long been the material for the dark humor of "sick" jokes. The comedian David Letterman was one of the first to gig the doctor when, on his *Late Night Show* of December 18, 1990, he made Kevorkian's suicide machine the topic for the show's famous "Top Ten" list. "Here," announced Letterman, "are the top ten promotional slogans for the suicide machine":

10. Just try it once—that's all we ask.

9. The quicker putter downer.

8. Isn't it about time you took an honest look at your stinking, miserable life?

7. From the people who brought you the clapper.

6. Impress the chicks in hell.

5. Claus Von Bulow says, "I liked it so much, I bought the company!"

4. While I'm killing myself, I'm also cleaning my oven.

3. Dammit! It's time you did something for *you!*

2. If you're not dead in thirty minutes—it's free!

1. We're *not* the Heartbeat of America.

Letterman could speak of the suicide machine in this way because, like the pop-culture sayings and figures it is associated with, its inventor was equally well known. Five months earlier Kevorkian had first used his machine (named by him the "mercitron") to help a fifty-four-year-old woman who had recently been diagnosed as being in the early stages of Alzheimer's disease commit suicide. The ensuing and intense media coverage of this unprecedented event made Kevorkian a celebrity. His face and the story that went with it were exposed in newspapers, magazines, and television news programs around the world. It thus was not difficult for Letterman to use Kevorkian to his advantage, for here was a real character whose calling involved him with a topic that was not only controversial but that also entailed a concern (death) that was (and still is) easier to laugh at than to take seriously. Letterman helped to make Kevorkian into a source of "entertainment."[19]

But, of course, Kevorkian is still taken seriously by those who, for various reasons, either commend his actions or fear and condemn them. Quill, for example, tells us that "Through his extreme actions, Dr. Kevorkian has forced medical ethicists and physicians to think more carefully about the rights and restrictions regarding a potential role in assisting the death of severely suffering patients." Quill too wants more of such thought to occur, but he also strongly disagrees with Kevorkian's way of bringing it about. This doctor, Quill continues, "has . . . deeply frightened us by the ease with which he helps patients to die, and by his apparent lack of doubt, uncertainty, or careful analysis of his patients and their problems. . . . He has used . . . [his patients' deaths] to gain publicity to promote his own unusual ideas and approach to death. He appears more interested in challenging society and the medical profession than in engaging with individual dying patients in their struggle to find their own path."[20] With this way of thinking, Kevorkian is no hero; rather, he is a selfish individual who has become famous by performing unprofessional, unethical, and illegal deeds and who has made a mockery of the euthanasia debate.

Kevorkian, to be sure, has adopted the deconstructive ways of mockery, of being indecorous, insulting, and contemptuous in an effort to call people and practices into question and ridicule them. His mocked subjects include the religious right, the Supreme Court, the American Medical Association, the media, the prescribed methods of suicide promoted by Derek Humphry, and basically anyone who does not recognize and accept the "truth" of his "rationalist" approach for understanding the morality of physician-assisted suicide.[21] One of the more perceptive and creative descriptions of Kevorkian that I know of is offered by the ethicist Kenneth Vaux, who describes the doctor as a "Rigoletto-like figure" that "a society that is in trouble [because of its being in 'death denial'] coughs up" and who is "given license by the king" to "dance around the edges" and to say "bizarre" and "provocative" things "that normally people in suits and coats can't say."[22] Kevorkian is a standout when it comes to acting in inappropriate ways. Notice, however, that Vaux, like Quill and many others, is still willing to admit that Kevorkian is not without some value; in his own provocative way this doctor does encourage us to think more carefully about certain matters of importance.

Medicine, law, the media, and the American public have had to come to terms with the doings and sayings of Kevorkian. Is he the heroic and needed caregiver that he claims himself to be, a person committed to giving voice to the call of conscience, or—especially now that he is locked up—is it more correct to say that with this "Rigoletto-like" character we essentially have before us the face of a murderer? An answer to this question is found not only in his many acts of assisted suicide but also in the rhetoric that he employs to justify these acts and that, as I hope to show, reveal some of the essential features of his overall character: his face. This face certainly warrants special attention from anyone who is interested in what the euthanasia debate is all about and where it might be taking us.

The rhetorical artifact that guides my reading of Kevorkian's face is an address that he and his long time lawyer, Geoffrey Feiger, were invited to give to the National Press Club on July 29, 1996. Borrowing a construct from Kenneth Burke, I take this address to be a "representative anecdote" of Kevorkian the crusader, orator, and entertainer.[23]

The president of the National Press Club, Sonja Hillgren, began her introduction of the featured speakers by noting: "When Victor Borge, the noted comic, stood at this podium just a few months after Dr. Kevorkian's visit to the National Press Club in October 1992, he quipped, 'When I heard that Jack Kevorkian was recently here, I thought I would be speaking to an empty hall'" (2). Such humor had been going on for six years. Kevorkian's presence was oftentimes depicted as a sick joke, and a grin made it easier to stand face to face with this imposing figure. Kevorkian held back no punches when speaking to people he considered his opponents and who, like the press, were more than willing to stand their ground. Contributing to Kevorkian's imposing face was his ever-present defender and legal counsel, Mr. Feiger—a medical malpractice attorney known for his histrionics and brash manner in the courtroom and during television interviews and presentations. Before Kevorkian took the podium, Feiger was given the opportunity to set the stage; and he made clear with a host of ridiculing remarks about his client's opponents—including the "yellow journalism" of the press—that he and the doctor were "involved in a fight" that was not about "the right to commit suicide" or "the right to obtain the right to suicide, physician-assisted suicide," but rather was about "the right not to suffer" (3). According to Feiger, Kevorkian's unending struggle to protect this right is what places him above the medical crowd: "He agreed to stand up, he agreed to be counted, he agreed to put himself ahead of the dangers of going after his medical license, throwing him in jail, trying him for murder five times. He agreed to stand up and be counted, and I thought that was what America was all about." Indeed, continued Feiger, Dr. Kevorkian "didn't go to medical school to watch himself on *ER;* he went to medical school for the rights of the patient" (6–7).

Feiger would certainly have his audience understand his client in such heroic terms rather than in terms that distorted Kevorkian's "genuine" professional and personal character. Hence, right before introducing the featured speaker, he announced: "I would like to take this opportunity to show you a part of Jack Kevorkian that you rarely see and what he's really about." A videotape of an AIDS public service announcement featuring Kevorkian was then played. The message was meant to be simple yet provocative:

> I'm not about death, I'm about life and about helping people. That's what I'm about. I'm into helping people. You want to talk about people who are really into death? You want to talk about people who are truly interested in committing suicide? People who have sex and don't use condoms. Those are the folks who are going to kill themselves. Damn effective way of doing it, too. Have sex and don't use a condom and you might contract AIDS. Once you have AIDS, the immunologists won't be able to save you. The internists won't be able to save you. The oncologists can't save you. Why perfectly healthy people would want to commit suicide is beyond me. (8)[24]

Of course! Compared to the irrational, careless, and suicidal behavior that could lead to contracting and spreading a deadly disease, Kevorkian's way of being for others respected their dignity. He was into life, not death; he was into mercy, not murder.

Right after being introduced by Feiger and offering a kind and respectful thank-you, Kevorkian was candid: "I have mixed feelings appearing here. I didn't want to come. Geoffrey twisted my arm, seriously. The mixed feelings stem from the fact that I appreciate [the] personal commitment of many of you to welcome me here, to talk to you, which in itself is an honor. That's individually. But collectively, representing the media, I do not consider it an honor to address the media, because they've been, to put it mildly, meretricious—the media itself" (8–9). This indictment serves as a somewhat awkward segue for Kevorkian's first major topic: ethics. Kevorkian had long complained about how the media prostitutes itself by telling stories about him that manipulate and distort the truth so as to turn it into a more profitable spectacle. Such "meretricious" behavior is, of course, unethical. "Ethics," according to Kevorkian, "is doing and saying what's right at the time. That's what people forget." That is, they forget that ethics, at least as Kevorkian would have it, is situational. Hence, if "you have eternal ethics based on some mythology you invent, you're going to have crises if you think that's eternal, as society changes" (9). How this last point specifically relates to the media is not developed by Kevorkian; instead, he goes on to make some additional remarks that eventually allow *his* ethical endeavors to be the center of attention.

Kevorkian speaks of Thomas Jefferson, a hero of his who, he maintains, emphasized how "things change" and thus how "we've got to be prepared to change the Constitution and amend it." Kevorkian argues, however, that Jefferson's teachings have become inconsequential because, "according to the philosophy dominating our secular legislative activity, there's an eternal ethics that dictate . . . what our laws will say. Despite television, superhighways, medical advances, miracles of space, we have eternal ethics. That's the problem" (9).

Kevorkian is out to expose what he perceives to be a fundamental contradiction that marks everyday, secular society: with the help of technology, society is constantly changing, but it still adheres to an eternal ethics and fails to understand how ethics is a matter of "timing." Nothing more is said about Jefferson for the time being, so that Kevorkian can clarify this matter with the following examples: "If I wanted to be very nice to you as a reporter, and I say, 'Hey, I got a gift for you for your birthday. I'm going to give you this little portable mechanical typewriter.' And you'd say, 'Wow, What a nice gift'—you know, cynically—whereas 40 years ago, 50 years ago, if I had said that, you'd be pleased. The action would seem more ethical to you than it would today. Or I'd say, 'Hey, this Christmas I'm going to have five tons of coal delivered to your house as a gift.' You wouldn't say that's an ethical action; you'd considered it an insult. Timing is important—timing" (9).

The major point here is, of course, as old as the rhetorical tradition itself. Certainly after Aristotle and Cicero we know that, at its best, rhetoric offers itself as a response to the contingent demands of a situation; it functions with an eye and ear attuned to the needs of others. In the midst of disputational contexts, rhetoric provides an opportunity for collaborative choice; its ultimate aim is not merely manipulation and persuasion but the enactment of deliberation and judgment, and the cultivation of practical wisdom and *kairotic* appropriateness. Indeed "timing" (*kairos*) is important, especially when the orator seeks to utter a call of conscience whose urgency is supposedly undeniable.

Although Kevorkian's audience may not have known the history of this phenomenon, I suspect that these media professionals were well aware of its obvious importance to their vocation. Perhaps it was the case, then, that at this moment in his address, when he was emphasizing the topic of "timing," his audience found his remarks inappropriate, if not a bit insulting to their intelligence. And if this is so, then what we have before us is a speaker who is rhetorically incompetent when it comes to actually practicing what he is preaching. His timing is off; he moves about in an indecorous way.[25]

This problem is partly resolved with Kevorkian's next move to the topic of physician-assisted suicide, but one must be patient as Kevorkian brings things together. Yes, "timing is important." And then Kevorkian immediately informs his audience: "What we're doing is long overdue. We're not leading, we're following" (9). One is able to make sense of this claim only after Kevorkian strings together some additional thoughts:

> Five hundred years before Christ, in ancient Greece, this was widely practiced by physicians, openly. The whole society accepted it as medical practice, except the Pythagoreans, and they were kooky, in a way, you know. They used to smoke secretly, too, you know. (Scattered laughter.) The Pythagoreans said, "No, no, no. By our faith, abortion is a sin, assisting a suicide is a sin." "But," they said—to this degree, see, they were still rational Greeks—"that's for us only." You can't make that for the whole society because society couldn't function that way. You see, they were rational. What do you say? "That's a sin. That's a sin for everybody." Even the whole world! So, the Greeks were smarter than we are. Well, it doesn't take much to know that if you know history. What—the timing of an ethical code is important. We are behind the times. All we're doing is struggling to get back to where the Greeks were; rational medical practice devoid of religious mythology. (9–10)

Kevorkian is attempting to make a connection between ethics, timing, physician-assisted suicide, and the ancient and "rational Greeks." Apparently, however, he is not especially concerned with "narrative coherence" and thus with composing well-constructed transitions that can help his audience keep their (and his) thoughts together.[26] No, what he explicitly admits that he wants his audience to realize is this: "I'm not against religion. I'm basically an agnostic. What you have is fine. But when you foist that on me as a law, then I object strenuously—stridently. And I'm known to be strident" (10). Indeed. But what exactly is Kevorkian referring to when he speaks of having something foisted on him as a law? As best as I can tell, it must be something that prevents him from being like those ancient Greeks who developed a "rational medical practice devoid of religious mythology."

But who where these Greeks? The Hippocratics? Throughout this book I have had a number of things to say about these first men of medical science whose oath and code of ethics are based in the religious doctrine advocated by the Pythagoreans. Hence, unless he is a poor historian, Kevorkian cannot be referring to the Hippocratics, for they certainly did *not* create a medical practice devoid of religious mythology. Kevorkian indicates his awareness of this fact when he admits: "Hippocrates didn't write the Hippocratic oath. That's a Pythagorean manifesto" (10). So who is Kevorkian's revered referent? Something of an answer comes with his next sentences: "So, you see, we still can't separate medicine and religion. The ethics are not medical ethics. What I'm doing is medically ethical. What the AMA says to do is theologically ethical. I mean, in what other profession . . . do you get another profession dictating your ethics?" (10). Kevorkian's referent is not ancient; rather, it is no further away from him than his own self. Genuine *medical* ethics does not come on the scene until Kevorkian gets things right.

Once again, I find Kevorkian lacking in rhetorical competence. The call of conscience that he attempts to utter is unclear and disjointed; its argument is poorly arranged. He formulates his narrative with speed and efficiency, like the physician who wrote "It's Over, Debbie"; but unlike that author, Kevorkian is more incoherent than he is ambiguous. His prose seems to come more from off the top of his head than from a carefully constructed manuscript or set of notes. He is trying to make the point that he is truly more professional and ethical than are physicians who, like those associated with the AMA, adhere to the ancient tradition that the body is "sacred." Kevorkian writes: "I never studied sanctity in a medical school. Sanctity is an invention of the human mind. Define 'sanctity'! I'll bet you don't get any kind of consensus in this audience. What is sanctity? Divinity, holiness, the whole body's sacred?" (11).

Kevorkian calls this traditional way of conceiving the body "mythologic borborygmus" (intestinal rumbling caused by moving gas), and he maintains that the condition will continue as long as people remain confused because of the theology of medical ethics. With this theology, insists Kevorkian, "we're trained to lie as we get older. That's the way you survive. That's a grease of society . . . lying: to yourself and to others. And the epitome of lying is in the epitome of society: the government." Kevorkian would stop such unethical behavior by insisting that society and its physicians answer such simple questions as this: "When I take the gallbladder out of the body, or a surgeon does, when it's removed is that gallbladder sacred? Better yet: when I take a baboon's heart and put it into [a human being], does that heart become sacred? Or do you have a sacred body with . . . a profane heart? As if that makes any sense. . . . You know what sanctity is, don't you? Can the body be partly sacred? Is the fecal material in your intestines sacred?" These questions, according to Kevorkian, beg for a simple and rational answer: "You're a human body, you're a biological organism like every other biological organism. You bleed when you're cut, and when you die, you stink. Now, what's sacred about that?" (11–12).

Kevorkian sees himself as being truthful, whereas the AMA is "dishonest, disingenuous" (12). Their problem can be traced back to the ancient Greeks, the Hippocratics, who, in the name of science, sought to develop a rational and empirical understanding of the body and its diseases. Kevorkian champions such an understanding, for it sticks to the facts of reality. Medical science can flourish only if it is true to this enlightening orientation. The Hippocratics hindered themselves, however, by allowing religion a place in their program; hence, their commitment toward telling good body stories was hampered by the belief that the body is sacred. So began an over-two-thousand-year-old episode of "mythologic borborygmus."

For the sake of what he maintains he is, a "medical scientist" and *only* that, Kevorkian would put an end to this chronic ailment. "You bleed when you're cut, and when you die, you stink"—that's it! Cured of the ailment, physicians and their patients could now realize that suicide is neither a sin nor even a right, but only something that is "inherent" to the body. "Everyone can kill himself—or herself." And this said, Kevorkian goes on to state what he considers to be the real problem at hand: "infringing the autonomy of the person who wants to actively help [another to commit suicide] without being asked or forced or coerced or feeling that he has an obligation to fulfill" (12).

"Absolute personal autonomy": these are the terms used by Kevorkian to identify the "philosophy" that underlies and directs his way of being. "I'm an absolute autonomist," declares Kevorkian. "Do and say whatever you want to do and say at any time you want to do or say it, as long as you do not harm or threaten anybody else's person or property" (18). The law against *assisted* suicide is one that, as Kevorkian sees it, is "irrational" because it restricts the freedom of people like himself who know that suicide is not a sin and who want to use their freedom to help others commit this nonsinful act that is "inherent" to their being. To get at what he terms the "nitty-gritty" of the matter, Kevorkian offers the following example: "The ancient Christians in Rome, they were all healthy. They weren't suffering physical disease. I think they were suffering mental disease—but not physical. And they had assisted suicide. Why? To alleviate the pain, mental pain, of having to renounce their faith. If I did that today—if I helped a person today under those circumstances I'd be strung up. And yet these people you call almost divine had assisted suicide in lion's jaws. If I did that with a patient, you know what would happen? If I had a lion to assist my suicide?" (12).

But how does this example get at the "nitty-gritty" of absolute personal autonomy? Kevorkian seems to be suggesting that because the thought of having to renounce their faith was so excruciatingly painful, Christians used their freedom to choose a less horrible fate—being eaten alive by lions. And yes, a person who today used a lion to assist in another's suicide would be charged with a horrible crime. But what does this have to do with the issue at hand? Where is the parallel between Christians being forced by their tormentors and executioners to "choose" their fate and a physician wanting to overcome any restrictions on his personal autonomy that would prevent him from helping another to commit suicide? Is this a "rational" way to make an argument about the importance of absolute autonomy and its relationship to assisted suicide, or is this but another instance of rhetorical incompetence?

I must admit that Kevorkian is not always so confusing (off the wall?) when making his case for assisted suicide. Consider, for example, what he has to say about dying a dignified death and the use of his much-publicized Volkswagen van:

> Let's take what people think is a dignified death. Christ—was that a dignified death? Do you think its dignified to hang from wood with nails through your hands and feet bleeding, hang for three or four days slowly dying, with people jabbing spears into your side, and people jeering you? Do you think that's dignified? Not by a long shot. Had Christ died in my van . . . with people around Him who loved Him, the way it was, it would be far more dignified. In my rusty van. Anyone disagree? And yet it's okay, because it's the good guys and it's our God. He died and He was born among the animals who stink and humans who haven't bathed in a month, and manure all over the floor. Very dignified birth. If He were born in my rusty van with people around him—clean, rusty van—more dignified. But I guess it wouldn't make a nice story for religion. See? Have I said anything wrong? If it offends you is it wrong? Or have you ever thought of these things? (14)

Kevorkian certainly has a point. Christ's death was not dignified; and I know of no rational human being who would opt for such a death over a more peaceful one, or who would want to be born and die on a floor covered with manure. Moreover, I would beg for Kevorkian's assistance if I had to die by way of crucifixion. His van would be a welcome sight. Once inside the vehicle and hooked up to a suicide machine, I would have a doctor by my side who would not let me suffer, who would not allow to happen to me what, as the story goes, God allowed to happen to his son. Is this to say that Kevorkian would be my true savior? Given what he says about dying a dignified death, he certainly seems to think so; for he is an "absolute autonomist" who, at least as he tells it, is no different than his hero, Thomas Jefferson. This founding father, writes Kevorkian, "advocated not only suicide, [but also] assisted suicide and euthanasia" in cases where people are suffering from such illnesses as cancer.[27] "It's all right to kill yourself if you're suffering from cancer, and it's all right for someone to give you the drug to do it." Kevorkian then notes that "when I learned that, it didn't matter what any Supreme Court justice here in Washington says—not one can match Jefferson!" (14).

So Kevorkian is like Jefferson, more merciful than God, and thus a hero of sorts. That this strategic way of defending and displaying his character and actions may have offended those in his audience who knew that his way of telling the story was rather incomplete did not seem to bother Kevorkian. Indeed, as he ends his presentation, he makes clear to his audience once again what he thinks of them, as well as of himself:

> You're wimps—all of you—all of you—as a media. And that's why I consider it no honor to be here talking to you as an abstraction, media. It's not meant as a personal insult. That's exactly why I didn't want to come here. I've learned that words don't mean much, because people either don't care or they're just too stupid. I don't like the printed word, I don't like the spoken word. My talking here isn't going to change much—never has in five or six years. The only thing that has changed anything is the action—and I am not on a crusade. I am a doctor. The patient in front of me is all that counts, and I help one patient at a time.[28]

Kevorkian tells it like it is. But notice that, with his concluding remarks, he employs a deconstructive tactic that, as discussed in chapter 4, was first used by the author of the Hippocratic and rhetorical treatise *The Art*. That is, Kevorkian has been using rhetoric to make a point that calls into question the true worth of this art: "words don't mean much"; all that really counts is "action." I thus suspect that Kevorkian would not mind being called "rhetorically incompetent." So what if he is lacking when it comes to arranging and constructing arguments, defining terms, telling stories, and showing some respect to an audience; for as he puts it, there is still his "manifesto" (*Prescription Medicide*) that "wasn't written for public consumption," which details his historical struggle and foretells the future. "I wrote it for the future. Whatever happens in the future will be in my book, and that's why I wrote it" (21).[29]

Kevorkian knows that he is right: he is a physician, a man of science who defies religious interference and who thereby can maintain an unclouded vision of where society will end up on the issue of physician-assisted suicide and euthanasia. Rhetorical incompetence, indeed! Why waste time with the art when one already has the truth that sets you free from wimps and stupid people and that guides you in doing what you know to be ethical and dignified? Listening to Kevorkian is not the key. His real character shows itself whenever he assists others with their suicide. We hear his call of conscience most clearly when his patients die.

The rhetorical tradition has long stressed the importance of the "good man speaking well." The practice of rhetoric can help build character and promote the civic virtue that makes it possible to join others in deciding what ought to be done for the good of the community. Kevorkian, for his part, is content just to be the "good man." And that is what, for me, makes him more of a danger than a hero. This danger, which comes with the abandonment of rhetorical competence, is again evident in those particular actions of Kevorkian that most recently led him to jail.

On November 22, 1998, the CBS news show *60 Minutes* aired a segment titled "Death by Doctor." Here, with Kevorkian's permission, they showed a videotape made by the doctor two months earlier that shows him killing one of his patients, Mr. Tom Youk, who was suffering from ALS (Lou Gehrig's disease) and who requested Kevorkian's services because, as explained during the news segment, he had lost the use of his legs and arms, was in terrible pain, had trouble breathing and swallowing, and was terrified of choking on his own saliva. During his interview with co-anchor Mike Wallace, Kevorkian explains how he saw it as his duty "to dispel that terror." Youk's family—wife, mother, and two brothers—supported his decision. Youk's wife admits she "was so grateful to know that someone would relieve him of his suffering. I don't consider it murder. I consider it humane; I consider it the way things should be." When asked by Wallace if she wanted her husband to be "a poster boy for euthanasia," Mrs. Youk was emphatic: "Oh, exactly not. Tom's very private and . . . he believes it's a private issue. . . . And I'm shocked that it's come to this, that in the '90s, we have to make such an issue out of something that a person should be in control of—their own life and death."

According to Kevorkian, he wanted the tape aired so that the issue of euthanasia would "be raised to the level where it is finally decided." Hence, Kevorkian tells Wallace, "I've got to force [the authorities] to act. They must charge me, because if they do not, that means they don't think it's a crime. Because they don't need any more evidence, do they? Do you have to dust for fingerprints on this?"

The portion of the tape when Kevorkian begins and ends his procedure is chilling. Youk is sitting in his wheelchair facing the camera.

KEVORKIAN: Tom, do you want to go ahead with this?
YOUK: Yes.

KEVORKIAN: Shake your head "yes" if you want to go.

YOUK: (Shakes head yes).

KEVORKIAN: All right. I'm going to have you sign again your name and I'm—and we're going to date it today, OK?

YOUK: OK.

KEVORKIAN: And we're ready to inject. We're going to inject in your right arm, OK? Okey-doke.

(The first injection contained Seconal which quickly put Youk to sleep.)

KEVORKIAN: Sleepy, Tom? Tom, are you asleep? Tom, are you asleep? You asleep? He's asleep.

(Then Kevorkian injected a muscle relaxant to stop Youk's breathing.)

KEVORKIAN: [This] paralyzes the muscles.

WALLACE: But he's still alive at this point.

KEVORKIAN: He's still alive, but—and that's why . . .

WALLACE: Now I can see him breathing just a trifle.

KEVORKIAN: That's why I have to—yes. Now you see—now that there's a —lack of oxygen getting to him now, but he's unconscious, deeply, so it doesn't matter.

WALLACE: Is he dead now?

KEVORKIAN: I'm—he's dying now, because his oxygen's cut off. He can't breathe. So I'll—now I'll quickly inject the potassium chloride to stop the heart.

WALLACE: He's dead.

KEVORKIAN: Yep. The heart has stopped.

Dr. Mark Siegler, director of the Center for Medical Ethics at the University of Chicago, also appears on the news segment. Having already watched Kevorkian's videotape with Wallace, Siegler, a staunch opponent of Kevorkian, is heard to say: "I was shocked, almost speechless, as we watched the tape. It was—it was such a frightening spectacle." Responding to Wallace's reminder that Youk wanted to die at the hands of Kevorkian, Siegler admits: "Yeah. And the—the heartwrenching case is—is the hardest case to argue against. I—I guess the argument against it is that we can do better than kill people when—when they're near the end of life. We—we can do better with end-of-life care." At the end of the segment, Wallace is once again interviewing Kevorkian about his actions. The doctor's response is different than Siegler's: "If you don't have liberty and self-determination, you got nothing. That's what this country is built on. And this is the ultimate self-determination: to determine when and how you're going to die when you're suffering. . . . That's why I'm fi— I'm fighting for me, Mike. Me. This is a right I want when I'm 71. I'll be 71. You don't know what'll happen when you get older. I may end up terribly suffering. I want some colleague to be free to come and help me when I say the time has come. That's why I'm fighting, for me. Now that sounds selfish. And if it helps everybody else, so be it."

For Kevorkian—the medical scientist, the patriot, the hero—the thinking here, although it might sound a bit paradoxical, is rational and thus makes perfect sense. Selfishness can lead to altruism when performed by a person who, like Kevorkian, believes in "absolute personal autonomy" for one and all. Kevorkian is doing us all a great favor; he is willing to sacrifice his freedom so that others might be free. It is all stated in his manifesto that foretells the future. If Kevorkian was a religious soul, one might conceive of him as a "god," given that he could have written such a book. If not a god, then at least a needed caregiver. As he stressed during his trial for the murder of Tom Youk, his intent "was not to murder" this man but to "end his torture, finally and definitively. . . . The aim was a final solution to internal agony."[30] Although I think the word choice here could have been better, Kevorkian's understanding of himself is clear: he is no murderer, but rather he is first and foremost a person who heard the call of conscience coming from a seriously ill patient and who was determined to say "Here I am!" and thereby bring about a dignified death. In his closing arguments (Kevorkian was his own legal counsel), he offers a warning to those members of the jury who would disagree with him: "History will judge you for what you do today. We can make a little progress in our society, but if you think I'm a criminal, then you must do what the law says. Honestly now, do you see a criminal? Do you see a murderer? If you do, then you must convict. And then, take the harsh judgment of history, and the harsher judgment of your children and grandchildren if they ever come to need that precious choice."

Kevorkian's strategy during his trial was not new. Despite the fact that his ways of ending the suffering of patients (for example, with potassium chloride) were commonly recognized by medicine and law as not having any medical and therapeutic value other than that of causing death, Kevorkian had earlier been acquitted by juries who had heard his caregiving defense and who had witnessed his histrionics when, for example, he once appeared in court dressed as Thomas Jefferson, thereby presenting a visual declaration of the tradition of individual rights that he championed as a patriot and caregiver.[31] What was missing in his last trial, however, was a key ingredient that his lawyer (Feiger) had always used in constructing his defense and that the media consistently employed in its coverage of Kevorkian: the emotionally packed and vivid details of a patient's person story—details that put a face on the abject misery of death and that thereby helped juries and the general public identify with, and gain a more heartfelt feeling for, people whose right to die with dignity warranted the utmost respect.[32] Siding with the prosecution, the trial judge refused to allow such details to be admitted as evidence because Kevorkian's active role in Youk's death (all previous assisted suicides had been performed by the patient with Kevorkian as a mere facilitator) made Youk's condition and his consent irrelevant. Hence, the jury was instructed only to consider the limited evidence they had witnessed when watching Kevorkian's tape and its quick and "okey-doke" account of death.

Kevorkian thus had to rest his case without having the Youk family tell their side of the story, which was unquestionably supportive of the doctor and which perhaps could have helped neutralize chief prosecutor David Gorcyca's perception of the tape: "What disturbed me most about the tape was the total lack of compassion shown in the last moments of a terminally-ill man's life. What I saw was a nonchalant, callous, business-like approach not to ease a man's suffering but to satisfy an attention-crazed ego."[33] Listening to Gorcyca's take on the entire matter, the jury was asked to see Kevorkian, not as a patriotic and heroic caregiver, but only as a criminal whose ways of "showing off" (with the help of the media) had now *really* gone too far beyond the boundaries of common decency. Kevorkian is a murderer; he killed a man in front of millions of people. Look at the tape!

Kevorkian did, however, mount a defense with the help of "medicine." In his closing arguments he told the jury: "You heard the medical examiner say, "Oh yes I do a cut here when I open the body, and I do a cut through the scalp." That's a mutilation. Isn't it? Why not a crime for the medical examiner? Why isn't he charged with mutilation of a body? Why? Because he's exempt. Because of his position, his profession. It's a medical service. Anyone else does that to a body and it's a crime but not for a medical doctor. He [the prosecuting attorney] calls this a murder, a crime, a killing. I call it a medical service. Medical service is exempt from certain laws."

Like his colleagues who conduct autopsies, Kevorkian claims, he is a medical doctor performing a medical service; he has not done anything wrong in the performance of his duty. The analogy, of course, did not work. Telling a less abstract person story would have made more sense, but this Kevorkian could not do, for the law excluded this option. All that Kevorkian had to go on, then, was his self-image as a physician who, in serving the community, was wrongfully accused by a prosecutor whose rhetoric was not scientific, not objective and unbiased, but was instead overly emotional and manipulative. "You notice he loves the words *kill* and *murder*," insisted Kevorkian in his closing arguments: "He's addicted to that word. Repeating over and over, 'killing, murder.' I intended to kill him. 'You did kill him.' You saw him kill him on the tape. Why did he use the words *kill, murder*? They're negative words. They're ugly and disparaging words. And that's what he intends to do."

Dr. Kevorkian offers a "medical service"—and that, he insists, is the correct and fair way to put it. Yet for one who claimed "that words don't mean much, because people either don't care or they're just too stupid," Kevorkian's emphasis on the use of appropriate terms seems lame. Borrowing a phrase from Tada, one might say that Kevorkian "had to drain the horror" from the prosecutor's words in order to gain an acquittal. But he had to do this with words that were not allowed to be inspired by a certain kind of story whose well-defined argument is heart-moving and humane. Kevorkian's face looks hard, uncaring, and arrogant when it is without a person story to help it show what is its better and more heroic side.

The jury looked at Kevorkian's face and saw a murderer. Perhaps matters would have been different if, as in the past, the man known as "Dr. Death" had been allowed to make use of whatever rhetorical competence he possessed to construct a story that helped others see him as the needed caregiver he thought himself to be. As Anatole Broyard struggled to survive prostate cancer, he wrote of his need to have a talented doctor who was both a well-trained physician and metaphysician: "Someone who can treat body and soul. There is a physical self who's ill, and there is a metaphysical self who is ill. When you die, your philosophy dies along with you. So I want a metaphysical man to keep me company."[34] I imagine that this is the wish of most dying patients. It certainly is my wish. Kevorkian, however, is no such man. Trained as a pathologist, his "patients" (before he began his new calling) were already dead; their metaphysical needs were therefore moot. The accounts that Kevorkian had to offer about these patients were, of necessity, scientifically grounded body stories. Kevorkian was trained to see, not a person with a soul, but only something that bleeds when you cut it and stinks when it dies. The request "have a heart" takes on a specific and concrete meaning in the context of such training. When doing his or her professional duty, the pathologist has no reason to be compassionate. If there is a heart to have, then let's give it to one who requires the transplant and move on.

Kevorkian became a part of the right-to-die movement as first and foremost a doctor who believed that euthanasia was justifiable if it facilitated the saving of lives through organ transplantation.[35] Once involved in the movement, he learned to speak (with the help of his lawyer and the media) the rhetoric of person stories, especially those whose characters begged for mercy and a dignified death. Kevorkian is into putting an end to human suffering; he wants to be seen as a needed caregiver—one who, like the hero, arrives in the nick of time to prevent and eliminate injustice. Yet only by way of a good person story can others gather necessary evidence and gain confidence about the genuine motivation that guides Kevorkian's would-be heroic actions. With this point in mind, it is hard not to wonder if Kevorkian—whose relationships with live patients were rather brief—could by himself tell a rhetorically competent person story.[36] I think he should have been given the chance to do so at his trial. Thomas Youk and his family, at the very least, deserved as much. They admitted they needed Kevorkian; and he certainly needed them.

In the euthanasia debate heroes—be they patients, family members, friends, or medical personnel—must be able to share stories of significant existential worth, stories that educate and instruct others about the meaning of life and death. Joseph Campbell emphasizes the significance of this rhetorical task when he tells of how the hero has an obligation to return to "the land of common day . . . where men who are fractions imagine themselves to be complete." The hero's calling includes being a teacher who knows how "to confront society with his ego-shattering, life-redeeming elixir, and take the return blow of reasonable queries, hard resentment, and good people at a loss to comprehend."[37]

I have been questioning Kevorkian's hero/teacher status. Granted, he is a master showman when it comes to confronting society, breaking its rules, and intimidating and humiliating any number of its members. Kevorkian knows how to play the game of deconstruction; he delights in calling things into question with actions and words that are so out of the ordinary, so interruptive, that at times they are laughable. That is how "Rigoletto-like" characters entertain; and entertainment, as humorists and satirists have long known, can be an excellent way to sound a call of conscience. Here, for example, is Mark Twain making fun of a topic that he knows to be of importance for humankind: "Good friends, good books and a sleepy conscience: this is the ideal life."[38]

Twain and Kevorkian would awaken us to the same thing. But in Kevorkian's case, the call that awakens always comes from one who is preoccupied with death—the ultimate deconstructive event. The call of conscience that lies at the heart of human existence, however, speaks not only of this event but also of its reconstructive counterpart: life and its need for acknowledgment and respect. Out of respect for a person's life, liberty, and pursuit of happiness, Kevorkian advocates euthanasia as a moral way of eliminating human suffering. His gift of reconstruction, then, is but an act of deconstruction—in both word and deed.[39]

Human existence calls for more than that. Those like Tada and Quill understand this point, and they demonstrate their understanding with the same hope and care and compassion that they write about in their stories. Both Tada and Quill are far more rhetorically competent than is Kevorkian; but he, unfortunately, does not care. "Action," not "words," is what really counts for Kevorkian in the euthanasia debate. Yet the practice of rhetoric *is* a type of action, and thus the same can be said about the telling of person stories. As told mostly by his lawyer, captured on videotape, and expanded on by the media, such stories provided a way for Kevorkian to make himself look less like a murderer and more like a friend, caregiver, and hero. I believe we need heroes in the euthanasia debate—people who, among other things, are good at telling emotional and well-argued stories that help others gain a better understanding of what it means to live a good life and to die a good death. Look what happened to Kevorkian when he didn't have the chance (or ability) to tell such a story. He now resides in jail, far less a hero than a celebrity, a show-off, whose last televised performance proved to be too outrageous and inappropriate for a jury of his peers.

The rhetorical construction of heroic faces is something that, for the benefit of all concerned, must take place in the euthanasia debate. For although these faces (of patients, family members, friends, caregivers) are not always joyful, they nevertheless allow us to see, hear, and judge things that have a crucial role to play in defining who we are as beings who can perceive and respond to the call of conscience and who can thereby sustain and develop humankind's moral consciousness. Where would we be without this consciousness and the rhetoric that formulates and displays its wisdom? What would life be like if nobody acknowledged your existence? How long could your good life continue once others no longer cared enough to say to you with all their hearts, "Here I am!"? Such questions have been raised throughout the present study—which now, I think it is fair to say, has come full circle in its investigation of how the relationship that exists between the call of conscience and the practice of rhetoric shows itself in everyday existence.

Chapter 8

Where Art Thou?
Here I Am!

I specifically designed this book on the call of conscience so that it might contribute to a literature concerned with finding ways of healing a long-standing rift between the enterprises of philosophy and rhetoric. This rift is apparent whenever philosophers feel obliged to remind their colleagues that rhetoric should be more devoted toward ascertaining the "truth" than toward, for example, inventing "strategic" and "flowery" discourse to manipulate and please an audience. The rift is also evident whenever rhetoricians feel obliged to return the favor by reminding philosophers that their obsession with the "truth" means little if their discoveries cannot be communicated and applied to everyday existence such that the members of a given community can better understand how to judge and act in a right and good manner. One of Heidegger's most distinguished students, Hans-Georg Gadamer, has a nice way of stating the rhetorician's reminder: "What man needs is not just the persistent posing of ultimate questions, but the sense of what is feasible, what is possible, what is correct, here and now. The philosopher, of all people, must, I think, be aware of the tension between what he claims to achieve and the reality in which he finds himself."[1]

Heidegger's and Levinas' philosophies of conscience contribute the theoretical foundations of the project. These two thinkers can (and must) go together. Levinas recommends that Heidegger be read before one turns to his own project. I agree. Levinas without Heidegger has too many holes; Heidegger without Levinas, however, is too dangerous, especially when considering a topic—euthanasia—that is as much about others as it is about the self.

Although neither of these philosophers associates his theories with a specific and sustained case study of everyday public moral argument, their phenomenological analyses of the call of conscience certainly lend support to the making of such a move. In both analyses the realm of everydayness is recognized as the place where conscience comes to call as an interruption of the typical spatiotemporal and emotional ways we exist with and for things, and with and for others. With the call of conscience comes a question—Where art thou?—in need of an answer: Here I am! The various ways that such an answer can be enacted include a certain type of know-how: rhetorical competence. The call of conscience is itself an eloquent rhetorical interruption that makes itself known in the euthanasia debate. In making this move from theory to practice, much was made of four related "rhetorical" phenomena emphasized by Heidegger and Levinas in their investigations of the interruption: the call's deconstructive/reconstructive nature, acknowledgment, the power of language, and the discursive construction of heroes.

With the call of conscience ringing in my ears, I would not claim that the "essence" of the rhetoric of the euthanasia debate can be reduced to these specific phenomena. Nor would I claim that my reading of texts wherein these phenomena show themselves captures the complete complexity of their presence and interrelatedness. My goal was not that ambitious. I only wanted to begin clarifying how texts mean as announcements of conscience; and with the debate in question, the materials are rich and abundant. The euthanasia debate defines a rhetorical situation that is awesomely telling when it comes to educating us about our ontological, moral, and ethical way of being in the world. We are, to be sure, creatures whose finitude calls us into question, who need to be needed, who require the life-giving gift of acknowledgment, who have the power to give this gift, and who may in the process warrant being called a hero. Although such acclaim may prove embarrassing, there nevertheless is something satisfying and good to be experienced here. When recognized for our heroic behavior, we are essentially being told that we have done something that our own existence calls us to do every day: be a stand-out who knows that being such a noble soul requires being open-minded to all who would say with a "good" conscience that we have yet to get matters right. We are creatures who are fated to move about in a deconstructive and reconstructive manner.

The euthanasia debate thrusts this fate in our face as it speaks to us of bodies that, owing to illness or accident, are themselves a testimony to the ways of deconstruction. With the fallibility of finitude comes an anatomy that sooner or later is bound to break down. The interruptive force at work here can come without warning, and the immediate result may be having to exist in a state of "living death." The euthanasia debate is before us because of this consequence and because of our failure, so far, to agree on how to deal with it in the most conscientious, ethical, and moral way possible. I do not believe that we will reach this agreement in the near future. I do believe, however, that we must never stop trying. Who does not want to live in peace and to die in peace? A "perfect" world would surely include this possibility. Have we reached that point in human evolution where we are even capable of knowing all that must be at work if such a world is to become a reality? As long as conscience calls as it does now, the question must remain before us, at least to some extent.

Yet because I believe in the importance of trying to get things right, I have developed a notion of perfection from my study of the euthanasia debate that I would gladly share. Recall the story I told of my father when introducing part 2: he suffered terribly as a dialysis patient for four years, his heart gave out because of the strain, and the doctors offered my mother the option of keeping him alive with a pacemaker at least until I could see him alive one last time. She took the chance, but the operation failed, and my father died without ever telling us exactly how he wanted to go in peace. In a more perfect world none of this would have happened. That it did does not, however, put an end to my dreams of perfection. I wish I knew more about how my father had come to terms with the meaning of life and death. I wish I knew if he wanted the pacemaker. If he did, and if it had worked, I wish I had made it home in time to share at least another day with him—a day of his recognizing my face and telling me stories that made clear that he was (or perhaps was not) ready to go, that he loved me very much, that he knew of my love for him, that he expected me to act correctly when the time came, and that he knew that I knew he was speaking the truth and understood perfectly where he was coming from.

If all this could have happened, I would have continued wishing for support from a caring medical staff who knew and appreciated the story of my father's personhood and who, like loving and giving family members and friends, would be there as I answered my father's call and would have uttered one too. Where art thou? Here I am, Pop! Where art thou? In the best of all possible worlds, my father and mother and I would have looked forward to having people around like Jory Graham, Anatole Broyard, Reverend Robert Fraser, Leon Kass, the Cruzans, Justice Brennan and Justice Stevens, members of Not Dead Yet!, Joni Eareckson Tada, and Timothy Quill. There would be disagreement going on in my father's room, of course, but it would be worth it. In the best of all possible worlds, the Hyde family would sit back and enjoy what all these visitors had to say as they took turns telling stories that made us laugh and moved our hearts and presented compelling arguments about the meaning of life and death. Maybe my father would have gained hope and strength from such stimulating conversation. Maybe then he would have had complete peace of mind as he repeated, "I want to live on!" or "I want to die a dignified death before it's too late!"

I wish I knew what my father really wanted. I wish I had the chance again to get things right. I wish my father had been an active participant in a conversation filled with rhetorical competence. My mother did the right thing in light of the family's Jewish heritage. I, however, broke the law by keeping a promise to my father regarding his remains. Was this the work of the devil? I wish my father could have addressed this question in front of his visitors. Recalling what he knew of the tradition of Kabbalah—the mystical core of Judaism, and ultimately of Christianity and Islam—perhaps he would have reminded his visiting caregivers that the serpent (Satan) in the story of Adam and Eve means more than what those like Tada claim it to be. The kabbalistic teaching is that Satan is not merely the lowly and horrible creature who rules the underworld, but he is instead "the force of fragmentation" that operates in the physical universe as a crucial element required for creation. Without this force, everything would unite with God and thus become one. According to Rabbi David Cooper, this does not mean, however, "that the splintering force of Satan is separate from the unity of God, but, paradoxically, that it is contained within the oneness of the Divine." Whenever the force of fragmentation (the serpent's bite) makes itself known in our lives by way of serious illness, for example, we are given the chance to develop "messianic consciousness" and thus an awesome sense of what life and death are all about. "Without the serpent," writes Cooper, "without the energizing of creation, we would never have the opportunity to follow a path returning us to our Divine Source."[2]

It would have been wonderful to see my father holding court, smiling and feeling good as he sensed that what he was saying was making a difference to his caregivers. What a proud moment: my father the stand-out, the good man speaking well, the teacher, the hero. My father deserved to be acknowledged in this way. "And what," someone would ask him, "does your understanding of the matter suggest to you concerning your ongoing treatment?" Hearing his answer, I would now feel secure in knowing what more to do for my father. More importantly, my father would feel secure in knowing that his final chapter would be well worth remembering for its goodness.

A great story, a dream of perfection: conscience calls, and all goes well. Why isn't the world always this way? Because conscience calls, human existence has yet to evolve into a state that can thrive without an ongoing process of deconstruction and reconstruction directing the way. Our inevitable involvement in this process allows for the rewards that were given to my father in my dream: genuine acknowledgment, the opportunity to cultivate one's rhetorical competence, the chance to become and to be remembered as a great teacher and hero who took seriously the ethical and moral responsibilities that come with existence itself. We are creatures whose existence *is* a being with and for others. We have a need to be needed, to be both the sender and receiver of the life-giving gift of acknowledgment. That certainly is one of the ways we develop character, moral consciousness, and the civic virtue that holds us together so that we can be clearly heard when we call out, "Where art thou?" and when we answer, "Here I am!"

Notice, then, that the notion of perfection that I am offering here is one that is not totally unattainable. Existence offers us some of what it takes to build a perfect world. That we have yet to complete the task, and that as finite beings we can never know for sure how long it will take to do so, are credible reasons for discouragement. And as long as we think of ourselves as being the center of a universe that we now know is at least as big as the time it takes for light to travel many billions of years, I think it is fair to say that the discouragement will linger and grow. Clearly, we are already at the point of recognizing how existence may be but a "game" whose end is nothing more than rot and stench. The euthanasia debate contains this view. It might be right, but what a waste. Yet there is reason for hope: the call of conscience indicates as much.

Religion is borne from such hope (and fear). What I have been saying about perfection is not, however, intended as an argument for allowing the institutions of religion to have the final say in the euthanasia debate. Rather, I would merely have religion be employed as an indicator for gauging how well the euthanasia debate is going. I think that, overall, the debate is going rather well. It certainly is providing us with opportunities for demonstrating and developing those abilities and visions that are needed in order to build a perfect world out of one that is filled with too much pain and suffering.

Yet let it not be said with this positive evaluation that I have no desire to discover the best solution for ending the debate. That would make me too much of a selfish rhetorical critic. Situations like the euthanasia debate provide rhetoricians (and, to be sure, philosophers) with a good reason for being. It makes them feel needed. In a perfect world, however, they would be of no significant use: we would already know everything there is to know and thus would have no reason to perfect our rhetorical competence other than that of wanting to engage in an entertaining and rather foolish ritual that once served the important purpose of fostering collaborative deliberation in the face of uncertainty.

I will have to live the rest of my life feeling uncertain about my father. By attending to the rhetoric of the euthanasia debate, I have nevertheless gained some understanding of what must be nurtured if human beings are to have any hope at all for things turning out for the better. Finite beings are not fated to live in a perfect world, although they are fated to be constantly confronted with the task of trying to get things right so that they might improve their circumstances. Conscience calls whether we like it or not.

Recently I was reminded of how there is room for improvement in the euthanasia debate. An act of reconstruction showed me the way—an act that was so well done, so rhetorically competent, so evocative, that I stood in awe of what I heard and saw. On February 28, 1999, the CBS news program *60 Minutes* did a follow-up segment to its earlier piece on Thomas Youk, the ALS patient who was euthanized by Jack Kevorkian. Mike Wallace, once again serving as anchor, introduced the segment ("Choosing Life") by telling how the Youk/Kevorkian story had generated more controversial responses than any other story on *60 Minutes* in the show's thirty-one-year history. According to Wallace, many people with ALS contacted the show's producers to let them know that, unlike Youk, "they still enjoy positive lives" and they would welcome interviews whereby they could explain "why we are choosing life and not death."

"Choosing Life" shares the stories of six patients suffering from ALS.

Although all of the stories make clear that their central characters are in desperate situations because of their fatal disease, they nevertheless also stress how people with ALS are capable of "choosing to thrive, not just survive" and thereby "can make a difference." As one patient put it, tragedy can "embitter us or enrich us," and the second alternative is worth fighting for. Listening to the patients was like reading Tada's book, although without all the religion. At least in the edited television version, each person was depicted as a highly spirited individual cherished by family and friends. Some admitted that early on they had considered suicide but had decided against this option as their various caregivers helped them develop hope and a sense of purpose.[3]

"Choosing Life" is, to be sure, inspirational, especially if one can bracket out any well-deserved cynicism toward *60 Minutes* and the media in general.[4] Of course, no respectable, objective rhetorical critic would ever approach a text without first warming up with this exercise in bracketing. For me, however, the cynicism did not disappear until I saw the face of the fourth patient. It was the face of a dentist and sportsman whose disease had brought him "close to suicide" as it made it impossible for him to move anything but his eyes. There he sat, strapped in his wheelchair, breathing with the help of a ventilator, and wearing on and around his head a high-tech device that covered his right eye. His presence was disconcerting, especially since the only visible sign of life was his flickering left eye. His faced showed no expression; his lips never moved. He was able to "talk" by way of a voice synthesizer that uttered words as he pointed the pupil in his right eye toward specific letters on a computer screen attached to his headset. He looked more like a cyborg than a human being. While answering one of the questions that CBS had sent him prior to the interview so that he would have time to formulate his thoughts, the patient reflected on his existence and shared what went through his mind when he decided not to commit suicide: "Technology is my salvation. . . . This can be the greatest adventure of your life. Think of what you may learn and what you will be able to teach others about life and living. Don't blow it now. I have never regretted that decision for one minute."

Deconstruction, resoluteness, courage, reconstruction, acknowledgment, being-for others: the patient's story said it all. Here was a patient who conceived of his situation as offering "the greatest adventure" of his life. That made sense to me. A patient in such a massive state of deconstruction might be capable of seeing the world in a "new" way, one that perhaps would be especially revealing of what humanity is really all about. As an academic who enjoys being on the lookout for relevant and exciting data, I could not help but think that this patient was indeed on an amazing journey of discovery—one that would let him see through the ritualized good showings of everyday life that can and do cover up the truth. The patient was devoting his life to getting things right. Religion was not mentioned in his story, so certain packaged notions about the "goodness of suffering" did not transform what I was hearing and seeing: a nearly motionless man who was so dedicated to meeting the challenge posed by the call of conscience that he was willing to live a life that the voice in my head told me I could never live. When I asked myself why, I heard hints: "You don't have the courage"; "You would never want to be such a burden to others." Still, I was soothed by the well-known fact that this way of thinking about oneself, in light of the disabled, is not uncommon. Human beings typically have a difficult time looking death in the face, and this difficulty is right before us when we are in the presence of those who remind us of our mortality and of how life can become a living death. The disabled are thus further condemned to a social death so that we "normal" folks need not be burdened and delayed by scenes of sadness.

Yet as I continue to watch the taped "Choosing Life" segment, I am less preoccupied with sadness and more taken with the stories' overall thought-provoking and inspirational qualities. The fourth patient continues to be the catalyst. Every time I look at this man and squirm over his cyborg existence and voice, I get caught up in the perspective of incongruity that takes shape between us. I am not at all sure that I could or would want to live such a heroic life. The fourth patient *is making a difference* as his face and its story continue to remind me of my shortcomings and limitations while at the same time evoking in me a sense of wonder for just how important heroes are. With heroes comes resoluteness, courage, reconstruction, acknowledgment, and a being-for others. We are never more authentic than when we struggle to be this way.

The fourth patient presented in "Choosing Life" allowed me to understand that more of the perfect world that I described above could become a reality. Owing to the help of devoted caregivers (and the media), the patient could show himself to be a person whose outlook on life struck a chord in my heart. With the fourth patient in mind, I am reminded of my father and of a dream that did not come true: "Let's try to spend more time together, son, before it's too late." "You bet, Pop. Whatever you need. Whatever you want. Here I am!" These words would be said knowing full well what was on my father's mind and without a second thought about what sacrifices would have to be made in order to get things right for *him*. Oh, to be a hero to my father, to my teacher, to one who never tired of being a hero to me!

I hope all of this does not sound too sappy, for it is my way of splitting the difference between the hard-core right to life and the hard-core right to die. Perhaps the following will prove helpful:

During his interview with the fourth patient, Wallace asked if he thought those like Thomas Youk should have the right to seek assistance in committing suicide. A "yes" is heard coming from the voice synthesizer. Another patient who could write but who could not talk agreed, but she also felt that Youk "wimped out." Cutting to an interview with Youk's wife, Wallace seeks a response to such a feeling. "It really hurt to have people think that Tom wimped out," she said. "Tom was very strong through this; he was very determined through this." Cutting back to his interview with another patient, Wallace emphasizes that all the patients in his story "were also determined." The point being? Wallace never says. That's good media logic: let the audience figure it out; it's more interesting and entertaining that way. The media thrives on unsettled controversy. If it is not there, then perhaps a loaded question or a nifty edit will do the trick.

I do not know how much manipulating and editing went on to help make "Choosing Life" a more captivating news segment than it otherwise might have been. But some of the rhetoric of the piece, and especially that of a particular patient, certainly hit home. I agree with the patient: Thomas Youk had the right to seek release from a life filled with too much suffering and pain. And from what I know about Mr. Youk's story, he came to this decision in the company of loved ones who were there to struggle with him, to give him hope, and to say "Here I am" whatever his decision. Kevorkian's and the media's use of Youk, however, made it all look too simple and easy. That, I believe, was wrong; it was *too* deconstructive. The call of conscience does not work that way. We have an obligation to do all we can to acknowledge others, to make them feel wanted, to help them reconstruct and feel good about their lives before we agree to pull the plug. The sacrifice should never be merely on the shoulders of the wounded storyteller. That allows things to become too imperfect, too impersonal and immoral. In a country that has yet to figure out how it will solve its much-talked-about "healthcare crisis," I do not think it wise to be overly zealous about the goodness of euthanasia.

What we need instead are efforts on the part of people who are willing to engage in more reconstructive tasks—one of which is developing the rhetor-ical competence that is needed to educate us about how we might best answer a call that comes from the ill and dying: Where art thou?[5] Of course, if we ever come up with a perfect answer to the question, there will no longer be any need for the rhetoric of euthanasia. In a perfect world uncertainty and ambi-guity would no longer exist, and thus rhetoricians would be out of business. But so would philosophers and doctors and nurses and lawyers and theolo-gians; for in a perfect world we would know it all, we would never get sick and die, nobody would break the law, and there would be no need for religious doctrine and dogma. Indeed in a perfect world the call of conscience would never be heard again, because its work would be done and we would all be One. I think it is fair to say, however, that we have a way to go before we reach such a state. In the meantime we would do well to cultivate those abilities and virtues that rhetorical situations like the euthanasia debate demand as they sound a call that speaks to our ability to advance humankind's moral goodness.

Notes

Introduction: Bringing Together Theory and Practice

1. Erich Fromm, *Man for Himself: An Inquiry Into the Psychology of Ethics* (New York: Henry Holt, 1947), 141–42.

2. See James Q. Wilson, *The Moral Sense* (New York: Free Press, 1993).

3. Ernest Becker, *The Denial of Death* (New York: Free Press, 1973), 150.

4. Although there are many other authorities that one can point to when considering the topic of conscience, the ones discussed here should be sufficient to clarify the dispute in question. For a wonderful lexical and historical discussion of "conscience," see C. S. Lewis, *Studies in Words,* 2d ed. (New York: Cambridge University Press, 1967), 181–213.

5. All biblical quotations are from the King James Version. For a discussion of the relation between the "heart" and "conscience" in the Old Testament, see Steven S. Schwarzschild, "Conscience," in *Contemporary Jewish Religious Thought,* ed. Arthur A. Cohen and Paul Mendes-Flohr (New York: Free Press, 1987), 87–90; and R. J. Zwi Werblowsky, "The Concept of Conscience in Jewish Perspective," trans. R. F. C. Hull, in *Conscience,* ed. Curatorium of the C. G. Jung Institute, Zurich (Evanston: Northwestern University Press, 1970), 81–109.

6. Abraham Joshua Heschel, *God in Search of Man: A Philosophy of Judaism* (New York: Noonday Press, 1955), 76–78.

7. Ibid., 112.

8. Ibid., 160.

9. Robert Jewett, *Christian Tolerance: Paul's Message to the Modern Church* (Philadelphia: Westminster, 1982), 43–67.

10. *Quodlibetum,* 3, 27, quoted in F. C. Copleston, *Aquinas* (New York: Penguin, 1955), 228.

11. See Jewett, *Christian Tolerance,* 68–91. See also C. A. Pierce, *Conscience in the New Testament* (London: SCM Press, 1955).

12. For an excellent historical study of the approach, see Albert R. Jonsen and Stephen Toulmin, *The Abuse of Casuistry: A History of Moral Reasoning* (Berkeley and Los Angeles: University of California Press, 1988).

13. Immanuel Kant, *Religion Within the Limits of Reason Alone,* trans. Theodore M. Greene and Hoyt H. Hudson (New York: Harper and Row, 1960), 3.

14. Immanuel Kant, *Grounding for the Metaphysics of Morals* with *On a Supposed Right to Lie Because of Philanthropic Concerns,* 3d ed., trans. James W. Ellington (Indianapolis, Ind.: Hackett, 1993), 30.

15. Immanuel Kant, *Religion Within the Limits of Reason Alone,* 174.

16. Immanuel Kant, *Ethical Philosophy,* trans. James W. Ellington (Indianapolis: Hackett, 1983), 59–60.

17. David Hume, *A Treatise of Human Nature,* 2d ed., ed. L. A. Selby-Bigge (Oxford: Clarendon Press, 1978), 458, 470.

18. Adam Smith, *The Theory of Moral Sentiments,* ed. D. D. Raphael and A. L. Macfie (Indianapolis, Ind.: Library Fund, 1982), 113.

19. Ibid., 126.

20. Ibid., 130–32, 134–37.

21. Kant, *Grounding for the Metaphysics of Morals,* 34, 46.

22. Charles Darwin, *The Descent of Man and Selection in Relation to Sex* (Princeton: Princeton University Press, 1981), 70–106.

23. Ibid., 72.

24. Ibid., 392–94.

25. Ibid., 101.

26. Friedrich Nietzsche, *Untimely Meditations,* trans. R. J. Hollingdale (New York: Cambridge University Press, 1983), 127.

27. Friedrich Nietzsche, *The Will to Power,* trans. Walter Kaufmann and R. J. Hollingdale, ed. Walter Kaufmann (New York: Vintage Books, 1968), 162.

28. Friedrich Nietzsche, *The Gay Science,* trans. Walter Kaufmann (New York: Vintage Books, 1974), 239.

29. Nietzsche, *Will to Power,* 548–50.

30. Friedrich Nietzsche, *On the Genealogy of Morals and Ecce Homo,* trans. and ed. Walter Kaufmann (New York: Vintage Books, 1969), 84–87.

31. Nietzsche, *The Gay Science,* 263–64.

32. Sigmund Freud, *New Introductory Lectures on Psycho-Analysis,* trans. James Strachey (New York: W. W. Norton, 1964), 74–81; Freud, *An Outline of Psycho-Analysis,* trans. James Strachey (New York: W. W. Norton, 1949), 62.

33. Sigmund Freud, *Civilization and Its Discontents,* trans. James Strachey (New York: W. W. Norton, 1961), 84.

34. Freud, *New Introductory Lectures on Psycho-Analysis,* 99.

35. Freud, *An Outline of Psycho-Analysis,* 64.

36. Freud, *Civilization and Its Discontents,* 84.

37. Ibid., 85–90; see also Freud, *The Ego and the Id,* trans. James Strachey (New York: W. W. Norton, 1960), 30–33.

38. See, for example, Freud, *Civilization and Its Discontents,* 106–9.

39. For a fuller discussion of this issue, see, for example, Hans Sluga, *Heidegger's Crisis: Philosophy and Politics in Nazi Germany* (Cambridge: Harvard University Press, 1993); see also Hugo Ott, *Martin Heidegger: A Political Life* (New York: Basic Books, 1993); and Rüdiger Safranski, *Martin Heidegger: Between Good and Evil,* trans. Ewald Osers (Cambridge: Harvard University Press, 1998).

40. This phrase, as is well known, is used in Heidegger's *An Introduction to Metaphysics* when he writes: "The works that are being peddled about nowadays [summer 1935] as the philosophy of National Socialism but have nothing whatever to do with the inner truth and greatness of this movement (namely the encounter between global technology and modern man)—have all been written by men fishing in the troubled waters of 'values' and 'totalities'" (199). This specific conception of the movement was not articulated when Heidegger first gave the lecture in 1935. He appended the parenthetic explanation to the 1953 German edition of his book so to clarify how, in his personal opinion, "the inner truth and greatness" of National Socialism was far different than the fascist rhetoric that claimed to know what this truth and greatness actually was. For what I take to be one of the best and most thorough discussions of how Heidegger's philosophy is affected by and speaks to the encounter between global technology and modern man, see Michael E. Zimmerman, *Heidegger's Confrontation with Modernity: Technology, Politics, Art* (Bloomington: Indiana University Press, 1990).

41. In chapter 1 I develop the argument that this way of being is contradicted by what Heidegger has to say in *Being and Time* about the call of conscience and what this call requires of human beings. At this point, however, I would merely stress, especially to those

not familiar with the literature that is devoted to discussing and critiquing Heidegger's (in)actions here, that this literature is quite large and continues to grow. I have found the following works to be especially enlightening in their treatment of the issue and the history of scholarship that surrounds it: Jean-Francois Lyotard, *Heidegger and "the jews,"* trans. Andreas Michel and Mark Roberts (Minneapolis: University of Minnesota Press, 1990); Berel Lang, *Heidegger's Silence* (Ithaca: Cornell University Press, 1996); Sluga, *Heidegger's Crisis;* John D. Caputo, *Demythologizing Heidegger* (Bloomington: Indiana University Press, 1993); Fred Dallmayr, *The Other Heidegger* (Ithaca: Cornell University Press, 1993); and Safranski, *Martin Heidegger.* For an excellent collection of essays dealing with the question of Heidegger's silence, see Alan Milchman and Alan Rosenberg, eds., *Martin Heidegger and the Holocaust* (Atlantic Highlands, N.J.: Humanities Press, 1996). For an equally excellent collection of documents, letters, memoirs, testimonials, lectures, interviews, and statements by Heidegger himself and by many other intellectuals who commented on his philosophy and politics, see Gunther Neske and Emil Kettering, eds., *Martin Heidegger and National Socialism: Questions and Answers,* trans. Lisa Harries and Joachim Neugroschel (New York: Paragon House, 1990).

42. I say this especially as a Jew who is always being pushed by students and colleagues who are aware of my Jewish heritage to explain my turn to Heidegger. I trust this book offers a decent answer.

43. John D. Caputo, *Against Ethics* (Bloomington: Indiana University Press, 1993), 227. Lawrence Vogel also has a nice way of putting it: "Just as there is a danger in becoming an apologetic or obscurantist disciple of a thinker—a danger to which too many 'Heideggerians' have succumbed—so there is the equally unfortunate prospect that the promise of someone's thought will be disregarded because his character turns out to be disappointing" See his *The Fragile "We": Ethical Implications of Heidegger's "Being and Time"* (Evanston: Northwestern University Press, 1994), 9–10.

44. In speaking about Heidegger's "existential analysis of death"—which, as will be shown in chapter 1, is intimately related to his analysis of the call of conscience—Derrida claims that such an analysis maintains no "competence" with respect to such ethical and political issues as "euthanasia." See his *Aporias,* trans. Thomas Dutoit (Stanford: Stanford University Press, 1993), 59–60. I disagree. The "competence" is there to be found, as is the "incompetence," especially if one is willing to go beyond Derrida's philosophical and theoretical argument and apply Heidegger's thinking on death and conscience to *the actual* workings of the euthanasia debate.

45. Plato, *Apology* (40a), trans. Hugh Tredennick, in *The Collected Dialogues of Plato,* ed. Edith Hamilton and Huntington Cairns (Princeton: Princeton University Press, 1961). Further references to this work will be cited in the text.

46. Hans Blumenberg, "An Anthropological Approach to the Contemporary Significance of Rhetoric," trans. Robert M. Wallace, in *After Philosophy: End or Transformation?,* ed. Kenneth Baynes, James Bohman, and Thomas McCarthy (Cambridge: MIT Press, 1987), 441.

47. Cicero, *De oratore* (3.16.61), trans. H. Rackham (Cambridge: Harvard University Press, 1942). Further references to this work will be cited in the text.

48. Cicero, *Orator* (33.118), trans. H. M. Hubbell (Cambridge: Harvard University Press, 1962). Further references to this work will be cited in the text.

49. Cicero, *De officiis* (1.7.22), trans. Walter Miller (Cambridge: Harvard University Press, 1913). Further references to this work will be cited in the text.

50. For two treatments of Cicero that I found especially helpful when thinking about

how his understanding of rhetoric is related to the call of conscience, see Brian Vickers, *In Defence of Rhetoric* (Oxford: Clarendon Press, 1989); and Michael Leff, "Decorum and Rhetorical Interpretation: The Latin Humanistic Tradition and Contemporary Critical Theory," *Vichiana,* 3d series, 1 (1990): 107–26.

51. My use of the term *physicianship* follows Karl Jasper's appreciation and use of the term when describing the moral nature of "the concrete professions": "Where the idea of physicianship is lost . . . the profession has become a mere technique and its social conditions are accidentally set by heterogeneous interests which utterly ruin its substance" (*Philosophy,* trans. E. B. Ashton [Chicago: University of Chicago Press, 1970], 2:332).

52. Thomas B. Farrell, *Norms of Rhetorical Culture* (New Haven: Yale University Press, 1994), 78.

53. Plato, *Phaedo* (64a), trans. Hugh Tredennick, in *The Collected Dialogues of Plato.* Further references to this work will be cited in the text.

54. In 1994 the state of Oregon approved as law its "Death With Dignity Initiative," which allows physicians to assist in a patient's suicide by prescribing certain drugs. "Lethal injections," however, are not permitted under this law. The margin of approval was 51 to 49 percent. The Oregon State Legislature worked to stall its implementation, sending the act back to the people for repeal. In 1997 the voters, by a margin of 60 to 40 percent, chose not to repeal the law.

55. W. H. S. Jones, *Hippocrates,* vol. 1, *The Oath* (London: William Heinemann; New York: G. P. Putnam's Sons, 1923), 299.

56. W. H. S. Jones, *Hippocrates,* vol. 2, *Law* (London: William Heinemann; New York: G. P. Putnam's Sons, 1923), iv.

57. My interest in the euthanasia debate has been going on ever since my father died of renal failure and its complications in 1984. (Some of my father's story will be told in introducing part 2 of this book.) After spending seventeen years monitoring the development of the debate and collecting its rhetorical artifacts, I have learned, of course, that no one book on the topic is ever enough to form a complete understanding of all that the debate entails.

Chapter 1: Heidegger and the Call of Consience

1. For a more in-depth discussion of how this "hermeneutic" process is related to Lincoln's address as well as to public address in general, see Michael J. Hyde and Craig R. Smith, "Hermeneutics and Rhetoric: A Seen but Unobserved Relationship," *Quarterly Journal of Speech* 65 (1979): 347–63; see also Michael Leff, "Hermeneutical Rhetoric," in *Rhetoric and Hermeneutics in Our Time,* ed. Walter Jost and Michael J. Hyde (New Haven: Yale University Press, 1977), 196–214.

2. W. B. Macomber, *The Anatomy of Disillusion: Martin Heidegger's Notion of Truth* (Evanston: Northwestern University Press, 1967), 31.

3. Hubert Dreyfus, *Being-in-the-World: A Commentary on Heidegger's Being and Time, Division 1* (Cambridge: MIT Press, 1991), 155.

4. Calvin O. Schrag, *Existence and Freedom: Towards an Ontology of Human Finitude* (Evanston: Northwestern University Press, 1961), 7.

5. H. F. Ellenberger, "A Clinical Introduction to Psychiatric Phenomena and Existential Analysis," in *Existence: A New Dimension in Psychiatry and Psychology,* ed. R. May, E. Angel, and H. F. Ellenberger (New York: Basic Books, 1958), 110–11.

6. Eric J. Cassell, *Talking with Patients,* vol. 2, *Clinical Technique* (Cambridge: MIT Press, 1985), 15.

7. W. H. S. Jones, *Hippocrates,* vol. 2, *Law* (London: William Heinemann; New York: G. P. Putnam's Sons, 1923), IV.

8. Anatole Broyard, *Intoxicated by My Illness and Other Writings on Life and Death* (New York: Ballantine, 1992), 41.

9. For analyses of these three phenomena, see Daniel J. Boorstin, *The Image: A Guide to Pseudo-Events in America* (New York: Atheneum, 1975); Kathleen Hall Jamieson, *Eloquence in an Electronic Age: The Transformation of Political Speechmaking* (New York: Oxford University Press, 1988); Neil Postman, *Amusing Ourselves to Death: Public Discourse in the Age of Show Business* (New York: Viking Press, 1985).

10. Equating idle talk with rhetoric is, of course, a way of thinking about the practice that is as old as the teachings of Socrates and Plato. As I intend to show in chapter 2, however, Heidegger, influenced as he is by Aristotle, is not one to see the practice of rhetoric as merely an exercise in the spreading of idle talk.

11. According to Jan Aler, "After one finishes reading *Being and Time,* he no longer needs to be a 'wise man' to recognize the presence of the voice of conscience as early as on page [206]," where the "voice of the friend" is first introduced. See his "Heidegger's Conception of Language in *Being and Time,* " in *On Heidegger and Language,* ed. Joseph J. Kockelmans (Evanston: Northwestern University Press, 1972), 59. See also Jacques Derrida, "Heidegger's Ear: Philopolemology (*Geschlecht IV*)," trans. John P. Leavey Jr., in *Reading Heidegger: Commemorations,* ed. John Sallis (Bloomington: Indiana University Press, 1993), 163–218. Derrida's essay is devoted to a deconstructive reading of the "voice of the friend," a reading that does not directly associate this voice with the relationship (between the call of conscience and the practice of rhetoric) that is crucial for the present project.

Chapter 2: The Ontological Workings of the Call of Conscience

1. Michael E. Zimmerman, *Eclipse of the Self: The Development of Heidegger's Concept of Authenticity* (Athens: Ohio University Press, 1981), 74.

2. Theodore Kisiel, *The Genesis of Heidegger's Being and Time* (Berkeley and Los Angeles: University of California Press, 1993), 435. See also Charles E. Scott, *The Question of Ethics: Nietzsche, Foucault, Heidegger* (Bloomington: Indiana University Press, 1990), 106–11.

3. Sören Kierkegaard, *Either/Or,* vol. 2, trans. D. Swenson and L. Swenson (Princeton: Princeton University Press, 1959), 146. (Original work published 1843.)

4. With conformism, then, we have the situation where one's "irresponsible" actions can be accounted for and defended by merely pointing out that "everybody else does it."

5. Heidegger makes this point when he notes, for example, that the instrumentality of any item of equipment "always is *in terms of* . . . its belonging to other equipment: inkstand, pen, ink, paper, blotting pad, table, lamp, furniture, windows, doors, room. These 'Things' never show themselves proximally as they are for themselves, so as to add up to a sum of *realia* and fill up a room. What we encounter as closest to us . . . is the room; and we encounter it not as something 'between four walls' in a geometrical spatial sense, but as equipment for residing. Out of this the 'arrangement' emerges, and it is in this that any 'individual' item of equipment shows itself. Before it does so, a totality of equipment has already been discovered" (BT 97–98).

6. Heidegger's distinction between emotions and moods was discussed in chapter 1, when analyzing the world of "everydayness." Anxiety functions as both an emotion and a mood. For the sake of simplicity, I refer to the emotion of anxiety in what follows.

7. In his critique of Heidegger, Richard Wolin, for example, would have us believe that Heidegger has nothing to say about the significance of this process; hence, according

to Wolin, "The existential phenomenology of *Being and Time* is devoid of a *Bildungsprozess* whereby the They in its fallen state could elevate itself to the sublimity of authentic existence" (*The Politics of Being: The Political Thought of Martin Heidegger* [New York: Columbia University Press, 1990], 45). I think Wolin is very much mistaken. The process is there; it is acknowledged when Heidegger admits what critics like Wolin omit in their discussion: "Only in communicating and in struggling [with others] does the power of destiny become free." On page 62 of his text, Wolin quotes from page 436 of *Being and Time:* "'Our fates have already been guided in advance, in our Being with one another in the same world and in our resolve for definite possibilities. . . . Dasein's fateful destiny *in and with its generation* goes to make up the full authentic historicizing of Dasein.'" Wolin replaces Heidegger's admission concerning communication and struggle with an ellipsis! Jacques Taminiaux also fails to acknowledge the admission and thus ends up presenting a very skewed critical analysis of Heidegger's thinking on the process involved in establishing "authentic community." See his *Heidegger and the Project of Fundamental Ontology,* trans. and ed. Michael Gendre (Albany: State University of New York Press, 1991), 131–32.

8. That Heidegger recognizes (albeit briefly) how Dasein exists as "a Being-with for Others" is significant; for, in so doing, he admits a point that many of his critics (e.g., Levinas) accuse him of neglecting. Yet the recognition is certainly there, thereby opening additional possibilities for interpreting the scope and application of his overall philosophical project. As will be discussed in chapter 3, Levinas does not grant Heidegger such "hermeneutic charity."

9. Kenneth Burke, *Permanence and Change* (New York: Bobbs-Merrill, 1965), 37.

10. *The Republic of Plato,* trans. Francis M. Cornford (New York: Oxford University Press, 1979), XXI, vi, 487b–497a.

11. Henry W. Johnstone Jr., *Validity and Rhetoric in Philosophical Argument: An Outlook in Transition* (University Park, Pa.: The Dialogue Press of Man and World, 1978), 72.

12. Martin Heidegger, *Being and Time,* trans. Joan Stambaugh (Albany: State University of New York Press, 1996), 130.

13. For a discussion of how this point is first developed in Heidegger's 1924 summer semester lecture course on Aristotle, see P. Christopher Smith, *The Hermeneutics of Original Argument: Demonstration, Dialectic, Rhetoric* (Evanston: Northwestern University Press, 1998).

14. Recall that metaphysics, as noted in the beginning of chapter 1, traditionally understands "Being itself" by focusing its outlook primarily on the present status of beings. For two of Heidegger's early works that deal specifically with the issue of metaphysics and that begin to clarify his move beyond the initial investigations of BT, see his KPM and FCM.

15. Joseph J. Kockelmans, *On the Truth of Being: Reflections on Heidegger's Later Philosophy* (Bloomington: Indiana University Press, 1984), 205–7.

16. John D. Caputo, *Demythologizing Heidegger* (Bloomington: Indiana University Press, 1993), 68.

17. Richard J. Bernstein, *Philosophical Profiles* (Philadelphia: University of Pennsylvania Press, 1986), 208, 219.

18. With this point in mind, I am inclined to ask: Was Heidegger's "silence" concerning the Jews his way of paying homage to the "truth" of Being? This question speaks to the problem of taking ontological inquiry too far, especially when circumstances demand a more appropriate response. That Heidegger was too conditioned by Being's call to offer such a response is suggested by a comment that he made in a 1949 lecture wherein he suggests how technology not only changes everyday existence but also, at times, brings out the worst in human beings: "Agriculture is today a motorized food industry, in essence the

same as the manufacture of corpses in gas chambers and extermination camps, the same as the blockade and starvation of countries, the same as the manufacture of atomic bombs" (quoted in Wolin, *The Politics of Being,* 168). Wolin goes on to argue that what Heidegger is saying here "is not only a monumental *non sequitur* in historical reasoning; it [also] suggests a fundamental incapacity for both moral and theoretical discernment." Giving Heidegger the benefit of the doubt, one could say, however, that his statement does exhibit some such discernment, for it at least acknowledges how misdirected human beings can become under the influence of technology; hence, the horror of the Nazis and the Holocaust. Still, the statement hardly amounts to a fitting and appropriate response to the practical consequences of such horror. Directed by the call of Being, Heidegger displays an amazing lack of rhetorical competence.

With this last point in mind, it is interesting to note how various authors over the years have tried to save Heidegger (the philosopher) from himself (as a political animal) by emphasizing how his thinking on the related topics of "communication" and "language" lends itself to a theory of communal life that calls into question the close-mindedness of fascism. See, for example, Fred R. Dallmayr's, *Polis and Praxis: Exercises in Contemporary Political Theory* (Cambridge: MIT Press, 1984), 104–32; and his *The Other Heidegger* (Ithaca: Cornell University Press, 1993). See also Werner Marx, *Is There a Measure on Earth? Foundations for a Nonmetaphysical Ethics,* trans. Thomas J. Nenon and Reginald Lilly (Chicago: University of Chicago Press, 1987); and his companion volume, *Towards a Phenomenological Ethics: Ethos and the Life-World,* trans. Stefaan Heyvaert (Albany: State University of New York Press, 1992); Lawrence Vogel, *The Fragile "We": Ethical Implications of Heidegger's "Being and Time"* (Evanston: Northwestern University Press, 1994); Simon Glendinning, *On Being with Others: Heidegger—Derrida—Wittgenstein* (New York: Routledge, 1998); Frederick A. Olafson, *Heidegger and the Ground of Ethics: A Study of Mitsein* (New York: Cambridge University Press, 1998).

The present work also constitutes an attempt to save Heidegger from himself. But the specific way I have tried to do this—by concentrating on the relationship between the call of conscience and the practice of rhetoric—provides, I believe, a more explicit and revealing study of how Heidegger's politics are contradicted by his philosophy. Defenders of Heidegger are being too kind when they only go as far as his thinking on "communication" and "language." The relationship between the call of conscience and the practice of rhetoric also warrants close attention, especially since it forces Heidegger to call himself into question.

19. Jürgen Habermas, *The Philosophical Discourse of Modernity: Twelve Lectures,* trans. Frederick G. Lawrence (Cambridge: MIT Press, 1987), 159.

20. All that was said in note 18 above is thus also applicable here.

21. One of Heidegger's most famous students, Hans-Georg Gadamer, states the matter this way: "What man needs is not just the persistent posing of ultimate questions, but the sense of what is feasible, what is possible, what is correct, here and now. The philosopher, of all people, must, I think, be aware of the tension between what he claims to achieve and the reality in which he finds himself" (*Truth and Method,* 2d rev. ed., trans. Joel Weinsheimer and Donald G. Marshall [New York: Crossroad, 1991], xxxviii). Indeed, Gadamer's point here is as old as Aristotle's and especially Cicero's critique of Plato's philosophy of rhetoric.

22. Employing Heidegger's own language, one might therefore accuse him of being a "coward" (BT 311) as he continued throughout his life to avoid offering a clear-cut rhetorical interruption that clarified his lack of judgment (*phronesis*) in the 1930s.

23. Thomas B. Farrell, *Norms of Rhetorical Culture* (New Haven: Yale University Press, 1993), 298.

Chapter 3: Levinas and the Call of Conscience

1. Throughout my discussion of Levinas, "the other" will refer to persons, while "the Other" will refer to "the otherness" (or "alterity") of the other. The two are sometimes indistinguishable in Levinas. Also note that the French *conscience* can mean both "consciousness" and "conscience" (*conscience moral*). My reading of Levinas is thus concerned primarily with the second of these two meanings.

2. For what is perhaps Derrida's most influential discussion and comparison of the two philosophers, see his "Violence and Metaphysics: An Essay on the Thought of Emmanuel Levinas," in his *Writing and Difference,* trans. Alan Bass (Chicago: University Press of Chicago, 1978), 79–153.

3. Erving Goffman, *Interaction Ritual: Essays on Face-to-Face Behavior* (New York: Anchor Books, 1967), 5, 44.

4. Although Levinas is certainly aware of phenomenology's commitment to "the thing itself" (TIHP), he nowhere, as far as I know, offers a discussion of "the movement of showing" that is as explicit as one can find in Heidegger.

5. Derrida, "Violence and Metaphysics," 137–38.

6. Abraham Joshua Heschel, *Man Is Not Alone: A Philosophy of Religion* (New York: Noonday, 1976), 296.

7. Calvin O. Schrag, *Communicative Praxis and the Space of Subjectivity* (Bloomington: Indiana University Press, 1986), 198–99.

8. See John Llewelyn, *The Middle Voice of Ecological Conscience: A Chiasmic Reading of Responsibility in the Neighborhood of Levinas, Heidegger and Others* (New York: St. Martin's Press, 1991). See also his *Emmanuel Levinas: The Genealogy of Ethics* (New York: Routledge, 1995).

9. David J. Wolpe, *In Speech and in Silence: The Jewish Quest for God* (New York: Henry Holt, 1992), 120.

10. Ernest Becker, *The Denial of Death* (New York: Free Press, 1973), 33–34, 147.

11. For what I take to be one of the most even-handed and relevant critiques of deconstruction, see Eugene Goodheart, *The Skeptic Disposition in Contemporary Criticism* (Princeton: Princeton University Press, 1984).

12. See, for example, Michel Foucault, *Politics, Philosophy, Culture: Interviews and Other Writings,* trans. Lawrence D. Kritzman (London: Routledge, Chapman, and Hull, 1988); Jean-François Lyotard and Jean-Loup Thebaud, *Just Gaming,* trans. Wlad Godzich (Minneapolis: University of Minnesota Press, 1985); Jacques Derrida, *Limited INC* (Evanston: Northwestern University Press, 1988), esp. 111–54.

13. Jacques Derrida, "Deconstruction and the Other" (interview with Richard Kearney), in *Dialogues with Contemporary Continental Thinkers: The Phenomenological Heritage* (Manchester: Manchester University Press, 1984), 107–26.

14. Jory Graham, *In the Company of Others: Understanding the Human Needs of Cancer Patients* (New York: Harcourt Brace Javanovich, 1982). Further references to this work will be cited in the text.

15. Susan Sontag, *Against Interpretation and Other Essays* (New York: Farrar, Straus and Giroux, 1966).

16. Michel Foucault, *The Birth of the Clinic: An Archaeology of Medical Perception,* trans. A. M. S. Smith (New York: Vintage Books, 1975), xix.

17. The essay quoted here is M. V. Gerbie, "Malignant Neoplasms of the Vulva, " in

Gynecology and Obstetrics, ed. J. J. Sciarra (Hagerstown, Md.: Harper and Row, 1977), 1:1–10.

18. See Robert Solomon, *The Passions: The Myth and Nature of Human Emotion* (New York: Anchor/Doubleday, 1976), 284.

19. Hans Blumenberg, "An Anthropological Approach to the Contemporary Significance of Rhetoric," trans. Robert M. Wallace, in *After Philosophy: End or Transformation?* ed. Kenneth Baynes, James Bohman, and Thomas McCarthy (Cambridge: MIT Press, 1987), 442.

20. John Dewey, *The Public and Its Problems* (Chicago: Swallow Press, 1954), 27.

21. Quoted in Richard Wolin, *The Politics of Being: The Political Thought of Martin Heidegger* (New York: Columbia University Press, 1990), 168.

22. Heschel, *Man Is Not Alone,* 36–37.

23. Margaret D. Zulick, "The Active Force of Hearing: The Ancient Hebrew Language of Persuasion," *Rhetorica* 10 (1992): 367–80.

24. Ibid., 373, 374.

25. Ibid., 375.

26. Rabbi David A. Cooper, *God Is a Verb: Kabbalah and the Practice of Mystical Judaism* (New York: Riverhead Books, 1997), 54, 55.

27. Ibid., 58.

28. Wilbur S. Howell, ed., *Fenelon's Dialogues on Eloquence* (Princeton: Princeton University Press, 1951), 23. For three thought-provoking discussions that suggest how rhetoric, despite Levinas' arguments to the contrary, still has a positive role to play in his philosophy, see Steven G. Smith, "Reason as One for Another: Moral and Theoretical Argument," in *Face to Face with Levinas,* ed. Richard A. Cohen (Albany: State University of New York Press, 1986), 53–71; Susan A. Handelman, *Fragments of Redemption: Jewish Thought and Literary Theory in Benjamin, Scholem, and Levinas* (Bloomington: Indiana University Press, 1991), 226–62; Susan E. Shapiro, "Rhetoric, Ideology, and Idolatry in the Writings of Emmanuel Levinas," in *Rhetorical Invention and Religious Inquiry: New Perspectives,* ed. Walter Jost and Wendy Olmsted (New Haven: Yale University Press, 2000), 254–78. In what follows in the text, I too will be arguing for a positive conception of rhetoric in light of Levinas' philosophy—a conception that extends the thinking of Smith, Handelman, and Shapiro by emphasizing a matter that escapes their attention: how the call of conscience defines an interruptive, epideictic, and rhetorically eloquent event. See also Lawrence W. Rosenfield, "The Practical Celebration of Epideictic," in *Rhetoric in Transition: Studies in the Nature and Uses of Rhetoric,* ed. Eugene E. White (University Park: Pennsylvania State University Press, 1980), 131–55. Although Rosenfield turns to Heidegger as a guide for understanding the workings of epideictic rhetoric, his consideration of the matter (which omits a careful assessment of how the call of conscience and rhetoric are related) nevertheless proved helpful in my thinking about how Levinas' philosophy provides an opening for developing a fundamental appreciation of rhetoric.

29. Henry W. Johnstone Jr., *Validity and Rhetoric in Philosophical Argument: An Outlook in Transition* (University Park, Pa.: Dialogue Press, 1978), 129.

30. Raphael Demos, "On Persuasion," *Journal of Philosophy* 29 (1932): 229.

31. Colin Davis, *Levinas: An Introduction* (Notre Dame: University of Notre Dame Press, 1996), 50.

32. Although he has nothing specific to say about this art, Simon Critchley does provide support for the point I am making here in his discussion of Levinas' notion of the "third party." See his *The Ethics of Deconstruction: Derrida and Levinas* (Cambridge, Mass.: Blackwell, 1992), 219–36.

Part II—Practice: Conscience, Rhetoric, and the Euthanasia Debate

1. Friedrich Nietzsche, *Human, All Too Human: A Book for Free Spirits,* trans. Marion Faber, with Stephen Lehmann (Lincoln: University of Nebraska Press, 1984), 60–62.

2. Friedrich Nietzsche, *Twilight of the Idols / The Anti-Christ,* trans. R. J. Hollingdale (New York: Penguin, 1990), 99–100.

3. Martin E. Marty and Ron Hamel, "Part Three: Some Questions and Answers," in *Active Euthanasia, Religion, and the Public Debate,* ed. Ron Hamel (Chicago: Park Ridge Center for the Study of Health, Faith, and Ethics, 1991), 41.

Chapter 4: The Call of Conscience/Rhetoric/Medicine

1. Plato, *Gorgias,* trans. W. D. Woodhead, in *Plato, The Collected Dialogues,* ed. Edith Hamilton and Huntington Cairns (Princeton: Princeton University Press, 1961), 456b–c.

2. Plato, *Phaedrus,* trans. R. Hackforth, in *Plato, The Collected Dialogues,* 270b–272b.

3. Aristotle, *Rhetoric,* trans. W. Rhys Roberts (New York: Random House, 1954), 1358b13. Further references to this work will be cited in the text.

4. Ludwig Edelstein, *Ancient Medicine,* trans. C. Lilian Temkin, ed. Owsei Temkin and C. Lilian Temkin (Baltimore: John Hopkins University Press, 1987), 87–110. See also Werner Jaeger, *Paideia: The Ideals of Greek Culture,* vol. 3, *The Conflict of Cultural Ideals in the Age of Plato,* trans. Gilbert Highet (New York: Oxford University Press, 1986), 3–45.

5. Plato, *Laws,* IV, 720c–e, trans. A. E. Taylor, in *Plato: The Collected Dialogues.*

6. W. H. S. Jones, *Hippocrates (The Art),* vol. 2 (London: William Heinemann; New York: G. P. Putnam's Sons, 1923), XIV. Edelstein, *Ancient Medicine,* describes this text as "the [Hippocratic] treatise which documents the physician's rhetorical stance and his rhetorical battle detached from all specifically medical objectives" (101). But notice how the author of this treatise *deconstructs* its rhetorical worth as he emphasizes seeing over hearing.

7. See Pedro Lain Entralgo, *The Therapy of the Word in Classical Antiquity,* trans. L. J. Rather and John M. Sharp (New Haven: Yale University Press, 1970), 139–70. See also Michael Frede, *Essays in Ancient Philosophy* (Minneapolis: University of Minnesota Press, 1987), 232–39; and Albert R. Jonsen, *The New Medicine and the Old Ethics* (Cambridge: Harvard University Press, 1990), 8–9.

8. W. H. S. Jones, *Hippocrates (Decorum),* vol. 2 (London: William Heinemann; New York: G. P. Putnam's Sons, 1923), V.

9. W. H. S. Jones, *Hippocrates (Law),* vol. 2 (London: William Heinemann; New York: G. P. Putnam's Sons, 1923), V. With the Hippocratic oath, the physician swears "to impart precept, oral instruction, and all other instruction to my own sons, the sons of my teacher, and to indentured pupils who have taken the physician's oath, but to nobody else." See W. H. S. Jones, *Hippocrates (The Oath),* vol. 1 (London: William Heinemann; New York: G. P. Putnam's Sons, 1923), 299.

10. W. H. S. Jones, *Hippocrates (The Art),* III, VIII.

11. In the Hippocratic oath one reads: "I will use treatment to help the sick according to my ability and judgment, but never with a view to injury and wrong-doing. Neither will I administer a poison to anybody when asked to do so, nor will I suggest such a course." This prohibition against harming patients is the basis for medicine's ethical stand against euthanasia.

12. W. H. S. Jones, *Hippocrates (Law),* IV.

13. Stanley Joel Reiser, "The Machine at the Bedside: Technological Transformations of Practices and Values," in *The Machine at the Bedside: Strategies for Using Technology in Patient*

Care, ed. Stanley Joel Reiser and Michael Anbar (New York: Cambridge University Press, 1984), 4–6.

14. For a fine discussion of this "anti-humanist" attitude of medicine, see Jonsen, *The New Medicine and the Old Ethics,* 17–37.

15. See Reiser, "The Machine at the Bedside." See also his *Medicine and the Reign of Technology* (New York: Cambridge University Press, 1982).

16. See Lewis Thomas, *The Lives of a Cell: Notes of a Biology Watcher* (New York: Penguin, 1982), 32–33. See also Jay Katz, *The Silent World of Doctor and Patient* (New York: Free Press, 1984).

17. Joseph Fletcher, *Morals and Medicine: The Moral Problems of the Patient's Right to Know the Truth, Contraception, Artificial Insemination, Sterilization, Euthanasia* (Princeton: Princeton University Press, 1979), 172–210.

18. In 1991 the federal government implemented the Patient Self-Determination Act, which requires federally funded hospitals, nursing homes, and home care agencies to inform patients of their rights under state law to sign advanced directives about whether artificial life-sustaining procedures should be used.

19. One sees this most dramatically with Oregon's "Death with Dignity" initiative made into law in 1997. See also D. E. Meier, C. A. Emmons, S. Wallenstein, T. Quill, R. S. Morrison, and C. K. Cassell, "A National Survey on Physician-Assisted Suicide and Euthanasia in the United States," *New England Journal of Medicine* 338 (1998): 1193–201.

20. W. H. S. Jones, *Hippocrates (The Art),* III.

21. See note 11 above.

22. Willard Gaylin, Leon R. Kass, Edmund D. Pellegrino, and Mark Siegler, "Doctors Must Not Kill," *Journal of the American Medical Association* 259 (1988): 2139–40.

23. Robert Moss, "Reflection," in *Active Euthanasia, Religion, and the Public Debate,* ed. Ron Hamel (Chicago: Park Ridge Center for the Study of Health, Faith, and Ethics, 1991), 97.

24. *Journal of the American Medical Association,* 259 (1988): 272.

25. See Mark Bloom, "Article Embroils JAMA in Ethical Controversy," *Science* 239 (1988): 1235–36. In this article Lundberg is quoted as saying, "The purpose of doing an editorial is to diminish the debate. An editorial would have been at counterpurposes to what we were trying to do. It's an easy way out, journalistically, but we would not have stimulated the debate" (1235). More will be said about this issue shortly.

26. George D. Lundberg, "'It's Over, Debbie' and the Euthanasia Debate," *Journal of the American Medical Association* 259 (1988): 2142.

27. Major newspapers reprinted the case. See, for example, Bill Richards, "AMA Journal's Letter from Mercy Killer Raises Legal Debate on Source Protection," *Wall Street Journal,* 22 February 1988, 21; and Isabel Wilkerson, "Essay on Mercy Killing Reflects Conflict on Ethics for Physicians and Journalists," *New York Times,* 22 February 1988, A16. Newspapers also reprinted reader-responses to the case that were initially published in *JAMA.* See, for example, Victor Cohn, "The Story of 'Debbie's' Death Isn't Over," *Washington Post,* 12 April 1988, Health section: 10. The case was also read and debated on the PBS Mac-Neil/Lehrer Newshour, 2 March 1988.

28. For example, see "Letters" in *JAMA* 259 (1988), especially those submitted by Charles B. Clark, Watson Kime, Susan D. Wilson, Diane Davis, and Eileen Moran (2095, 2097–98). According to Lundberg, at "press time" *JAMA* had received "more than 150 letters" concerning "Debbie." "Most of the early letters were from physicians and tallied about 4:1 against the action the physician described and 3:1 against *The Journal* for publishing the essay. Reactions from the public and media were delayed but were extraordi-

nary in volume and duration" (Lundberg, "'It's Over, Debbie' and the Euthanasia Debate," 2142).

29. See "Letters" in *JAMA* 259 (1988): 2096. The "requirements" read: "1. There must be adequate legal documentation that the euthanasia was requested by the patient well in advance of its occurring. 2. The physician who aids the patient in dying must have known the patient and must have been fully aware of his/her medical history and desire for aid-in-dying in the event of terminal illness. 3. The physician must have a second opinion from another qualified physician that affirms that the patient's condition is indeed terminal. 4. The rights of physicians who cannot in good conscience perform aid-in-dying are to be fully respected, providing they in no way obstruct the practice of physicians who in good conscience give such aid."

30. The AMA argued that the subpoena was contrary to the First Amendment and the Illinois Reporters Privilege Act. The subpoena was eventually quashed by the chief judge of Cook County Criminal Court.

31. Eugene F. Diamond, "Abhorrent," *Chicago Sun-Times,* 17 February 1988, Commentary section, 34.

32. See, for example, Howard Wolinsky and Tom Brune, "Experts believe 'mercy killing' essay a hoax," *Chicago Sun-Times,* 9 February 1988, 3; also Jon Van, "Essay on mercy killing may have fatal flaws," *Chicago Tribune,* 21 February 1988, sec. 4, pp. 1, 4.

33. Gaylin, Kass, Pellegrino, and Siegler (see note 22 above). For a similar line of "reasoning," see Charles Colson, "It's Not Over, Debbie," *Christianity Today* 33 (1988): 80.

34. Mark Siegler, "The AMA Euthanasia Fiasco," *New York Times,* 26 February 1988, A35.

35. Quoted in "JAMA: Editorial Freedom or License?" *Illinois Medicine* 10 (1990): 12.

36. As indicated, for example, in some of the reader responses cited above. I will continue to illustrate this point throughout this essay in both the text and the notes.

37. I put matters this way ("is the case") because with "Debbie," as I hope to show, speculation is inevitable. My critical reading of the case will thus often be written in the speculative mode—that is, by raising questions in order to make my case as compelling and as "truthful" as possible.

38. Jean-Francois Lyotard's description of "postmodern" art and prose is fitting here: "The postmodern would be that which, in the modern, puts forward the unpresentable in presentation itself; that which denies itself the solace of good forms, the consensus of a taste which would make it possible to share collectively the nostalgia for the unattainable; that which searches for new presentations, not in order to enjoy them but in order to impart a stronger sense of the unpresentable. A postmodern artist or writer is in the position of a philosopher: the text he writes, the work he produces, are not in principle governed by preestablished rules, and they cannot be judged according to a determining judgment, by applying familiar categories to the text or to the work. Those rules and categories are what the work of art itself is looking for. The artist and the writer, then, are working without rules in order to formulate the rules of what *will have been done.* . . . Post-modern would have to be understood according to the paradox of the future (*post*) anterior (*mondo*)" (*The Postmodern Condition: A Report on Knowledge,* trans. Geoff Bennington and Brian Massumi [Minneapolis: University of Minnesota Press, 1985] 81). With this in mind, one might begin to wonder whether "Debbie" is a "truth" or a "fiction." I deal with this matter in some detail later in the chapter.

39. Many readers perceived the slippery slope phenomenon at work in "Debbie." Here, for example, is a particularly extreme reaction to this phenomenon offered by the Reverend Robert L. Barry, professor of religious studies, University of Illinois, Urbana: "Would not legalization of suicide and euthanasia make it a little bit easier for a resident to

say to Debbie, I am sick and tired of you, you are ruining my reputation, you are taking away my sleep and I am fed up with you? Would not legalization of suicide and euthanasia make it easier for that physician to slip her another injection? . . . I must also ask what sort of people this legalization of suicide and euthanasia would bring to the medical profession. We know that there are many people out there who simply love to kill. They love the excitement of bringing others to death. Would not these people, often very intelligent, very cunning and astute, would not they be attracted to the medical profession precisely because it would be within the medical profession that they could practice the killing art with the full protection of the law?" ("The Dawning of the Brave New World," transcript of "Sustaining Life or Prolonging Death: A Symposium Presented by the Illinois State Bar Association's Standing Committee on Interprofessional Cooperation, Hyatt Regency O'Hare, Rosemont, Illinois, 13 May 1988, 30–31). For a more analytic and formal assessment of "slippery slope" arguments and their presence in the euthanasia debate, see Douglas Walton, *Slippery Slope Arguments* (New York: Oxford University Press, 1992), 161–67.

40. In short, the physician adhered to none of the "requirements" listed in note 29 above. Responding to the lack of remorse on the physician's part, Gaylin, Kass, Pellegrino, and Siegler write: "This is no humane and thoughtful physician succumbing with fear and trembling to the pressures and well-considered wishes of a patient well known to him, for whom there was truly no other recourse. This is, by his own account, an impulsive yet cold technician, arrogantly masquerading as a knight of compassion and humanity" (2139).

41. The uncertainty here speaks (albeit indirectly) to the question of how family members and close friends may be a factor in a patient's "personal" decision to request some form of euthanasia. For a well-informed examination of this issue, see David C. Thomasma and Glenn C. Graber, *Euthanasia: Toward an Ethical Social Policy* (New York: Continuum, 1990), 84–117.

42. The issue of a patient's "competence" is a recurring one in the euthanasia debate since, as many experts point out, patients who are suffering from a painful terminal disease or from a severe and incapacitating injury may become so depressed that they lose the ability to think "rationally" about their situations.

43. For example, one might imagine them saying: "God created human beings to live and not to die. Death in any form is inimical to what God originally had in mind for his creation. Death is the last great enemy to be overcome by the power of the risen Lord (1 Cor. 15:26). To speak of 'death with dignity' or 'merciful release, ' therefore, consists of engaging in unholy rhetoric." See Ron Hamel and Edwin R. DuBose, "Part Four: Views of the Major Faith Traditions," in *Active Euthanasia, Religion, and the Public Debate,* 61, where the authors are discussing the views of the Lutheran Church–Missouri Synod. With specific reference to "Debbie," see Joseph Cardinal Bernadin, "Action in 'Debbie' case was immoral," *Chicago Tribune,* 10 March 1988, sec. 1, p. 20, where it is declared that "No situation or set of circumstances may justify the intentional taking of innocent human life."

44. On January 15, 1999, Lundberg, who had been the editor of *JAMA* for seventeen years, was fired by the AMA for publishing an article that surveyed college students' definitions and understandings of "sex" and that coincided with the impeachment trial of President Clinton. The trial, as is well known, centered around Clinton's lying about his extramarital sexual activities. The AMA justified its action by emphasizing that Lundberg, according to E. Ratcliffe Anderson Jr. (the AMA's executive vice-president), "inappropriately and inexcusably" interjected "JAMA into the middle of a debate that has nothing to do with science or medicine." Reacting to the AMA's actions, Arthur Caplan, the director of bioethics at the University of Pennsylvania, was quoted as saying: "I think this is a tragedy, since George Lundberg is a giant in the field of American medical publishing, and

under his leadership the journal flourished." See "AMA journal editor fired over timing of publication of 'what-is-sex' survey," *Winston-Salem Journal,* 16 January 1999, A4.

45. Lundberg, "'It's Over, Debbie' and the Euthanasia Debate," 2142.

46. Lundberg admitted that "Debbie" "proceeded through two cycles of peer review, and was subjected to rigorous staff discussion prior to a decision to publish that was not unanimous" (Ibid., 2142). Still, Lundberg is the editor of *JAMA;* he thus has the final say in publishing decisions and must therefore assume responsibility for essays that appear in his journal. See also Jon Van, "'It's Over, Debbie,' and Doctor Takes a Life," *Chicago Tribune,* 31 January 1988, sec. 1, pp. 1, 24, wherein it is reported that Lundberg published the essay "over the objections of several members of his staff" (24).

47. Van (see note 46 above) admitted this to me in a phone interview (25 October 1988) concerning his article. He said he was informed of "Debbie" by an "outraged" physician from the University of Chicago. He also said that he typically didn't read "A Piece of My Mind."

48. Cf. Thomas, *The Lives of a Cell,* 78.

49. Eugene Kennedy, "It's Over, George: 'Debbie' Is Too Dubious to Support Serious Debate," *Chicago Tribune,* 19 February 1988, sec. 1, p. 17.

50. Ibid., 17.

51. The phrase "a champion of readers' rights" is taken from Mary Louise Pratt, "Interpretive Strategies/Strategic Interpretations: On Anglo-American Reader-Response Criticism," in *Postmodernism and Politics,* ed. Jonathan Arac (Minneapolis: University of Minnesota Press, 1987), 45. During an interview (13 April 1988) granted to me by Dr. Lundberg so that I could talk to him about "Debbie," I asked him, "How in the world would a *physician* come to know about and appreciate 'reader-response theory' and 'deconstructionist literary theory'?" He told me that his wife had been writing her dissertation in these areas and was giving him her chapters to review. If one reads the dissertation, one can learn a lot. It is a fine piece of work. (See Patricia Lorimer Lundberg, "Gendered Reading Communities: The Feminization of Reader-Response Criticism and a Dialogics of Reading," Ph.D. diss., Loyola University of Chicago, 1988.) During the time he was involved in reading and discussing his wife's work, he received the "Debbie" essay. He would not say for sure that his decision to publish the essay was influenced by his "new" education, although he did say this: "Just sitting within the walls of the AMA would have in no way prepared me for 'Debbie.'"

52. Kennedy made this point during a phone interview with me on April 6, 1988. For Lundberg, however, it is not that simple. In his editorial in *JAMA* he reminds readers that "as its title implies, the popular weekly column A Piece of My Mind is the site of opinion pieces: prose and poetry, anecdotes and reflections, some humorous, some sad, nostalgic, or angry. We allow the authors great flexibility and encourage freedom" (2142).

53. See "Letters" in *JAMA* 259 (1988): 2095.

54. Kennedy makes this very point during his attack on Lundberg, whose "cavalier attitude about the truth of an anonymous contribution also does a disservice to the art of fiction." According to Kennedy, "Great novels live precisely because they are built on the truth observed keenly, often at the price of great suffering by their authors. It is not difficult to distinguish between works of fiction that are rooted in human truth and those that are not. The true ones, we say, speak with authority. . . . It is well to remember that the words 'author' and 'authority' are related; they come from the Latin *augere,* which means to increase, to be generative. That author who does not speak the truth cannot have authority, cannot enlarge our lives."

55. Elliot G. Mishler, *The Discourse of Medicine: Dialectics of Medical Interviews* (Norwood,

N.J.: Ablex, 1984); Arthur Kleinman, *The Illness Narratives: Suffering, Healing and the Human Condition* (New York: Basic Books, 1998); Kathryn Montgomery Hunter, *Doctors' Stories: The Narrative Structure of Medical Knowledge* (Princeton: Princeton University Press, 1991); Richard M. Zaner, *Troubled Voices: Stories of Ethics and Illness* (Cleveland: Pilgrim Press, 1993).

56. For an informative discussion of the stylistic nature of medical case histories, see Hunter, *Doctors' Stories.*

57. In the fast-paced world of modern medicine—where, for example, the night life of an on-call physician can easily conform to what one reads in the first paragraph of "Debbie"—speed and efficiency make sense. But can the rigorous pace of such a life-style also pose a threat to conscientious patient care? Some readers of "Debbie" raised such a question in light of the story's first paragraph. See, for example, Joan Beck, "Do sleep-starved hospital residents endanger patients?" *Chicago Tribune,* 4 February 1988, sec. 1, p. 25. According to Beck, "This case does . . . make a powerful argument in another continuing medical controversy, this one over whether hospital interns and residents are working such long hours that chronic fatigue and stress increase the risk that they will harm a patient by making a mistake or using bad judgment."

58. See the letter submitted by Harold Y. Vanderpool in *Journal of the American Medical Association* 259 (1988): 2094.

59. I think it is fair to say that "Debbie" encourages one to ask such questions. Elsewhere I have dealt with the questions in light of other case studies. See my "A Rhetoric of Risk: Medical Science and the Question of 'Wrongful Life,'" in *Argument and Critical Practices: Proceedings of the Fifth SCA/AFA Conference on Argumentation,* ed. Joseph W. Wenzel (Annandale, Va.: Speech Communication Association, 1987), 129–36; and "Experts, Rhetoric, and the Dilemmas of Medical Technology: Investigating a Problem of Progressive Ideology," in *Communication and the Culture of Technology,* ed. Martin J. Medhurst, Alberto Gonzalez, and Tarla Rai Peterson (Pullman: Washington State University Press, 1990), 115–36. For two quite moving essays whose "rhetoric" speaks to the importance of the questions, see Andrew H. Malcolm, "The Ultimate Decision," *New York Times Magazine,* 3 December 1989, 39–40, 50, 54–55, 146; and Charles Siebert, "The Rehumanization of the Heart: What Doctors Have Forgotten, Poets Have Always Known," *Harper's* (February 1990): 53–60. See also Jared Goldstein, "Desperately Seeking Science: The Creation of Knowledge in Family Practice, *Hastings Center Report* 20 (November/December 1990): 26–33. Goldstein turns to "the postmodern movement of literary criticism known as poststructuralism or deconstructionism" as a way of exploring the tensions that exist between medical "science" and medical "practice" (29–31).

60. See "Letters," in *Journal of the American Medical Association* 254 (1988): 2094–95.

61. Sidney H. Wanzer, Daniel D. Federman, S. James Adelstein, Christine K. Cassel, Edwin H. Cassem, Ronald E. Cranford, Edward W. Hook, Bernard Lo, Charles G. Moertel, Peter Safar, Alan Stone, and Jan van Eys, "The Physician's Responsibility Toward Hopelessly Ill Patients: A Second Look," *New England Journal of Medicine* 320 (1989): 845.

62. With Jacques Derrida one would see the use of this deconstructive act of "self" criticism as a way of "destabilizing" the "conventionalized" and discursive "power" of the scientifically oriented voice of medicine. See, for example, his *Limited INC,* trans. Samuel Weber and Jeffrey Mehlman (Evanston: Northwestern University Press, 1988), 147. See also his "Deconstruction and the Other" (an interview with Richard Kearney), in Richard Kearney, *Dialogues with Contemporary Continental Thinkers: The Phenomenological Heritage* (Dover: Manchester University Press, 1986), 107–26, wherein he says such things as: "Every culture and society requires an internal critique or deconstruction as an essential

part of its development. . . . Every culture needs an element of self-interrogation and of distance from itself, if it is to transform itself" (116). With all this in mind, one might begin to wonder about the "rhetorical motivation" at work in "Debbie." Perhaps the author is trying to tell us something here. I deal with this matter in the conclusion of this chapter.

63. See the "letter" from Dr. Sheldon T. Berkowitz in *JAMA* 260 (1988): 788. See also Diane M. Gianelli, "JAMA article on lethal dose given 'Debbie' generates wave of controversy," *American Medical News,* 19 February 1988, 1, 88, 90, wherein Dr. Matthew E. Conolly, a pain control specialist and a professor of clinical pharmacology, is quoted as saying that today "nobody uses an alcohol drip for sedation" (88).

64. Pointing to the alcohol drip, Berkowitz (see note 63 above) suggests that this "incident" may have occurred twenty-five years ago since the sedation therapy "has not been in use for at least that long." He then speculates further: "I wonder if this physician was presumably doing the best that he could at the time, without all the knowledge that we now have about pain control. If this is the case, public scrutiny was not as intense as it is now, and thus an act like this could be carried out in relative privacy" (788). This is an interesting speculation. However, if it is all that simple, then it seems reasonable to ask: Why didn't the author simply admit this instead of engaging us in a narrative filled with uncertainty and ambiguity? What I have to suggest in the remainder of my reading speaks to this question and thus also to the shortcomings of Berkowitz's speculation.

65. *Journal of the American Medical Association* 260 (1988): 787. Berkowitz fails to take this point into account. The point certainly undermines the possible "truth" of his position.

66. Kenneth L. Vaux, "Debbie's Dying: Mercy Killing and the Good Death," *Journal of the American Medical Association* 259 (1988): 2140. See also his "The Theologic Ethics of Euthanasia," *Hastings Center Report,* Special Supplement on "Mercy, Murder and Morality: Perspectives on Euthanasia" 19 (Jan/Feb 1989): 19–22, for a further elaboration of this point. Vaux published a number of supportive commentaries on the "Debbie" case, thereby helping to spread the word about the story and its surrounding controversy. See, for example, his "If we can bar the door to death, can't we also open it?" *Chicago Tribune,* 10 February 1988, sec. 1, p. 23; and "Debbie's Dying: Euthanasia Reconsidered," *Christian Century* 105 (1988): 269–71. Vaux's efforts received much praise for their "eloquence" and "brilliance." See, for example, the "letters" of doctors Max Spital and Aaron Spital, in *Journal of the American Medical Association* 260 (1988): 788–89.

67. With this interpretation the physician's actions would, of course, no longer be "controversial."

68. As explained to me by a physician, a doctor does not try to control pain by purposefully "attacking the patient's center" (depressing the respiratory drive).

69. See Howard Wolinsky and Tom Brune, "Experts Believe 'Mercy Killing' Essay a Hoax," *Chicago Sun-Times,* 9 February 1988, 3; Jon Van, "Essay on Mercy Killing May Have Fatal Flaws," *Chicago Tribune,* 21 February 1988, sec. 4, pp. 1, 4. See also Charles Krauthammer, "The Death of Debbie," *Washington Post,* 26 February 1988, A23.

70. See her "letter" in *Journal of the American Medical Association* 259 (1988): 2098.

71. Krauthammer, "The Death of Debbie." Meursault, one may recall, is the protagonist of Albert Camus' *The Stranger.*

72. Gaylin, Kass, Pellegrino, Siegler, "Doctors Must Not Kill."

73. See the "letter" from Dr. Peter A. Singer in *Journal of the American Medical Association* 259 (1988): 2096. The Nazi analogy at work here is often employed by opponents of euthanasia. That the analogy lacks credibility should not go unnoticed, however. See, for

example, James Rachels, *The End of Life: Euthanasia and Morality* (New York: Oxford University Press, 1986), 175–78. See also Michael Burleigh, *Death and Deliverance: 'Euthanasia' in Germany c. 1900–1945* (New York: Cambridge University Press, 1994). For two excellent collections of essays that deal with the issue, see George J. Annas and Michael A. Grodin, eds., *The Nazi doctors and the Nuremberg Code: Human Rights in Human Experimentation* (New York: Oxford University Press, 1992), and Arthur L. Caplan, ed., *When Medicine Went Mad: Bioethics and the Holocaust* (Totowa, N.J.: Humana Press, 1992).

74. Lyotard, *The Postmodern Condition,* xxv.

75. Ibid., xxv. See also Lyotard's and Jean-Loup Thebaud's *Just Gaming,* trans. Wlad Godzich (Minneapolis: University of Minnesota Press, 1985): "What is at stake in artistic language today is experimentation. And to experiment means, in a way, to be alone, to be celibate. But, on the other hand, it also means that if the artifact produced is really strong, it will wind up producing its own readers, its own viewers, its own listeners. . . . It is the message itself, by its form, that will elicit both the one who receives it and the one who sends it. They are able then to communicate with each other. And, as you know, sometimes this takes centuries, sometimes twenty years, sometimes three, and there are times when it happens right away" (10).

76. Gerald Dworkin, R. G. Frey, and Sissela Bok, *Euthanasia and Physician-Assisted Suicide* (New York: Cambridge University Press, 1998).

77. I say this with the "proto-postmodernist" theorist Friedrich Nietzsche in mind. For it is Nietzsche, as is well known, who informs us that "truth" is nothing if it is not *rhetorical.* See, for example, his "On Truth and Lie in an Extramoral Sense," in *The Portable Nietzsche,* ed. and trans. Walter Kaufmann (New York: Viking Penguin, 1986), 42–47.

78. Gaylin, Kass, Pellegrino, and Siegler, "Doctors Must Not Kill," 2139.

79. Lundberg, "'It's Over, Debbie' and the Euthanasia Debate," 2142.

80. My thinking of "Debbie" as being a *pharmakon* is certainly indebted to Derrida's discussion of this "ambiguous" term in "Plato's Pharmacy," in *Dissemination,* by Derrida, trans. Barbara Johnson (Chicago: University of Chicago Press, 1981), 63–171.

81. See, for example, "letter" cited in note 70 above.

82. Rabbi Joseph Edelheit, "Reflection," in *Active Euthanasia, Religion, and the Public Debate,* 82. See also H. Tristram Engelhardt Jr. "Fashioning an Ethic for Life and Death in a Post-Modern Society," in *Hastings Center Report,* special supplement "Mercy, Murder, and Morality: Perspectives on Euthanasia," 7–9.

83. Shortly before publishing "Debbie," *JAMA* did reject a signed essay whose physician-author told how he helped "hasten" the death of his cancer-stricken mother-in-law by making arrangements with one of her attending physicians to increase her morphine injections (for pain relief) and to withdraw other medications. The mother-in-law wanted it this way. See Howard Wolinsky, "Signed 'mercy killing' article's rejection told," *Chicago Sun-Times,* 21 February 1988, 5, 34. The physician's essay is included in this newspaper article. He publicized his essay's rejection by *JAMA* because of the "Debbie" case. In the essay the physician made it a point to say that the case of his mother-in-law was not an instance of "active euthanasia." No mention is made, however, of how the case could be seen as an instance of "passive euthanasia." Hence, although the essay is quite moving, it nevertheless works to close off the ongoing controversy concerning whether there is truly a moral difference between passive and active euthanasia.

84. Jane P. Thompkins, "An Introduction to Reader-Response Criticism," in *Reader-Response Criticism: From Formalism to Post-Structuralism,* ed. Jane P. Thompkins (Baltimore: Johns Hopkins University Press, 1980), xxv.

85. Zygmunt Bauman, *Postmodern Ethics* (Cambridge, Mass.: Blackwell, 1993), 245.

86. Kenneth Burke, *Counter-Statement* (Berkeley and Los Angeles: University of California Press, 1968), 167–70.

87. Zygmunt Bauman, *Mortality, Immortality, and Other Life Strategies* (Stanford: Stanford University Press, 1992), 129–30. Here I wish to send a blessing to a colleague and friend, the late Robert Hopper of the University of Texas.

88. I thank Mr. Andy Carvin for the example here.

89. See Philippe Aries, *Western Attitudes Toward Death: From the Middle Ages to the Present,* trans. Patricia M. Ranum (Baltimore: Johns Hopkins University Press, 1974).

90. See Kathy Eden, "Hermeneutics and the Ancient Rhetorical Tradition," *Rhetorica* 5 (1987): 59–86.

91. Jack Kevorkian, *Prescription: Medicide, the Goodness of Planned Death* (New York: Prometheus Books, 1991), 206.

Chapter 5: Reconstruction

1. Sherwin B. Nuland, *How We Die: Reflections on Life's Final Chapter* (New York: Alfred A. Knopf, 1994), 154.

2. Ibid., 156.

3. Hans Zbinden, "Conscience in Our Time," in *Conscience,* ed. The Curatorium of the C. G. Jung Institute, Zurich (Evanston: Northwestern University Press, 1970), 15.

4. Ibid., 29

5. For a fascinating collection of essays that display the evolution of a philosopher's thinking from being strictly analytical to being more rhetorically astute, see Henry W. Johnstone Jr., *Validity and Rhetoric in Philosophical Argument: An Outlook in Transition* (University Park, Pa.: Dialogue Press, 1978).

6. Charles Mangel and Allen B. Weisse, *Medicine: The State of the Art* (New York: Dial Press, 1984), 196.

7. It should be noted, however, that these genres often draw on each other when making a case. That should not be surprising since the euthanasia debate is rooted in the physiological/biological/psychological conditions of people who are suffering from the consequences of some illness or accident and whose philosophical (for example, spiritual) outlook on life and death, as articulated by themselves or others, typically plays a significant role in the decision-making process. My analysis of the chosen artifacts should make this clear.

8. Robert Fraser, "A Plea for the Right to Die with Dignity," *Hemlock of Illinois Newsletter* 2 (Spring 1988): 1. First published in the November 1984 issue of *Preventive Medicine.*

9. David J. Wolpe, *In Speech and in Silence: The Jewish Quest for God* (New York: Henry Holt, 1992), 170–71.

10. Raphael Demos, "On Persuasion," *Journal of Philosophy* 29 (1932): 229.

11. David Hume, *Essays: Moral, Political, and Literary,* ed. Eugene F. Miller (Indianapolis, Ind.: Liberty Classics, 1985), 583.

12. Ibid., 583.

13. Walter J. Ong, *The Presence of the Word: Some Prolegomena for Cultural and Religious History* (New York: Simon and Schuster, 1967), 323. For a classic analytic approach and discussion of the topic, see also Richard Robinson, *Definition* (New York: Oxford University Press, 1954).

14. For a discussion of how definitions are themselves arguments, see Edward Schiappa, "Arguing About Definitions," *Argumentation* 7 (1993): 403–17.

15. For the insight concerning how the enthymeme correlates with "*enthumeisthai,*" I

am indebted to P. Christopher Smith, *The Hermeneutics of Original Argument: Demonstration, Dialectic, Rhetoric* (Evanston: Northwestern University Press, 1998), 26.

16. Leon R. Kass, "Death with Dignity and the Sanctity of Life," in *A Time to Be Born and a Time to Die*, ed. Barry S. Kogan (New York: Aldine de Gruyter, 1991), 117. Further references to this work will be cited in the text.

17. Kenneth Burke, *Language as Symbolic Action: Essays on Life, Literature, and Method* (Berkeley and Los Angeles: University of California Press, 1966), 44–62.

18. Kass's discussion and argument are quite enlightening and also a bit "thick." Capturing some of this thickness requires that I try not to be too stingy with his actual words.

19. See, for example, Leon R. Kass and James Q. Wilson, *The Ethics of Human Cloning* (Washington, D.C.: American Enterprise Institute (AEI) Press, 1998), 8–9.

20. For example, Wolpe, in *In Speech and in Silence*, 72–102, tells the story of Moses in this context. For a critique of the "cruelty" that can be associated with this position, especially as it is formed in Christianity, see James Rachels, *The End of Life: Euthanasia and Morality* (New York: Oxford University Press, 1986), 160–65.

21. Admittedly, it might come off as quite silly and inappropriate (not to mention tedious and perhaps boring) if leaders of the right-to-die movement spent much time carefully formulating a philosophical justification of their position while arguing a "grassroots" understanding in public forums (television, newspapers, Internet websites and chat rooms).

22. I trust this is clear from what has been said so far (especially with Heidegger in mind) about the relationship that holds between human being (Dasein) and its particular way of showing itself in a person's biological and existential history. For an excellent phenomenological analysis of the narrative structure of human existence, see David Carr, *Time, Narrative, and History* (Bloomington: Indiana University Press, 1986).

23. Ronald M. Green, "Good Rules Have Good Reasons: A Response to Leon Kass," in *A Time to Be Born and a Time to Die*, 152.

24. Martin Foss, *Death, Sacrifice, and Tragedy* (Lincoln: University of Nebraska Press, 1966), 43.

25. Kenneth Burke, "Literature as Equipment for Living," *The Philosophy of Literary Form*, 3d ed. (Los Angeles: University of California Press, 1971), 293–304. The phrase "equipment for dying" was suggested to me by my friend and colleague Wade Kenny. See his "The Rhetoric of Kevorkian's Battle," *Quarterly Journal of Speech*, forthcoming.

26. Leon R. Kass, *Toward a More Natural Science: Biology and Human Affairs* (New York: Free Press, 1985), 348.

27. Ibid., 348.

28. Commenting on how the question of truth has been handled by the humanities, Kass writes: "Over the last century, and alarmingly so in the last two decades, most humanists and many teachers of religion have been declaring bankruptcy regarding truth: Even leaving aside the recent malignant politicization of humanistic disciplines, with its denial of the independence of mind and its insistence that everything can be reduced to power, the humanities have long been in retreat from the pursuit of wisdom. Analytical clarity, logical consistency, demystification, and refutation; source criticism, philology, and the explication of thinkers solely in terms of their historical and cultural contexts; and the devotion to theoretical dogmas—formerly romanticism and historicism, nowadays Marxism, deconstructionism, multiculturalism, feminism, and many other 'isms'—all these preoccupations keep humanists busy with everything but the pursuit of wisdom about our own humanity" (*The Hungry Soul: Eating and the Perfecting of Our Nature* [New York: Free Press, 1994], 6–7).

29. Woody Allen, "Death (A Play)," in *Without Feathers* (New York: Random House, 1975), 99.

30. Anatole Broyard, *Intoxicated by My Illness and Other Writings on Life and Death* (New York: Ballantine, 1992), 19–20. Further references to this work will be cited in the text.

31. Cf. David Appelbaum, *Voice* (Albany: State University of New York Press, 1990), esp. 1–13 ("The Cough"). Appelbaum does not speak of "the call of conscience"; rather, he conceives of bodily functions such as the cough as being indications of a more primordial "voice" that underlies our being.

32. Wolpe, *In Speech and in Silence,* 72.

33. B. J. Nelson, "Mother's Last Request: A Not So Fond Farewell," *Harper's* 292 (March 1996): 35–43. Further references to this essay will be cited in the text. The essay was also published as a chapter in Nelson's *Keepers: A Memoir* (New York: W. W. Norton, 1998).

34. Barry L. Nelson, "Letters," *Harper's* 292 (June 1996): 81–82.

35. Here, of course, I am once again recalling the position advocated by Raphael Demos.

36. Ernest Becker, *The Denial of Death* (New York: Free Press, 1973), 152–53.

37. Nelson, "Letters," 82. I deal with the case of Kevorkian in chapter 6.

38. Libby Cone, "Letters," *Harper's* 292 (June 1996): 81.

39. In chapter 6 I deal specifically with such a story of heroism.

40. See, for example, Lonny Shavelson, *A Chosen Death: The Dying Confront Assisted Suicide* (Berkeley and Los Angeles: University of California Press, 1995).

Chapter 6: The Rhetorical Construction of Heroes

1. Joseph Campbell, *The Hero with a Thousand Faces* (Princeton: Princeton University Press, 1968), 58.

2. Ernest Becker, *The Denial of Death* (New York: Free Press, 1973), 4–5.

3. Ibid., 6.

4. David J. Wolpe, *In Speech and in Silence* (New York: Henry Holt, 1992), 98.

5. Daniel J. Boorstin, *The Image: A Guide to Pseudo-Events in America* (New York: Atheneum, 1975), 48.

6. Ibid., 57–58.

7. Ibid., 63.

8. Ibid., 76.

9. Joshua Meyrowitz, *No Sense of Place* (New York: Oxford University Press, 1985), 273.

10. Joseph Campbell, *The Hero with a Thousand Faces,* 390.

11. Although much has been written about the history of the Cruzan case, an especially moving account is offered by her father, Joe Cruzan, in *Trends in Health Care, Law, and Ethics* 8 (Winter 1993): 70–74.

12. George Annas, "The Insane Root Takes Reason Prisoner: The Supreme Court and the Right to Die," in *Trends in Health Care, Law, and Ethics* 8 (Winter 1993): 22–23.

13. See his account (note 11): 72.

14. Ibid., 74.

15. Ibid.

16. Ibid.

17. *Cruzan v. Director, Missouri Department of Health,* 497 U.S. 291 (1990). Further references to the case will be cited in the text.

18. Leon R. Kass, "Death with Dignity and the Sanctity of Life," in *A Time to Be Born and a Time to Die,* ed. Barry S. Kogan (New York: Aldine de Gruyter, 1991), 134.

19. Kass writes: "I have no illusions that it is easy to live with a . . . Nancy Cruzan. . . . I think I sufficiently appreciate the anguish of their parents or their children, and the distortion of their lives and the lives of their families. I also know that, when hearts break and people can stand it no longer, mercy-killing will happen, and I think we should be prepared to excuse it—as we generally do—when it occurs in this way. But an excuse is not yet a justification, and very far from dignity" (Ibid., 140).

20. Abraham Joshua Heschel, *Man Is Not Alone: A Philosophy of Religion* (New York: Noonday Press, 1951), 296.

21. See note 11 above: 71.

22. Quoted in Joseph Fletcher, *Morals and Medicine* (Princeton: Princeton University Press, 1954), 209.

23. Michael Heim, *The Metaphysics of Virtual Reality* (New York: Oxford University Press, 1993), 102.

24. Some of the rhetoric of the right to die that was expressed during the controversy to be examined here will be included and commented on later in the chapter. As I hope to show, this rhetoric was at times more ethical than that expressed by members of "Not Dead Yet!"

25. See, for example, Derek Humphry, *Dying with Dignity: Understanding Euthanasia* (New York: Carol, 1992).

26. For a good historical discussion of this point, see James M. Hoefler and Brian E. Kamoie, *Deathright: Culture, Medicine, Politics, and the Right to Die* (Boulder, Colo.: Westview, 1994).

27. This and all other postings included in this section were retrieved from the ERGO listserv (http://www.right-to-die@enf.org). As of early December 1996, all ERGO postings are archived at http://www.reference.com.

28. Which is to say that the list manager (Humphry) did not censor contributions.

29. The notion of "wounded storytellers" is adopted from Arthur W. Frank, *The Wounded Storyteller: Body, Illness, and Ethics* (Chicago: University of Chicago Press, 1995).

30. Ibid., 49.

31. Ibid., 17.

32. Ibid., 25.

33. See, for example, Diane Coleman, "Withdrawing Life-Sustaining Treatment from People with Severe Disabilities Who Request It: Equal Protection Considerations," *Issues in Law and Medicine* 7(1992): 55–79; Carol Gill, "Suicide Intervention for People with Disabilities: A Lesson in Inequality," *Issues in Law and Medicine* 8 (1992): 37–53; A. I. Batavia, "Disability and Physician-Assisted Suicide," *New England Journal of Medicine* 336 (1997): 1671–73.

34. Frank, *Wounded Storyteller,* 2 (emphasis added).

35. However, as a deeply religious Jew, Levinas must necessarily stand against the practice of physician-assisted suicide. See, for example, Abraham S. Abraham, "Euthanasia," in *Medicine and Jewish Law,* ed. Fred Rosner (Northvale, N.J.: Jason Aronson, 1993), 1:123–36.

36. In a phone interview (17 November 1998), Steven Drake admitted that his way of initiating contact with the listserv members of ERGO was intentional.

37. In *Washington* plaintiffs argued that liberty interests under the fourteenth amendment protected the personal choices by mentally competent, terminally ill adults to commit physician-assisted suicide. The District Court agreed. The Ninth Circuit Court of Appeals reversed, reheard the case en banc, and then reversed their previous ruling and affirmed the District Court's decision. The Supreme Court, granted certiorari and

reversed the decision, stressing relevant historical legalities and highlighting the vulnerable nature of groups who would be affected by the ruling. Using the slippery-slope argument, with evidence from the practice of physician-assisted suicide in the Netherlands, the Supreme Court concluded that a right to physician-assisted suicide does not overwhelm the state's interest in preserving life.

In *Vacco* the arguments were quite different. The District Court upheld the New York statute only to be reversed by the Second Circuit Court of Appeals. The plaintiffs argued that the statute violated the requirement of the Equal Protection clause that individuals similarly situated be treated alike in that mentally competent adults in the final stages of terminal illness and on life-support had different end-of-life decisions than those who were not on life-support. Once more focusing on legal traditions, the Supreme Court reversed the Second Circuit, highlighting both legal tradition and the government interest in the preservation of life, while disputing the distinction between terminally ill individuals on and off of life-support. Different cases, same conclusion.

38. *Amici Curiae Brief of Not Dead Yet and American Disabled for Attendant Programs Today in Support of Petitioners, Vacco v. Quill* 117 S. Ct. 2293 (1997).

39. Ibid., 4.

40. See Introduction, note 54, for more information concerning this initiative.

41. D. E. Meier, C. A. Emmons, S. Wallenstein, T. Quill, R. S. Morrison, and C. K. Cassell, "A National Survey on Physician-Assisted Suicide and Euthanasia in the United States," *New England Journal of Medicine* 338 (1998): 1193–201.

42. Heschel, *Man Is Not Alone,* 193–95.

Chapter 7: The Face of the Needed Caregiver

1. Ronald J. Glasser, *The Body Is the Hero* (New York: Random House, 1976), 26.

2. Ibid., 229, 248.

3. Quoted in "Career Opportunities," *Winston-Salem Journal,* 5 March 1999, A2.

4. Joni Eareckson (with Joe Musser), *Joni* (Grand Rapids, Mich.: Zondervan, 1976), 7.

5. Joni Eareckson Tada, *When Is It Right to Die? Suicide, Euthanasia, Suffering, Mercy* (Grand Rapids, Mich.: Zondervan, 1992), 17. Further references to this work will be cited in the text.

6. The picture, of course, literally "puts a face" on the author and thus, as my students continually point out, makes a reading of her book more "personal" and "realistic."

7. Derek Humphry, *Final Exit* (Secaucus, N.J.: Carol, 1991).

8. See Viktor E. Frankl, *Man's Search for Meaning: An Introduction to Logotherapy* (Boston: Beacon Press, 1959). Although I find Tada's reading to be acceptable, I would also stress that there is much more to Frankl's book than she admits. For additional works that expand and clarify Frankl's philosophy, see, for example, his *The Doctor and the Soul: From Psychotherapy to Logotherapy,* 2d expanded edition (New York: Alfred A. Knopf, 1965); and *The Will to Meaning: Foundations and Applications of Logotherapy* (New York: World, 1969).

9. Larry McAfee was referred to in chapter 6 when discussing the case of NDY.

10. Timothy E. Quill, "Death and Dignity: A Case of Individualized Decision Making," *The New England Journal of Medicine* 324 (1991): 691–94.

11. Timothy E. Quill, *Death and Dignity: Making Choices and Taking Charge* (New York: W. W. Norton, 1993), 25. Further references to this book (and to the story of Diane) will be cited in the text.

12. Quill's presentation ("Death and Dignity") was given as part of a program ("Dying Well in the Late Twentieth Century") sponsored by the Garrett-Evangelical Theological Seminary, Northwestern University, 26 May 1994. He opened the presentation with a

series of slides that pictured Diane and her family. This rhetorical strategy certainly helped the audience to identify more closely with Quill's eloquent account of his patient's story. In my response I made much of the importance of telling stories in the euthanasia debate. Being the master storyteller that he is, Quill took no exception to my remarks, or what some might call "a fat pitch."

13. In his book Quill makes much, for example, of his early training and experiences (29–56); the reader thereby is offered a very personal and humanizing perspective on the doctor that works to his persuasive advantage. See also Timothy E. Quill, *A Midwife through the Dying Process: Stories of Healing and Hard Choices at the End of Life* (Baltimore: Johns Hopkins University Press, 1996).

14. Joseph Harontunian, "Life and Death among Fellowmen," in *The Modern Vision of Death,* ed. Nathan A. Scott Jr. (Richmond, Va.: John Knox Press, 1967), 84–85.

15. Sherwin B. Nuland, *How We Die: Reflections on Life's Final Chapter* (New York: Alfred A. Knopf, 1994), 155, 157.

16. Ibid., 268.

17. Lonny Shavelson, *A Chosen Death: The Dying Confront Assisted Suicide* (Berkeley and Los Angeles: University of California Press, 1995).

18. I have been collecting information on Kevorkian since 1990. The "popular" literature from newspaper and magazine articles and essays and cartoons (not to mention television specials) detailing, commending, and criticizing his activities is, to say the least, immense. I thus make the assumption that readers are not totally unfamiliar with this well-known character. The only book that I know of that is devoted totally to detailing (in journalistic form) Kevorkian's story is Michael Betzold, *Appointment with Doctor Death* (Troy, Mich.: Momentum Books, 1993). What I have to say about Kevorkian in the following pages will include material that updates this story to 2000.

19. Cf. Jack Lessenberry, "Death and the Matron," *Esquire* 127 (April 1997): 80–85, 130–31; Michael Betzold, "The Selling of Doctor Death," *New Republic* 216 (26 May 1997): 22–28.

20. Timothy E. Quill, *Death and Dignity,* 124–25.

21. Kevorkian offers an early account of his activities and the "rationale" that supported them in his *Prescription: Medicide, The Goodness of Planned Death* (New York: Prometheus Books, 1991). For an early "philosophical" treatment of this rationale, see his *Beyond Any Kind of God* (New York: Philosophical Library, 1966).

22. Vaux offers this description during an interview in my documentary film, *Negotiating Death (A Rhetorical Perspective on the Euthanasia Debate),* directed by Andrew Carvin and Susan Cornwall, Northwestern University, School of Speech, 1993.

23. Kenneth Burke, *A Grammar of Motives* (Berkeley and Los Angeles: University of California Press, 1969): 59–61. Further references to Kevorkian's and Feiger's address are based on the transcript provided by the Federal News Service, Inc., 1996, and will be cited in the text.

24. When the videotape was first played, technical difficulties made it impossible to hear the first two sentences. They were later provided by Feiger when he spoke again during the presentation.

25. I have Cicero especially in mind in saying this. My reading of Cicero on "decorum" is much indebted to Michael Leff, "Decorum and Rhetorical Interpretation: The Latin Humanistic Tradition and Contemporary Critical Theory," *Vichiana* 3 (1990): 107–26.

26. For a more detailed discussion of "narrative coherence," see Walter Fisher, *Human Communication as Narration: Toward a Philosophy of Reason, Value, and Action* (Columbia: University of South Carolina Press, 1987).

27. According to Kevorkian, "In 1812 [Jefferson] wrote a letter to a Dr. Butler, saying, you know, I hear that they have this new poison in France—it was capsicum—that really works well—it's easy to take and it's fast, and you just go to sleep. And I found out that the aristocracy there have it with them in case they are going to be guillotined, so they take it so they don't [*sic*] be guillotined. And Jefferson says, boy, I'd like to get some of that. In the letter he said I'd like to get some of that—what a wonderful thing it would be for those suffering from the 'inverterate cancer'—those are his exact words, 'inverterate cancer'" (13). Kevorkian claims that he discovered this fact in a book that he bought for ten cents at a book sale. When he looked through the index for euthanasia, he found "Jefferson's letters." This is as far as Kevorkian goes in referencing his "research."

28. Kevorkian's presentation was followed by a "question/answer" period wherein Feiger once again chimed in. The substance and style of their answers were consistent with their earlier remarks.

29. The full citation for the "manifesto" is contained in note 21 above.

30. Opening Arguments, Michigan v. Kevorkian, 1999. This case was televised on *Court TV.* Transcripts were obtained from the website http://www.courttv.com/trials/kevorkian/032599_pm_ctv.html. To keep abreast of new developments in the Kevorkian case, refer to http://www.courttv.com.

31. For a unforgiving critique of Kevorkian's histrionics and everything they stand for, see Wesley J. Smith, *Forced Exit: The Slippery Slope from Assisted Suicide to Legalized Murder* (New York: Random House, 1997), passim.

32. For what I take to be the best documentary on the lives and times of Kevorkian and some of his patients, see the PBS Special: "The Kevorkian File."

33. Bryan Robinson, "In Wake of *60 Minutes* Death Tape Prosecutors Vow Not to Be Baited by Kevorkian's Taunts," *Court TV:* 13 par. Internet. 29 April 1999. Available: http://www. courttv.com/national/1998/1123/kevorkian_ctv.html.

34. Anatole Broyard, *Intoxicated by My Illness and Other Writings on Life and Death* (New York: Ballantine Books, 1992), 40.

35. See his *Prescription: Medicide,* 17–99.

36. Ever since Kevorkian began his crusade in 1990, he has been criticized for his procedure of only getting to "know" his patients as he talked with them about their rationale for wanting his assistance. According to Quill, for example, Kevorkian "has been willing to act without a deep or long-standing relationship with the patient, and therefore may not have the emotional investment in his patient's well-being that should underlie such a profound decision to help. He has shown little interest in working with or learning from dying patients who are finding alternatives to suicide." See Timothy E. Quill, *Death and Dignity,* 124.

37. Joseph Campbell, *The Hero with a Thousand Faces* (Princeton: Princeton University Press, 1972), 216.

38. Samuel Langhorne Clemens, *Mark Twain's Notebook* (American Biography Series) (New York: Library Binding, 1927).

39. One could argue, however, that Kevorkian's activities do indeed have a reconstructive dimension to them if one grants that assisted suicide can lead to the saving of lives through organ transplantation. See his *Prescription Medicide,* 17–99. I am unaware, however, of any cases wherein Kevorkian emphasized this procedure to justify a patient's assisted suicide.

Chapter 8: Where Art Thou? Here I Am!

1. Hans-Georg Gadamer, *Truth and Method,* 2d rev. ed., trans. Joel Weinsheimer and

Donald G. Marshall (New York: Crossroad, 1991), xxxviii. Gadamer also addresses the importance of "rhetoric within social life" in such essays as "Rhetoric and Hermeneutics," trans. Joel Weinsheimer, in *Rhetoric and Hermeneutics in Our Time,* ed. Walter Jost and Michael J. Hyde (New Haven: Yale University Press, 1997), 45–59; and "Rhetoric, Hermeneutics, and Ideology-Critique," trans. G. B. Hess and R. E. Palmer, in *Rhetoric and Hermeneutics in Our Time,* 313–34. Still, Gadamer is a philosopher who is also on record as describing rhetoric as an art that "is other than the factical matter of our propositions," "possesses the purely operational and ritual function of exchange through speaking, whether in oral or written form," and that thus is a "pseudotext" that "is devoid of meaning." See his "Text and Interpretation," trans. Dennis J. Schmidt and Richard Palmer, in *Dialogue and Deconstruction: The Gadamer-Derrida Encounter,* ed. Diane P. Michelfelder and Richard E. Palmer (Albany: State University of New York Press, 1989), 106.

2. David A. Cooper, *God Is a Verb: Kabbalah and the Practice of Mystical Judaism* (New York: Riverhead Books, 1997), 43, 58.

3. Three of the patients make brief mention of their being religious but do not clarify exactly how this affected their decision.

4. CBS aired the program during "sweeps week."

5. Bill Moyers's recent four-part, six-hour PBS series "On Our Own Terms: Moyers on Dying" (September 10–13, 2000) and this series's use of the Internet (http://www.pbs.org/wnet/onourownterms/about/index.html) to encourage discussion and public moral argument on such related issues as American culture's denial of death, the evolution of palliative ("comfort") care, the ethics of euthanasia and physician-assisted suicide, and this country's current healthcare crisis, provide an outstanding example of how such an effort may take form. I viewed Moyers's series and its Internet component as I was reviewing the typeset page proofs of this book; hence, I am unable to offer here a detailed rhetorical assessment of his work. I would note, though, that in his series Moyers employs his highly acclaimed journalistic and documentary talents to tell and interconnect with great rhetorical competence moving stories of patients, family members, physicians, and healthcare providers caught up in the struggle of trying to decide the "best" course of action for coping with the ontological assault of life-threatening illness and disability. Although Moyers does not advocate specific solutions to the problems under consideration, his series certainly admits a powerful call of conscience: Where art thou? Witnessing this call, it is difficult not to turn on one's computer in order to explore the supplementary and well-arranged Internet material and to join the unfolding conversation about the issues at hand.

Index